K·I·S·S

The Only Guides You'll Ever Need!

THIS SERIES IS YOUR TRUSTED GUIDE through all of life's stages and situations. Want to learn how to surf the Internet or care for your new dog? Or maybe you'd like to become a wine connoisseur or an expert gardener? The solution is simple: just pick up a K.I.S.S. Guide and turn to the first page.

Expert authors will walk you through the subject from start to finish, using simple blocks of knowledge to build your skills one step at a time. Build upon these learning blocks and by the end of the book, you'll be an expert yourself! Or, if you are familiar with the topic but want to learn more, it's easy to dive in and pick up where you left off.

The K.I.S.S. Guides deliver what they promise: simple access to all the information you'll need on one subject. Other titles you might want to check out include: Playing Guitar, Playing Golf, the Internet, Living with a Dog, and Astrology.

GUIDE TO

Windows MICROSOFT®

COVERS WINDOWS 98 AND WINDOWS 98 SECOND EDITION

RICH LEVIN

Host of *Rich Levin's PC talk* on CBS Radio

Foreword by Guy Kawasaki

A Dorling Kindersley Book

Dorling Kindersley

LONDON, NEW YORK, SYDNEY, DELHI, PARIS,
MUNICH AND JOHANNESBURG

Dorling Kindersley Publishing, Inc.
Editorial Director LaVonne Carlson
Series Editor Beth Adelman
Editor Joseph Gonzales
Copyeditor James Lubin

Dorling Kindersley Limited
Editorial Director Valerie Buckingham
Senior Editor Bridget Hopkinson

Managing Art Editor Stephen Knowlden
Jacket Designer Neal Cobourne

Created and produced for Dorling Kindersley by
THE FOUNDRY, part of The Foundry Creative Media Company Ltd,
Crabtree Hall, Crabtree Lane, Fulham, London SW6 6TY

The Foundry project team
Frances Banfield, Lucy Bradbury, Josephine Cutts, Sue Evans, Karen Fitzpatrick,
Douglas Hall, Sasha Heseltine, Dave Jones, Jennifer Kenna, Lee Matthews, Ian Powling,
Bridget Tily, Nick Wells, and Polly Willis. Very special thanks to Martin Noble and all at CMYK.

Copyright © 2000
Dorling Kindersley Publishing, Inc.
Text copyright © 2000 Rich Levin
2 4 6 8 10 9 7 5 3 1

Published in the United States by
Dorling Kindersley Publishing, Inc.
95 Madison Avenue
New York, New York 10016

A CIP catalog record for this book is available from the Library of Congress
ISBN 0-7894-5982-5

A CIP catalog record for this book is available from the British Library
ISBN 0-7513-2025-0

Dorling Kindersley Publishing, Inc. offers special discounts for bulk purchases for sales promotions or premiums.
Specific, large-quantity needs can be met with special editions, including personalized covers,
excerpts of existing guides, and corporate imprints. For more information, contact Special Markets Department,
Dorling Kindersley Publishing, Inc., 95 Madison Avenue, New York, NY 10016 Fax: 800-600-9098.

Color reproduction by David Bruce Imaging and The Foundry
Printed and bound by Printer Industria Grafica, S.A., Barcelona, Spain

For our complete catalog visit

www.dk.com

Contents at a Glance

CONTENTS

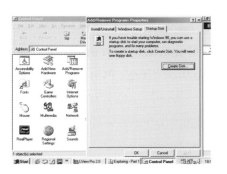

PART THREE *Welcome to Productivity City 220*

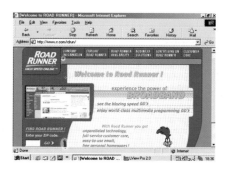

Foreword

*LIKE YOU, I WAS A NOVICE when I first sat down at a
personal computer back before I care to admit. Today I'm the CEO
of a Silicon Valley firm that assists high-technology startups find
venture capital using the Internet, and I'd be lost without my
computers or, I should say, I'd be lost without my computing skills.*

*Starting and running a business requires more than a good idea, a
sound business plan, a dollop of venture capital, passion, hard work,
dedication, and a little luck. It also requires a mastery of the
personal computer. That wasn't the case as little as five years ago,
when executives and business managers could sidestep the need to
understand computing by delegating tasks or using traditional
organizational and communications methods.*

*Day planners, tickler files, Dictaphones, U.S. mail, fax machines,
the telephone ñ they were the standard weapons in the business
warrior's arsenal. Today personal computers have displaced many
of these technologies, and the revolution isn't over yet. Computers
are the modern business person's communications, organizational,
and information hub. If you don't have strong computing abilities,
you're at a critical disadvantage in today's business environment.*

*There are 1001 ways to get started with computers, and 999 aren't
right for people "with lives." Sure, you can take night classes,
attend corporate training sessions, or try to memorize step-by-step
instructions offered by any one of the legions of "how to" books.
Or you could hire your own personal computer trainer to sit down
beside you and work with you at your own pace.*

But let's get real: No one can learn to use a computer this way.

The real world way to use a personal computer is to impart the fundamental skills that provide a baseline understanding of the beast. With time, patience, and exploration, this baseline can blossom into a mastery of computing. That's the approach you'll find in this book. Rich Levin has bottled over 20 years of experience mentoring everyday people between these covers. He assumes no previous computer knowledge, and tackles computer training in an entertaining, practical, and understandable way. His unconventional approach reminds me of the earlier days of personal computing; when users helped users for the sheer pleasure of making the world a better place. So read this book and reap the benefits of Richard's knowledge and of personal computing.

G Kawasaki

GUY KAWASAKI

Guy Kawasaki is CEO of Garage.com, a Silicon Valley firm that assists high-technology startups find venture capital using the Internet. A notedcolumnist for Forbes magazine, speaker, and founder of various personal computer companies, Kawasaki is the author of seven best selling books, including his latest, Rules for Revolutionaries. Kawasaki currently serves on the board of directors of Garage.com, WebOrder, and Startups.com.

Introduction

You're Smart. Your Computer is Stupid.

Who gets the blame for making computers confusing, annoying, obnoxious, and just plain hard to use? Most computer book publishers think YOU get the blame. The evidence is in plain sight, lining the shelves of your favorite bookseller. There you'll find aisle after aisle of self-help computer books, the majority of which boldly assess your intellectual capabilities right on their covers. The titles say it all: inexperienced computer users are dummies, morons, or complete idiots.

This perverse notion that only dimwits find computers hard to use has long permeated the computer industry. It's a form of institutionalized brainwashing that PC makers and software developers use with lethal effectiveness to subjugate the masses. By convincing the public that computers are easy to use – meaning folks who can't get them to do their bidding are stupid – the industry sidesteps its responsibility to deliver the increased productivity, higher earnings, and paperless communication it promises PC buyers.

If you feel you can get more work done with pen and paper than your PC, it must be you, not the computer. If you find it easier to use the telephone than e-mail, it must be you, not the computer. And if you still trot out the fax machine rather than use your computer's built-in faxmodem, it must be you, not the computer. It's about time you learned the dirty little secret computer industry power brokers don't want you to know: It's not you. It's the computer!

You're not stupid. The real dummies, morons, and complete idiots are the people who engineer, manufacture, and sell these cartons of junk we call "PCs," then have the audacity to brand their ornery offspring "user friendly." For all of their supposed brilliance, after 60 years of trying, the computer industry's best minds still haven't figured out how to build a PC that mere mortals can use on day one, straight out of the box.

Computer technology continually evolves

The secret to mastering computers rests not in oversimplifying the myriad tasks computers are capable of, and boiling them down to sets of steps that users can memorize. In fact, rote memorization is perhaps the worst path you can take to becoming computer savvy. The reason: Computer technology continually evolves.

There's a good chance that features you memorize today will be history tomorrow. When step-by-step processes change, those who memorized those steps will be *fundamentally lost. This is why some users are always baffled by new software and require hours of advance training, while the office guru clacks away at the keyboard seconds after first encountering a new program.*

Gurus don't rely on manuals or memorization. On the contrary, they develop and continually hone deductive reasoning skills and coping mechanisms that allow them to size up computing tasks quickly and dive in without fear. Master the deductive reasoning skills and coping mechanisms that guide the most experienced users, and there are no tasks you can't accomplish, no programs you can't dominate, and no software you can't govern.

Six laws of computing

Acquiring these talents demands you first acknowledge the basic building blocks of computer wizardry; six laws of computing that I will delve into in greater detail later in these pages:

1. *Computers are not now, never were, and never will be easy to use.*
2. *Computers bomb, crash, bug out, and misbehave. Don't fear it. Deal with it.*
3. *Any computer problem can be solved through stubborn determination.*
4. *When a problem can't be solved, refer to rule 3.*
5. *What you don't know today, you will know tomorrow.*

Each and every computer user, from Bill Gates to John Doe, no matter how knowledgeable or well-trained or experienced, was at one time a complete novice. They, like you, had their "day one" at the computer, sitting nervously before the keyboard for that very first time. And they, like you, were utterly clueless about what to do next.

But being clueless is a passing phase – the first step on your path to computing enlightenment. With every new day, you'll conquer more computing tasks, and slowly glide up, up, and away from the novice's launch pad. Persevere, and it won't be long before you too are considered the computer expert among your friends and colleagues. That's when you'll be able to share with other newbies the sixth and most important law of computing:

We're all novices once, but we're experts forever.

This book aims to help you on that journey, but not with page after eye-numbing page of procedural guidance. Doing so would simply serve up the step-by-step manual that, by rights, Microsoft should have included with Windows. Rather, the K.I.S.S. Guide to Windows 98 will teach you mastery of your computer, so no matter how often Microsoft or third-party vendors change features, processes, interfaces, etc., you'll be capable of grabbing the reins and getting your work done. Here you'll find practical advice that gets you working quickly, while imparting the values, reasoning, and coping mechanisms critical to achieving guru status.

How to use this book

The K.I.S.S. Guide to Windows 98 contains a wealth of easy-to-read, jargon- and acronym-free information that's accessible to all, regardless of your level of computer expertise. Beginners will benefit most from this book, because I've assumed that its readers will have no computer knowledge or skills whatsoever.

Unlike "how to" computer books, you don't have to read the K.I.S.S. Guide in front of your computer. The book is designed to be read in the comfort of your favorite easy chair, or wherever else you enjoy reading and relaxing most. As you wind your way through the book, dog-ear any exercises, and run through them whenever you find yourself sitting at your personal computer.

A leisurely pace will deliver the best educational results. Don't fret when you don't find legions of screen shots and "how to" bulleted lists. If you work your way through the various exercises, you'll wind up with stronger skills and a deeper, fundamental understanding of computing – which no "how to" guide can impart.

Windows 98 SE

Note that my K.I.S.S. Guide covers the latest version of Windows 98, dubbed "Windows 98 Second Edition." To take advantage of everything this book has to offer, you'll need an IBM-compatible personal computer running Windows 98 SE. If your PC has Windows 95, get yourself the Windows 98 Second Edition upgrade. Even if your PC has Windows 98, note that Windows 98 SE includes a number of worthwhile improvements. To get the most out of the book, Windows 98 users should also purchase and install the Windows 98 Second Edition upgrade.

But even if you don't own a personal computer, fear not. I'll prepare you to select and buy your very own personal computer.

Thanks for choosing my K.I.S.S. Guide over all those other computer books. I hope you enjoy reading it, and using it, as much as I enjoyed writing it for you.

RICH LEVIN

Philadelphia January, 2000

Dedication

To Mark
7/23/59–11/20/93

Disclaimer

The author expressly wishes it to be known that the inclusion of particular web sites in this book does not necessarily contsitute any approval or personal recommendation unless specifically stated otherwise. All images in this book are for the purpose of illustration only and serve to provide examples of specific points or issues raised in the text.

What's Inside?

THE K.I.S.S. GUIDE TO WINDOWS 98 will take you by the hand and walk you through each and every step of the computing experience. Each chapter is designed to both illuminate and educate you in the ways of Windows computing. Instead of boring step-by-step instructions, this K.I.S.S. Guide will entertain you with informative narratives and train you with interactive exercises.

PART ONE

In Part One I will ease you into the world of Windows 98, explaining how to build up your knowledge, one skill at a time. If you haven't yet bought one, I'll show you the best way to purchase a new personal computer. I'll tell you how, with the right attitude, you'll be able to identify your requirements and specify the PC that's right for you. Then I'll walk you through purchasing your new computer and powering it up for the first time. Along the way, I'll also get you signed onto the Internet.

PART TWO

I will talk in Part Two about getting started with Windows 98 — a highly flexible and complex piece of software. I'll explain how you can take charge of Windows and organise things your way. You're probably itching to explore the Internet, so I'll be covering connecting, browsing, shopping – not forgetting e-mail. As well as a survey of Windows' library of software, there's a full explanation of getting stuff out of your computer.

PART THREE

In Part Three I will really get down to business and show you how to be productive with your PC. I'll tell you how to get fast access to your software, and discuss the "Win" key and other important commands. I'll cover the essentials of word processing, and explain what a spreadsheet is and what you can do with it. I'll even delve into databases, uncovering the power of this oft-ignored type of application. And I'll also show you the basics of a very useful calendar program.

PART FOUR

I'll explain in Part Three just how important the safety and maintenance of your PC is. Ultimately, it will probably hold some or all of your most important information. I'll explain how keep your data safe from cyber-thieves or accidents. Next up, I'll cover tools and techniques for keeping your PC working in peak condition, and tell you how to upgrade it. And finally ... I won't let you forget computing's Golden Rule: Back-up!

The Extras

TO MAKE SURE YOU HIT ALL the important data points included in the book, be on the lookout for these helpful road signs and billboards you'll find along the way. Watch for these road signs:

Very Important Point

This symbol points out a chunk of critical knowledge you'll need to succeed. Pull over and check out the information whenever you see a VIP icon.

Complete No-No

It's just that: Don't do it, and don't say I didn't warn you! Watch out for Complete No-No icons and avoid these natural computing disasters.

Getting Technical

Consider the Getting Technical icon a pit stop where I pause to explain the meaning of otherwise over-technical mumbo jumbo.

Inside Scoop

Here's the stuff you won't find anywhere else: inside information that dishes the dirt, squeezes the secrets, and takes you behind the scenes.

You'll also find some little boxes that include information I think is important, useful, or just plain fun.

Trivia...
These are cool facts and background info that add an extra bit of color to the subject.

DEFINITION
Here you'll find definitions of buzzwords, technical terms, acronyms, and more. They're short, they're sweet, and they're ultimately descriptive.

INTERNET
www.internet.com
These provide useful resources on the Internet. As well as web sites, they can include e-mail addresses, FTP sites (libraries of downloadable files), or other resources.

PART ONE

YOU NEED TO GET YOUR HANDS ON A PC WITH
THE WINDOWS 98SE OPERATING SYSTEM

FROM PLANNING TO PURCHASE POWER

BEFORE YOU can get started in computing, you need to get your hands on a PC with the Windows 98SE operating system. It's *easy* enough to study up on the latest models, hit the Sunday newspapers, poke around for the best deal, and stake your claim. But clinching the best deal might be the  worst way to get started with Windows. I'll show you why this is so in Part One, and how the most *experienced* computer users go about selecting, buying, and setting up a new PC.

When you've finished Part One, you'll be ready to spec, *source*, and set up any computer purchase, from new systems to upgrades to outright replacements.

Chapter 1

A Prescription for Success

SURPRISING AS IT MIGHT SEEM, success with computers doesn't start with a computer. It doesn't start with software, schooling, mentoring, experimenting, or on-the-job training, either. And as much as I hate to admit it, it doesn't start with a good book. Success with computers starts with a "can do" attitude, coupled with a sound plan of attack, tempered with realistic goals and expectations. These attributes are shared by every successful computer user, from self-taught enthusiasts to elite computer scientists, I begin, then, with an attitudinal overview, a war-torn but proven computing battle plan, and a simple discussion of what to expect when you embark on your journey into computing with Microsoft Windows 98.

In this chapter...

✓ One skill at a time

✓ First things first

✓ Identifying your requirements

✓ Great expectations

WITH A GOOD PLAN, YOU'LL BE READY FOR YOUR JOURNEY INTO COMPUTING

One skill at a time

PIGGING OUT AT A PICNIC *may be fun, but it'll give most folks a good case of indigestion. If you have an iron stomach, or you manage to chug enough pink stuff in time, most of what you overeat will stay down. In most cases, though, the body quickly rejects what it can't digest.*

■ **Just take it** *one bite at a time.*

Your mind works the same way, especially when it comes to soaking up computer knowledge. There's a mountain of information you need to consider well before you attempt anything productive, such as getting on the Internet, sending e-mail, managing investments, writing letters, and so on. Undertake too many tasks at once, and you'll give yourself a good case of cranial indigestion. Much of what you attempt to take in simply won't stick, because your brain will reject what it can't assimilate.

Don't make the mistake of trying to get up to speed too fast, pointing and clicking your way around the computer screen with abandon. That's a surefire way to fail at some or all of the tasks you're trying to accomplish.

It also risks breaking your spirit, and hinders the "can do" attitude that's essential for achieving success with computers. Pace yourself, and you give your mind time to digest the cyber-tasks at hand. By acquiring one new skill at a time, you slash the number of potential pitfalls, and bolster your chances of achieving success. That feeds your "can do" attitude, and fuels your ability to take on subsequent tasks with lots of confidence.

First things first

THE JOURNEY OF *a thousand miles begins with a single step. But if your first step is the wrong step, you'll end up taking a thousand-mile journey in the wrong direction — and never reach your final destination.*

■ **If your first step** *is wrong, you'll never know how to reach your final destination.*

Keep selection simple

Most people kick off their journey to computing by shopping for a new PC. That's the wrong first step for one reason: Nearly everyone overcomplicates the process of buying a computer. Folks waste weeks studying up on MIPS, MHz, megabytes, modems, and other maddening details, boning up on every conceivable aspect of PC technology they can uncover, ultimately turning their minds into whirlwinds of techno-confusion. Worse, while buying computers by the numbers may ensure that you get a machine with the latest bells and whistles, it's no guarantee the PC is right for you.

■ **Beware** - *all computer advertisements contain jargon.*

You'll end up with a computer that makes magazine reviewers swoon, but doesn't add a bit of value to your workday, or fails to simplify your overall computing experience.

You could turn to family, friends, colleagues, and associates to enlist their advice, but they'll further confuse the issue. When it comes to computers, everybody's an expert, and their expert opinions often differ radically as to which constellation of PC specifications is "right" for you. Ask a carpenter how the physics of a hammer work, and he (or she) will likely stare back at you as if you were nuts. Ask a carpenter how to use a hammer, and you'll get a practical and memorable lesson. Know anybody who researches a television purchase by first studying the TV's schematic drawing? Know anybody who cares how many revolutions per minute their VCR's rewind spindle is capable of, or how much memory their microwave oven's controller uses? Me neither.

Focus on the nuts and bolts of computer technology, and you will learn a thing or two about what makes computers tick, but you won't learn anything about how to make computers do your bidding.

It's no wonder so many newbies end up with marvelous PCs and flashy software, yet can't get the darn things to do more than play a game of solitaire. Here's the stone cold truth: the first step to computing has nothing to do with buying a computer, and everything to do with preparing to live with one. Take the right steps in the right order, and you'll expedite your journey from newbie to knowledgeable. So before you lay your hands on a keyboard and a mouse, take the following steps first.

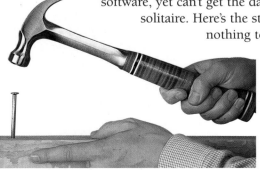

■ **You don't need** *to understand physics to use a hammer.*

Steps for a successful purchase

Step 1. Assess your computing requirements. In other words, what do you plan to use the computer for? Some people buy a PC just to play on the Internet, while others want to track their investments, run their business, conduct research or do homework, create presentations, or learn to program. Cogitate a bit on the reasons why you need a PC, and you won't make the mistake of buying an over- or under-powered computer.

Step 2. Determine the ideal balance of *hardware* and *software* programs to support your computing requirements.

■ **Before buying your computer** *it is important to establish exactly what you will be using it for.*

Step 3. Choose the Internet service provider that best meets your computing requirements. Internet service providers are to the Internet what telephone companies are to the phone system, your onramp to the network. America Online, CompuServe, the Microsoft Network, and AT&T WorldNet are all examples of Internet service providers. There are hundreds of Internet service providers to choose from, including local companies in your neighborhood.

Step 4. Buy the computer.

Step 5. Take it home and set it all up.

These are the actions that separate the winners from the whiners. These are also the steps I'll explain, define, and cover in far greater detail – and in that exact order – over the next few chapters.

■ **Some Internet** *Service Providers, such as AOL, provide exclusive content for members.*

> **DEFINITION**
>
> *Computers and their various components (disk drives, monitors, printers, etc.) are also known as* hardware. *They're "hard" because you can put your hands on them and touch them. To upgrade them requires disassembling the physical unit, removing old components, and installing new ones. Programs you run on a PC, such as Windows 98 or a word processor, are also known as* software. *They're "soft" because they exist only in cyberspace, and can be updated and changed merely by running a Setup program.*

The bottom line: Focusing on developing practical computing methods will teach you how to use computers as a tool, much like the carpenter uses a hammer and the painter uses a brush.

Identifying your requirements

BIOLOGISTS WILL SAY it was the egg, and not the chicken, that came first. Old-time merchants will tell you the horse comes first, followed by the cart. All pursuits in the physical universe, including the banal pursuits of humans, are ordered by their natural requirements. In other words, put the cart before the horse and you won't get very far very fast.

If you set a goal, but you don't know what's required to attain it, chances are you'll flounder around until you (A) eventually figure out the requirements, wasting loads of valuable time in the process, or (B) die trying. Both options are less than desirable. As I said in the previous section, the first step in your journey to computing know-how is learning how to assess your computing needs (a process referred to by industry insiders as "assessing your *application* requirements.")

Users who are driven by their application requirements typically wind up buying the right stuff, and become productive with their computers quickly and painlessly. That's because their computer hardware and software are well suited to their needs.

COLOR PHOTOGRAPHS

Consider two people, for example, who plan to send, receive, and print color photographs transmitted over the Internet. One guy just buys a PC by the numbers, assuming that having the latest Internet-ready technology means the computer is equipped to process digital photography. The other guy treats digital photography as a requirement, and makes sure the computer is properly equipped for digital photography. That means his computer gets outfitted with a high-resolution digital photograph printer, in addition to a traditional color business printer. It also means he investigates digital image editing software and chooses a package that meets his experience level, as opposed to being stuck with freebie software that comes with the PC.

It could also mean he adds more workspace memory and permanent storage to the PC, even going so far as to tack on a rewriteable CD drive so he can burn his own photo CDs.

If the pics he'll be exchanging are huge, it could mean he needs a high-speed dedicated Internet connection, as opposed to the low-speed dial-up modem most PCs include. A modem is the device that connects your computer to other computers over the Internet. It's called a modem because it converts digital data from your PC to an analog (sound) signal that can be handled by a telephone. This process is technically called "MOdulation/DEModulation," hence the term "modem." Some modems automatically dial your telephone to get an Internet connection, while others have no dialing capability (such as cable TV modems). Those that dial the telephone to get on the Internet are called "dial-up modems."

Contrast this to the guy who bought his PC by the numbers. He brings home a fire-breathing, award-winning computer, only to later discover it's ill equipped to handle the digital photo editing work that turned out to be of crucial importance to him.

Your application requirements

How, then, do you assess your application requirements? It's actually quite easy. Grab a pencil and paper, and break down all of the things you plan to use your computer for into three distinct categories:

THINK FIRST

1 Things I need to do right away
2 Things I need to do in the near future
3 Things I can see myself doing in the future.

In creating your list, don't be swayed by all the bells and whistles of computer technology. For example, if you've never used an answering machine, or you're happy with the machine you own, don't list "voice mail" as a requirement simply because you found it listed as a feature in some PC catalog. In other words, don't build your requirements list by comparing one manufacturer's computer to another. Forget about the computer features you read about in magazines and advertisements, or hear about on the radio, TV, or through family and friends.

■ **Do you really** *need all those bells and whistles?*

Focus on tasks you believe the computer will help you get done faster and easier than you accomplish them now.

Anything less will channel you into buying a PC by the numbers, at which point you're headed down the path of no return. Once you have assembled your application requirements, you are prepared to match them to the various computer hardware and software technologies that meet them. Make sure that the PC you buy can deal with all of the requirements in the "Things I need to do right away" and "Things I need to do in the near future" categories. Further, insist that it meet (or can be effortlessly upgraded to deal with) the "Things I can see myself doing in the future" category as well.

In the future

Perhaps you envision yourself traveling with a pocket organizer at some point in the future. If that's the case, look at computers that feature an infrared data eye. When the day comes, you'll be able to point your portable device at your PC, and automatically transfer your contacts, appointments, and other data. While you're "beaming" data, the guy who didn't put his requirements in the driver's seat will be futzing around with cables and power supplies, hoping he has an available connector to plug into, and then waiting while the data is ever-so-slowly sent across the old-fashioned wire.

Or, suppose you or your kids will be playing the latest computer games. Any Windows PC can play computer games; however, if you want your gaming to compete with the best dedicated console devices (such as the Sony PlayStation), you'll need special video, audio, speakers, controllers, and *I/O* ports. While you're wowing the kids with eye-popping 3D graphics and window-rattling surround sound, your neighbor will be wondering why the games on his "state of the art" PC flicker like a vintage silent movie.

Getting to know your application requirements, and lining them up with your new PC, will certainly maximize your man/machine interactions, and minimize frustrations and delays.

But nothing is perfect. No matter how diligent you are about following this step-by-careful-step approach to computing, computing is a problem-prone pursuit. It's for this reason you need to proceed without harboring unrealistic expectations.

■ **Your multimedia PC** *shouldn't flicker like a vintage silent movie.*

Great expectations

AS SIR ISAAC NEWTON, *the father of Newtonian
physics, tells us in his third law of motion, "for every action
there is an equal and opposite reaction." Little did Newton
know that his third law would also apply to computers in
the year 2000. "For every action your computer performs
correctly, it will mess up something else." On second thought,
maybe that's Murphy's first law of computing. You might think
that what separates proficient computer users from beginners
is their level of frustration. You'd be wrong.*

■ **Sir Isaac Newton:**
*"For every action there
is an equal and
opposite reaction."*

*Computers frustrate even the most accomplished users,
often on a daily basis.*

I've been computing for over 20 years. I know many programming languages,
can set up and administer networks, and can build a PC from the parts up. Yet
today I had to resist the urge to smash my PC to smithereens on not one, not two,
but three occasions.

Computer frustrations

Today my computer refused to copy CDs; erroneously decided
it was out of disk space and declined to save my files; and forgot
how to logon to my e-mail server (which prevented me from
retrieving my e-mail). My telephone bill also arrived today, and
revealed that my PC repeatedly dialed a random number last
month that, as luck would have it, was home to another PC.
It proceeded to run up 200 minutes of toll charges, at a cost
of $90.

This was one red-hopping mad and frustrated "experienced"
user. Yes, I was as ticked off as any beginner. So what separates
the know-it-alls from the know-nothings is not frustration, but
the BTDT factor: "Been There, Done That." In other words,
experienced users expect their computer to blow up, mess up,
and foul up. They accept it as a way of computing life. Novice
users, on the other hand, tend to feel they've done something
wrong, or are lacking some mystical skill that, if only they
possessed it, would cause the computer to behave.

Be realistic

As I said at the beginning of Part I, success with computers starts with a "can do" attitude, coupled with a sound plan of attack (your application requirements list), tempered with realistic goals and expectations. So set your expectations properly. Understand going in that things will go wrong. Really wrong. No user escapes unscathed. Software won't work as it's supposed to. Important data will be lost or seem to disappear. Certain web sites won't work. E-mail attachments won't open. Your PC will crash. You'll suffer down time. It's not you. It's the computer.

Getting started with PCs is akin to scaling a bell curve. You will not be productive on day one, week one, or even month one. But with each passing day, you're one day closer to knowing everything you need to know to remain productive on a PC. Perhaps by the end of year one, you'll have a good grip on all of the "Things I need to do today." Then it's on to the "Things I need to do in the near future" category.

In upcoming days, weeks, and months, you'll learn how to embrace new software and get up to speed fast. But you'll also be forced to learn how to cope with belligerent PC behavior.

Through it all, remember Levin's Credo: "There isn't a computer user on Earth, no matter how experienced, who wasn't baffled the first time he or she wrestled with a belligerent computer." That includes me. We're all novices once, but we're experts forever.

A simple summary

✓ Maintain a positive "can do" attitude. Lack of knowledge is no excuse for lack of determination.

✓ Tackle each computing task one step at a time. Bite off more than you can chew, and you'll either choke or spit up.

✓ As you move forward through the computing experience, don't let frustrations get you down.

Computers are sometimes more frustrating than they are useful.

✓ Take the right steps in the right order. The #1 reason new users fail is because they take the wrong steps first.

✓ Figure out what your goals and objectives are. Develop them into a requirements list that drives your entire computing strategy.

Chapter 2

Designing Your PC

SUCCESS WITH COMPUTERS doesn't start with a computer, but it sure helps to have one. Now that you have developed a strong "can do" attitude, determined your requirements list, and set your goals and expectations, it's time to go shopping. The PC market is a complicated one, with many options to choose from. In this chapter, I'll cover the various PC offerings you'll encounter in the marketplace and the essential apparatus you'll need no matter what. I'll also compare pre-installed software to custom-fit solutions, and help you design your personal computer center.

In this chapter...

✓ The PC market then and now

✓ The cost of "free" PCs

✓ The essentials you'll need

✓ A custom-fit solution

✓ Your computer room

The PC market then and now

THE FIRST COMPUTER *I bought was an Atari 800. That was around 1981, when Atari was one of the personal computing kings. That computer set me back over $1,500, yet delivered a fraction of the computing power people can now get for a few hundred bucks, or even for free. I gave my local Sam Goody record store $1,500 (they didn't have computer stores in those days), and took home a 2MHz terminal with 48K of RAM, no monitor, no disk drives, no modem, and no printer. It did include a converted cassette recorder that could be used to store programs and data.*

■ **That's me at** *my first computer, an Atari 800, circa 1981, smiling the smile of a happy novice.*

THE LITERATURE OF COMPUTING

It's unavoidable; the literature of computing is filled with upper and lowercase K's, M's, and G's. These letters represent storage or speed capacities. A lowercase letter refers to capacity measured in thousands (k), millions (m), or billions (g) of data "bits." A bit is the smallest amount of data a computer handles; it's literally one piece (or bit) of information, always a 1 or a 0. An uppercase letter represents thousands (K), millions (M), or billions (G) of data "bytes." One byte equals eight bits of information, such as 00001111. Computers need one byte of storage to store one alphanumeric letter, such as an A, B, or C, in memory. In practical terms, a 10G hard drive stores 10 Gigabytes of information, or roughly 10 billion characters, whereas a 56k modem sends and receives data at 56,000 bits per second – or 7,000 bytes per second. It's a strange and confusing nomenclature that, unfortunately, we're stuck with.

Today you can buy a fully equipped brand-name PC system for $1,500, including a high-speed Pentium-class processor, 64M or more of RAM, floppy and hard drives, a CD-ROM or DVD drive, a built-in 56k modem, upgrade slots, I/O ports, high-performance video, and a monitor. (Don't worry if you're slightly confused by all these alien acronyms, such as RAM, ROM, MHz, CPU, and so on. I'll soon explain them all in great detail.)

In fact, many vendors will even throw in a color printer and software packages including dozens of programs. Clearly the computer industry is a case study of the law of supply and demand. Demand and supply are high and getting higher, and that's driving prices downward. Down as low as . . . free!

Thanks to wacky Internet marketing schemes, you can snag a brand-new computer for absolutely no money down.

On the flip side, if you don't get suckered by – er, I mean, take advantage of the free PC deals, you can spend $1,000, $2,000, $3,000, or more on a complete PC package. Trying to divine the differences between a free PC and those other price points can become very confusing, very fast. But there is a way to cut through the confusion and boil things down to a manageable set of facts. We'll start, then, with the hottest trend in computing today, the free PC.

The cost of "free" PCs

THE COMPUTER INDUSTRY *has a history of misrepresenting its products. Things labeled quick, easy, or new have a tendency to be slow, hard, or rehashed. So it is with the word "free."*

Virtually every free PC offer on the market today will entangle you with strings attached.

One approach, pioneered by Free-PC.com gives you a free computer in exchange for your privacy. The folks at Free-PC.com monitor your web surfing habits and feed them, along with other personal data, back to advertisers.

Freebies from your ISP

In another approach, pioneered by Internet service providers such as Gobi.com, DirectWeb.com, and others, you get a free computer in exchange for signing up for three or more years of Internet services at rates ranging from $20 to $50 a month. In some cases, these deals also hit you with a $100 or more setup charge. Nearly all hide a fat cancellation fee, which can approach $600 to $1,000, usually covering the cost of the computer.

Not to be outdone, major national Internet service providers (ISPs) such as CompuServe (owned by America Online), Prodigy, and the Microsoft Network (MSN) have climbed aboard the free PC bandwagon. Their deals are a little better, but not much. These companies offer rebates of up to $400 in exchange for a three-year commitment to their online service. The rebates can be used for anything, or just put in the bank. In most cases, users apply them to the cost of a new computer.

The dark cloud

Combined with other offers, such as manufacturer and retailer rebates, the net cost of a new PC can be driven down to $500, $200, or even $0. Look closely at these marketing schemes, however, and you'll find there's much less to them than meets the eye. Topping the list: the computers themselves. In the cases of Gobi, DirectWeb, and other regional ISPs, the computers are usually the cheapest tin boxes they can get their hands on. They often carry no brand name and are warranted solely by the ISP. In other words, if you don't like the PC's performance, if it proves incompatible with upgrades, or if the ISP itself tortures you with busy signals, slow connections, or disconnects, you're stuck. Worse, there's no opportunity to adapt the PC to your requirements. What features and components you get are those the ISP puts in the box. No more, no less.

The rebate approach offered by the national ISPs is slightly more flexible, and therefore better, but it still suffers from serious potential drawbacks. With rebates, you can use the cash refund in any way you see fit. That means you can pick and choose your PC from among all the available brands. That's good, because it means you can align the computer's design with your requirements list. But you're still stuck with the ISP for three years at $20 or so per month, and that's bad. In the event you discover a need to access the Internet at high-speed, and want to switch to cable or other more capable, faster Internet connections, you'll be locked into the national ISP's pokey dial-up service.

In a nutshell, virtually all of the free PC deals limit your PC purchasing flexibility, restrict your upgrade and online options down the road, or compromise your privacy and security.

Plus, when you add them up, they ultimately cost between $700 to $2,000 in monthly service and other fees. You're better off buying your new PC with cash or credit, and using one of the many free, advertiser-supported Internet services to access the Net (more on this later). They don't cost a penny, and if you don't like their service, there's no contract preventing you from switching to another free or for-pay ISP.

Scratch the free PC deals off the list, and that leaves computers ranging in price from a few hundred dollars to thousands. How to differentiate among these? Once again, it's easier than it looks. Your requirements list will drive the specifications you demand. Don't scour the market, comparing zillions of vendor offerings point for point, spec for spec, dollar for dollar.

■ **Some "free PC"** *vendors will give your details to advertisers or salespeople.*

The essentials you'll need

NO MATTER HOW UNIQUE your requirements are, there are certain fundamental elements every PC needs. In addition to the basics, there are particular devices, peripherals, programs, and upgrades you're better off buying sooner rather than later. Get the essentials out of the way at the time of purchase, and you won't need an emergency upgrade.

What follows are the absolutely essential components for any desktop or laptop PC. To keep things neat and orderly, I've broken out the core essentials list as follows:

✓Essentials for all PCs　　　　　　　✓Essential extras
✓Essentials for desktop PCs　　　　　✓Non-essentials worth noting
✓Essentials for laptop PCs

If you're in the market for a desktop PC, you'll need, at least, the core essentials for all PCs and desktop PCs. Similarly, laptop users will want the core essentials for all PCs, plus those for laptop PCs. If your computing needs are limited to word processing, spreadsheet, database, e-mail, and web access, you can base your purchasing decision on these core essentials alone.

Essentials for all PCs

Windows 98 compatibility. You need it. You want it. You can get it. Above all, you want a PC that's fully compatible with Windows 98. Believe it or not, some PCs are more compatible than others. Here's how you tell: Look for the "Designed for Windows 98/Windows NT" logo on the box.

The Windows logo is your guarantee the PC has passed a rigorous testing procedure that ensures it is fully compatible with Windows.

The CPU

The Central Processing Unit (also known as "the processor") is your computer's electronic brain. It defines your computer and your computing experience. Look for PCs with Intel Celeron, Pentium II, or Pentium III processors, or with AMD K6-2, K6-III, or Athlon CPUs.

Don't be fooled by marketing pitches put out by CPU vendors. As long as Microsoft certifies the CPU as compatible with Windows 98 (just look for the "Windows 98" logo on the box), it will run all of your Windows programs, and control all of your PC hardware as well as any other chip.

The CPU cache. This is a tiny amount of workspace memory, usually on or near the CPU chipset, that allows the CPU to store the results of recent computations.

It's the CPU equivalent of a paper tape for your calculator. Rather than have to rerun calculations, the CPU can look up the results in the cache. That saves time, and makes the computer finish tasks faster. Generally, the larger the cache, the better, but don't get bogged down on cache size. Virtually all PCs today feature an appropriately sized cache

Clock speed

The relative speed of a computer is rated in megahertz (MHz) – and coming soon, in gigahertz (GHz) – which means millions – or billions – of clock cycles per second. Every computer's central processor (its "brain," if you will, e.g., the Intel Pentium) is synchronized to an on-board clock. When the computer's clock "ticks," the central processor grinds out some work. Obviously, the more clock ticks a computer can generate per second, the more work it can do per second. That's why a 300MHz computer is, technically, slower than a 500MHz computer.

■ **The faster your** *computer's clock can tick, the better.*

Here's the catch: higher speed is not always better, in terms of bang for the buck. As you'll learn later, a 500MHz computer can be configured to run circles around a 700MHz computer.

Don't be lured into spending more for a PC with a faster clock speed. Let your requirements list drive the clock speed decision. That said, it is essential that your PC feature at least a 300MHz processor, which is plenty fast to run 99.999% of software today.

RAM

Your computer's "chip memory." is called RAM. Consider it the computer's blackboard. This is where your computer stores programs and information you're working on, only to erase and discard it all when you move on to something else.

The greater the PC's RAM, the more tasks the computer can work on simultaneously. Also, some tasks, such as editing digital images, audio, or video, are what we computer nerds call "memory intensive." Such tasks run best when lots of RAM is available. Most PCs today ship with at least 32M (that's 32 megabytes, or "megs") of RAM. This stands for "millions of characters." The English alphabet consists of 26 characters, or 26 bytes, in computerese.

DEFINITION

RAM stands for "Random Access Memory," which means the computer can read and write to the memory chips. (There's another form of memory, called Read-Only Memory [ROM], which can only play back information.) It's sort of like the difference between a cassette tape and a music CD. You can read (play) and record (write) to cassette tape, but you can only play (read) the music CD.

A PC with 32M of RAM can work with 32 million characters (bytes) of information in memory at a time. While that's adequate for the big 5 basic computing tasks, plan for the future, and go with a PC that offers 64M minimum. (My PC has 128M.) The bare essentials: make sure your PC has at least 32M of RAM.

Hard disk

Consider this your electronic filing cabinet. It's where all your programs and personal data are permanently stored and retrieved. The bigger the hard disk, the more information you can pack into the computer.

INTERNET

www.thechipmerchant.
com/cpuspecs.html

www.tomshardware.
com/busspeed.html

Don't take my word for it. Check out these web sites for the complete lowdown on CPU speeds and specs.

Hard disk drives are sized in terms of "gigabytes" (also called "Gs" or "GBs," or "gigs"). This stands for "billions of characters." A 10G hard drive, then, stores 10 billion characters (bytes) of information. Obviously, the greater the drive's capacity, the better. Drive capacities keep climbing. By the time you read this, any recommendations I could make regarding size will be obsolete. But I can safely say this: it's essential that your computer has a hard drive capacity of 10G or more.

CD or DVD drive

Virtually all desktop and many laptop computers today include a CD-ROM drive, capable of loading and running Windows software and playing music CDs. Growing numbers of PCs today are offering DVD drives, which can store full-length movies, as well as computer data and music.

Considering that nearly all commercial software is delivered on CD-ROM, it's essential that your PC have a CD-ROM drive. Many laptop PCs, especially the ultra-light models, don't offer integrated or plug-in CD-ROM drives. If you're considering a laptop, be prepared to buy an add-on CD drive. If your requirements list calls for full-screen movies and video, or you plan to be playing the latest computer games, you want a DVD drive. If not, a conventional CD-ROM drive will do (it will be many years before they become obsolete). Considering CDs are the past and DVDs are the future, if the PC you're interested in offers a DVD as part of the package, there's no reason not to grab it. And remember: It's always easy to add a DVD drive later. Bottom line: it's essential that your PC have a CD-ROM drive, and having a DVD drive isn't a bad idea, either.

Trivia...

Contrary to popular belief, DVD doesn't stand for Digital Video Disk. The "V" stands for "versatile," because a DVD disk can be used to playback music, video, software, or data. Now that's versatile!

Audio

Every PC on the market today includes CD quality digital audio, usually built into the motherboard. With few exceptions, the default audio circuitry integrated into most PCs is ideal for nearly all audio recording and playback tasks. Some PCs, however (especially laptops) don't offer the full complement of audio jacks. It's essential for the computer to have a microphone input jack, a stereo line-in jack, and a stereo speaker or headphone output jack. The best computers will also offer a stereo line-out jack, and a MIDI port. Don't sweat the audio specs (such as FM versus wave table synthesis, number of MIDI channels, etc.) unless your requirements list calls for extra audio capability. For example, if you're planning to play high-end computer games or connect a musical keyboard to the PC, it's worth exploring these options.

Faxmodem

Nearly all computers ship today with a built-in 56k faxmodem, also known as an "internal modem." This device allows you to connect to the Internet and transfer data at 56,000 bits per second, and send and receive faxes. Better computers also offer a faxmodem that can do double duty as a voice mail system. It's not essential to have a faxmodem unless you plan to get on the Internet using a dial-up telephone connection, send and receive faxes, or use the PC as an answering machine. However, your PC will probably come with a faxmodem anyway.

Make sure, however, that the faxmodem is not a so-called "WinModem." WinModems use software that simulates hardware, and are notorious for poor performance and cranky operation.

Printer

You need a computer to compute, and you need a printer to print. If your output requirements are basic, such as letter quality personal and business correspondence, any under-$200 color printer from Canon, HP, Lexmark, Xerox, or Epson will do. If your output needs are more demanding (digital photos, posters, banners, newsletters, mass-mailings, desktop publishing, etc.), you'll need to fall back on your requirements list to help drive your printer purchase. Don't get bogged down in printer specs such as dots per inch, printer technology ("laser" versus "ink jet"), pages per minute, and so on. Compare real-world printed color text and graphics output side by side, and go with the printer you like best. Note, however, that it's sometimes easier to find replacement ink and toner cartridges and other supplies for Canon and Hewlett-Packard models than for some other manufacturers' printers. Laptop users may want to consider portable printers. The print

■ **Companies like Canon** (*www.ccsi.canon.com*) *will sell you printers online.*

quality is usually less than stellar, and the printers are very slow. They'll fit in a laptop PC case, though, so you can take them with you on the road.

✓Bottom line: you'll need a printer and a printer cable to connect it to the PC. If your needs are basic, go for the best deal you can find.

USB ports

The Universal Serial Bus, a-k-a "USB," is the latest rage to hit personal computing. It's the future upgrade path for all modern computers. Most desktop and laptop PCs today offer two USB ports. Devices that you can connect to the USB ports include scanners, digital cameras, *Web cams*, external storage drives, personal organizers, displays, keyboards, mice, game devices, speakers, other computers, and much more. One nice feature of USB is that it supports "plug & play." This means you just plug USB devices into the computer, and they're automatically recognized and enabled – without having to power-cycle the PC (computer-speak for "turning the computer on and off").

■ **With the Universal** *Serial Bus (USB) you can "plug & play" a wide range of devices.*

> **DEFINITION**
>
> A Web cam *is a video camera connected to a PC that broadcasts its pictures over the Internet.*

✓Universally essential: insist on a computer with two USB ports.

The core essentials for desktop PCs

It doesn't matter whether you're buying a portable or a desktop PC. All of the above equipment is essential. But if you're buying a desktop PC, you'll also need the following core essentials.

Fast bus speed

Similar to the clock speed, this is how fast the computer can transfer data between the processor and other PC components, such as a hard disk drive. The pathway between the CPU and the components is called "the bus," because it shuttles data back and forth like a bus. You'll find PCs today offering bus speeds ranging from 50 to over 133MHz. (Laptop users might find it tough to figure out a unit's bus speed. It's safe to assume that all major-brand laptops today offer bus speeds of 66MHz or faster.)

The faster the bus speed, the faster the computer — in theory. In practice, the bus speed often has little impact on the computer's real-world throughput. Let your requirements list drive this decision.

✓Bottom line: make sure your PC features a 66MHz or faster bus.

Video card

The video adapter conjures up everything your PC needs to display, and sends it to your monitor (the screen) for output. Every PC includes a built-in video card, which can be upgraded later. For most users (those attacking the basic big five requirements), the default video support will be fine. If your requirements include playing video games; working with digital images, photographs, or video; or using computer-aided design tools, the stock video might not be sufficient. Consider an extra-cost upgrade. One important

■ **If you want** *to edit your video movies, you might need to upgrade your video card.*

point for laptop users: you're stuck with whatever video chipset is embedded on the motherboard. If you're considering a laptop, make sure the video card can handle the jobs you'll be throwing at it, because you won't be able to upgrade later.

✓ The clear essentials: let your requirements list drive any video upgrades.

Monitor

Your computer's display screen is one of the most important components, because you'll be staring at it for hours on end. Don't skimp here. Make sure the monitor is large enough for you to view comfortably. Most people prefer a 15" to 17" screen. Make sure, too, that the monitor's "dot pitch" is .28 or lower. That's the measurement, in millimeters, of the spacing between the on-screen dots that make up the image. The lower the dot pitch, the tighter and clearer the image.

A good monitor also offers a "refresh rate" of 60Hz (Hertz, or cycles per second) or greater. That's how many times per second the entire screen is redrawn. Low refresh rates cause flickering and distortion. Better displays offer between 75Hz and 85Hz. The best go above 100Hz.

If you're after the finest screen display, consider a flat-panel LCD. These monitors cost more, but they're worth it. LCDs aren't susceptible to at least 12 imaging problems that plague conventional monitor tubes, such as pin cushioning, barrel distortion, nonlinearity, and fuzzy focus.

✓ The essential pitch: Make sure your monitor offers a .28 dot pitch and a vertical refresh rate of 60Hz or higher.

COM ports

These are the PC's external COMmunication ports, one or more 25-pin plugs found on the back of the system. This is where you can connect communication devices such as modems, digital cameras, and printers. Some salespeople will try to confuse you by saying your computer contains "internal" COM ports or "USB" ports that "do the same thing." Don't be fooled.

Good computers offer one external COM port, dubbed COM1. The best PCs offer two, labeled COM1 and COM2. It's essential to have at least one external COM port.

INTERNET

www.zdnet.com/reviews

Look here for reviews of the latest PC monitors and other computer technology.

Input device ports

You control your computer using a keyboard and mouse, otherwise known as your input devices. The best PCs offer a dedicated keyboard port and a mouse port. Some newer, so-called "*legacy-free*" PCs do not include these traditional ports, which means that users must tap their USB ports for all input devices. PCs that offer dedicated input device ports are preferred over those that rely on the USB ports.

DEFINITION

Ultra-modern computers have come to be called legacy-free *PCs by the industry. In such computers, the PC's legacy (classic) technologies are downplayed in favor of the latest and greatest stuff. Unfortunately, legacy-free PCs aren't as expandable or upgradeable as PCs that support both legacy and more modern technologies.*

✓Input device ports are essential. Which flavor to use is up to you.

Input devices

Make sure your desktop PC comes with a 104-key "Windows keyboard," and a three-button "Windows mouse." You'll know your keyboard is Windows 98 compatible if it features a Windows logo key on both sides of the space bar. You'll know your mouse meets the latest Windows 98 standard if it features two buttons, plus a small "scroll" wheel between the two buttons (which doubles as a third button). Some PC makers cut corners by including older 101-key keyboards and two-button mice.

✓Make sure your PC comes with a Windows 98 standard keyboard and mouse.

Parallel port

If you're planning to print things on paper (and who isn't?), you'll need a parallel port. Also referred to as a printer port or "Centronics" port, this is where you'll plug in your printer. You can also connect many nonprinting devices such as scanners, digital cameras, and external storage devices, to your parallel port, without affecting your ability to use it for the printer.

■ **Some PC makers** *supply the older style of two-button mouse.*

Some legacy-free PCs do away with parallel ports, and use USB ports for printing instead. This results in one less USB connection for other uses, and is not recommended.

✓PCs that offer a dedicated parallel port are preferred.

Speakers

Most PCs include a cheap pair of stereo speakers, either as stand-alone units or integrated into the display monitor. If you're planning to play computer games, listen to CD music, or produce professional audio, then your audio quality is important to you. In that case, ditch the bargain basement bundled units, and upgrade to a professional computer audio rig. Vendors to consider: Altec Lansing, Yamaha, Bose, Benwin, or Creative.

■ **Most computers** *come with a pair of speakers.*

INTERNET

www.alteclansing.com
www.bose.com
www.benwin.com

Check out Altec Lansing speakers, for the audiophile in you, and Bose for better sound (and bigger bucks) through research. (The Benwin flat-panel speakers are the ones I use)

The core essentials for laptop PCs

When portability is your goal, you'll want a computer that packs a desktop PC punch, and then some. Add the following core essentials to your list if you're in the market for a portable computer.

Display

Insist that your laptop PC feature an "active matrix" backlit (or side lit) color LCD display. That's the best and brightest screen offered today. Alternate display technologies, such as "passive matrix" or "dual scan," will give you washed out, hard-to-read images.

VIP

Laptop displays come in a range of sizes, from 10in to 14in or even larger. As with most PC specs, bigger is better. Use your eyes to determine which screen size is best for you. Remember: you'll be staring at it for hours on end. Don't compromise on image quality.

The best laptops sport a video-out port (called a *VGA* or *SVGA* port) that allows you to connect a conventional desktop monitor to the computer. This can be a boon for people who need to work on the road but prefer a full-size display when at home or in the office.

PC Card slots

A good laptop provides no less than two PC Card slots. These slots accept credit card-sized plug-in upgrades that allow you to connect all manner of devices to the PC, such as scanners, external storage devices, extra modems, network cards, and more.

✓Make sure the laptop has 2 PC Card slots, both unused and available for future upgrades.

DEFINITION

VGA stands for "Video Graphics Array," a marketing term coined by IBM for the PC video standard it invented. SVGA is "Super VGA," another marketing term, this one dreamed up by video card makers who successfully improved on IBM's standard.

Full-size keyboard

You'll be typing on it all day, so make sure it's comfortable, and has full-sized keys. Corner cutting to watch out for: half-sized arrow keys, or arrow keys that do double duty as page up/page down keys, or laptop keyboards with fewer than 84 keys (the laptop standard). Also insist that the keyboard feature a "Windows" logo key, which is used by Windows for special functions. Note, however, that most laptops don't provide full-size function keys.

If you don't like the keyboard, you'll hate the computer after a short time. Get lots of hands-on time with the laptop before you buy it, and make sure you love the keyboard. The best laptops also offer a keyboard port that allows you to plug in a full-size keyboard when you're not on the road.

Pointing device

Most laptop PCs provide a mouse port that allows you to plug in and use a desktop mouse, but when you're mobile, there's often no place to set the mouse down. That's why you'll find a variety of pointing devices on laptops today. They range from little eraser-style pointing sticks, to flat and smooth touch pads, to trackballs, and more. Some laptops even offer two or more alternative pointing devices. Most people either love or hate the various alternative devices, so make sure you experiment with them before buying the PC.

Memory upgrade panel

The best laptop PCs make it easy to upgrade RAM. Look for a RAM upgrade panel on the bottom of the laptop. If upgrading the RAM requires a trip to the dealer, scratch the laptop off your list.

Essential extras

There are certain extra-cost items that most users ignore, or simply don't know about. Certainly you don't need every option known to man. But certain components that are considered optional are actually essential.

Backup power

When the power goes out, you lose your data. It's that simple. Laptop PC users don't have to worry, because the laptop's battery will automatically kick in. Desktop PC users aren't so fortunate, and should invest the extra $100 or so in a backup battery. There are only two brands to consider: Tripp-Lite and American Power Conversion.

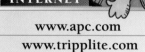
■ **It's worth** *investing an extra $100 on desktop PC backup batteries. Try APC's site at www.apc.com.*

Backup device

In the event of a fire, flood, or other catastrophe, you can always replace your hardware and software. But if you don't have backups (copies of your data), you can't replace lost data. Don't waste one red cent on a PC unless you're prepared to invest in a backup device. The best backup device is a CD-RW (CD Read/Writeable) drive, which can be used to create standard data CDs that contain your personal data. The advantage of a CD-RW is this: any computer with a CD-ROM or DVD drive can access the backups.

■ **CD-RW recorders** *from manufacturers like Yamaha (www.yamaha.com) are a popular backup solution.*

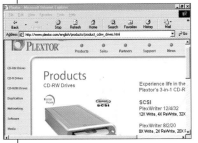

■ **Free Internet** *storage services such as http://Backup.com allow you to backup and share large files.*

Other backup options include tape drives, Zip drives, Jaz drives, and floppy drives. I strongly encourage you to avoid these alternatives. With the exception of floppy drives, virtually all require proprietary hardware and software to recover backed up data. Floppy drives are not recommended because they are slow, and can store only relatively small amounts of data. Tape, Zip, and Jaz drives can store much more data, but are notorious for having high failure rates. Remember, you buy a backup device not to backup your data, but to restore it when the time comes. Today, the closest thing to a fail-safe solution is a CD-RW drive. CD-RW brands to look for (in order of my preference): Yamaha, Plextor, LaCie, Hewlett-Packard, MicroSolutions, Sony, Ricoh, and Panasonic.

Nonessentials worth noting

Floppy disk drive

A carry over from an earlier PC era, the floppy disk drive (FDD) reads and writes 3.5in pocket-size disks that can hold up to 1.44M of data. Now at the end of its lifespan, the floppy disk drive may or may not be a feature of your PC.

Some PC makers are following the lead of Apple Computer, which moved the floppy disk from a standard to an optional item when it introduced the iMac in 1998.

Frankly, few users today will have use for a floppy disk drive, preferring to use 100M or 250M Zip or 120M SuperDisk drives instead. It's not essential that your computer feature a FDD, but if it has one, that's OK, too.

Zip or Jaz disk drives

These popular removable drives are manufactured by Iomega. The Zip drive is sort of like a floppy disk drive on steroids, capable of holding 100M or 250M of data per disk.

The Jaz drive is a removable hard drive, available in 1G and 2G capacities. If you need to share large amounts of data with other users, the Zip drive is the most popular way to go. If you need to share more than 250M of data with other users (or more than 650M, the maximum capacity of a CD-RW disc), then a 1G or 2G Jaz drive is the smart choice.

Before investing in a Zip or Jaz drive, note that free Internet-based storage services are emerging. These allow you to backup or share large files with other users, using nothing more than your Internet connection.

■ **A Zip drive** *is like a storage bodybuilder.*

Ethernet port

An industry-standard connection to a computer network. You might need this if you plan to use a high-speed Internet connection, such as cable, or if you plan to connect multiple computers together as part of local area network.

IrDA port

An infrared transmitter/receiver used to create wireless connections between your PC and portable devices, such as laptops, personal organizers, and palm-top computers. An IrDA port exchanges data at up to 4mb. If you're planning to use any form of pocket-size computer, an IrDA port is probably essential.

SCSI port

The Small Computer System Interface, a.k.a. SCSI (pronounced "scuzzy") is perhaps the fastest and most flexible connection technology available today. It can cost under $100 to add a SCSI adapter to your system. Once you do, you can string up to 16 devices to the adapter card. Scanners, Zip and Jaz drives, high-capacity external hard drives, CD-ROMs and CD-RWs, DVDs, digital photo and video cameras . . . nearly all high-performance devices are available in easy-to-use SCSI models.

SCSI differs from USB in that it's a high-speed connection, offering data transfer rates of up to 160MB per second. Compare that to USB's sluggish maximum throughput of 1.5MB per second. SCSI is one of the smartest upgrade paths you can follow, and well worth installing in your new PC, desktop or laptop, from day one. If you choose to do so, there's only one SCSI card vendor to consider: Adaptec.

TV ports

As if having the World Wide Web at your fingertips weren't distracting enough, now some PCs are offering TV-in ports. This lets you watch the boob tube while you work on the PC tube.

■ **A TV port** *lets you watch TV on your PC.*

Scanner

Computers are great for outputting data on paper. You can print it, fax it, e-mail it, or post it on the web. But getting paper into the computer is another matter entirely. If you need to capture paper-based reports, forms, photos, or images, you'll need a scanner. Scanners can be connected to your parallel, USB, or SCSI ports. (The fastest connection is SCSI, followed by USB.) For basic paper capture requirements, any brand-name scanner under $200 will do. If you demand high-resolution and the utmost in color accuracy, you'll need to bone up on scanner specs to find the model that's right for you. The best way to choose a scanner is by its resolution, rated in "dots per inch," or "DPI." The higher the DPI, the sharper the scanned image.

Watch out for vendors who artificially boost their DPI ratings through software. Make sure the DPI rating is the "optical" DPI, and not "dithered," "interpolated," or "enhanced."

All these terms refer to software gimmicks that artificially boost the DPI rating. Regardless of the price point you're after, consider scanners from Visioneer, Hewlett-Packard, and Canon. They're the top quality, safe buys.

Gaming devices

If you plan to play computer games, you'll need at least two different kinds of gaming devices. Look for a game pad and a joystick. The best brands are Logitech and Microsoft.

Removable drives

On certain laptop models, you can remove and replace the hard drives, floppy drives, and CD or DVD drives. This seems like a cool feature, but it's not. The drive connections are always proprietary to that manufacturer, meaning any expandable drives you purchase will be worthless the day you ditch the laptop. Also, the drive upgrades are prohibitively expensive. A better path: if and when the time comes to upgrade a drive, buy one that supports the laptop's industry-standard USB or PC Card slots. That way, the new drive will work with any future laptop PC you may buy.

MIDI/game port

The MIDI (Musical Instrument Digital Interface) port used to be a standard feature of PCs, tacked onto the audio card. Because it doubled as a gaming device port, it was used mostly to plug joysticks and such into the computer. Most gaming devices today connect via the newer USB port. As a result, many computer makers are doing away with the MIDI port (now considered a "legacy" device). If you plan to connect a musical instrument or device to the computer, you'll want a PC that offers a MIDI port.

A custom-fit solution

PCS ARE COMMODITIES, *pure and simple. It's often tough to tell one vendor's offering from another, beyond exterior design, perceived quality, and price. That's why PC makers have turned to free software deals to attract buyers. Given the choice between two relatively equal $1,000 PCs, buyers will generally opt for the model that offers more pre-installed "free" software. But free software doesn't mean good software.*

With the notable exception of general-purpose office productivity suites from Microsoft (Office 2000, Works 2000), Corel (WordPerfect Suite), and Lotus (Smart Suite), most bundled software suites are more hype than substance.

Further, for folks going about their PC purchase the right way – building their PC platform based on carefully constructed requirements – using one-size-fits-all freebies is akin to hammering a nail with a wrench. It's a random tool for the job. Even worse, much pre-installed software is provided without backup installation CDs. This means that when you need to upgrade to a new PC, or if you suffer a disaster, there's no way to re-install the free software short of going out and buying it. Practically every user needs a word processor, spreadsheet, database, presentation graphics tool, and other business computing basics. If you find a PC that meets your needs and happens to offer a free version of Microsoft Office 2000, Microsoft Works 2000, Corel WordPerfect Suite, or Lotus Smart Suite, grab it. Just make sure the package includes the manufacturer's installation CDs, or provides a low-cost option to get them. Short of that, don't be swayed by any – and I do mean any – other pre-installed packages on your PC.

Your computer room

WE SPEND THOUSANDS OF DOLLARS *on our computers and software. We invest hours daily working on them and with them. Yet few people dedicate more than a passing thought to the quality and ergonomics of the most important place of all: your computer room.*

Invest a little time and money to insure that your workplace is biometrically and ergonomically sound, and you'll dramatically reduce or even eliminate the risk of computer-related bodily injuries.

Preventing repetitive stress injuries

Those mysterious work-related aches and pains are called repetitive stress injuries or RSIs. Recent government studies show that increasing numbers of computer users are afflicted with repetitive stress injuries. Unfortunately, most folks never realize their discomfort is caused by extended computer use – nor do their doctors. Physicians often prescribe painkillers to patients complaining of aches and pains. But while medication may offer short-term symptom relief, continued pill-popping allows RSIs to fester unabated. When the fundamental cause of RSIs remains untreated, the injuries become serious and permanent, and can cost employers and insurers millions in time off and long-term disability claims.

Fortunately, you don't have to be a victim of the information age. There are some low- and no-cost strategies, techniques, and products that together can protect you from computer-induced repetitive stress injuries.

Most important, to reduce or eliminate RSIs, target their Achilles' heel: leaning. Virtually every RSI is caused by long-term leaning on a keyboard, desk, mouse, telephone, or chair. Eliminate the leaning, and you eliminate the possibility of getting stress-related injuries.

Ergonomically correct hardware

First case in point: the keyboard. Leaning on a wrist rest might feel better than bearing down on a cold hard desk, but it does little to prevent wrist, arm, and shoulder injuries. A better solution: move your keyboard to the edge of your desk, and type with your wrists in the air, without leaning. This eliminates the possibility of wrist pain and injury, because it removes all pressure from your wrists. It may look and feel odd at first, but if you suffer from a keyboard-related RSI, you'll get relief in days.

A soft-touch keyboard, preferably with a sound ergonomic design, can also help. Microsoft, Logitech, IBM, and others offer ergonomically designed keyboards (dubbed "natural" keyboards) that sell for $50 to $130. Also try putting a couple of thick foam mouse pads under your keyboard. These absorb and diffuse typing shock, which can reduce or eliminate pins and needles in fingers. Next in line: your mouse. To move it, you have to lean on it. Clicking on it eight hours a day can put your shoulder, elbow, and upper back on fire. Even ergo-mice require users to bear down on their desks for hours on end, and mouse pads won't help.

The solution: toss your mouse out the window (be sure to open the window first), and switch to an airborne pointer. Some of the best are Logitech's TrackMan Live!, Interlink's RemotePoint, Gyration's GyroPoint, and Mind Path's F/X IR50. These $100-$200 pointing devices operate in midair, freeing you from bearing down to mouse around. Mousing-in-space eliminates leaning on your desk and shifting body posture in unnatural ways. The result can be pain-free pointing and clicking. Yes, airborne pointers take some getting used to, but once you get the hang of it, they'll work as well as your favorite desktop mouse, without the discomfort.

Last up: your telephone. If you're one of the millions who cradles your phone between your ear and your shoulder, stop! Invest in a headset telephone or adapter. This allows you to sit naturally while you're working, especially when you're typing at the computer. Using a headset phone isn't as convenient as a conventional handset, but the choice is one of comfort, not convenience. Likewise, switching to an office chair that doesn't have armrests will keep you from leaning on your elbows, yet another common cause of RSI pain.

Avoiding leaning during the business day as much as possible, switching to ergonomic computer hardware, maintaining proper typing posture, and using a damn good chair are simple, yet very effective ways to reduce the risk of RSIs. It also helps to do some stretching exercises before you settle in at the keyboard. After you've been working for 20 minutes or so, get up and take a break. Do more stretching exercises, or take a stroll around your workplace. That deadline can wait.

A simple summary

✓ There's no such thing as a free lunch, or a free PC. All free PC offers end up costing you big money or your privacy. Review these offers carefully.

✓ Don't be motivated by steals and deals. Get to know the core essentials every computer user needs.

✓ It's worth paying a little extra for the essential extras, such as a backup power supply and a data backup device.

✓ Stick with your personal application requirements, and make sure the software you get is tailored to meet your unique needs.

✓ Using a computer can be detrimental to your health. Don't bring a PC into your home or office until you've arranged your work area for proper ergonomics. Plan to invest a few extra bucks on an ergonomic keyboard, mouse, chair, and telephone. It really is worth it.

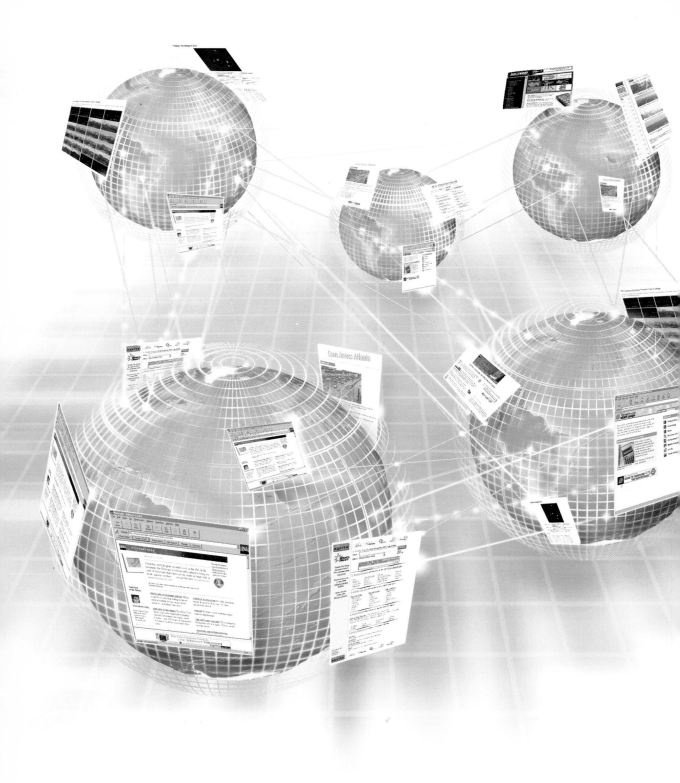

Chapter 3

Signing on to the Internet

A S WITH LONG DISTANCE telephone companies, all Internet service providers are not created equal. While people usually apply plenty of thought, reasoning, and research to the choice of a long-distance service provider, first-time Internet users often don't think twice about how they'll access the Internet. Like herded cattle, they blindly accept whatever services the PC maker bundles with their new computer. Most of the time, that means choosing one of the online services featured on the Windows Desktop. In this chapter, I'll explain the different kinds of ISPs and their various service offerings, and help you determine which ISP and connection technologies are right for you.

In this chapter...

✓ I want my web PC

✓ Big toe or big splash?

✓ Never judge an ISP by its cover

✓ Internet connection options

THE INTERNET IS FULL OF SERVICES AND TECHNOLOGIES TO CHOOSE FROM

I want my web PC

QUICK: WHAT'S THE #1 REASON people buy a PC today? If you said games, word processing, accounting, homework, or running a business, you'd only be partly right. It's the Internet or, more correctly, everything the Internet has to offer. People are after e-mail, web surfing, chatting, shopping, 24-hour investing, and multi-user gaming. They want instant news, sports, weather, and gossip. They want downloadable *music and videos, up-to-date TV and movie listings, and more.*

DEFINITION

Downloading *gets data, uploading sends data. When data is coming into your PC, it's said to be "downloaded." When you transmit data in any way, shape, or form, you're said to be "uploading" data.*

For some folks, the PC is simply a means to an end; the standard appliance used to navigate the all-popular "Information Superhighway." For others (perhaps you), the PC is much more than a simple Internet terminal. But no matter which camp you fall into – PC web surfer or PC power user – the Internet represents a crucial collection of technologies and services that will surely play a pivotal role in your everyday computing. Considering, then, that the Net is crucial to all PC users, and that service levels vary wildly among Internet providers, it makes sense to invest a little time assessing your Internet access requirements and options. If you don't, you could get stuck with an Internet service provider who not only doesn't meet your computing needs, but also provides horrible service. And I do mean stuck. Many of the Internet access plans offered today actually lock you in for 24 to 36 months or more, or require that you pay a year or more in advance.

If you try to switch ISPs before the plan's term is up, you'll get hit with stiff cancellation charges that can amount to hundreds of dollars.

There are also other ways in which picking the wrong ISP can be a mistake you can't escape. For example, many users can't get or stay on the web due to busy signals, painfully slow connections, or sessions that repeatedly hang up or crash. But they'll tolerate these service problems simply because switching ISPs means changing their e-mail address. Unlike the US Postal Service, there is no change of address form you can file when you change your e-mail address. Any mail on its way to your *inbox* will be lost.

DEFINITION

Your inbox *is your Internet mailbox. It's the electronic place where you pick up your Internet mail.*

Any mail sent to you after you change ISPs will be lost. And dozens, perhaps hundreds of people and web sites that have added your e-mail address to their address book will lose their electronic connection to you.

■ **When you** *download a file, you can choose where to save it.*

Still others find they'd rather suffer the pain of poor service than lose the familiarity of their particular online provider's software. After spending months cozying up to the various windows, icons, and menus that make up a service's e-mail and other offerings, who wants to go back to square one and learn everything over again?

Proprietary online services

Then there's the familial lock, most commonly found among folks who signed up with one of the so-called *proprietary* online services, such as America Online (AOL), CompuServe (CS), Prodigy, and the Microsoft Network (MSN). Your spouse or kids, for example, may demand that you stick with a service because all of their friends are on AOL, CS, Prodigy, or MSN. Of course, these friendships blossomed on the service, and wouldn't exist had you not made the mistake of signing up in the first place.

Clearly, choosing an ISP is not unlike getting married. Plan on getting hitched for life, because breaking up is hard to do.

Get it right the first time, and you'll never have to suffer the pain of divorcing your ISP. Before you hit the stores in search of a new PC, you need to figure out which Internet service provider you're going to settle down with. Doing so means that, once again, you have to assess your personal requirements, and learn a thing or two about the various service options available to you.

■ **Your inbox is** *your Internet mailbox.*

■ **Choose your ISP** *partner with care – divorce can be messy and painful.*

Talk is cheap on the Internet

It's a fact: You don't have to be an AOL, CompuServe, Prodigy, or MSN user to chat with or e-mail other users on those systems. All you need to know is their e-mail address, and you can exchange messages with them in a flash. There are also tens of thousands of free chat rooms on the Internet, if you're interested in chatting with other users. Yes, even AOL's famous chat rooms can be had for free, and accessed from any ISP – not just AOL. You can also exchange "instant messages" without signing up with AOL or other proprietary online services. Here's a sampling of some of the more popular chat rooms, bulletin boards, and instant messaging services. Try them all, and settle in with those you like best.

FREEBIES

Free Internet chat rooms

Chat rooms allow you to engage in live electronic conversations with other users around the world, 24 hours a day. What you type on your keyboard is seen by other members in the chat room, and you can see what they type.

aim.aol.com	irc.icq.com	www.talkcity.com
chat.msn.com	irc.webmaster.com	www.yack.com
chat.yahoo.com	www.go.com/chat	

Free Internet bulletin boards

Bulletin board systems are similar to chat rooms, except that you "post" a message to the bulletin board and return in a few hours or days to read replies. Bulletin board systems are also called BBS's, forums, message boards, news groups, and conferencing centers.

boards.talk.city.com	www.delphi.com	www.icq.com/boards
clubs.yahoo.com	www.go.com/community/	
communities.msn.com	message	

Instant messaging services

Messages sent over an instant messaging (IM) service pop up instantly on the recipient's screen. You can IM with one or multiple people at the same time.

aim.aol.com	messenger.yahoo.com
messenger.msn.com	www.icq.com

Big toe or big splash?

JUST AS YOU SHOULD *get a grip on your application requirements before rushing out to buy a new PC, it's equally important to understand your Internet requirements before speeding on to the information superhighway.*

It's easy to pay two, three, even four times more than need be for your Internet access. For people who will be accessing Internet sites and services infrequently, it doesn't make sense to pay $20, $40, even $60 a month for online service. It's a little known fact that most Internet service providers offer "bare-bones" (stripped down) service plans for sporadic surfers for as little as $9 a month, and sometimes even less. These plans provide full access to the Internet for a fixed number of hours per month.

Bare bones vs. unlimited use Internet plans

In most cases, bare-bones plans include everything the higher cost plans feature, including multiple e-mail accounts, web access, a personal web site, chat rooms, newsgroups, "instant messaging," and more. The only difference between bare bones and "unlimited" use plans: If you use more than the allocated hours in a given month, the ISP will charge a fee for each additional hour online. For example, an ISP might offer 10 hours a month for $9, with each additional hour costing $1. Bare-bones plans also have one distinct advantage over other plans. You can always upgrade later to increased hours or higher performance. If you're not sure how much Internet you need, bare-bones plans are a great way to sample the Net, and decide later how much you need. If your Internet requirements are minimal to start with, it pays to shop around for a bare bones plan. If you know in advance you'll be making heavy-duty use of the Internet, it makes sense to contemplate higher cost, higher performance services, and prepaid plans that deliver unlimited hours at low, amortized rates.

Suppose you're planning to set up a home office, and you'll be working at the computer for most of the day. You know you'll be sending and receiving e-mails, and jumping on and off the web repeatedly to conduct research. This scenario reflects an online access requirement of eight hours a day, five days a week (or more). Clearly a person in this situation would benefit from a $20 to $30 per month flat-rate unlimited access service plan. But you can actually amplify the savings. Many ISPs (especially local providers in your neighborhood) offer steep discounts for customers who prepay. Paying one or more years in advance can cut your aggregate monthly cost from 10 to 40 percent, sometimes even more. In fact, some ISPs are even offering rebates of up to $400 for customers who sign up for three years of unlimited online access at about $20 a month. Do the math! With the rebate in play, the monthly service charge is actually $8 a month for unlimited web surfing.

High-speed Internet connections

There's one other factor to consider when selecting an Internet service provider: bandwidth. Simply put, bandwidth is the term used to describe the speed of an Internet connection. The higher the bandwidth, the faster the connection. A telephone modem, which connects to the Internet using your phone line, is a low bandwidth connection. A cable modem, which uses your cable TV line, is high bandwidth.

There are many other bandwidth options between telephone and cable (and beyond) which I'll delve into later. For now, suffice it to say that the more intense your Internet requirements are (and the deeper your pockets), the more bandwidth you'll need. If you're planning on sending and receiving huge data files, such as digital photos, videos, or audio clips, you had better plan as well on spending at least $40 to $100 a month for a high-speed Internet connection. You'll need the same capability if you want to take advantage of multi-user computer gaming, Internet audio or video teleconferencing, Internet television and radio, downloadable music, web serving, and other high-bandwidth functions.

These options have to be carefully weighed, however. Unlike bare-bones dial-up plans, when you sign up with a high-speed Internet service provider, it's all or nothing: With few exceptions, you can't throttle back to a lower cost, lower speed plan without changing ISPs. Which brings up perhaps the most important aspect of choosing an ISP: Upgradeability.

Look for an ISP that offers a full complement of service offerings, from basic dial-up to high-speed fireball connections.

The ability to upgrade gives you the flexibility to make mistakes. If you start off with too much or not enough bandwidth, you can change your service level without losing your e-mail address or encountering other pain. In a nutshell: Invest the time to work out your actual Internet requirements, then find a reliable ISP whose services can meet your present and future needs. It could be the single most important step in your thousand-mile computing journey.

■ **Hotmail.com** *is the world's most popular e-mail service.*

Never judge an ISP by its cover

HERE'S THE SCENE: *It's Saturday night, and you're on the hunt for something to do, somewhere to go. An advertisement for a local seafood restaurant catches your eye. "All you can eat for $20," it screams, in big, bold type. It's a done deal! You and the spouse grab your hats, don your coats, and zoom over to the local eatery. There you indulge in a few hours of gluttonous delight. Shrimp. Crabs. Lobster. Beer.*

That's when it hits you. No, not indigestion. The fine print. Just as you're washing down the last of the peel 'n eats, you notice a tiny disclaimer at the bottom of the coupon: "All food must be consumed within 60 minutes of arrival." You've been munching for three hours. Game over. Of course, in the real world, no restaurant could get away with this kind of scam for long. But ISPs get away with it all the time. It's one of the many ways they mislead new users aiming for the Internet.

Beware of ISP marketing tricks

Take a recent America Online ad campaign. The mailers, which looked strikingly similar to a bright orange box of Tide detergent, included a free CD-ROM with the latest version of the AOL software. On the cover and in six places overall, in large lettering,

AOL promised new users 100 free hours of online access just for signing up. Sounded like a great deal, until they read the fine print. There, in letters so small you needed an electron microscope to read them, AOL noted that the 100 free hours had to be used within the first 30 days after signing up.

Unless users went on a non-stop AOL binge during their first month of access, chances are they'd consume far fewer than the 100 free hours they thought they were entitled to.

In fairness to AOL, many other online services are also playing this bait-and-switch game. That doesn't make it right. Worse, it's not the only gimmick national and regional ISPs are using to lure unsuspecting consumers. Pulling a close second is the "unlimited access" offer many ISPs make. This ploy entices users with "unlimited" Internet access at flat monthly rates – often in the $20 range, but sometimes as low as $5. Surf an hour a day – pay the same rate. Surf 24 hours a day – pay the same rate. Sounds like a great deal, until you try to use it. Most users interpret "unlimited access" to mean they can dial in and log on in the morning and keep their connection alive all day. There are numerous advantages to logging on once in the morning and staying connected. For one, you can set your computer to continuously poll for e-mail. The moment a message arrives, you'll be alerted. You can also use Instant Messaging as a business communication tool, sending and responding to IMs all day. And of course, whenever you need to tap the web for news and information, you can switch to your browser and start surfing instantly.

But that's not how many ISPs define unlimited access. Put the ISP's access agreement under the magnifying glass, and you'll find it defined as unlimited INTERACTIVE access.

That little play on words means the ISP can and will disconnect your call if you're not actively typing at the keyboard. Walk away from your computer to take a phone call, write a letter, grab a sandwich, or answer nature's call, and the ISP will drop your session like a hot potato. This is especially annoying when you're one hour into a two-hour download, and the ISP kicks you off line. Dig a little further, and you'll find that most ISPs do offer a true unlimited service option – for about twice the cost of what they advertise as unlimited.

That's not the end of the ISPs' bag of tricks. Some ISPs allow you to set up multiple e-mail accounts, so you can put the entire family on the web for one low monthly fee. Other ISPs charge extra for each additional mail account you set up. The amount of "free" web storage space also varies wildly among ISPs. Some give you 5M of storage, while others offer 10M, 20M, 30M, or more – all for the same $10 to $30 a month. The more web storage space you get, the easier it becomes to create your own web site, when and if you so desire.

Know your ISP's privacy and access policies

ISPs can differ dramatically in how they treat your privacy. In addition to your name and address, ISPs have a record of every e-mail you send and every web site you surf.

Some promise never to provide advertisers with access to this incredibly sensitive personal information. Others earn a pretty penny selling to the highest bidder.

The flip side of this equation: The best ISPs do everything they can to protect you from SPAM, Internet-ese for junk e-mail. Other ISPs are known as "SPAMhauses," because they provide a haven for SPAMmers (junk mailers). These ISPs not only promote SPAMming, they'll allow your inbox to overflow with junk mail. But perhaps the most important aspect of selecting an ISP is often the most overlooked: access numbers. No matter how wonderful an ISP's pricing, services, and, privacy policies, it all adds up to zero if you can't get online.

■ **There are two kinds of SPAM:** *The kind you eat and the kind you find in your e-mail.*

Some ISPs have points of presence throughout the United States, and even around the world, while others are limited to your local region. Even more disturbing, almost all of the high-speed services, such as cable and DSL, don't provide remote dial-up access, or charge exorbitant hourly fees for the privilege. That means if you're on the road, you're out of luck. You won't be able to log in, retrieve your e-mail, and surf the web using a portable PC – or if you can, it will cost you an arm and a leg. (For example, the cable modem service Excite@Home charges $9 an hour for roaming access. Ouch!)

The lesson: Don't judge an ISP by its offers. Read the fine print in an ISP's advertising, and ask about the company's privacy and access policies. Better still: Get the policies in writing and read them carefully. You want straight answers to the following questions:

✓ How much time do I have to use the free hours?
✓ How much does it cost for unlimited INTERACTIVE access, and how much does it cost for totally unlimited access?
✓ Will I be logged off if I am not using the computer?
✓ How many free e-mail accounts do I get?
✓ How much free web storage space do I get?
✓ What's your privacy policy?
✓ What's your SPAM policy?
✓ Where are your points of presence?
✓ Do you support dial-in access outside of the local market, and if so, is there an extra charge for dialing in from the road?
✓ What's the fastest Internet connection you offer?
✓ Can I upgrade to faster Internet access down the road?

Internet connection options

IN ADDITION TO *choosing an ISP, you also need to decide which Internet connection technology is right for you. This is actually easier than it might seem at first glance. There are, essentially, six basic Internet connectivity technologies that most consumers and small businesses can affordably choose from.*

The "seminal six" Internet connectivity options cost from $5 to $250 or more a month, and offer data transfer rates (speeds) from 56k to 3m. Surprisingly, paying more doesn't guarantee faster or better service. For example, depending upon where you live, an ISDN line can cost upwards of $250 to $500 a month, but delivers only a 128k connection. Contrast that to a cable modem, which delivers a connection between 700k to 3m, at $40 a month – about 1/6th the cost. Setup charges also vary widely among the various Internet connection technologies. Basic dial-up service using a plain Jane 56k modem often costs $5 to $20 to set up. ISDN can cost $500 or more, while cable runs anywhere between $100 and $700. There are other, even faster ways to get on the Internet, but technologies above and beyond the seminal six are way too expensive (as much as $1,000 per month) for the average computer user or business manager.

KEEP THIS IN MIND

Two rules to keep in mind when determining which type of Internet connection technology you need:

First: Generally, the more hours you intend to spend on the Internet, the faster your Internet connection should be. If you're planning to use the Internet to send a few e-mail messages a day or to check up on your investments a few times a week, a plain 56k modem connection is probably fine for you. On the other hand, if you're preparing to day trade, conduct research, send and receive large data files, then a faster Internet connection is absolutely essential.

Second: It's not always easy to do, but try to find an Internet service provider who offers a variety of connectivity technologies. This enables you to start slow, and ramp up to faster performance as your needs grow – without having to change your e-mail address. To help you get started, here's a breakdown of the seminal six Internet connectivity technologies at your disposal.

Dial-up

This is how the vast majority of users everywhere get on the Internet: with a modem and a telephone line. Technically, the fastest connection you can get is 56k, although due to archaic FCC regulations, no 56k modem can deliver more than a 53k link. Actually, due to the nature of dial-up technology, most 56k modem users never link up above 40k to 50k. If your phone lines are old, or too far from the telephone company central office (CO), you may find that the best connection you can get is between 28.8k and 33.6k.

Windows 98 includes built-in support for dial-up connections, and nearly all computers today include a 56k modem as a standard feature. Dial-up requires only a regular phone line, which makes it the easiest way to get on the Internet from anywhere in the world.

But its reliance on old fashioned telephone lines means that a dial-up connection is also the slowest (some would say most painful) way to surf the Net. To get the most out of a 56k connection, upgrade to a top-quality external modem, such as those offered by 3Com's U.S. Robotics division. Note that external modems connect to your computer's COM or USB ports; you do not have to open the computer up and remove or install any hardware to upgrade to an external modem.

Most Internet service providers support 56k dial-up access. Cost varies from about $5 a month to as much as $30 a month. Prepaying a year or more in advance can reduce the average monthly fee. When shopping for a dial-up connection, make sure the ISP offers multiple local access numbers in your area. This avoids toll charges, and ensures you have extra numbers available in case you encounter a busy signal on your primary dial-in line.

Some ISPs offer free dial-up connections. In exchange for the free connection, you're subjected to a nonstop barrage of advertising. Most users report that the free services are reliable, which means they're a viable option for moderate Internet requirements.

INTERNET

www.altavista.com
www.freeweb.com
www.juno.com
www.netzero.com

You can't get a free lunch, but you can get a free ISP by signing up with one of these services.

ISDN

These letters stand for "Integrated Signal Digital Network." ISDN lines transmit data digitally (and more reliably than plain dial-up connections) at either 64k or 128k (your choice). For this type of service, you'll need a special ISDN modem and a visit from the phone

■ **3com.com** *provides full details of the high-quality range of U.S. Robotics external modems.*

company to reconfigure your telephone line and switch type and to assign you something called a "SPID."

ISPs characteristically charge a hefty setup fee for this entire up-front configuration. Then they hit you with fat monthly rates, "line charges," and hourly usage fees (not to mention toll charges, if the ISDN dial-in number isn't local).

Clearly, ISDN can become very expensive very fast. Depending upon where you live and the ISP involved, ISDN costs can hit $500 (or more) a month. It's not available everywhere, although most major telephone companies and regional ISPs offer it. In general, ISDN connections are poor value; avoid them if you can.

Multilink PPP

The third connection option is known as multilink point-to-point protocol (or MLPPP for short). The best kept secret of the Internet, MLPPP lets you combine multiple dial-up modems for faster access. Any number of modems can be "bonded" together with MLPPP, although most people combine no more than four. MLPP can be used in one of two ways: with Windows 98's built-in "multilink" feature and several separate modems, or by way of a dedicated device known as an "MLPPP *analog* router."

■ **ISPs like AltaVista.com** *offer a free dial-up connection but will bombard you with advertising.*

I recommend going the MLPPP router route. A router is easier to install and configure than multiple modems, and it can expand with your needs.

Plus, if you need technical help, the MLPPP router vendor will be there for you, whereas Microsoft's "multilink" feature isn't well supported. In addition to the MLPPP router itself, you'll need one telephone line for each modem you're going to connect, an Ethernet networking card in the PC, and an ISP that supports MLPPP connections (most do).

DON'T NIX THE NIC

Try to make sure that your new PC features an Ethernet networking card, also known as a Network Interface Card, or NIC. Ethernet cards provide very fast 10-megabit (10mb) connections between multiple computers. That's much faster than the maximum 56k connection possible with dial-up modems. Most high-speed Internet connections – including MLPPP, DSL, and cable – require or work best with a NIC. Even if your PC doesn't have a NIC, any local PC dealer can add one in minutes. The best Ethernet cards are manufactured by 3Com (www.3Com.com) and SMC (www.SMC.com). Linksys (www.Linksys.com) also makes a good line of NICs.

DEFINITION

AUX is shorthand for auxiliary port. It's a receptacle in the back of the router (or any device) that's used to connect add-on (auxiliary) options.

MLPPP routers cost between $200 to $600. Some include two internal 56k modems, providing 112k Internet access. You can boost that to 160k by adding a third external modem, which plugs into the MLPPP's *AUX* port. Other router models don't include pre-installed modems, but allow you to plug in from one to four external modems.

Whether they include built-in modems or not, all MLPPP routers operate the same way, from your PC's perspective. Simply connect the MLPPP router to the phone lines, and plug your Ethernet networking card to the router. Then run the setup software, enter your ISP's settings, and you'll be surfing the Internet between 112k to 216k. If you choose to use MLPPP, save money by instructing your local telephone company to provide minimum service for your 2 to 4 lines. Assuming your ISP provides a local dial-in number for MLPPP service, asking for minimum service will keep your monthly line charges low.

Another advantage of MLPPP routers: They're actually networking "hubs," offering 4 to 8 network connections. This means you can connect up to eight other computers in your home or office to the MLPPP router, and share files, drives, printers, and your Internet connection. MLPPP also goes with you.

If you move your home or office, all you need are three new phone lines to get your MLPPP connection back up and running. Further, MLPPP routers support dial-in access, which lets you connect to the Internet when you're on the road. The best MLPPP routers are those offered by Netopia and Ramp Networks. Another option is the new 4-modem router from Linksys. Or, you can do MLPPP without a router, using multiple modems and Windows 98's built-in support for the technology.

Another well-kept secret of the Internet, satellite modems capture Internet data at 400k and send it out at 56k. With satellite, surfing the Internet is fast and sending data is slow.

But that's not as bad as it sounds, since most people send nothing more than keystrokes and mouse clicks over the Internet. For simply interacting with web sites and services, satellite's 56k *upstream* connection is more than sufficient.

The only time you'll feel constrained by satellite's 56k uplink is when you have to transmit a large file to someone or some service. And I'm not talking documents, spreadsheets, and other general office communications that "weigh" just a few kilobytes. I'm talking videos, music files, photographs, and other heavy-duty items that consist of more than just basic text and numbers. These data types often consume vast amounts of hard disk space, measured in megabytes. Obviously, sending a 10k document over a 56k connection will take under a second. Sending a 10M video, on the other hand, will take quite a while indeed. But for most folks, this is not an issue. For the majority of users, the main advantage of satellite connections is their nationwide availability. That's good news for people who have been waiting for years for high-speed cable or DSL hookups, with no end in sight.

As long as your home, apartment, or office has room for the satellite dish, and the dish can be positioned to get an unobstructed heavenly view to the south, you're a candidate for high-speed satellite access.

Another advantage of satellite: The same dish can serve up both the Internet and digital satellite TV. But satellite isn't perfect. As I mentioned earlier, it requires the use of your computer's 56k modem. Also, satellite presently supports only Windows 98 PCs, and requires an available USB port or expansion slot. (Support for other Windows versions is coming.) Lastly, some users report problems trying to share their satellite connection with other PCs on a home or business network.

■ **Routers such as** *those supplied by Linksys.com provide fast connections between multiple computers by linking modems via a Network Interface Card.*

INTERNET

www.diamondmm.com

www.linksys.com

www.netopia.com

www.ramp.com

You'll find everything you need to know about MLPPP, with or without routers, at these sites.

■ **Windows 98** *provides limited help on Microsoft's multiple modems feature, but ISPs that offer MLPPP routers generally provide better support.*

Satellite connections are fast, but they're also more costly than similarly performing options and more complicated to set up. Unless you're handy, you'll need to have the satellite dish professionally mounted and installed. That can cost from $100 to $250. The basic hardware starts at about $300, with monthly fees of $30 for 25 hours of access, $35 for 100 hours, and $110 for 200 hours a month. Each additional online hour per month costs $2.

■ **It's probably best** *to have a satellite dish professionally installed.*

Unlimited service is not yet available, so you'll have to watch your time, or suffer the stiff hourly surcharges that kick in after you consume your basic hourly allocation for the month.

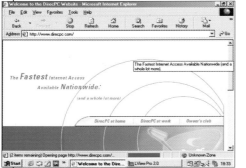

■ **Try DirecPC.com** *for answers to your questions about Internet access via satellite.*

But for people who need more than 216k connections, and who live in areas not served by cable or DSL, satellite remains the best game in town. Currently, there is only one satellite modem service: DirecPC. It's a part of Hughes Network Systems, the same company behind the DirecTV satellite service.

INTERNET

www.direcpc.com.

You'll find everything you ever wanted to know about satellite Internet but were afraid to ask on DirecPC's home page.

DSL

Long on promise, short on delivery. That's DSL in a sold under a variety of names: DSL, ADSL, SDSL, xDSL, and a dozen others. Whatever it's called, Digital Subscriber Line technology is a way to provide high-speed digital Internet transport using your existing analog telephone lines. (In some cases, however, an additional phone line is required.) DSL performance varies according to the type of DSL you buy, the type of phone cable used in your neighborhood, and your proximity to the phone company's central office.

DEFINITION

In symmetric data transfer, information is sent and received at the same speed. In asymmetric data transfer, data is sent and received at different speeds, which usually means that uploads are slower than downloads.

The fastest DSL available is ADSL (asymmetric DSL) which, technically speaking, can download data up to 7.1mb, and upload at about 1.1mb.

But most ISPs cap all DSL connections, including ADSL, between 100k and 700k. SDSL (*symmetric* DSL) tops out at 1.5mb both upstream and downstream, but it's also commonly capped at around 600k to700k.

The bottom line is, most DSL flavors are pre-configured to grab data somewhere around 700k and to send it around 100k. Again, your DSL mileage may vary, depending upon how close you are to the telephone company CO. The farther you are from the CO, the slower and less reliable your DSL connection will be. Also note that regional telephone companies have a horrendous track record for fouling up DSL installations. DSL itself is notorious for high levels of downtime, worse than any other high-speed Internet option available today.

DSL costs vary, but expect to pay about $50 a month for 600k to 700k access, $100 a month for 1.5mb, and $200 monthly for the full 7mb. You'll also be hit up for an installation charge and the cost of a DSL modem – about $200 all told.

DSL providers frequently require buyers to sign a long-term contract, ranging from 12 to 24 months. If it turns out DSL technology is not for you, you could be stuck with it for a lot longer than you care to be. Make sure you know the contract terms going in.

The end game: Consider DSL if you need the fastest connection available, cable modems are not available in your area, and you're prepared to undergo the hassle of dealing with miscreants at your local telephone company.

Cable

Surprise! Perhaps the perfect solution for most web surfers comes from the company you love to hate: Your cable TV provider. It turns out the cable that brings television signals into so many homes is also ideal for carrying computer data. Technically, cable modem connections could be as fast as a true business network. In practice, the cable companies limit their downstream bandwidth to between 1.5mb and 3mb – still plenty fast for virtually all Internet applications. Upstream bandwidth is often capped at 128k, although some cable providers are permitting 1mb, 1.5mb, or greater upstream links – just right for running a personal web server right out of your home or office (but don't tell them that).

As with all technology, cable isn't perfect. Cable networks are broken down into neighborhood-sized nodes. Like any business network, as more users log on and bat data back and forth, the network slows down – in theory. In practice, cable companies have attacked this fundamental law of networking by applying "managed network" technology. This allows them to guarantee minimum service levels – about 700k downstream and 128k upstream – to each and every user.

Like satellite and DSL, cable service is available only where the cable line is installed. You'll need a dial-up modem to access the Internet on the road, and you'll have to pay by the minute for that luxury, or use a separate dial-up ISP.

Cable service averages about $40 a month, plus a one-time installation fee that varies between $100 and $700. You'll also have to buy or lease a cable modem. Leasing runs about $10 a month, while the modems themselves cost about $300. As with satellite, your TV signal can share the cable line with your Internet data.

Unlike DSL, cable providers don't require long-term commitments. You can cancel cable service at any time.

Cable is ideal for users who don't travel a lot, and need the fastest, most reliable Internet connection money can buy. It's clearly the best all-around value. The leading providers are Excite@Home and AOL/Time-Warner's Road Runner.

INTERNET

www.home.net

www.rr.com

Check out the sites where the cable Internet revolution begins.

One word of warning: Avoid cable service providers who use so-called "hybrid" cable modem systems. These systems use a cable modem connection to download (surf) web data and a modem to upload (send) data. Unlike satellite, which has perfected this hybrid technique, the cable companies haven't quite gotten it right. Users who opt for hybrid cable systems often wind up pulling their hair out over frequent down time, poor performance, system crashes, and incompatibilities.

■ **Excite@Home** *(www.home.net) is a leading provider of cable Internet access, the best all-round value where cable is already installed.*

In addition to the basic six, new connectivity technologies are slowly becoming available. Microwave (MW) and MW-DSL, for example, deliver T1-class speeds for a fraction of the cost. But for now, dial-up, ISDN, MLPPP, satellite, DSL, and cable are your only options.

What do I use? I was one of the first people to jump on the cable bandwagon; in fact, I was a beta tester for the @Home service way back when.

I loved my cable modem service (provided by Comcast in Philadelphia), but had to drop it when I moved out of the city. Unfortunately, unless you live in a major metropolitan area, cable modem access is tough to come by. I now use MLPPP, and

■ **AOL/Time Warner's** *Road Runner (www.rr.com) is another major provider of cable modem access.*

have little to complain about. I also have a DirecDuo satellite dish installed and ready to go (that's TV and Internet). I plan to transition my Internet connection over to the satellite as soon as I have some free time. And I wouldn't sign up for DSL or ISDN even if they offered it to me for free.

■ **Unless you live** *in the city, cable modem access isn't easy to find.*

A simple summary

✓ Choose your Internet service provider the same way you choose your PC and your programs: based on your unique needs, not based on free online time, free computers, or other come-ons.

✓ Seek out an ISP that offers a variety of services, so you can start by dipping your big toe into the Internet waters and dive in later – without having to change your e-mail and web settings.

✓ Make sure you know what you're getting into before you get into it. Read the contract before signing up. Look for an ISP that doesn't lock you into long-term contracts and that doesn't limit your online access to so-called "interactive" use.

✓ Avoid ISPs that don't respect your privacy or don't provide remote dial-up access.

✓ Select the type of Internet connection technology that's best suited to your individual requirements, be that dial-up, ISDN, MLPPP, satellite, DSL, cable modem, or something even fancier and faster down the line.

■ **Some ISPs try** *to lock you into a long-term contract.*

Chapter 4

Purchasing Your Computer

I N STARK CONTRAST to most new computer buyers, who sign up for the computing revolution without spending one minute in basic training, you have invested time in learning to formulate a cogent plan of attack. It's time to venture forth into the battle zone we call "computer shopping." Yet no matter how well-prepared you are, your opponents – also known as dealers – have the strategic edge. They'll field wave after wave of highly trained sales people at you, all of them experts in pushing products, clouding minds, and closing sales. Before you head off to battle, here are a few last-minute thoughts to tuck away in your mental duffle bag. They could mean the difference between pain or victory on the retail battlefield.

In this chapter...

✓ Bad advice from good friends

✓ Brand name or cheap clone?

✓ Beware salesmen bearing offers

✓ Warranties, service plans, and the restocking charge

BE ARMED TO THE TEETH WITH INFORMATION WHEN YOU GO COMPUTER SHOPPING

Bad advice from good friends

THE FIRST CHALLENGE *you'll encounter when shopping for a new PC won't be posed by salespeople, vendors, or your credit card limit. No, the most taxing aspect of buying a new PC is warding off the mountains of advice from friends, family, and associates. The moment word leaks out that you're in the market for a new PC, suddenly everyone you know becomes a computer expert. The first wave of attacks often comes from the Macintosh users — also known as "Mac addicts" — in your personal circle.*

■ **They hear you're** *buying a PC — suddenly everyone wants to offer advice.*

Duck and cover when the Mac fanatics swoop in. They're fully experienced in guerilla warfare and cult programming. They'll literally kick your butt in an all-out effort to sway you from the dark side of Windows toward the enlightenment of Macintosh.

Macs are wonderful computers, and well worth your consideration. But you bought this book because you probably made up your mind to enter the world of Windows. Rather than endure a Holy War with Mac warriors, here are the only magic words known to douse their fires: "My boss wants me to get a Windows PC." Mac users know they can eventually win one mind at a time, but they can't change your company's computer standard.

Telling them you'll be using the PC on the job, with special software that won't run on a Mac, will call off the Mac dogs.

After the Mac pack disperses, you'll be hit by a wave of advice from PC technologists. You see, every PC user who has read three or more issues of any computer magazine believes he or she is fully qualified to act as your personal computer consultant! One friend will tell you that a 700MHz Intel Pentium III PC is a must, and warn you about compatibility problems with Pentium clones. Another will say he or she has an AMD Athlon 750MHz Pentium clone that leaves the genuine Intel Pentium in the dust. Still another will chime in with the notion that it's not the processor that determines your PC's speed at all, but rather, it's how much RAM is installed. That opens the floodgates for the RAM debate, in which one expert claims 128 megs of RAM is a must, and another says anything

---

Trivia...

Guy Kawasaki administered an Internet mailing list called the Evangelist, which was sent daily, sometimes multiple times a day, to tens of thousands of Mac lovers and otherwise interested parties. The Evangelist contained true stories of Macintosh successes in the field, and provided a true shining light for Mac users who were trying, sometimes desperately, to keep the Mac platform viable and alive. Apple returned to profitability with a vengeance in 1998, and has been flying high ever since. Its work done, the Evangelist was retired that same year.

over 32 megs is a waste. If there are specs that can be spoke, they'll be thrown your way. From the motherboard to the chipset to the video type to the modem, everyone has an opinion as to what makes or breaks a good PC.

My advice: Ignore everyone's advice. Stick to your application requirements list, and don't allow anyone or any publication to weaken your resolve.

The moment you deviate from being requirements-driven to technology-driven, you're buying technology for technology's sake. That's why some people take ten minutes to find a phone number in a "pocket organizer," while others are dialing the phone in ten seconds because they looked up the number in a pocket telephone book (or they used their brain, and memorized it).Some things are better left uncomputerized. And some friends are better off left unconvinced. Stick to your guns, stick to your requirements, and you won't get stuck with a computer that makes techies swoon, but doesn't meet any of your needs.

Brand name or cheap clone?

WHEN SHOPPING FOR A NEW PC, *there's one question that tops all others in difficulty. Its answer is tougher than working out your application requirements, tougher than figuring out which Internet technology is best for you, and tougher than finding the ideal ISP. The question is: "Where do I shop for my computer?"*

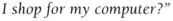

Figuring out what you need is the easy part. Actually heading out into the world and shopping for a computer can be one of the most confusing experiences you'll ever have, and certainly one of the most expensive.

Unlike practically any other product you'll shop for, computers are available through not one, not two, but at least four different sales channels: Retail dealers, mail order/direct marketers, the web, and local computer consultants. Within those groups, you can buy from distributors, discounters, resellers, direct marketers, traveling computer shows, TV infomercials, national superstores, department stores, mall stores, neighborhood boutiques, or direct from the manufacturer.

> ## Trivia...
> *Who makes the fastest CPU? It depends on which day of the week you ask the question. AMD bested Intel when it released its 750MHz Athlon processor in late 1999. Barely two weeks passed before Intel introduced its 800MHz Pentium III. By the time you read this, both companies may have introduced 1,000MHz CPUs (that's 1GHz!). You can expect them to continue playing CPU leapfrog through 2000 and beyond.*

You'll also be amazed at the number of computer brands you'll have to choose from. By my estimate, there are over a thousand different computer brands being actively marketed in the USA alone. Add to this mix a wide variety of prices, return policies, warranty plans, support services, store locations, and financing plans, and you have a recipe that can confuse the most experienced computer shopper.

SORTING THROUGH THE CHOICES

The process of buying a PC doesn't have to be confusing. There's a simple way to choose a quality PC vendor you can trust. To illustrate it, I've devised the following painless quiz. Check off the one statement you agree with:

1 [ ] I would buy a TV from a guy down the street who builds them from scratch.
2 [ ] I would buy a TV from a company I never heard of to save a few bucks.
3 [ ] I would only buy a TV from a major international brand, such as GE, RCA, Sony, Toshiba, or Zenith.

I'm willing to bet that you didn't select #1, and probably didn't select #2. The truth is, most people will only buy a television from a company they know and trust. The notion of buying a hand-wired TV from a neighborhood hacker appears ridiculous, but that's exactly how many people acquire a PC. For some reason, folks are easily convinced that brands don't matter when it comes to buying a computer. Nothing could be further from the truth. All PCs are not created equal, and the difference between a top-quality unit and junk is often only a few dollars.

Here's the hard and fast rule that will always guide you to the best PCs your money can buy: Buy a PC the same way you would buy a TV. Look for a brand name you know and trust, and then shop around for the best price.

Sure, a *white box* builder might be able to save you $100 on a PC. But what would you rather have, a computer that was quickly assembled from cut-rate parts, or a box that was engineered to uphold the quality standards of an internationally respected vendor?

■ **White box computer**
equipment does not have labels.

DEFINITION

White box *PCs have no label and are handmade one at a time by a local dealer or consultant in your neighborhood. Off-brand PCs, on the other hand, are products from companies you never heard of. Believe it or not, white box PCs are often of much higher quality than off-brand products. It's rare, but some even compare favorably with major brands*

The pitfalls of white-box and off-brand PCs

A disturbingly high number of off- and no-brand PC clones don't meet FCC standards for radio frequency emissions, and haven't been examined or approved by Underwriters Laboratories (UL) for meeting safety standards.

■ **The UL mark** *on computer products is a sign of reliability.*

And it gets worse. Many generic PC clones offered by local dealers (and some national players) are often pre-loaded with illegal, "pirated" copies of Microsoft Windows 98and other software. If you want to sell PCs on the cheap, these are the corners that get cut.

There's more to the name-brand vs. off-brand and no-brand argument than basic quality. When you buy a computer that carries a major manufacturer's logo, you also get the advantage of their national or international support network. That includes 24-hour support lines, spare and repair parts inventories, global service networks, next-day on-site service options, and more. Better still, if you don't like one dealer, you can take the computer to any authorized location.

Try that with a box that was "custom" built by a mail order shop, chain store, or local box kicker. With generic white box PCs, you're stuck with the dealer for life (or until they go bankrupt) – like it or not.

Honestly, it's wiser to spend $100, $200, even $300 more on a brand-name box that sports a major manufacturer's label, and meets established safety and radio frequency emissions standards, than to save a few pennies on no-name junk that contains who-knows-what parts. For those who haven't kept an eye on the computer industry, the accompanying chart lists the top-selling PC brands in the USA. With perhaps the exception of Acer, these brands should be familiar to most Americans. (Acer is one of the world's largest PC makers, but many of their models are sold under other brands, such as IBM, Texas Instruments, and Apple!) A computer manufactured by any one of these vendors is a safe and smart buy.

INTERNET

www.ul.com
www.fcc.gov

Only products that are periodically checked and approved by UL at the vendor's manufacturing facility are eligible to carry the UL mark. The same goes for FCC certification. More information on both of these important topics can be found on these web sites.

Top ten U.S. brand-name PC makers

Vendor	Shopping Site	Phone
Acer	www.shopacer.com/us	800-368-2237
Compaq	www.compaq.com/showroom	800-888-0220
Dell	www.dell.com	800-WWW-Dell
Gateway	www.gateway.com	800-846-4208
Hewlett-Packard	www.shopping.hp.com	888-999-4747
IBM	commerce.www.ibm.com	888-411-1WEB
Micron	www.micron.com	888-208-1937
NEC	www.nec-computers.com	888-863-2669
Sony	vaiodirect.sel.sony.com	800-236-1877
Toshiba	www.csd.toshiba.com	800-Toshiba

Some final words on off-brand white box clones: There are many national and local dealers who do, in fact, build PCs from off-the-shelf parts that rival the quality of the name-brand manufacturers. The tough part is finding them. One way to separate the good clone makers from the junkyard dealers is to ask for a company history, and check their references. Building PCs is a tough business with intense competition. Make sure your computer vendor has been in business five years or more, and can prove it. Ask for a list of 10 customer references, and call them. Inquire about the manufacturer's quality, technical support, and after-sale service.

It's also a good idea to call your local Better Business Bureau to see if any complaints have been lodged against the vendor.

Perhaps most important, press the vendor for information about the PCs they offer. Find out if they're using brand-name parts from companies you recognize, or see advertised in major publications such as *PC Magazine*, *PC World*, and *Wired*. If their PCs don't offer brand-name motherboards, hard disks, floppy drives, sound and video components, shop elsewhere. And don't buy that off-brand or white box PC unless it sports a UL mark and is FCC certified for home and business use. PC clone makers that can meet all of the above requirements are clearly conscientious about quality and safety, in addition to price. That said, your smartest, safest, and easiest move is to stick with the big industry players.

The computer types

Listed here, from highest to lowest risk, are the six types of PCs you'll encounter when you set out to buy a PC:

6 Any computer you get for free.
5 A product that has no brand name whatsoever, but is built

INTERNET

www.bbbonline.com

Even the Better Business Bureau is online. You'll find them at this address.

by a local computer company or consultant, or one of the ten zillion computer mail order houses.

4 A product from a company whose brand you never heard of, but your friend's cousin's mother's son (who happens to work for a computer company; was it Micro-something?) recommends.

3 A product from a company whose brand you never heard of, but some web site, magazine, TV, or radio show recommends.

2 A product from a company whose brand you might have heard of or seen in stores, but don't know much about (such as eMachines, TriGem, Pionex, Quantex, Micron, etc.).

1 A product from one of the top ten PC makers, companies whose brands you know and trust (such as Acer, Apple, Compaq, Dell, Gateway, Hewlett-Packard, IBM, NEC, and Toshiba).

Beware salesmen bearing offers

GETTING STARTED WITH PCS *doesn't require a mortgage or a student loan, but it's not free, either. Computing costs money. All of the up-front planning I have urged so far will be severely devalued if you run off and buy more computer than you can reasonably afford.*

Overbuying is an easy mistake to make, and most new computer shoppers make it. Now that you've fleshed out your reasons for needing a computer, boned up on the technology and vendor essentials, it's time to touch on the one requirement that drives the rest: Your budget. It's easy to get carried away by convincing sales pitches, special offers, fantastic deals, magnificent bundles, freebies, and the like. Professional computer sales people will not think twice before they mentally tear up your carefully formulated requirements sheet, and route you straight to the make and model they're pushing hard that day. They'll weave influential pitches that explain why particular PCs are ideally suited to the kinds of things you want to do. They'll enlighten you on the scientific details of computing in such a way that your confidence in their technical acumen will be assured. They'll entice you with free printers (if you buy a specific model), free scanners (if you buy a specific model), free monitors (if you buy a specific model), and even free computers (if you buy a specific model). Then, once you're hypnotized by their deal making, they'll slam dunk you into a power-packed PC that makes propeller heads faint, and credit card bankers dance with glee.

Don't end up spending hundreds, even thousands of dollars more than you initially intended. Think you're immune? You're not. Many an experienced PC shopper has been suckered by a sweet deal.

But there are seven magic words that, I promise you, will ensure your new computer meets all of your requirements, and doesn't break the bank: Set a budget, and stick to it. No matter what the computer sales gurus tell you, set a budget, and stick to it.

Considering that nearly all computing tasks today can be tackled by fully outfitted PCs priced between $800 to $2000, a budget in that range is absolutely realistic for the vast majority of shoppers.

Figure out what you can afford, and don't let any amount of politicking cause

■ **The seven magic words:** *"Set a budget and stick to it."*

you to deviate from your budget. That way, when you're in the checkout line, you can watch the other guys and gals nervously tap their fingers as they await the credit card verdict. You, on the other hand, will have known from day one what the verdict will be: A computer that fits your budget. Because that's the

#1 requirement.

Warranties, service plans, and the restocking charge

AT ROLL CALL, kindly head sergeant Phil Esterhaus would kick off NBC's classic television series, Hill Street Blues, *with these words of warning to the officers of Hill Street Station: "Be careful out there."*

The same should be said to computer shoppers as they pound the dangerous PC retailers' beat. After all is said and done, few computer shoppers are trained and prepared for the final "gotcha's" computer retailers have in store for them. Even if you meticulously developed your requirements list, painstakingly selected an ISP, and doggedly stuck to your initial spending budget, you can be stung – and hard – by the tricks and tactics of computer retailers. There are three primary weapons retailers use to separate you from your money, even after you've decided on the PC you want, negotiated a final price, or even purchased it and brought it home.

The extended warranty

Offered under a variety of names, such as "Extended Service Protection" or "Computer Support Plans," the store's pitch for the extended warranty usually begins seconds before the sales rep is about to ring up your order. In fact, as a rule, the pitch kicks off right at the cash register. It goes something like this: "For only a few hundred dollars, you can protect your investment with our store's extended support plan! It's more than an extension of the manufacturer's warranty. Our extended support plan covers you from keyboard to power cord, and covers things the manufacturer doesn't. This includes protection from power surges, brownouts, and other dangerous power-line conditions. We'll also provide fast, fast, fast on-site service for desktop PCs; and overnight repairs for laptops shipped back for repair. We'll also cover your PC for a full three years, which is, of course, much longer than the standard one year manufacturer's warranty." Don't bother to object. The sales reps are trained to deliver the complete pitch.

Here are the facts: All new PCs today are protected by comprehensive warranties that cover defects in materials and workmanship for one to three years. The cost of supporting the warranty is built in to the price you pay for the computer.

Further, every component, peripheral, and add-on is also covered by a manufacturer's warranty, usually for at least 12 months. Should an item fail within the warranty period, the manufacturer will repair or replace it, for free.

What if a part fails after the warranty has expired? With computer product pricing in a free fall, the cost of repairing or replacing virtually any component is nearly always substantially less than the price of an extended warranty. In the rare event your computer gets fried by a power surge, most homeowner's insurance policies will cover it. Check with your agent to be sure. If your policy is old, it might need updating. Ask that it be updated to reflect the standard $10,000 of home electronics and PC coverage most new policies include today. Lastly, if a brownout zaps your data, you can recover it with the backup device you bought with your PC (you did buy a backup device, right?).

Extended warranties are nothing more than a way for retailers to boost income in an extremely competitive marketplace. Watch out for them, and avoid them at all costs.

Service plans

A service plan is a variation on the extended warranty. It's simpler in that it strictly provides for on-site service in the event your computer needs repair.

INTERNET

www.safeware.com

One company has actually specialized in providing PC insurance policies for over a decade. It's Safeware. You'll find them on the web or call them at 800-800-1492.

STRAIGHT FROM THE HORSE'S MOUTH

Regular listeners of my weekly PC Talk show on Talk Radio 1210 WPHT (Infinity Broadcast [CBS] in Philadelphia) regularly hear me rant about the evils of extended warranties. Here's an unedited letter I received from a listener who actually works for one of the country's biggest consumer electronics retailers. It's a real eye-opener (the names have been changed to protect the guilty):

Rich,

I work at [store name deleted], and the place is awful!!! Tell your listeners and readers, however, that we rip them off majorly. Example, we sell basic IEEE-1284 printer cables for $19.99. I have had a few people comment to me that the same exact cable was $5 at Wal-Mart. Also, do an investigation on our [extended warranty/service plan]. I have heard from a great many people that 90% of things that go wrong with your PC are not covered under the plan, although we are told to tell our customers that the plan covers EVERYTHING except viruses, and things caused by installing software. I have heard that these are a major ripoff.

Just some thoughts

Billy

The evil restocking charge

It may be the most insidious scam ever promulgated on unsuspecting consumers. It's illegal, immoral, downright unethical, and out to bite you. "It" is the evil restocking charge. Consider this scenario: You spend a few thousand dollars on a new brand-name PC, only to get it home and discover it's defective. You head back to the major national retailer where you bought it, and hit the customer service desk for your rightful refund. That's when you discover that you can't get your money back. Or at least, not all of it. The store will refund 85% of your purchase, you learn, but will withhold 15% as a "restocking charge." The restocking charge supposedly covers the retailer's cost of repacking the product and shipping it back to its maker. Never mind that the manufacturers and distributors nearly always refund 100% of the returned product costs to their dealers. Never mind that the cost of returns is a burden that, by rights, should be shouldered by retailers and manufactures, and not consumers. Never mind that restocking charges are not disclosed to consumers before the sale. And never mind that, according to the US Uniform Commercial Code and the Magnuson-Moss Warranty Act, restocking charges are illegal. Unless you're prepared to haul the retailer into court, you're stuck with a 15% shopper's tax for the luxury of returning defective product.

That is, unless you ask about return policies before handing over your cash, check, money order, or credit card. It's the single most important question to ask when scouting for a new computer . . . or any technology purchase, for that matter.

Ask retailers about their return policies, and you will quickly separate the good guys from the bad. You'll find there are many national and local retailers who offer their customers 100% money-back guarantees, and surprisingly manage to remain in business.

Imagine that. So, to protect yourself, always invoke the consumer's magic words before you pay for any computer product: "What's your return policy?" You might be surprised to find some of the most respected national retailers are always ready to rip you off.

Now that you've pondered the options and heeded the warnings, go out there and buy yourself a nice computer! Bring it home, and get ready to power up!

A simple summary

✓ Gird yourself against Mac attacks.

✓ Ignore the controversy and advice from your computing friends, and stick with your requirements when shopping for a new PC.

✓ Buy your PC the way you would buy your TV or automobile: Stick with the major national brands you know and trust.

✓ The probability of problems increases dramatically with no-name and off-brand PC products.

✓ If you must buy a white box generic PC, make sure it's FCC and UL certified.

✓ When dealing with white box vendors, make sure they have no complaints against them with the BBB, have been in business for five years minimum, and can provide a list of verifiable references.

✓ Don't buy a PC based on how great the deal is. Buy a PC based on how well it meets your application requirements.

✓ Don't opt for the extended warranty or service plan.

✓ Before you fork over your cash, check, or credit card, ask about the seller's return policies, and get the policy in writing.

Chapter 5

Power Up!

A<small>LL THAT REMAINS</small> before you start working with your new PC is to set it up, and make sure it all works. Let's do it!

In this chapter...

✓ Setting it all up

✓ Windows keyboard and mouse

✓ Making sure everything works

✓ Burn in and back up

✓ Installation and configuration

✓ Windowing tricks

✓ Explore the Control Panel

✓ Personalizing Windows

Setting it all up

YOU'RE JUST MINUTES AWAY *from unpacking and powering up your new computer. But as the infamous Murphy said, "If something can go wrong, it will." You can, however, minimize Murphy's chances of being right.*

First, carefully unpack and remove the computer, keyboard, and mouse from their box. Take care to save all packing material. Stack the manuals, warranty registration cards, bundled software CDs, cables, and disks atop the closed box.

Everything in its place

Put the computer on your desk with the floppy and CD-ROM drives facing you. If you're right handed, the drives should be to your right (and vice-versa if you're a lefty). This will make it easier to swap disks in and out of the PC. It's also ergonomically correct (meaning it's healthier for your mind and body). Don't put the computer smack-dab in front of your work chair. That spot is reserved for your monitor. No, the monitor doesn't go on top of the PC, for a variety of reasons. One, it's heavy, and can warp your computer's case. Two, when the day comes that you have to open your PC case for a repair or upgrade, it's infinitely easier when you don't have to first remove a 35 pound (or heavier) monitor. Third, ergonomically speaking, it's better for the monitor to be at eye level, not perched atop a PC.

As I suggested earlier, position the bottom edge of the computer keyboard smack-dab against the edge of your desk. This will encourage you not to lean on your wrists, and helps prevent a common (and painful) computer-related injury called carpal tunnel syndrome. After the computer is in place, unpack the monitor, again taking care to keep all packing materials, cables, and documentation nearby. Plop the monitor down dead-center in front of your workspace, leaving room for the keyboard.

Sitting in your work chair, look at your reflection in the monitor's screen. Position the monitor so that the reflection of your face is perfectly centered, with your reflected head and chin touching the top and bottom of the monitor's frame, respectively.

This orients the monitor in such as way as to minimize eye and neck strain. Use the same care with every other – component – mouse, printer, scanner, drives, other peripherals – carefully unpacking and organizing their materials, and positioning the devices where you plan to use them. Ideally, all peripherals (printers, scanners, and such) should be within arm's reach. This will make it easier for you to spin around in your chair and pull out a document, scan in a form, or whatever, then flip right back to your PC screen, without ever standing up.

Plugging into the computer

After all the components are placed, it's time to wire them up. Don't plug them into AC power just yet. One by one, plug the devices into the computer. Some PCs color code the main plugs and ports, which makes jacking-in the keyboard, mouse, and printer easier. If you're not sure which port to jack a device into, check the computer's manual (which should be sitting atop the box). All brand-name makers include a diagram that illustrates the computer's ports.

Never force a plug into a port. You know a plug is in the right port when it slides in easily. Make sure all the connections are snug, but don't overtighten the thumbscrews you'll find on some cables. Doing so can break the computer's receptacle straight off the frame, making it impossible to tighten the plug in the future. After all the connections are secure, double-check them. Also check the floppy drive, if your computer has one, and remove any protective cardboard sheets that might have been inserted there to protect the drive during shipment. Make sure to check the printer for hidden cardboard or foam packing materials as well. You'll often find them tucked away in the paper-path, and where the ink cartridge goes.

This is a common reason why new printers don't print! Check other devices for cardboard or foam packing materials, or plastic overlays as well.

Starting up your PC

At this point it's safe to plug the computer and all the accessories into the AC power. Then, one by one, turn on all the devices, saving the computer for next to last and the monitor for last. As soon as you power-up the PC, press the eject button on the CD-ROM and/or DVD drive. This will allow you to remove any packing materials that were jammed in there as well.

If you did everything right, the computer should come to life with a loud "beep!" and will display some copyright and manufacturer information on the screen. It will then start a memory test, counting up from zero to however much RAM you have installed, and do a check of its disk drives, keyboard, ports, settings, and other essential components. The computer will perform this Power-On Self-Test (POST, for short) whenever you turn it on.

If there are any severe configuration problems with the computer, you'll find out about them right now. The computer will beep again and display an error message on the screen. Considering that the computer is brand new, any configuration errors mean one of two things. Either you plugged something into the PC incorrectly, or the computer is defective in some way. Read the error message, and try to make sense of it. If it says, for instance, "Error: Keyboard failure," that's your clue that the keyboard isn't plugged in, or is stuck in the wrong socket.

If the computer generates incomprehensible error messages and you can't deduce what's wrong, contact your dealer immediately. You'll learn how to troubleshoot your PC in due course, but that's certainly not what you want or should be doing on day one. Today your PC should fire up perfectly. If it doesn't, that's a job for the dealer to handle. On the other hand, if your computer started smoothly, it will complete the memory test, perhaps beep happily a few more times, and proceed to load Windows 98.

Be patient, and let the PC go through its startup motions. The first time you fire up Windows might take longer than subsequent runs. Also, be prepared to answer some basic questions the computer might pose on its first run. For example, it might ask you for your name, company or organization name, *computer name*, and some other information.

The computer will also ask you for your Windows "OEM code." That's Microsoft-ese for the product's serial number. You'll find the Windows OEM code on the back of your Windows 98 CD, which should be tucked away with your computer's other stuff on top of the PC box.

Note that some PCs will ask more questions than others, including the current date, time, country, and time zone you're in. Others might ask if you want to set up a printer now, or get on the Internet now.

In fact, I have a dozen new Windows 98 computers from a dozen different computer vendors in my lab. Guess what? Each and every one has a different out-of-the-box startup process.

Different manufacturers have their own ideas about how Windows 98 should startup. In its ongoing effort to keep its vendor customers happy, Microsoft has made Windows 98 flexible enough so that each vendor can customize the startup process to some extent. That's great for vendors, but confusing for users (and book authors)!

If you don't know the answers to your computer's setup questions, or how to work the various on-screen computer controls, it's safe to use your mouse to click the "No" button (or click the Cancel button), or press the Esc key on your keyboard. Doing so will skip any setup questions that don't have do with your personal info. Don't worry: We'll be tackling all of that technical stuff a little bit later. In the interim, feel free to type in your personal info using the computer's keyboard. Also, note that Windows 98 might ask you to enter your user name and password. I'll be covering this topic in a bit. For now, if this happens, use your mouse to click the Cancel button, or press the Esc key on your keyboard.

Windows keyboard and mouse

BEFORE YOU CAN DO ANY *of this stuff, however, a brief tutorial on the Windows 98 keyboard and mouse is in order. Let's jump on the keyboard first. Following is a brief explanation of some keys that will make entering information for the first time a little easier.*

Keyboard components

✓ The TAB Key
Each time you hit the Tab key, the computer's *focus* will jump to the next item. For the fun of it, hold the Tab key down and watch the focus zip all over the screen. Don't be scared! You can't hurt anything.
✓ The QWERTY keys
Use these standard typewriter keys to type in your information. Press and hold the SHIFT key while you're typing for capital letters and "shifted" characters such as $ and *.
✓ The BACKSPACE Key
Use Backspace to erase something you just typed by mistake. Each time you press backspace, the last character you typed will be erased.
✓ The ESC Key
The Escape key gets you out of trouble. Press Esc if you want to cancel what you just entered, and go back to a previous screen. Note that Escape doesn't always work (it depends on the screen you're on), but most of the time, it does. The Esc key usually reacts no matter where the focus is, and no matter what you're doing. If you want to cancel something, whack Esc a few times – even if there is no "Cancel" command on the screen. The Esc key will usually bail you out.

> **DEFINITION**
>
> The focus *is often incorrectly referred to as the "cursor" or the "pointer." The cursor is the blinking vertical or horizontal line that indicates where you're typing. The pointer is the arrow that moves when you jostle the mouse. The focus is whatever element on the screen has the computer's attention.*

WINDOWS 98 KEYBOARD

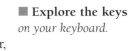

✓ The ARROW Keys

Left, right, up, and down, the arrow keys do exactly what you expect them to. Use them to move around within any data entry field.

✓ The ENTER Key (sometimes labeled as "Return")

The most powerful key on your keyboard! Enter does just what it says: It enters information into the computer. Press Enter when you're sure you want to send the information to the computer, and move on to the next screen. Like Esc, Enter reacts no matter where the focus is.

■ **Explore the keys** *on your keyboard.*

✓ The SPACE BAR

The Space Bar is the longest key on your keyboard, on the bottom row. Use the Space Bar to enter a space between words. But be careful! Sometimes the Space Bar works like the Enter key. For example, if the focus is on a button, press Enter or the Space Bar.

✓ The INSERT & DELETE Keys

As explained earlier, the arrow keys move the focus left, right, up, and down. If you want to delete a character, use the arrow keys to move the focus beneath the letter you want to delete, then press the Delete (or Del) key on your keyboard. Similarly, to insert a character or a word, use the arrow keys to move the focus where you want to start the insertion, and start typing. If what you type erases (overwrites) text that's beside it, press the Insert (or Ins) key on your keyboard.

✓ The HOME & END Keys

Pressing home moves the focus to the beginning of a line. Pressing End moves the focus to the end of a line.

✓ The PAGEUP & PAGEDOWN Keys

Pressing PageUp will jump the focus up one full page. PageDown does the reverse, jumping down one full page.

Your trusty mouse

Move the mouse to move the mouse pointer on the screen. In most cases, the mouse pointer looks like an arrow. Sometimes, though, the mouse pointer will change into different characters. Whatever moves on the screen when you move your mouse is the current mouse pointer. When the mouse pointer is where you want it, click the left mouse button to cause an action. For example, to press an on-screen button, position the mouse pointer over the on-screen button, then click the left mouse button. To type inside of a text field, position the mouse pointer over the field, and click the left mouse button. Note: From here on in, when I tell you to "click" something, it means to point at it with the mouse, then press and release the left mouse button. As you will soon discover, there are clicks, double-clicks, right-clicks, middle-clicks, click-drags, and scrolls. Leave it to computer engineers to complicate a device that was supposed to make computing easier. Some mice feature a third button, called a "wheel." Rolling the wheel up and down with your middle finger is the same as using the PageUp/PageDown keys, but easier, and more convenient.

■ **A standard** *Windows 98 mouse.*

Windows on-screen controls

As you study the on-screen displays, you'll probably be confused by this first encounter with the Windows "user interface." Instead of having to remember and type in computer commands, Windows is managed through zillions of on-screen "controls." You'll get to know all of these controls in due course. For now, though, the rule is, while it's safe to use your mouse to click on anything that makes sense to you, the time to explore and experiment will come later. At the beginning, limit your clicking only to those buttons that are required to complete the Windows startup setup process.

Don't let your curiosity cause you to start clicking randomly on some enticing picture or button. Doing so might cause the computer to run a program or launch a process that can ultimately get you into trouble. After your basic skills are developed, you'll be able to confidently explore your PC. Be patient.

After you have answered all of the computer's questions, it will proceed to finish its first *boot* of Windows. Before long, the computer will settle down, and you'll be staring at your new virtual workplace: The Windows 98 Desktop.

> **DEFINITION**
>
> *When a computer is first turned on, the first program it runs is called a "bootstrap loader," because the computer is, in a manner of speaking, pulling itself up by its boot straps. That's why you'll hear users say they* boot, *boot up, or reboot their computer. It's user jargon for start and restart.*

Making sure everything works

JUST BECAUSE YOU got your computer home, out of the box, assembled, and powered-up on your desk doesn't mean Murphy has left the room. It is only through careful planning and attention to detail that you've avoided Murphy's wrath so far. But there are still plenty of things that can, and possibly will, go wrong.

Murphy is lying in wait to strike. To usher him out of the picture completely, you need to test all the PC's components and make sure they work.

This falls into the "First things first" category. Sure, I could take you on a star-studded tour of your PC right now, and start exploring Windows, programs, tools, and such. But you'd be in for a rude surprise when you tried to print. That's because the printer hasn't been tested. Even though it's plugged in and powered on, it won't work – yet. Other indispensable components, such as your monitor, aren't initially configured – yet.

If one of your peripherals isn't set up properly or is (Heaven forbid) defective, it's better to find out right now than weeks later, when you first need to use it for a project. There's nothing worse than battling with an ornery peripheral when you have a deadline to meet. Following is a quick rundown of the key components you need to test before you can move on to bigger and better things and actually start using your PC. You know your keyboard and mouse are working OK, because you used them to enter your personal information when your PC was first booting up. So we'll skip them and start by testing your monitor.

But before you can do that, you need to establish a logon name and password with Windows 98. Failure to do so could cause the PC to forget some of your settings, and keep you from automatically logging onto the Internet.

The Windows logon password

It might not happen the first, second, or even the third time you start Windows 98, but at some point, Windows 98 will ask you to establish a logon name and password. Unlike most passwords you'll encounter in your computing travels, your Windows 98 password provides little in the way of access protection. Anyone can use your computer whether they know your password or not, simply by turning it on. But unless they know your Windows 98 logon and password, they won't be able to access the Internet using your ISP account, and they won't be able to access any other password-protected resources on your PC. Whenever Windows 98 first gets around to displaying its "Enter Windows Password" prompt, make sure you enter your user name and then choose a password. To enter your user name, just start typing it when the "Enter Windows Password" prompt appears.

■ **You can change** *your password.*

The shorter your user name, the better, because it will take you less time to type in the future. On my computer, my user name is "RBL." My wife uses "Sweetie," and my cat uses "Tigger."

When you're done typing your user name, don't press Enter. Press the Tab key to zip to the password *input box*. Enter a password between 8 and 10 characters long. The best passwords are combinations of letters and numbers, separated by a hyphen, or some other punctuation character. For example, "Orange-2001."

DEFINITION

Any on-screen area that accepts text typed at the keyboard is termed an input box.

Never use your last name, spouse or children's names, favorite team, or other obvious predilection for a password. Such passwords are easily cracked.

When you've selected your password, press the Enter key. Windows 98 will ask you to re-enter it, just to be sure it was entered correctly. Do so, then press Enter again, and the password will be accepted.

Testing the monitor

Next in line for "most important component" status is your monitor. Obviously, it's working, because you're looking at it. But is it working at its optimal settings? Make sure both the contrast and the brightness are cranked up to 100 percent (their maximum setting). This will reduce eye strain by keeping the display crisp and bright. If the display is too bright or its contrast too high, feel free to trim back the settings a little bit. Blacks should be black, not gray, and whites should be snow white, not blued or grayed. If your monitor lets you adjust other settings, such as horizontal and vertical size and positioning, tweak them for a perfect picture as well. Make the picture as large as you can, and center it on the picture tube. Confused by your monitor's front panel controls? That means it's probably a digital monitor. You'll have to refer to the owner's manual to learn how to call up the adjustments menu and tweak the various settings. A little later, I'll walk you through the steps of synchronizing Windows 98 software settings with your monitor's tube and other hardware. But for now, using the monitor's on-board controls is satisfactory.

Setting up and testing the printer

Before you can print anything, you need tell Windows what kind of printer you have. If your printer is connected to your USB port, Windows has already detected it, and attempted to set it up automatically. Not all printers use the USB port. In fact, most don't. If yours doesn't, you're going to have to actually click on some stuff on the screen, so don't get nervous! It's easy to do. Grab your mouse, and move the mouse pointer over the button labeled "Start."

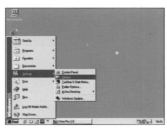

You'll find the Start button on the lower left-hand corner of the screen. When the mouse pointer is pointing at the Start button, click your left mouse button. (To reiterate: When I tell you to "click" something, it means to point at it with the mouse, and press the left mouse button.)

■ **To access your** *Printers folder, click Printers in the Settings Menu.*

After you click the Start button, "the Start Menu" pops up. Among the many options on the Start Menu is one labeled "Settings." Click it. Voilà! Out slides another menu, which features, among other things, a menu option labeled "Printers." Click the Printers option. The Printers window will appear on your screen. At this point one of the seminal laws of computing comes into play: RTFS, which stands for "Read The Fine Screen."

Add Printer Wizard

If you read the fine screen, you'll see Windows is trying to tell you what do next. There before you is an icon labeled "Add Printer." Double-click it. (In other words, click "Add Printer" twice in a row.) This activates the Add Printer *Wizard*. For now, click the Next button to push the Add

■ **The Printer Wizard** *asks if you're connecting to a local or network printer.*

Printer Wizard along. It will ask you if you're connecting to a local or network printer, with local preselected as the default. Click the Next button. The Wizard will chug for a moment or two, and will then present you with a *laundry list* of every printer make and model in the known universe. You'll see two panels. The left panel contains the printer manufacturers, while the right panel contains the various models.

On the left side of each panel will be small buttons with up and down arrowheads. On the left panel, click the down arrowhead to scroll down the list of manufacturers until you find your vendor (such as Hewlett-Packard, Canon, Xerox, Lexmark, etc.). The arrowheads themselves are technically called "scroll buttons" or "page buttons," and they move a page up or down one line at a time. The long gray bar in between the up and down arrowheads is called a "vertical scroll bar," because if you click it, an entire page (about 25 to 50 lines) will scroll up or down. Sometimes you'll see a scroll bar spanning the bottom of the screen. That's a "horizontal scroll bar," and it's used to move a page or window to the left or right. Vertical, horizontal, horizshmontal – most people just call the thing a "scroll bar."

■ **The Printer Wizard's** *laundry list of printers.*

If you have a "wheel mouse," you can roll the center wheel to scroll up and down. If you scroll past the one you're after, click the up arrowhead to scroll back up the list of manufacturers. When you see your printer maker's name, click on it. That will cause the manufacturer's various makes and models to appear in the right panel. Now click the right panel's down arrowhead, until you hit upon your printer's exact model. When you do, click on it. At that point, you will have selected both the manufacturer and model in the Add Printer Wizard.

If your printer make and model aren't listed, you'll have to use the SETUP disk provided by your printer manufacturer. Exit the Add Printer Wizard by clicking the Cancel button and, instead, carefully follow the instructions provided by your printer manufacturer to set up your printer. Once you've set up the printer, click the Next button. You'll be presented with a list of computer connections that can support a printer. There's only one that matters: It's "LPT1," which is computerese for "Line PrinTer #1." Click on LPT1, and then click Next. The Add Printer Wizard will now ask you for the printer's "name," and will suggest a name for the printer.

This name will be used to describe the printer in menus that you'll encounter later. It's best to accept the suggested printer name by clicking Next.

Finally, the Add Printer Wizard will ask you if you would like to print a test page. Why, certainly! First, though, check to make sure the printer is on, with an ink cartridge installed, and paper loaded. Then click Next. Windows 98 will chug for a moment before giving your printer its first workout. When it's done, a message will be displayed asking you if the test page printed properly. Click Yes if all went well, or No if the page didn't print. Clicking No will cause Windows 98's Print Troubleshooter to load, which at this stage of the game will probably confuse the living daylights out of you. Of course, if you're feeling brave and bold, you can try using Windows 98's Print Troubleshooter as well – but it can't solve anything more than minor printing problems. If you can't get the printer to print, call your dealer.

Hooking up the modem

You're only as strong as the weakest link in your technology chain. With all the technological riches the Internet has to offer, none within reach without the lowly modem. That is, if you didn't opt for a cable, DSL, satellite, or other high-speed connection.

If you did, your Internet service provider has or will soon visit your location, and will wire up your Internet connection for you. (How else can they earn their $150 installation fee?)

But if you, like me, are among the overwhelming majority of Internet users, you'll be surfing the web using an ordinary internal or external dial-up modem. If that's the case, verify that your telephone line is connected to the port on your modem labeled "line." If you're using an external modem, make sure it's plugged into one of your PC's COM ports or a USB port (which is really just a fancy COM port). Simply connect the modem's computer cable to the one port on the PC that fits it perfectly. External modem users should also confirm that the device's AC power supply is plugged into a wall outlet, the speaker's volume control is cranked up, and the power switch is in the "ON" position.

Now click the Start button on the lower left-hand side of your Windows Desktop. (Notice a trend? They don't call it "Start" for nothing! Most everything you'll do starts by clicking Start.) After you click Start, click Settings, then click Control Panel.

We'll be spending lots of time in the Control Panel later, but for now, just double-click the yellow telephone icon labeled "Modems" that appears in the Control Panel's window. One of two things will happen: If your modem was preinstalled at the factory, the "Modems Properties" *dialog* will appear. If you installed your modem, or if the factory did a half-baked job of installing it, the "Install New Modem" dialog will pop up.

■ **If your modem** has been correctly pre-installed, the Modems Properties dialog will appear.

To test the modem using the Modems Properties dialog, click the "Diagnostics" tab, then click on the picture of your modem, which will show up in the list. Next, click the "More Info" button. Windows 98 will communicate with the modem, and then display the "More Info" dialog that reports it's working properly. Click OK to close the More Info dialog, then click OK again to close the Modems Properties dialog.

To test the modem using the Install New Modem dialog, keep clicking Next until the Add New Hardware Wizard starts searching for your modem. After the Wizard finds your modem, click the Finish button to complete the installation.

When Windows 98 has wrapped up the installation, it's a good idea to revisit this section and follow the steps detailed here to test your modem. This double-checks the Wizard's installation, and confirms the modem's proper setup.

If the Wizard doesn't find your modem, you have a serious configuration problem, and should immediately contact your computer dealer.

Testing the sound card and speakers

Next in line are your PC's sound card and speakers. Assuming the speakers are plugged into their proper connections on the sound card, here's how to test the rig. First, look at the bottom right of your Windows Desktop. There, just below the clock, is a picture of a speaker. Click it once to make the "Volume" control appear. Make sure the volume is cranked up by pressing the "Page Up" key on your keyboard (it's usually located just above the arrow keys).

Now click the Start button (again!), then Settings, then Control Panel. Double-click the "Sounds" icon in the Control Panel. When the "Sounds Properties" dialog opens, click

■ **Click the speaker** *icon once to access the Volume Control.*

the down arrowhead button until you see a sound that has a speaker icon beside it. Select the sound with the speaker icon by clicking on it. In the center right of the Sounds Properties dialog is an arrowhead pointing right. That's the "Play" button. Click it. You should hear a sound come out of your speakers. If you don't, double-check your speaker connections. Make sure the speakers are on and powered up (most speakers require batteries or AC power). Also make sure any volume controls on the speakers themselves are cranked up.

If you're not getting any sound, it's possible your PC has a hardware conflict. Contact your dealer to have the problem checked and resolved.

Checking the disk drives

Your hard disk is working fine, because your computer started up. Windows 98 is stored on and loads from the hard disk, so if you're using the computer, the hard disk is fully operational. But you still have to test your CD-ROM and/or DVD drive and your floppy drive. To test the CD or DVD, simply press the load/eject button on the front of the drive (it's the only button on the drive). The drive caddy will slide out.

Drop a CD or DVD into the caddy, and press the load/eject button again. The caddy will "mount" the disc, and the drive's LED light will blink. In a few seconds, a program window will open, or a movie will play. This lets you know that the drive is working. To stop the program or movie, press the load/eject button again, and remove the CD or DVD. By the way, it's also a good idea to test the CD or DVD with a music CD.

All PCs can play music CDs. To see if your music CD subsystem is working, plop a music CD into the CD-ROM or DVD drive, and make sure it starts to play automatically.

To stop it from playing, eject the music CD. When you eject the disc from the drive, you might also have to click the X, cancel, Close, or Exit button on your Windows screen. If your DVD or CD had trouble completing any of these tasks, contact your dealer and have the hardware checked out.

Last up are your removable floppy and/or Zip drives. They're also a snap to check. Click the Start button, then click "Programs," and finally, click "Windows Explorer." Yowza! A really complicated and unfriendly window opens on your screen. You'll climb the Windows Explorer ropes soon. For the moment, though, take a gander at the left-hand panel, labeled "All Folders." That's a list of all the disk drives available on your system.

Topping the list should be one labeled "3.5 Floppy." Click on it. The disk's activity light (on your computer) should go on, and you should hear the drive grinding away. After a few seconds, Windows 98 will report, "The drive is not accessible." That's good news, not bad! It means Windows accessed the drive, and didn't see a disk in it. Repeat the above steps for every drive in your system. Just click the drive's name in the left-hand panel of Windows Explorer. Make sure the drive's light illuminates. Windows should also display a "not accessible" error, or show you a list of files that are stored on the drive. If the drive's light does not illuminate, contact your dealer immediately. That's it! You've successfully tested all of your PC's major common components. Note that your tests covered only the common components that literally all PC's have.

If you have any specialized hardware, such as scanners, digital cameras, musical interfaces, etc., now is the time to crack open the owner's manual's for each, and carefully follow the installation and test instructions. While doing so, remember computing's golden rules: RTFM and RTFS.
If you have software programs to install, hold off. I'll be getting to software installations further on. For now, leave the computer running as is, because it's time to . . .

■ **If your floppy** drive is empty, "A:\ is not accessible" is good news!

Burn in and backup

FEW THINGS ARE AS EASY as falling off a log. Burning in your computer is one of them. It's the last step before you can actually begin using your PC for anything productive.

Remember that many of your computer's parts, – and perhaps the entire PC itself – have circumnavigated the planet to arrive at your desktop. Chips, drives, circuit boards were manufactured in all four corners of the globe. Then they all get shipped by land, sea, or air to a final assembly facility somewhere in North America, Europe, South or Central America, or Asia. From there, the fully assembled and boxed PC is shipped to the manufacturer's US warehouse. Then it's boxed up again and shipped to a local retailer. Along the way, it's bumped, kicked, dropped, banged, shoved, and otherwise pummeled by warehousemen and shippers.

It's a wonder the PC arrives in your home or office in one piece. Doesn't it make sense to test the PC for a few hours before you invest time setting up all your software, and committing your personal data to it?

The burn-in test

You bet it does. In fact, the so-called burning-in process, in which the computer is left on and idle for several hours or days, is used by virtually all experienced users to make sure their PC's hardware is up to snuff and free of mechanical-, heat- or time-related defects. The time to do this is immediately after you've set up your PC.

In general, if a PC component is going to blow, it's going to do so within the first few days of regular use. Computer hardware that survives the first few days of use will usually deliver reliable performance for years to come.

Computers are also like light bulbs in one respect. If they're going to fail, they'll often do it when they're first turned on. Just as a light bulb will glow for years if it's never turned off, a computer will keep ticking longer if it's kept on all the time. The reason: Allowing a computer to run around the clock helps it to maintain its ideal operating temperature and keeps its components from constantly expanding and contracting – and perhaps seizing up – due to changing temperatures. Keeping the PC powered up also ensures a constant air flow through the case, which prevents dust and condensation from building up – another common cause of hardware failure.

DEFINITION

To power-cycle *simply means turning the computer off and then on again.*

To flush out any hidden problems, *power-cycle* the PC, then leave it sitting powered-up and idle for at least a full 24-hour period.

To power-cycle the PC, click the Start button, then click Shut Down. When the Shut Down dialog appears, make sure the button beside "Shut down" is selected, and then click OK. After a moment, the PC will either turn off, or will display a message telling you it is now safe to turn off your computer.

Note: Always use the Shut Down command to turn off your PC (click the Start button, then click Shut Down). Never turn your computer off without it.

The Shut Down command ensures that unsaved information is "flushed" out of RAM (temporary working memory) and recorded on the hard disk (permanent memory). If you turn off your PC without first using the Shut Down command, you can lose some or all of your work, and even cause serious damage to your computer.

■ **To power-cycle** *your PC, first shut it down by clicking Start and then Shut Down.*

After the PC powers off, switch off all of your external devices (monitor, printer, scanner, drives, etc). When everything is off, turn right around and power everything up again. Remember to power up the monitor last and the computer next-to-last. After a few minutes, the computer will complete its startup process, and settle down at the "Enter Password" prompt. Press the Esc key, or click the Cancel button. The PC will return to the main Windows screen, also known as the Windows Desktop. At this point, walk away from the PC, and allow it (and all connected components) to "burn in" for a few hours. After a few hours, power cycle the entire rig again. Do this repeatedly for at least a full 24-hour period. After all, you waited this long to buy a computer.

It's worth investing one more day to make sure that it, or its accessories, won't blow up in a week.

Obviously, if any of the components fail during this period, contact your dealer for a replacement. However, if the PC makes it through the 24-hour burn-in period (and it should), it's time to perform your first system backup.

Saving data

Your first backup won't be a complete backup of the PC's programs and data. You'll do that down the road. For the moment, you'll just backup your critical Windows "system" files, the bits and pieces Windows uses to actually fire up your computer. To do this, you'll need a few blank floppy disks. Once you have them in hand, click the Start button, then click Settings, and finally, click Control Panel. When the Control Panel opens, double-click (i.e. click twice) the Add/Remove Programs icon. In the Add/Remove Programs Properties dialog, click the Startup Disk tab. That will reveal the Create Disk button. Slide your floppy disk into its drive, and then click the Create Disk button. Windows 98 will chug and churn for an instant, and will then begin creating an emergency backup disk. After the disk is created, remove it, and label it with a Post-It marked "Emergency Startup Disk #1."

■ **Backup your critical** *Windows system files by making a Startup Disk.*

Never write directly on removable disks, including floppies, Zips, and CD-ROMs. Doing so can damage the media and render it unreadable by the computer.

Instead, jot your labels on a Post-It note (make sure the disk isn't beneath the Post-It when you're writing), and stick the Post-It on the disk. Store the disk in a cool, dry place whose whereabouts you won't forget. Repeat this process with another disk, just in case the first disk becomes corrupted over time. Then, in the event your computer ever fails, and can't startup, you can use an emergency startup disk to get the computer back in action. To do so, turn the computer off, slide the emergency startup disk into the floppy disk drive, and turn the power on. Again, that's the remedy for a rainy day. For now, store the disk, and let's hope you never have to use it. Now that your PC is burned in and backed up, you can turn your attention to loading up all of your software, and tweaking the PC's settings to suit your personal preferences.

Installation and configuration

SO CLOSE, AND YET, SO FAR. Having successfully picked off nearly every item on our pre-flight checklist, you're probably wondering if I'm ever going to turn you loose on your PC. The answer, of course, is yes – and soon! But just as you grab a snack, pour a drink, and fluff your easy chair before settling in for a good TV movie, a dash of self-indulgent digital pampering is in order before you flip on the PC for work or entertainment.

■ **Nearly done!** *But before you relax, there a little light configuration to do ...*

The task: Configuration, also known as customization or personalization. In fact, the ability to adapt to your distinctive predilections is one of Windows' greatest strengths. And yet, for reasons I don't understand, it's also one of Windows' least used capabilities. Unlike your easy chair, you'll only have to make Windows "just right" once. It will remember your individual preferences, and present you with the same personalized computing environment day in and day out.

And as your skills and knowledge grow, you can easily re-configure Windows to reflect a more mature state of computing.

Best of all, working your way through the configuration process will expose you to most, if not all, of Windows 98's on-screen system controls. Instead of numbing your mind with step-by-step examples, you'll experience the various Windows 98 rudiments first hand, one control at a time. By the time you're done, you'll not only have configured your PC; you'll have learned the ropes of controlling Windows.

Literally all of Windows configuration power rests in one place: The Settings menu on the Start button. To get there, click Start, then click Settings. You'll see five configuration areas, all of which we will traverse together. First up: the Control Panel. You've been here before, but this time you're going to give it a workout. Click Start | Settings | Control Panel to open the Control Panel. Before sampling the wares in the Control Panel, let's first make the window fill the screen.

Windowing tricks

AT THE TOP OF THE CONTROL PANEL *window, you'll see a blue title bar that reads "Control Panel." To the left is a mini-version of the Control Panel folder icon. To the right are three small buttons. Allow your mouse pointer to hover over each one of the three small buttons. As you do, you'll see a small box drop down with an explanation of each button. These drop-down boxes are called "Tool tips."*

Anytime you're wondering what a button or icon does, just hover your mouse pointer over it. Most of the time, a tool tip will drop down and describe the control. As you can see, button one (which looks like an underscore) is described as "Minimize." Button two, which looks like two boxes, is described as "Maximize." And button three, which looks like an X, is described as "Close." Try this: Click the middle button. Your Control Panel window zooms to fill the screen.

Now, if you hover over the middle button, its tool tip says, "Restore." Click it, and the Control panel window returns to its smaller size. Clicking the minimize button will zoom the Control Panel window to the bottom of the screen, turning it into a button. Click the Control Panel button, and the window will zoom back, and reopen. Similarly, clicking the Close button will remove the Control Panel window entirely. To get it back, click Start | Settings | Control Panel.

Play and discover more tricks

Why don't you try playing with those three little buttons for a few minutes. When you're done, click Start | Settings | Control Panel, and we'll resume our exploration of the Control Panel. Congratulations! Now you know how to control any Windows 98 window that opens on your screen! That's all there is to it. Well . . . almost. Here are a few extra windowing tricks, now that you've gotten your feet wet.

To move a window, point anywhere within the window's blue title bar, then click and hold your left mouse button down. Keeping the button held down, move the mouse, and watch the window move with it. When you release the mouse button, the window will "stick" to wherever you "dropped" it. To resize a window, point to any of the window's edges, then click and hold the left mouse button down. Move the mouse, and the window will move with you. Release the mouse button, and the window will snap to wherever you demand.

Note that some windows are not resizable, so if you try to size it and fail, it's not you, it's the window.

■ **Now that you've** *gotten your feet wet, there are a few more tricks in Windows.*

Now that you know how to open, move, and close windows, let's get the computer acclimated to you personally. By the time you're done, not only will your PC be personalized, but you'll also know how to respond to virtually every Windows control.

That's because, throughout this book, you'll be learning by doing — instead of being bored to tears studying step-by-step tutorials.

Explore the Control Panel

IF THE CONTROL PANEL isn't already on the screen, click Start | Settings | Control Panel. When the window opens, you're the proud beholder of Windows 98's nerve center. With rare exceptions, the Control Panel is where all of your Windows settings reside.

Depending upon your computer make and model, the Control Panel icons you see might vary. Some computers will have more Control Panel items; others will have fewer. It all depends on what hardware and software was pre-installed on the PC.

Without exception, your Windows 98 PC will feature some or all of the following Control Panel items. Before delving into these items in greater detail, take a look at this brief overview:

✓ Accessibility Options: Use this to activate a limited special feature set for disabled computer users. Feel free to explore.

✓ Add New Hardware: Rarely used. Starts automatically when you plug in or otherwise add new hardware to your PC.

✓ Add/Remove Programs: Use this to install or remove software from your computer.

✓ Date/Time: Used to set your PC's clock. Been here, done that.

✓ Desktop Themes: Use this to easily change the colors, icons, and other user interface elements of Windows. Feel free to explore here.

✓ Display: Use this to customize your monitor settings. Stay away, for now.

✓ Fonts: Contains a list of all the typefaces installed on your PC. It's best to stay out of this folder. There's literally nothing of value in here for most users.

✓ Game Controllers: This is the place where you can tinker with joystick, game pad, and other game controller settings. If you have a game controller hooked up to your PC, don't be afraid to peek inside.

✓ Infrared: If your computer has an infrared data port, this icon will provide access to the various IR options. Feel free to peruse these options.

✓ Internet Options: Your one-stop-shop for an assortment of Internet performance, security, integration, and other preferences. Don't touch, for now.

✓ Keyboard: Just what it says: A few tweaks for ye olde keyboard. Go ahead; dive in.

✓ Mail: If you're using Microsoft e-mail software, this icon will grant access to all your mail settings. Best left for later.

■ **An applet**
carries out a tiny task.

✓ Modems: Your modem setup is located here. Been here, done that.

✓ Mouse: Go here to tune-up your mouse's behavior and responsiveness, and choose any custom mouse pointers. Click away!

✓ Multimedia: All-important information and configuration options for your multimedia subsystem (audio, video, music) resides here. You'll rarely if ever need to peek in here.

✓ Network: Technical data and setup options for your Internet connection are located here. Only fiddle with these delicate settings if specifically instructed to by your Internet service provider, or a software or hardware vendor.

✓ ODBC Data Sources: Stuff only a rocket scientist could love. Avoid at all costs.

✓ Passwords: Contrary to what it says, your passwords aren't stored here. The Passwords applet is used to enable "profiles," which allows more than one person to use your computer. It also enables the computer to remember each person's individual preferences (such as screen colors, mouse pointers, etc.). A cool idea that doesn't work well. Best left as is.

DEFINITION

An applet is any program that handles a very small task. Think of applets as "lite" applications.

✓ Power Management: Options for controlling your computer's energy-saving features are placed here. It's OK to play with these settings.

✓ Printers: All of your printer profiles and system options can be found in this folder. Been here, done that.

✓ Regional Settings: You can tug, pull, and yank assorted internationalization aspects here, such as your home country, numeric displays, and currency displays. You'll also find date and time settings here (again). Been here, done that.

✓ Sounds: Just what it says – The central repository of all your system beeps, bleeps, buzzes, and boinks. Zip, zap, and pow your way through.

✓ System: More stuff that only a rocket scientist can appreciate. Stay away from this for the time being.

✓ Telephony: Used to inform Windows 98 of your country and area code. Feel free to set it.

✓ Users: The gentle sister of the Passwords program. A high-level, easier to use wizard that helps you set up your PC to support multiple user personalities. Best left alone for now.

That's the Control Panel in a nutshell. As you can see, some of these Control Panel options are best left alone. Windows automatically manages and optimizes their

settings. Others are begging for you to fiddle with them. As you gain experience with your PC, you'll be more inclined to experiment with various features, options, and commands.

There's an easy way to tell if a feature is safe to experiment with: If it doesn't boggle your mind, it's probably safe to experiment with.

Conversely, if you don't have a clue what the on-screen text is talking about, it's best to leave well alone.

Personalizing Windows

LET'S DIP INTO THE FRIENDLIER *Control Panel programs, and set some preferences. Your first task is to give your Windows 98 PC a look and feel that reflects your tastes. To do that, double-click the Desktop Themes icon.*

Desktop Themes applet

When the Desktop Themes dialog opens, you'll see a control panel that's titled "Themes." (For what it's worth, geeks call this type of control panel a "drop-down pick list," because it slides down to open.) Click the down arrowhead to the left of the pick list, and a long list of desktop themes appears. Click on any one that strikes your fancy, and a preview of the theme will appear. When you find one you like, click the OK button at the bottom right of the Desktop Themes dialog.

If you don't like any of the desktop themes, click the Cancel button. To return Windows 98 to its factory settings, go back into the Desktop Themes control panel, and select "Windows Default Settings" from the Themes pick list and then click OK. Now you know what to do when you encounter a drop-down pick list in Windows 98!

Display Properties applet

Next up are your Display Properties. Double-click the Display Properties icon, and you'll be greeted with an assortment of at least six *tabs*: Background, Screen Saver, Appearance, Effects, web, and Settings.

Background tab

On the Background tab, you can pick your Desktop Wallpaper and Desktop Patterns. To choose your wallpaper, click the down arrowhead and scroll down the list of designs. You can sample any design by clicking on it. That will cause a preview of the design to appear on the simulated monitor that takes up most of the Desktop Properties dialog. If you don't like a design, click on another, or use the up arrowhead to scroll back to [None]. If you decide to use wallpaper, be sure to click on the Display drop-down pick list, and sample the various options there. You can have your wallpaper centered, tiled, or stretched.

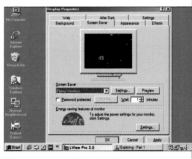

■ **You can choose** *from various Desktop Themes.*

If you don't care for any of the wallpaper designs, you might like the desktop patterns. They're similar to wallpaper, except that they can't be tiled, centered, or stretched.

They always fill up the entire desktop. To play with patterns, make sure the wallpaper selection is set to [None.] Then click the Pattern button, and work your way down the Pattern list box. Each pattern you click on will appear in the preview pane. If you find one you like, click OK. Otherwise, click Cancel.

Screen Saver tab

Now click on the Screen Saver tab, and click on the drop-down pick list labeled "Screen Saver." Work your way down the list, and click on a screen saver you'd like to preview. Then click the Preview button to see it in action. Press any key on your keyboard to stop the preview. When

■ **To preview and select** *a screen saver, select Display Properties | Screen Saver.*

you find one you like, point at the small up and down arrowheads beside the "Wait:" box, and click on them to set the amount of time you want the computer to wait before it kicks in the screen saver.

By the way, the little Wait box is called a "spinner control," because it spins numbers up or down, like a one-armed bandit. You can also click inside the spin box box, and type in a number directly. Depending upon the screen saver you select, you might be able to adjust some of its settings. Click the Settings button to see what options are available. Feel free to experiment with them, and see what they do by using the Preview button.

Lastly, on some computers, you'll see an "Energy Saving Features" option. Skip that for now. The same controls are tucked away beneath the Power Management icons, which we'll delve into momentarily.

Appearance tab

Next in line is the Appearance tab. Click it, then click the Scheme drop-down pick list. Work your way down the list using the down and up arrowheads. When you see a scheme you like, try it by clicking it. You'll see a sample of it in the main window above. When you find a scene you like, move on to the Effects tab. If you don't like any of the schemes, scroll down the list until you find the "Windows Default" scheme, and select that. Then go to the Effects tab.

Effects tab

Click on the Effects tab, and you'll unveil a short list of checkboxes that toggle certain user interface behaviors. To turn a visual effect on, click its checkbox, and a check mark will appear inside. To turn it off, click it's checkbox again, and the box will become empty. If you, like me, are nearsighted, turning the "Use large icons" feature on will double the size of certain Windows icons, making screens easier to read.

Turning on "Show icons using all possible colors" also makes certain Windows icons more realistic and pleasing to the eye. Turning on the "Animate windows" option causes program windows, menus, and tool tips to glide open slowly and smoothly. Turning the feature off makes windows, menus, and tool tips snap open and closed. To test the effect, click the Animate Windows checkbox on or off, and then click the Apply button. Double-click the Control Panel's blue menu bar, and watch it either swoop down or snap closed. Then click the Animate Windows checkbox again, and click the Control Panel's button, now at the bottom of the screen. The "Smooth edges of screen fonts" visual effect is supposed to make on-screen type sharper and clearer. In reality, it often makes type faces faded and blurry. For now, it's best to keep this option unchecked (off). After you've used the computer for a few days, return to the Display Properties and flip the "Smooth edges" feature on to give it a try.

You won't see the effect in all of your screens, but it will become evident as you surf the web and work on various word-processor documents.

Last up is the silly "Show window contents while dragging" option. This tells Windows 98 how to display windows when you move them. Click this checkbox to turn it on, then click Apply. To see the effect, point your mouse at the Display Properties title bar, then click and hold the mouse button down as you move the mouse. This is called *dragging* a window. As you can see, the entire window is visible as you move it around. Now uncheck the "Show window contents" checkbox, and drag the window again. This time all you see is an outline. A silly feature, indeed! Most users keep this option checked (on). Don't worry about the "Hide icons when the desktop is viewed as a web page" option. To increase Windows 98's reliability, you'll be disabling its ability to replace the standard Windows 98 Desktop with a web page. Doing so also disables this feature.

DEFINITION

Dragging *a window or other on-screen element is also referred to as "clicking+dragging," or "click+drag."*

Web tab

Stepping right up is the web tab. This one's easy. Uncheck the "View my desktop as a web page" box. Turning this feature off makes Windows 98 more reliable. After you're experienced with online access, you can return to this feature and give it a spin.

Settings tab

Bringing up the rear is the Settings tab. There are only two controls you need to concern yourself with here: The Colors drop-down pick list and the Screen Area slider. Click the Colors pick list, and select the level of color accuracy you want to work with.

Next, point the mouse at the Screen Side slider control. Click on and drag the slider control to the right, then back to the left. Notice how the amount of information you can display on your Windows 98 desktop increases and decreases. The farther to the right (towards the "More" setting) you drag the slider, the more information you pack on the screen. This is especially useful when viewing web pages, documents, photos, games, and movies.

■ **By moving the** *"Screen area" slider control to left or right in Display Properties | Settings you can decrease or increase the amount of information you can display on the screen.*

The more colors you tell Windows to work with, the sharper and more accurate your images will be when viewing photographs, web pages, and so on. The trade off: The higher the color depth, the longer it will take your computer to put pictures on the screen.

Generally, the best balance of color accuracy and performance is the "High Color (16 bit)" option. This works with a palette of roughly 65,000 colors, more than enough to render vivid photos and other images.

Anything less than 65,000 colors will generate choppy, blotchy displays. Going to "High Color (24 bit)" or "High Color (32 bit)" uses a palette of 16 million colors – clearly a lot of data for the PC's display adapter to calculate. If you're editing digital video or photos, or otherwise creating and editing graphic art, then it certainly makes sense to crank your color depth up as high as it will go. But if you're doing general computing (web, e-mail, word processing, etc.), stick with 65,000 colors.

Slide the slider to the extreme right. Next, click the Advanced button, and click on the little round button besides "Ask me before applying the new color settings" to select it. (This is called a "radio button.") Also make sure the "Show settings icon on task bar" is checked. If you see any other controls, ignore them for now; they're linked to your particular brand of computer, and are stock features of Windows 98.

Now click the OK button, then click Apply. Windows 98 will warn you that it is about to test your new display settings. Click OK. Windows 98 will then ask if you like the way the new settings look. You do? Click OK. You don't? Click Cancel. Keep playing with your display settings until you're happy with them. Then click OK to save all of your Display Properties settings, and close the Display properties dialog. (Just a quick aside: You now know how to use radio buttons and slider controls!)

Keyboard applet

Coming up next is the Keyboard control panel. Double-click it, and set the "Repeat delay," "Repeat rate," and "Cursor blink rate" slider controls as you like them. The repeat delay specifies how long it takes for a character to be displayed on the screen after you type it. The repeat rate is how fast the keyboard automatically repeats characters when you hold a key down. Most users crank the repeat delay to Short, and the repeat rate to fast. You can test your settings by typing in the box labeled "Click here and hold down a key to test." When you're happy with your settings, just click the OK button.

Mouse applet

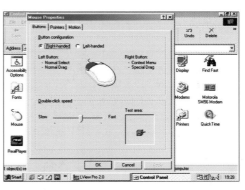

The Mouse control panel is your keyboard's best friend. Double-click it, and you can set your button configuration for left- or right-handed. You can also fine-tune your double-click speed by dragging the associated slider control, and double-clicking on the test area. When you're done, click the Pointers tab, and choose a mouse pointer scheme from those offered in the drop down pick list. Then click the Motion tab, and crank up your mouse pointer sensitivity up or down.

■ **Go to Control Panel | Mouse** *to configure the way your mouse behaves.*

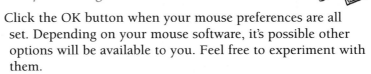

You can test mouse pointer sensitivity by clicking Apply, and moving the mouse around. For a cool effect, click the "Show pointer trails" checkbox, and drag the slider control all the way to the right.

Click the OK button when your mouse preferences are all set. Depending on your mouse software, it's possible other options will be available to you. Feel free to experiment with them.

■ **Feel free to** *experiment with your mouse preferences.*

Power Management applet

Experienced users often call this technology Power Manglement, because it's notorious for making computers act goofy. By design, power management is supposed to give you the ability to instruct various computer components to go to sleep when not in use. This, of course, conserves precious electrical resources. In practice, however, some computer hardware doesn't respond well to power management commands. As a result, using power management can cause your PC to lock up, run slowly, or turn in other aberrant behavior.

With that caveat in mind, double-click the Power Management icon. To disable Power Management entirely, select the "Always On" Power Scheme. Or, if you prefer, mix the various power schemes with the "System standby," "Turn off monitor," and "Turn off hard disks" drop-down pick lists.

If your computer seems sluggish or otherwise weird, return to the Power Management control panel and disable power management.

Sounds applet

It's a sound time to tune up your Windows 98 sounds. Double-click the Sounds icon, and choose any one of the sound Schemes from the drop-down pick list. To hear what the sound scheme sounds like, scroll down the Events list simply using the up and down arrowheads.

Note: Going forward, I'll often refer to double-clicking as "opening," "running," "launching," or "firing up" an item. That's how you'll hear most experienced folks refer to it. I'll also start referring to drop-down pick lists as just plain "pick lists."

Click on any event that has a speaker icon beside it, and then click the "play" button (that's the right arrowhead button beside the "Preview" box). After you click on a few sound events, you'll get an idea as to what the sound scheme sounds like. To turn off all sounds, choose No Sounds in the Schemes list. To choose a specific scheme, select it in the Schemes list, and then click OK.

That's a wrap. Your system is unpacked, set up, burned in, tested, and configured. In addition to whatever your computer vendor pre-installed on your new PC, you probably have additional software you purchased, and plan to use. Hold that aside for now.

Sometime after your basic computing skills are in place, you'll crack open those extra software boxes and CDs, and install your custom software solutions. Be patient! You'll get there soon enough.

A simple summary

✓ Unpack and set up your new PC with loving care. Keep all software, documentation, and paperwork tidy and organized. You might need those materials in the future. Store the boxes in case you have to ship a component for repair.

✓ Logically position the monitor, PC, keyboard, mouse, printer, and other peripherals within reach and for easy access. This will avoid health-related computing hazards.

✓ Get to know your keyboard. Its Backspace, Esc, Enter, Space bar, and arrow keys are the ones most often used for data entry and control.

✓ Your mouse is the easiest way to manipulate Windows 98's on-screen controls. Just click, double-click, or click+drag to make Windows 98 do your bidding.

✓ Exercise key components, such as the monitor, printer, modem, sound system, and disk drives, to make sure everything works.

✓ Burn-in your PC before configuring it or using it regularly. After it's all set up, let it sit fully powered up for at least 24 hours. This will isolate any heat- or stress-related manufacturing defects.

✓ Power-cycle new PCs repeatedly during the 24-hour burn-in cycle. This will flesh out any mechanical or electrical problems.

✓ After burn-in, make sure you back-up your critical Windows systems folders.

✓ You're now ready to hop through the Control Panel and set all your preferences.

✓ The prevailing Windows 98 controls are menus, buttons, title bars, scroll bars, list boxes, drop-down pick lists (a-k-a pick lists), and sliders.

✓ Don't install any additional software yet. The time for that will arrive after your basic computing skills are honed.

PART TWO

INVESTING THAT EXTRA EFFORT MAKES IT
ALL WORTHWHILE

NOVICES ONCE, EXPERTS FOREVER

THERE'S ONE THING you can say about Windows 98 that you can't say about any other computer operating system: People of all *experience* levels use it every day. Newbies, surfers, suits, T-shirts, hackers,  crackers, and hard-boiled experts alike find Windows 98 meets their widely divergent application requirements. From the family room to the boardroom, no other software product in history has proven so *flexible*

But Windows 98's adaptability comes with a high price: complexity. To address Windows' growing complexity, Microsoft introduced the START button in 1995 to help new users just like you. Unfortunately, getting started with PCs will require a tad more effort than just clicking the START button. Ready to *invest* that extra effort? Good!

Chapter 6

Getting Started

To help ease your transition into the electronic world, I'll show you why you're better off having joined the computing revolution later, rather than sooner. You'll go sightseeing on the Start Menu and once you gain your bearings there, you'll earn your Windows 98 wings by launching, flying, and landing programs solo.

In this chapter...

✓ A vast new world

✓ Don't start with START

✓ Surveying the Desktop

✓ Mastering the Taskbar

✓ START one step at a time

✓ 3, 2, 1 . . . launch program!

A vast new world

TAKE A GOOD HARD LOOK *at your new computer's screen. There are icons labeled My Computer, Network Neighborhood, Recycle Bin, My Briefcase, Online Services, MSN, Outlook Express, Internet Explorer, and more. There's a gray banner across the bottom with a bunch of other little icons on it, and they're not even labeled. When you click the button labeled START, up pops some kind of menu that has way too many options on it, none of which makes any sense.*

You're already thoroughly confused, and you haven't even scratched the surface of Windows 98! If you think this is bad, be glad you're getting started with computers in 2000, and not in 1981. Things were far more difficult for PC users 19 years ago. Back then, personal computers weren't friendly at all. Powering up the PC didn't result in a screen full of helpful icons, menus, buttons, and prompts. Instead, people were greeted by this obscure *user interface*: C>

That was it. The dreaded "C" prompt. To get the computer to do anything, you had to spend months learning how to talk to it. For example, to view a list of documents, users had to learn to say DIR*.DOC /S /P

Or perhaps you know someone who recalls FORMAT A: /S, used to prepare floppy disks for use; or the infamous FIND "target text" /I /N *.DOC, used to find text in a document file. There were hundreds of these arcane commands tucked away in PCs. Today, thanks to Apple's Mac OS and Microsoft Windows, almost anyone can sit down at a computer and become productive in minutes. Both the C> prompt (a-k-a the "command line") and the current WIMP (windows, icons, menus, pointer) user interfaces have proven equally difficult for new users to master. Where WIMP excels is in its consistency. With the old C> prompt, what worked in one program didn't work in another. With WIMP, when you learn how to do something once, you can apply that lesson over and over again, in every Windows 98 program.

■ **A computer screen** *1981-style: no windows, no icons, no menus. Just the "C" prompt. It wasn't pretty.*

Learning Windows 98 is like a bell curve, requiring more up-front effort, and much less long-term effort.

> ### DEFINITION
>
> *Computers communicate with other computers using 1s and 0s, but they also have to interface with humans. For that, they use sight and sound. Letters and images on the screen tell us what to do next, or provide us with options. Sounds are used to identify error messages or alerts and other system events. This is called the computer's* user interface.

Don't start with START

WHEN YOU FIRST *fire up your PC, keep an eye out for a little message that zips along the bottom of the screen, and reads, "Click here to begin." Beside the message is an arrow pointing to the Start button.*

It should come as no surprise that the button labeled "Start" is the last place a new Windows user should click.

By rights, Microsoft should relabel the Start button the "Start later" button. Before you engage the Start button, you need to learn a thing or two about the place where the Start menu resides: The Taskbar. And before you learn about the Taskbar, it's crucial to learn a thing or two about the place the Taskbar resides: the Windows Desktop.

Anything that appears on your computer's screen is said to appear on the Windows Desktop. It's called the Desktop because it's supposed to be the virtual equivalent of your office desktop. Just as your office desk has file folders, papers, tools, and electronic devices scattered over it, your Windows Desktop has file folders (also called "directories"), documents (papers), tools (programs), and electronic devices (fax, e-mail) scattered about. And just as your office has a trash can that you can rummage through to retrieve a document you accidentally tossed, your Windows Desktop offers the Recycle Bin as its digital counterpart.

Surveying the Desktop

ANY ITEM ON YOUR WINDOWS *Desktop can be opened, moved, copied, edited, and deleted (that's computerese for erased). You can also organize your Windows Desktop by dragging items around, or have Windows organize things for you.*

Try this: Click once on the Recycle Bin icon, and drag it to the lower left hand side of the screen. Next, click+drag the My Computer icon anywhere in the upper right area of the screen. Then click+drag the My Briefcase icon to the center of the screen. You've just rearranged your Windows Desktop! You could manually click+drag the three items you moved back to their original locations . . . or you can ask Windows to clean up your Desktop for you. Here's how.

Using context menus

Put the mouse pointer in any blank area of the display (that is, anywhere there isn't an icon). Now click your RIGHT mouse button (that's the button on the right side of the mouse). Up pops a little menu, which computer users call a "context menu."

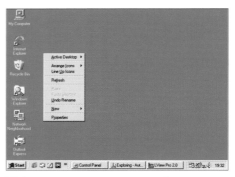

Any time you click your right mouse button, Windows will display a context menu that's custom tailored to the item you clicked on.

■ **A context menu** *pops up when you right-click on the Desktop.*

The context menu you're looking at now is custom tailored to the Windows Desktop. Click "Line Up Icons." Voilà! Your mishmash of icons instantly snaps to order. Want to sort icons by name?

Right-click the Windows Desktop again, and this time click "Arrange Icons," followed by the "By Name" option. Your Windows icons are now sorted by name. If you'd like Windows to keep your icons tidy, right-click the Desktop again, click "Arrange Icons," and then "Auto Arrange."

Creating a new Desktop folder

Right-click the Desktop once more, and this time select New, followed by Folder. Congrats! You just created your first file folder in Windows 98. In the box below the folder's icon (called the name box), you'll see the words "New Folder." Click once on the name box, and give the folder a name by typing "Folder Shmolder," and pressing the Enter key on your keyboard. (If you can't type the name, press the Esc key, click once on the name box, and try again.)

Suppose you mistyped the folder's name, or couldn't type it in for some reason. Right-click the folder, and select Rename. To give the folder a new name, type "Folder" in the name box and then press the Enter key on your keyboard.

Creating a new Desktop document

OK, let's create a new letter together. Right-click the Desktop, click New, and click Text Document. A new text document appears. In the box below the document icon (called the filename box), it reads "New Text Document.txt." Click once on the name box, and give the file a name by typing "Letter.txt," and pressing the Enter key on your keyboard. If you can't type the name, press the Esc key, then click once on the name box, and try again.

When naming or renaming files, never, ever, ever change their extensions.

The extension is any text that appears after the period in a file name; for example, .TXT. Windows 98 uses the extension to identify the file's type and connect the file to its creator programs. In other words, Windows 98 knows that a text editor creates .TXT files; that .DOC files are created by a word processor, and that a web browser creates .HTM files. If you change a file's type (i.e., its extension), Windows 98 won't know what program is supposed to use the file – and neither will you.

Drag+dropping documents into folders

To file the letter into the folder you created, click on Letter.txt, and drag it atop the folder. The folder will change color when the letter is precisely over it. When the folder changes color, let go of your mouse button. The letter will drop into the folder. The maneuver you just completed is called "drag+drop," because you dragged and dropped the letter into the folder. It is similar to click+drag, except that when you let go of the mouse button, you're "dropping" an icon on top of another icon.

Opening, editing, and saving a new document

What good is a letter in a folder if you haven't typed anything on it? Not much! Right-click the folder, and select Open. The folder opens into a window. As you would expect, inside the folder window is Letter.txt. Right-click Letter.txt, and select Open. The letter opens into a window. Anything you type will appear in the letter. Type THE QUICK BROWN FOX JUMPED OVER THE LAZY DOG. Click the letter's Close button (that's the little X in the upper right-hand corner). Windows will ask you if you would like to save the letter. "Saving" a document is computerese for "filing" it. Click the Yes button, and the Letter.txt window closes. Now right-click the Letter.txt icon again, and select Open. This time, it opens to reveal the text you typed. Click the letter's Close button again. You didn't type any new text, so Windows 98 will close the Letter.txt window immediately, without asking you if you'd like to save it. Next, click the folder's Close button, and the folder closes. How's that for amazing? You just created a new folder, a new letter, edited the letter, saved it, reopened it, closed it, and closed the folder. Are you feeling like a Windows 98 expert yet?

Deleting and restoring Desktop folders and documents

Don't get too cocky! There's lots more work to do. Imagine Folder and Letter.txt are part of a project that was cancelled. You don't need the documents any longer, and want to erase everything associated with the cancelled project. Click on the folder, and drag+drop it onto the Recycle Bin. Bang; it's gone. But wait – your spouse calls to tell you the project wasn't cancelled after all.

Crisis? What crisis? Right-click the Recycle Bin, select Open, and there's your folder. Right-click on the folder, and then click the Restore command. Your folder has just been miraculously returned straight to the Windows Desktop. To close the Recycle Bin, click the window's Close button. (Yep, that's the little X in the upper right-hand corner.)

There's one fundamental tool you can use to decipher anything that appears on the Windows Desktop: The right-click's context menu.

If you want to know what something is and what you can do with it, right-click it. All of the item's available options will pop up. You never have to remember commands, sequences, steps, or anything more than right-clicking.

Mastering the Taskbar

SEE THAT LONG GRAY *area at the bottom of your computer screen? That's the Windows Taskbar, and it's far more powerful than it seems.*

When you have various windows open on your screen, you can't see the Windows Desktop. But you can still see the Taskbar. After you use the Windows Start button, the Start Menu it reveals disappears. But you can still see the Taskbar. Whatever you do, wherever you go, you're going to go through it together with the Windows Taskbar. First and foremost, the Windows Taskbar makes it easy for you to switch between programs.

Switching from program to program with the Taskbar

To see how easy switching programs is, double-click the My Computer icon. When My Computer opens, grab its title bar and drag the window to the right of the screen. Go back to the Windows Desktop, and this time double-click the My Documents icon. Now you have two windows open at the same time. Gaze down at the Windows Taskbar. Two buttons, one for each open window, have materialized. Click the button labeled My Computer, and that window pops to the forefront. Click the one labeled My Documents, and up comes the My Documents window. No matter how many windows are cluttering your screen, you can always get your bearings and navigate among them by using the Windows Taskbar.

Managing window positions with the Taskbar

Ah, but there's even more power lurking beneath this unassuming tool. Right-click the Taskbar wherever there are no buttons. Up pops the Taskbar's context menu. Click the Tile Windows Horizontally option. Windows automatically resizes your windows for maximum viewable space. Try that again, this time right-clicking the Taskbar, and selecting Cascade Windows, or Tile Windows Vertically. Get the picture? Got it! What if you want to clear all of your open windows and get back to the Windows Desktop? Right-click ye olde Taskbar, and select Minimize All Windows. To restore all open windows at once, right-click the Taskbar again, and select Undo Minimize All. As if that's not exciting enough, the Taskbar can also house a clone of your entire Windows Desktop.

Cloning the Windows Desktop to the Taskbar

Replicating the Windows Desktop on the Taskbar keeps it at your fingertips at all times. Here's how you do it. Right-click the Taskbar, and select Toolbars, then Desktop. Next thing you know, every icon that appears on your Desktop will also appear on your Taskbar.

Double-clicking the vertical line beside the word "Desktop" on the Taskbar will show or hide the Desktop icons, which helps to save much-needed Taskbar space. Clicking the small double-arrow that appears on the right will scroll through all of the Desktop items now replicated on the Taskbar. Repeat these steps to reverse the process. To remove the Desktop clone from your Taskbar, right-click the Taskbar, select Toolbars, and click the Desktop option. The cloned Desktop items will go away.

Resizing, relocating, and hiding the Taskbar

If your Taskbar gets cluttered, it's easy to resize it. Move your mouse pointer to the upper edge of the Taskbar, until the mouse pointer changes. Now click+drag the Taskbar's edge to make it larger or smaller. And if you click+drag inside the Taskbar's body, you can move it to the top, left, right, or bottom screen edge.

But the Taskbar's coolest feature is dubbed "Auto Hide." This allows the Taskbar to slide out of your way when it's not in use, and pop back up when you need it.

Right-click the Taskbar, and click Properties. Make sure the "Always on top" and "Auto hide" checkboxes are checked, then click OK. Now click anywhere on the screen except the Taskbar, and watch the Taskbar disappear. To get it back, just move your mouse pointer to the Taskbar's edge of the screen. To disable Auto Hide, simply reverse the process: Right-click the Taskbar, click Properties, and uncheck the "Always on top" and "Auto hide" checkboxes. Click OK, and your taskbar is returned to normal.

One final Taskbar tidbit: You can bring up the Taskbar and the Start Menu at any time by pressing the Windows logo key on your keyboard.

That's the key usually jammed between those marked Ctrl and Alt, to the left of the space bar. And now, at last, it's time to START playing around with the START button.

START one step at a time

WITH THE WINDOWS DESKTOP *and Taskbar under your belt, it's safe to say you've conquered two of three big aspects of the Windows cyberscape. All that remains is the Windows Start button and the Start Menu that pops up when you click the button.*

During the course of your Windows 98 travels, you've had occasion to click the Start button and traverse the Start Menu a few times. This round, however, calls for more than merely visiting the Start Menu. This round, you'll come to understand it.

■ **The Start Menu** *pops up when you click the Start button.*

In the era before Windows 95 and 98, all computer users had to devise their own means to access programs. Some people used commands, typing the full program name at the C> prompt every time they wanted to run something. Other folks created lists of commands, called *batch files*, that allowed them to type in a letter or number, and the batch file would execute the command lists automatically. Still others built or bought menuing software that allowed them to load programs using their arrow and Enter keys (this was called, appropriately enough, "point and shoot").

Better access to programs

Microsoft's software engineers repeatedly tried to come up with a better way to access programs. First they delivered the MS-DOS Shell, introduced in DOS version 4.0, and entirely rewritten in version 5.0. Both flopped. Then there was the "MS-DOS Executive," which debuted in Windows 1.0. It was a stinker, too.

Microsoft almost got it right when they released Windows 3.0, which featured a mediocre menuing system called "Program Manager." Unfortunately, Program Manager wasn't properly integrated into the Windows file system. Menu items would quit working whenever users moved, renamed, or deleted programs and documents. (It's one of the main reasons Macintosh users dubbed Windows with the name "Windoze.")

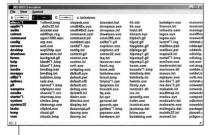

■ **MS-DOS Executive** *flopped – and you can see why.*

But with the release of Windows 95, PC users got the last laugh. Not only did Windows 95 give PC users a true desktop environment; it added the innovative Taskbar, and for the first time, served up an intuitive and flexible menuing system: the Start Menu.

Essentially, clicking the Start button to pop-up the Start Menu is akin to telling the computer, "Show me an organized list of everything I can do with this PC."

The Start Menu is much more than just a simple entry point for new users. It's more extensive than a program launch pad, and deeper than a "main" or "master" menuing system. The Start button is, in essence, the key to all that there is and all that will be in your Windows PC.

The Windows Start button gives you the complete top-down view of the vast software universe that exists on your PC.

It's also easy as pie to use and, like the Taskbar, possesses some powerful features that aren't immediately obvious. Before getting into advanced features, let's start with basic navigation.

The Start Menu defined

To take the helm of the Start Menu, first click the Start button, or press the Windows logo key (hereinafter referred to as the "Win" key) on your keyboard. Up pops the Start Menu, displaying its top level entries:

Programs: All installed software is organized under this heading.
Favorites: A list of web sites that you can customize.
Documents: A link to your My Documents folder, and a list of the most recent documents you worked on.
Settings: Links into your computer's "engine" room (system settings and preferences).
Find: A search engine for finding folders, files, web sites, and other personal data.
Help: Calls up the Windows Help system.
Run: Reveals the Windows command line (yes, the old C> prompt is still hiding under the covers)
Log Off: Appears only on systems connected to business networks; allows you to log-off the network.
Shut Down: Used to safely turn off or restart the computer.

Important note: Never turn your computer off without using Shut Down. If you turn off your PC without using Shut Down, you can severely damage your computer.

Traversing the Start Menu

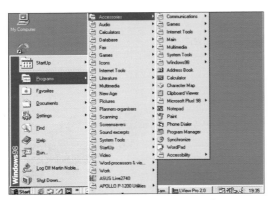

Notice those little right arrowheads beside certain Start Menu items? That's your cue to *hover* your mouse pointer over the item. Do so, and the Start Menu will cascade outwards, revealing even more items.

■ **When you hover** *your mouse over the Accessories entry in the Programs menu, a second menu cascades from the first.*

Give it a whirl. Click Start, then hover your mouse pointer over the Programs entry on the Start Menu. After a split second, the Programs menu appears. Don't click yet! Gently slide your mouse pointer above the expanded menu. Now run your mouse pointer up and down the expanded list. Depending on your computer's make and model, you will have anywhere from eight to dozens of programs, documents, folders, and other stuff listed here. If the list is too big to fit on the screen, Windows will add two small arrowheads to the top and bottom of the menu. Hover the mouse pointer over them, and the expanded menu will scroll up or down to reveal more entries.

Try it yourself: Hover your mouse over the Accessories entry. Out swoops yet another extended menu. In Windows parlance, you are now viewing the Start | Programs | Accessories menu (or the Accessories menu for short). Notice there are lots of menu items with right arrowheads. These are called "sub-menus." The items without an arrowhead beside them are called "executable objects." An *executable* item can be a program you run or a document you read or work on. Or perhaps it's a video you can watch or digital music you can play. It might even be a web site you can visit.

Spend a little time exploring the various menus and submenus that appear on the Start Menu – but don't click on anything! Hover your mouse pointer over as many menus and submenus as you can find.

Give each menu a gander, and see if you can guess what the various "executable objects" do – but remember, don't click any just yet! When you've finished exploring the Start Menu, then and only then is it time to take the next big step.

3, 2, 1 . . . launch program!

STEP INTO YOUR *fire-retardant suit. Slide on the Plexiglas goggles. Don your crash helmet. Strap on your parachute and your seatbelt. And take a deep breath. You're about to launch headfirst into the vast and often uncharted universe known as . . . Windows 98.*

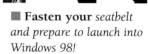

The preflight planning, purchasing, and preparation phase is over. All computer hardware and software have been tested and cleared for flight conditions. All systems are fully configured and "go" for takeoff. As you sit in the cockpit and survey the dashboard – er, I mean Desktop – before you, all that remains is to run down the

■ **Fasten your** *seatbelt and prepare to launch into Windows 98!*

last-minute checklist to make sure that you, the pilot-in-training, can safely take off, fly, and land this electronic bag o' bits. Believe it or not, you've already flown a few successful Windows 98 missions – albeit in a carefully controlled manner, with me as your copilot/instructor. This time around, however, I'm cutting you loose, kicking you out of the nest, and turning over the PC's controls.

Launching programs on the start menu

Rev up the engine by clicking the Start button, and pulling up the Start Menu. Head straight to the Programs menu, and click on it. When it opens, feel free to click on any program on any menu or sub-menu. After the program opens, return to the Programs menu on the Start Menu, and fire off a different program on any menu or sub-menu. Do this several times, until you have at least seven, different programs open on your screen.

Glance down at your Taskbar, and you'll notice seven (and preferably more) different buttons. Click on any Taskbar button. Notice its associated window pops to the top of the stack. Now click on another Taskbar button. Same thing happens again. No matter how many programs you launch via the Start Menu, the Taskbar will maintain a list of buttons that makes it easy for you to jump to and fro among their windows. Now let's clean up the mess we've made. Right-click the Taskbar and select Minimize All Windows. All the open program windows disappear, but their Taskbar buttons remain. Click on any Taskbar button, and now only that program's window appears on your desktop.

■ **You can switch** *between several programs by using the Taskbar buttons.*

Seven ways to leave your program

Now let's close the open programs, until they're needed again. In the process, you'll use one of seven (count 'em) ways to exit a Windows program. The first way to get out of a program is the one you're already familiar with: Pick any program, and click its Close button. That's the little X at the upper right-hand corner of every window. The program disappears, as does its Taskbar button. You know a program has been unloaded when its Taskbar button goes away.

Speaking of the Taskbar, right-click on any Taskbar button. Notice anything obvious? That's right: There's a "Close" command. Click the Close command, and the Taskbar button and its associated program window disappear. But there's more! Notice every program window on the screen has a tiny picture (i.e., an icon) in its upper left-hand corner. Click that icon once and a pop-up menu appears. Once again, there's a "Close" command. In fact, this is the same menu that came into view when you right-clicked a Taskbar button. Click Close, and the program will exit. You can also double-click the little icon on the title bar to close a program. That's four ways to close down, with three to go. The first runner up: The File menu's Exit command. By now you've probably noticed that most Windows 98 programs feature a list of commands across the top. This is called the "menu bar." Below the menu you'll often find a bunch of little buttons. This is called the "toolbar." The menu bar and the toolbar are two ways to do the same thing: Issue commands to software programs.

Menu bars and toolbars will differ from program to program, but there's one menu they almost all feature: The File menu. Click the word "File" on the menu bar, and the File menu drops down. In nearly all cases, the last command on the File menu will be Close or Exit. Click it, and the program will terminate. Try that now on one of the open windows. After the program exits, notice that the letter "F" on the File menu of another program is underlined. The underlined letter is called the "hot letter."

It's Windows 98's way of telling you that the File command can be activated by pressing the ALT key on your keyboard, combined with the letter F. Give it a whirl. Press and hold the ALT key down, and then tap the letter F.

This is called "Alt+F." Do it, and the file menu drops down. This time, notice the "x" in the word Exit is underlined (or the "C" in the word "Close" is underlined). Hold the ALT and F keys down, and then press X if there's an Exit command, or C if the featured command is Close. The program exits. So Alt+F+X or Alt+F+C can be used to quickly exit programs using the keyboard.

But there's more! There should be at least one more window still open on your screen. In nearly all Windows 98 programs, the keyboard combination of Alt+F4 is the universal Close command. Hold the ALT key down, then press the F4 key. Each time you press Alt+F4, another window closes. Press it enough times, and all of your open windows will close – including Windows 98 itself! That's the slam dunk, no-holds-barred, fastest way to close any windows program. Just give Alt+F4 a whack, and the program is gone until you need it again.

A simple summary

✓ No matter how difficult learning to use a computer is, it's far easier today than it was just a few years ago.

✓ We're all novices once, but we're experts forever.

✓ The Taskbar is your command center for hopping around whatever you're working on.

✓ When using the Windows Desktop and the Taskbar, you can inspect customized "context" menus for almost any item.

✓ You can move and rearrange items on the Windows Desktop simply by dragging+dropping them at any time.

✓ You can relocate the Taskbar by clicking on it and dragging it to any edge of the screen.

✓ The Start button reveals Windows 98's Start Menu, the master view of everything your computer offers. The Start Menu contains other menus, called sub-menus, which list available programs and documents.

✓ You can open programs using the Windows Desktop or the Start Menu, but there are seven different ways to close programs. Alt+F4 is the fastest.

✓ After a program loads, all of its commands will appear on a menu bar and toolbars. Menu commands and toolbar buttons can be activated by clicking on them.

✓ You can activate any command you see on the screen by holding down the ALT key on the keyboard while pressing the command's hot letter.

Chapter 7

Taking Charge of Windows

IF YOU'RE TRULY COMFORTABLE with the nuts and bolts of navigation, it's time to put your budding skills to the test, and actually navigate somewhere. In other words, get ready to shove off beyond the relative comfort of the Windows 98 Desktop. In this chapter, you'll leave the Windows Desktop behind, and take what some new users say is a rather frightening trip into the cavernous depths of Windows 98's file system. After that, you'll discover how to take advantage of Windows' intrinsic ability to automatically organize your work life – a feature most people, including advanced users, tend to overlook. Lastly, you'll find out how to share information between multiple Windows programs.

In this chapter...

✓ Getting organized: START now, benefit later

✓ Exploring Explorer

✓ Windows as your personal secretary

✓ Time for a dry run

131

Getting organized: START now, benefit later

LIFE WOULD BE INCREDIBLY DIFFICULT *were it not for internationally recognized standards. There are standards for electrical plugs and voltage, standards that dictate how telephones communicate, and standards for entertainment media, such as cassettes, CDs, and videos. In fact, nearly everything you see, hear, or touch is in some way impacted by global standards. What if those standards were to suddenly disappear? Imagine, for a moment, a world in which standards didn't exist.*

It's a place where your phone works with only one telephone company, your cassette tapes work only in one tape player, and every kitchen appliance requires a different electrical adapter. Need gas? Your gas tank's fill valve only fits the pump on your new car dealer's lot. Going on vacation? Make sure you bring plenty of film, because your camera only accepts the manufacturer's special format (and it has to be developed by the camera maker, too). Don't laugh. This scenario isn't as far-fetched as it seems.

■ **Standards make it** *possible for different telephone companies to communicate.*

Ask any owner of any laptop PC how hard it is to find replacement batteries, and how they get ripped off once they find them. Most laptop PC users are forced to visit their dealer or the PC maker to get replacement batteries. Worse, these proprietary batteries can cost ten times more than off-the-shelf rechargeables. For example, a battery that should cost $25 can run $250 – simply because there are no laptop battery standards. This allows manufacturers to lock customers in.

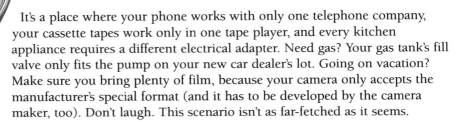

What does all this have to do with learning about Windows 98? Plenty. Every software company has its own unique ideas about how programs should look and operate, what the user experience should be, and how personal data should be stored, organized, and retrieved.

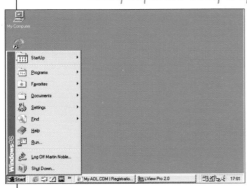

As you move forward in your Windows 98 experience, you'll discover that some programs put their startup icons on the Desktop, while others use the Start Menu, and still

■ **Some programs** *can be fired up in the Start Menu...*

others use the Taskbar – or go so far as to install their own proprietary menuing systems. Some programs save your personal data in the Desktop's My Documents folder. Others put your stuff in the same folder their program resides in. Still others ask you to specify a folder, or create a pseudo-folder that's not really part of the Windows 98 file system.

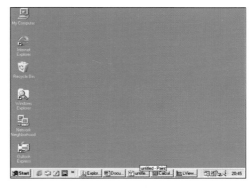

You can end up learning and suffering with 1,001 different, incompatible ways to manage your programs and personal data.

■ ...**while others** *can be started in the Taskbar.*

Or you can take charge, and establish your own personal standards for how information is handled by your PC. I obviously advocate the latter approach:

GET ORGANIZED

✓ Get organized now, before you have gigabytes of data scattered all over your hard drive.

✓ Get organized now, and save hours of wasted effort searching for lost folders and files.

✓ Get organized now, and you'll be able to access your programs and data in ways that reflect your personal work habits, and not the work habits of some faceless programmer.

✓ Get organized now, and work the same way, every day, the first time, every time.

It's easy to set your own computing standards, and keep your system organized. It's equally easy to fall into the trap of doing it someone else's way.

There's no better way to illustrate this equation, and learn how to organize your Windows 98 system, than to start working with Windows Explorer.

Exploring Explorer

FOR 60 YEARS AND COUNTING, *MGM's 1939 classic,* The Wizard of OZ, *has taught kids of all ages that things are not always what they seem. That timeless maxim is perhaps best illustrated in one of the film's final scenes. Standing inside the Wizard's Emerald City castle, Dorothy (Judy Garland) and her entourage quiver before a magnificent, larger-than-life, translucent image of the Great, Powerful Wizard. Amidst belching flames and smoke and the apparition's fearful ranting, Dorothy notices a small, portly fellow pulling levers and pushing buttons behind a shimmering green curtain.*

"Pay no attention to that man behind the curtain!" booms the Wizard's echoing voice. But it's too late. Dorothy and co. have exposed the Great, Powerful Wizard: He's nothing more than an elaborate carnival trick.

Windows 98 has a lot in common with the Great, Powerful Wizard. On the surface, it appears there's little more to the environment than Windows 98's friendly, emerald-colored Desktop, populated with colorful icons, buttons, windows, and menus. However, with just a few keystrokes and mouse clicks, you can part Windows 98's emerald curtain, and expose the unattractive machinery that makes its friendly facade tick.

■ **Explorer,** *the "guts" of Windows 98*

Look inside

Try this: Click Start | Programs | Windows Explorer. In a flash, the Windows Explorer opens, and presents you with what has to be one of the most imposing screens in all computing. There you see the nuts, bolts, wires, levers, bells, whistles, and wheels that make up the guts of Windows. Down the left panel is a list of every technical resource your computer offers. In the right panel is a list of folders and files and who knows what else. Across the top are 12 toolbar buttons, and no less than 7 commands on the menu bar. If you get the feeling that one misplaced keystroke can cause all manner of havoc, you're right. Explorer is one of the few tools in your PC that superbly empowers you to screw things up.

■ **Explorer reveals** *the nuts and bolts of Windows 98.*

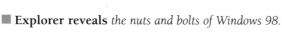

For instance, if you accidentally click the Delete button or the Delete key, you can send an important Windows component to never-never land. Then your PC might not be able to start up, or certain programs will crash and fail. It's also easy to unintentionally fall into Explorer. To wit: Close Windows Explorer by clicking its Close button. Note the Desktop icon labeled "My Computer." Right-click it, then click the Open or Explore commands. Bingo. You're back in Windows Explorer.

It looks somewhat different, because there's no right and left panel. But it's the same Explorer with a slightly altered, slightly friendlier face.

Don't let the friendlier face fool you. You're still one click away from screwing up your system.

Click the Close button to run away. Now try this: Click Start | Run, and type the word "Command" (without the quotes). Then click the OK button. A window labeled "MS-DOS Prompt" opens, and presents you with the lowly C> *prompt* of computing's past! Type the word DIR and press the Enter key. A jumbled list of computer commands appears. Type the wrong one, and you can blast your hard disk to smithereens.

> **DEFINITION**
>
> *Before there were menus, dialogs, and buttons, there were prompts. These terse, cryptic, sometimes incomprehensible teasers were the computer's way of asking users what to do next. Software engineers of the day believed prompts made computers friendlier. They didn't.*

Clearly Windows 98 is a deep and powerful operating system. There are low-level, powerful tools like Explorer and the C> prompt for advanced users. And there are high-level, friendly tools such as the Desktop, Start Menu, and Taskbar for folks like us.

My advice: If you wouldn't think of removing the case on your TV and poking around inside, avoid poking around the innards of Windows with Explorer at all costs. Stay away from the C> prompt, too.

Contrary to what some power users will tell you, you can tap all of Windows 98's muscle without first having to waste weeks learning to tiptoe around Explorer, or studying up on the obtuse intricacies of the legacy C> prompt. Earlier I stressed the importance of setting your own computing and organizational standards, instead of following some programmer or power user's idea of how things get done. Certain Windows 98 elements, including Windows Explorer, My Computer, and the MS-DOS Prompt, are clearly someone else's counter-intuitive notion of how best to navigate your computer's resources and manage your personal data. That's the bad news.

The good news: Windows 98 is an incredibly flexible environment. So much so that everyday users like us can easily adapt the system to deliver all its computing power without having to leave the safe confines of the Desktop, Taskbar, and Start Menu.

Windows as your personal secretary

YOU DON'T NEED A NEW PAIR *of glasses to see that it's easy to work harder, not smarter, with Windows 98. Allow the operating system, software vendors, and power users to lead you around by the nose, and you'll be doing things every way but the right way. The alternative is attractive: Dismiss the experts, and take charge of your Windows 98 computing environment. Make the computer handle all of the administrative and organizational tasks, so you don't have to. That's working smarter, not harder.*

■ **Don't let the** *operating system lead you by the nose.*

The first step in getting organized and leaving conventional computing "wisdom" behind is to adjust the Windows Desktop environment (including the Taskbar and the Start Menu) so that it works for you. To do this, you need to create a master personal folder, a central repository for everything you'll ever install, save, or retrieve. Your friends will be astonished when they see how easily you manage your PC with this powerful strategic computing concept.

■ **Too many folders** *within folders can get confusing.*

AVOID FOLDER HIERARCHIES

Most users fall into the trap of creating folder hierarchies; that is, folders within folders, scattered about their hard drive. When you think about it, that's nuts! Nobody uses a file cabinet that way. Most rational people simply organize files alphabetically, because that's the approach that makes the most sense. Similarly, I urge users not to fall into the trap of stuffing folders within folders here, there, and everywhere.

Creating your master personal folder

First, clear away any and all open windows by clicking their Close button, or hitting Alt+F4 repeatedly. When you're back at the Windows Desktop, right-click the Desktop, and select New. When the New menu glides out, click the Folder command. A new folder appears on your Windows Desktop. Click the folder's name box, and type in a short, memorable name, such as your initials. Press the Enter key to finish.

There's good reason for using a short name: You'll be referring to this folder often, usually by typing it's name.

Giving the folder a short and sweet name makes it easier to jump back to it when launching programs, or opening and saving files.

On my PC, my master folder is named "RBL." Compare how much time it takes to type that versus "Richard Bruce Levin," or "Rich's Folder," or even just plain old "Levin." Now expand that time savings over the course of a day, week, month, or year, and you'll see what I mean.

■ **Creating your** *personal folder.*

Some users actually name their master personal folder using just one letter, number, or character. In fact, I've seen entire families and businesses that organize their PCs with multiple master folders. A folder named "1" is for Dad, "2" is for Mom, "3" is for big sister, and "4" is for little brother. Everyone gets one-key access to their personal programs and data simply by typing their master folder number. That's as fast as it gets!

After you have named your master folder, you can click+drag it anywhere on your Desktop. Position it somewhere that's easy to get to, such as the upper right-hand corner of your screen. If it refuses to "stick" where you place it, right-click your Desktop, and select Arrange Icons. Then click the Auto Arrange command to uncheck arranging. Alternatively, if you want your Desktop icons to always be neat and tidy, turn Auto Arrange on.

Changing your master personal folder

Since this is your master personal folder, you want it to stand out from the other icons on your Desktop. Right-click your personal folder, and select Properties. Then click the Change Icon button. In the Change Icon dialog that appears, peruse the list of available icons by clicking on the left and right arrowheads. When you find an icon that strikes your fancy, double-click it to accept it. Click OK, and your master personal folder has a new look. (You can also change any icon the same way you changed your master personal folder.)

Now that you've created, named, and dressed up your master personal folder, let's put some stuff in it – starting with your programs. But before you can stock your master folder with programs, you have to open it.

Trivia...
Use the ` character as the first letter of a folder or filename, and the file or folder will always appear first in any on-screen listing. In the event you're viewing a listing that's not alphabetically sorted, pressing the ` key will jump to the first file that features the ` character. Pressing it again will jump to the next, and next, and so on. It's a great way to tag your most used or most important files and folders for faster access.

The many paths to your master personal folder

There are at least four ways to open your master personal folder. You can double-click it, or you can right-click it and select Open or Explore. (If you choose to right-click, Open is preferred. Explore drops you in Windows Explorer, which overcomplicates things.) You can also put a link to your personal folder on the Start Menu, and get to it by clicking the Start button.

Or you can create a hot-key that zooms your master folder to fill the screen, just by pressing a key on your keyboard.

ALL FOUR TECHNIQUES

Technique #1: the double-click. Point to your master personal folder, and double-click it. After it opens, close it by clicking the Close button. That's about as easy as it gets, and how most users open their master personal folder.

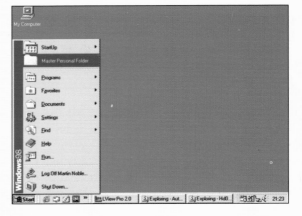

Technique #2: The right-click. Point to your master personal folder, right-click it, and select Open. Once again, close it by clicking the Close button.

■ **You can get** *a fancy icon for your master personal folder by clicking Display Properties | Effects | Change Icon.*

Technique #3: The Start Menu trick. Drag+drop your master folder directly atop the Start button. When done, click the Start button. There, at the top of the Start Menu, is an icon for your master folder! Click it, and your master folder opens. Close the folder by clicking Close.

And lastly, my personal favorite, technique #4: The hot key! To assign a hot key to the master personal folder, right-click it, and select Properties. Click once anywhere on the "Shortcut key" entry in the Properties dialog. Nearly any keyboard key or combination of keys can now be assigned as your hot key.

Most users assign the F12 key to their master personal folder, because other Windows 98 programs almost never use it.

To assign F12, just press the F12 key. The entry "F12" appears in the Shortcut key input box. Click the OK button, and the F12 key is now officially assigned to your master personal folder. If you want to assign a different key, by all means, feel free to do so. But be forewarned: You don't yet know which keys your programs need. It's safest to stick with F12 for now. You can change your hot key in the future, simply by repeating this procedure.

■ **Shortcut keys** *can be assigned to some folders.*

To test your new hot key, press it. Hit F12, and your master personal folder pops into view. Since you're using the keyboard to open it, hit Alt+F4 to close it. How's that for quick and easy? Most users find their hot key is the best way to call up their master personal folder.

No matter what you're working on, what programs are open, or where you're navigating within Windows 98, pressing your hot key will immediately open your master personal folder.

Second runner-up to the hot key in convenience is the master folder icon on the Start button (technique #3). The reason: the Start button is always in view. With double-clicking and right-clicking, you first have to return to the Desktop before you can open the folder. That means you have to close all open windows before you access the master personal folder – an inconvenient proposition. From here on, when I instruct you to open your master folder, I mean for you to bring it up by pressing F12, by clicking Start and then clicking on the folder's icon, or by double- or right-clicking the icon on the Desktop. It's your choice. (Me, I'll be hitting F12!)

To recap: Your master personal folder is set up, named, assigned a unique icon, positioned on your Desktop, installed on the Start Menu, and attached to a hot key. All that remains is to put it to good use.

■ **Once you can access** *your master personal folder with a hot key, you'll never want to do it any other way.*

Time for a dry run

WITH YOUR MASTER PERSONAL FOLDER at the ready, you're armed and dangerous. A quick flick of the wrist, and your personal folder pops up, reporting for active duty. Of course, there's not much you can do with it right now, as it pops up emptier than a football stadium in July. Let's populate it with some useful items. First up on the population agenda is to pour in some program icons. Doing so will give you instant access to your favorite applications, without requiring you to navigate the Taskbar and Start Menu, or having to close windows and head back to the Windows Desktop.

Filling up your master personal folder

■ **If you want** to copy, don't click Cut!

It's a snap to get going, and you can add more program icons at any time. Open your master personal folder using your preferred method (I press my hot-key, F12). With the folder open, click the Start button, then click Programs. Travel around the Start Menu's Program Menu until you come across a program you'll be using a lot. If you're not sure which program to pick, hold the mouse pointer over the Internet Explorer icon (that's what you'll be using to access the Internet), but don't click on it! Instead, right-click it, and select Copy.

Whatever you do, don't click Cut. Copy duplicates the item, whereas Cut erases it!

By clicking Copy, you've just put an invisible copy of the program's icon on an invisible Windows 98 tool called "the Clipboard." Every time you copy something, it goes on the Clipboard.

Whether it's letters, numbers, words, paragraphs, documents, spreadsheets, graphics, etc., if you copy it, it's clipped on the Clipboard. The Clipboard is always active, even though you can't see it.

Now call up your master personal folder by pressing its hot key (or however else you choose to bring it up). Right-click anywhere inside the blank area of the master folder, and select Paste. Poof! The program's icon appears. Whenever you want to run this program, all you have to do is call up your master folder, and double-click its icon. That's a maximum of two steps to get to any favorite program, and far superior to poking around the Start Menu.

Repeat this process for every one of the programs you know you'll be using a lot. Find them on the Start Menu, right-click and Copy them to the Clipboard, switch to your master folder, right-click and Paste away. If you don't know which programs you'll be using most, don't fret. You can Paste them into your master folder later, after you've discovered which programs you rely on most. To remove a program from your master folder, right-click it, and choose Delete.

Organizing your master personal folder

Keeping all of your programs in one place is only one function of the master personal folder. It's also the place where, ideally, you should store all of your personal data. From word processing documents to web site clippings to digital photographs and downloaded music, if it's computer data that you've captured or otherwise created, your master personal folder is the place to put it. It's sort of like a shoebox, where you can jam all your personal papers.

Unlike a shoebox, however, your master personal folder can automatically organize everything you put in it.

This powerful capability will become clearer to you further on, as you learn the ropes of web surfing, word processing, spreadsheets, and other productivity software. For the present, a brief demonstration is in order. Open up your master personal folder and maximize it to full screen. Next, right-click any blank area and select New. When the New menu slides out, click on Bitmap Image. This creates a new graphic file, just as if you created a chart or a drawing. Click again on any blank area, this time selecting New | Text Document. Repeat this twice more, right-clicking a blank spot, then creating a New | Wave Sound, and a New | WordPad Document.

By now you should have four new documents in your master folder: A bitmap image, a text document, a wave sound, and a WordPad document. That, plus however many program icons you added to the master folder. In a small way, this is how your master personal folder will evolve over time, as you add more programs and personal data to it. Take a gander at the toolbar on your master folder. Notice the View button. Click it.

■ **Your first** *files on the dektop.*

The display changes from large, colorful icons to small icons. Click the View button again, and the display switches to a top-down list. Click View once more, and the list adds technical details about each icon, such as the date and time it was created.

■ **The appearance** *of icons can be changed.*

Sorting items in your master personal folder

It's all well and good to view technical details, but that doesn't do much for your organizational abilities. Ah, but what the View button won't do, right-clicking will! Click View again to put the display back in large icon view. Then right-click any blank area, and select Arrange Icons. Look familiar? You've been here before. Once again, you're being presented with five options: Arrange by Name, Type, Size, Date, and Auto Arrange.

Clicking the "by Type" command sorts all of the icons according to their nature. Program icons are grouped together, text files are grouped together, graphics files are grouped together, and so on. This makes it incredibly easy to find what you're looking for. Of course, if you're an alphabetical kind of person (as I am), right-clicking any blank area and selecting Arrange | by Name will sort all the icons by their program, file, and folder names.

If you select the Arrange | Auto Arrange option, Windows 98 will remember your preference, and will automatically arrange items in your master folder accordingly.

Adding sub-folders to your master personal folder

Your master personal folder has one more trick up its sleeve: Sub-folders. Just as you can file multiple folders inside of a file cabinet, you can create multiple sub-folders inside of your master folder. Suppose you're working on year-end taxes, and you want to keep all tax files together. You could save them in your master personal folder, but that would co-mingle them with files unrelated to taxes.

The solution: Create a sub-folder dubbed "Taxes2000" (or something similar). Right-click any blank area in your master folder, and click New | Folder. In the folder name box, type Taxes2000, and press Enter. You'll learn later how to store files directly into your master personal folder or sub-folders. You can also drag+drop anything that appears in the master folder into a sub-folder. You can even create sub-folders inside other sub-folders! To step inside a sub-folder, double-click it, or right-click it and select Open. To leave a sub-folder, click the "Back" or "Up" buttons on the toolbar. You can also press the Backspace key on your keyboard, or press Alt+Left Arrow.

And if you want to move a sub-folder up a level, simply right-click on it, select Cut, then navigate to where you want to relocate it. Right-click, and select Paste. The organizational possibilities are endless.

With your Windows Desktop prepped and organized, your next logical move is to extend your reach into cyberspace, which is what we'll do in the next two chapters.

A simple summary

✓ There are two ways to organize your PC: your way, and everyone else's way. Instead of wasting your time adapting your work habits to every program's unique view of the world, set your own computing standards.

✓ Get organized now, and you'll reap the benefits later. Months from now, you'll still be enjoying the fruits borne of the organizational seeds planted today.

✓ The Windows Desktop, Taskbar, and Start Menu mask a deep, powerful, and complex computer operating system.

✓ Contrary to what rabid enthusiasts will tell you, you need never have to deal with Windows 98's technical innards. All of your computing goals can be realized through the friendly, safe confines of the Windows Desktop.

✓ The Windows Explorer, and programs like it, are easy to stumble into, and extremely risky for new users to be poking about. If you find yourself in a complicated system program, you can safely escape by clicking the Close button.

✓ Success with computing doesn't mean you know every acronym, buzzword, and propeller-headed program. Success with computing means you know how to use the computer to get your work done with an absolute minimum of fuss.

✓ Success with computing doesn't mean you know how computers work. Success with computing means you know how to work computers.

✓ Take control of Windows by creating your own master personal folder on the Windows Desktop. Think of your master personal folder as a digital shoebox. It's an easy to access, central location to tuck all of your favorite programs and data into.

Chapter 8

Destination: Internet

POP QUIZ: What's the #1 reason most people buy a PC today? Pop answer: Everyone wants to go online. Internet-mania is bigger than the Beatles, bigger than Pokémon, and bigger than the *Who Wants to Be a Millionaire* TV game show.

In this chapter...

✓ On becoming a cybernaut

✓ Hooking up to the Internet...

✓ Internet Connection Wizard

✓ Web browser basics

✓ Surfing the web

✓ Credit card safety on the web

THE INTERNET IS A WORLD WIDE WEB OF COMMUNICATION

On becoming a cybernaut

IN SOME WAYS, *life in the cyber-age parallels the Dark Ages. The Internet is a vast and uncharted new world, teeming with all manner of pitfalls and predators. No netizen is safe from the intrusive march of advertisers, vendors, SPAMmers, scam artists, and stalkers.*

Just as citizens in the Dark Ages had no ordinary rights, netizens surrender many of their supposedly inalienable rights the moment they connect online.

First to go: The right of free speech. When uttered online, unpopular, socially unacceptable, threatening, or "dirty" comments normally protected by the first amendment of the U.S. Constitution can result in the termination of your Internet access or land you in jail. Retailers must warn you when they're monitoring dressing rooms or showrooms with closed circuit TVs. Not so on the Net. Marketers can plant bugs in your PC that monitor your every move – and those of your kids, your husband or wife, or anyone else who happens to log in. Law enforcement authorities have to jump through legal hoops to wiretap your telephone line.

But all it takes is a phone call for your Internet provider to hand over a list of every site you've visited, and every message you've sent online. Most offensive, hiding in the Net's dark electronic alleys are countless thieves and thugs, poised to spring on every unsuspecting netizen who crosses their path. But every dark cloud has a silver lining, and the Internet is no exception. In the electronic world, it's actually easier to protect yourself from scum and vermin than it is in the real world. You won't have to pack heat, you won't need a bulletproof vest, and you won't need an alarm system. Rather, by taking full advantage of the privacy and security features built into Windows 98, and stirring in a dash of common sense, you'll be able to immerse yourself in the wonders of the Internet – without getting a virtual black eye.

Hooking up to the Internet...

BEFORE YOU CAN *buy that throw rug that glows in the dark with your state motto on it, you have to hop in the car and drive to the store. And before you can do anything online, you have to fire up your Internet connection and get online. Until recently, getting online was a royal pain for most users, requiring manual entry of a half-dozen arcane Internet settings.*

Luckily you started computing in the 21st century, because today, getting online is easier than nearly anything else you can do with your PC. Still, how you get online will vary depending upon who you selected as your Internet service provider.

. . . with AOL, CompuServe, MSN, or Prodigy

If you decided to use one of the major proprietary services, such as America Online, CompuServe, the Microsoft Network (MSN), or Prodigy, all you have to do is activate their software, and follow the easy on-screen instructions.

You'll find their software inside the Online Services folder on the Windows Desktop. Just double-click the folder, or right-click it and select Open. Then double-click the icon of the online service provider you want to use (or right-click it and select Open), and their sign-up process will begin.

Read and carefully follow the step-by-step instructions presented on the screen, and you'll be online in minutes. Skip to the next section when your sign-up process is complete.

. . . with AT&T WorldNet

If you want to use a "pure" Internet connection – that is, one that doesn't require you to use proprietary desktop PC software – and you haven't already decided on an internet service provider (ISP), go with AT&T WorldNet, featured in the Online Services folder. Double-click the AT&T WorldNet icon, and walk yourself through the easy sign-up process.

On the other hand, if you have decided on a dial-up ISP, now is the time to install its sign-up software. Put your ISP's setup disk in the appropriate disk drive. If it's a 3.5-inch floppy disk, slide it all the way in the floppy disk drive with the engraved arrow facing up and towards the PC. You'll know it's properly inserted when it snaps into the drive with a confident "click!" If it's a CD, press the eject button on the CD drive. When the tray slides out, drop the CD in, label-side up, and press the eject button again.

If the sign-up software doesn't load automatically, click Start | Settings | Control Panel, and double-click the Add/Remove Programs icon. Then click the Install button, and Windows 98 will automatically search for, find, and load the sign-up software. Follow the on-screen instructions to get wired with your new ISP.

When the ISP's setup process is complete, eject the floppy or CD by pressing the respective drive's eject button. Store the disk away in a safe, cool, dry place.

. . . via cable modem, DSL, satellite, MLPPP, ISDN, or other services

If your Internet connection uses a cable modem, DSL modem, satellite, or some connection other than a standard telephone line, your Internet service provider will most likely visit your location, and handle all the gory details of getting your PC wired up. The exception is MLPPP, which most users can set up on their own (although your ISP can also handle this for you).

Installation approaches differ with every hardware vendor and ISP. Regardless of which high-speed connection method you choose, carefully follow the instructions provided by your ISP and/or MLPPP router vendor to get the connection working with your system.

If the instructions are too complicated for you to follow, or require opening up the PC and messing around inside, it's worth paying your ISP or a local consultant to perform installation for you.

This will save you time and, quite possibly, a costly repair bill in the event you screw something up.

Internet Connection Wizard

IF YOU'RE ONE OF THE FEW USERS whose ISP doesn't provide a setup disk, but rather, gives you a list of strange Internet settings to enter into your computer, fret not. Microsoft planned ahead, and engineered Windows 98 to make manual Internet setup a piece of cake. Double-click the Internet Connection Wizard (ICW) icon that appears on your Windows Desktop. The ICW will give you a choice of (1) signing up for a new Internet account, (2) transferring an existing Internet account, or (3) setting up an account manually.

Note: If your modem has not yet been configured, Windows 98 will launch the Install New Modem wizard first. See the section entitled "Hooking up the modem," in Chapter 5, for instructions on how to manage the Install New Modem wizard.

■ **It's a piece of cake** to do a manual Internet setup in Windows 98.

■ The Internet
Connection Wizard
makes it easy to setup a
new Internet account.

Choosing the first option, "I want to sign up for a new Internet account," connects your PC to a Microsoft server somewhere in cyberspace, which transmits a list of Internet service providers hand-picked by Microsoft. If you want to keep things simple, choose this option, and sign up with any one of the major national ISPs featured. At the time this book went to press, these ISPs included the vendors introduced in the Windows Desktop's Online Services folder. Also included were Sprynet, Juno, Concentric Network, EarthLink, Netcom, Mindspring, and MCI WorldCom. All of these ISPs are roughly equivalent, and offer quality service. The second option, "I want to transfer an existing Internet account," doesn't apply to you, since this is a new PC, and you don't yet have an Internet account. Choose the third radio button, which reads, "I want to set up my Internet connection manually," and click Next. At this point, it's possible (though rare) that Windows 98 will issue a warning message about "file and printer sharing." Just ignore it, and click the OK button to get it out of the way.

DEFINITION

Connect two or more computers in your home or business, and you have a local area network, *or LAN. You can connect multiple PCs in multiple ways, using "network interface cards" (called NICs), or home networking systems that use your house's electrical wiring. After the computers are physically connected by hardware and wires, you can use Windows 98's built-in networking support to share disk drives, printers, and Internet connections among the connected PCs.*

Phone line or LAN

The ICW will then ask if you will connect to the Internet using a telephone line or a *local area network*. Choose the "I connect through a phone line and a modem" option (that's the first radio button), then click Next.

Specifying a phone number

Next up, the ICW will ask for the phone number of your ISP. This is the dial-in modem access number your ISP should have provided you. Click anywhere inside the "Area code" input box, and type in the area code of your ISP's dial-up access number. Follow by clicking anywhere inside the "Telephone number" input box, and type in the rest of your ISP's dial-up access number. Click on the "Country/region name and code" drop-down pick list, and make sure it's set to your corner of the globe.

If you want Windows 98 to use the area code and country code when dialing out (most people do), make sure the checkbox that reads "Dial using the area code and country code" is checked. If you want Windows 98 to dial only the number specified in the "telephone number" input box, uncheck the "Dial using the area code and country code" checkbox.

When you're done fiddling with these settings, click the Advanced button — don't click Next!

Advanced settings: PPP or SLIP

■ **If in doubt,** *leave the Connection Type set at PPP – 99 percent of ISPs use this.*

The Advanced Connection Properties dialog is now revealed. On the Connection tab, you can specify a "Connection type," either PPP or SLIP. If you don't know which connection type your ISP uses, leave it set at PPP. It's the one nearly all ISPs use.

Every computer connected directly to the Internet transmits information by slicing it into multiple TCP/IP "packets."

The packets are sent over a network connection, where they are reassembled and read by the receiving computer. Each packet contains the "IP address" of the sending (originating) computer, a slice of the actual raw data being shared, and some control codes that allows the receiving computer to confirm that the packet was transmitted without error and to reassemble the packets in the proper order. But your personal computer isn't really directly connected to the Internet. Rather, it's connected to an ISP's server that's directly connected to the Internet. Your PC needs a way to share information with the ISP's server, which then puts your data on the Internet, or retrieves the Internet data you're after, and sends it back to your PC. A circuitous route if ever there was one! That's where PPP comes in.

PPP

PPP stands for Point to Point Protocol. It defines how two computers – a client (you) and a server (your ISP) – connected over the Internet by way of a telephone line (your modem) should communicate. In a nutshell, PPP packages your computer's local *TCP/IP* packets, and forwards them to the server where they are put on the Internet. It also accepts TCP/IP packets back from your ISP's server, and unpacks them for use on your PC. Before PPP was introduced, there was SLIP: The Serial Line Internet Protocol. SLIP is similar to PPP, except that it can only communicate in one direction at a time (transmit or receive), and lacks error detection. PPP can transmit and receive packets simultaneously, and supports error correction. This

---

DEFINITION

The Internet works because every computer connected to it adheres to a standard set of communication protocols. A protocol is a documented, repeatable procedure that two or more computers understand. For example, protocol dictates that you shake someone's hand upon first meeting them. Similarly, computer protocols dictate how computers sync up their connections and share information. Regardless of whether the computer runs UNIX, Windows, the Mac OS, or whatever, they all "speak" the same language: TCP/IP, the principal Internet protocol. TCP/IP stands for "Transmission Control Protocol/Internet Protocol." This is sometimes referred to as "IP" for short.

DEFINITION

Programmers can create special documents that contain lists of computer commands. These command lists are called scripts, because they tell a computer what to do, just like a Broadway script tells an actor what to do.

Unlike a stage actor, computers aren't playacting. They'll perform the scripted commands precisely the same way every time. ISPs that have nonstandard log-on procedures will use scripts to automate the process, to save users the pain of manually entering multiple log-on commands.

makes PPP faster and more reliable than SLIP, and is why 99% of ISPs use it. You can also specify your "Logon procedure" here, as well. If you're not sure which type of log-on your ISP uses, leave this set at "None." It's rare for ISPs to require manual or *scripted* log-ons. Selecting None logs on automatically, the default for most ISPs.

Advanced settings

The Addresses tab of the Advanced Connection Properties dialog lets you specify your IP and DNS addresses.

Your IP address is a long code number that uniquely identifies your PC on the Internet. Most ISPs assign this automatically, and change it every time you log on, in part to protect your anonymity. Your DNS (Domain Name System) server address is similar to your IP address. Just as your PC is assigned an Internet address (a-k-a an IP address), your ISP's DNS servers need to be addressed as well. These DNS servers act as an invisible address book for computers. They contain the path to every known web site and e-mail system on the Net.

When you enter the address of a web site or a person, your ISP's DNS server "resolves," or translates, it from a "dot-COM" or dot-whatever name to a numeric IP address computers can understand.

■ **Like actors,** *computers can perform "scripts."*

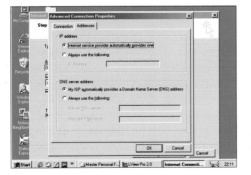

■ **You can specify** *your IP and DNS addresses in ICW's Advanced Addresses tab, though most ISPs assign them automatically.*

Naming domains

A unique number, known as an Internet Protocol (IP) address, identifies every computer connected to the Internet. Rather than force people to remember a zillion arcane IP addresses, the Internet's architects came up with the DNS, the Domain Name System. The DNS maps (translates) plain English names to IP addresses. When you type in Microsoft.com (or www.microsoft.com), the DNS invisibly translates (or "resolves") that to 207.46.130.150 – Microsoft's Internet server's IP address. It's certainly easier to remember Microsoft.com than 207.46.130.150! Domain names are further organized into multiple levels, to help users better understand the kind of site they're surfing. Whatever appears after the second dot in a web site address is said to be part of the Internet's "top-level domain," or TLD. For example, my web site at www.rblevin.net is part of the .NET top level domain. Microsoft.com belongs to the .COM top-level domain. The most common top-level domains are .COM for COMmercial ventures, .NET for NETwork services, .ORG for non-profit ORGanizations, .EDU for sites run by EDUcational institutions, .GOV for US GOVernment sites, and .MIL for sites run by the US MILitary. Many countries outside of the US have their own national TLDs. Sites in the United Kingdom end in .UK, sites in France use .FR, Israeli sites end with .IL, and so on.

The "RBLevin" or "Microsoft" portion of a domain name is referred to as the second-level domain name. Put the two levels together, and you have what is known as a "fully qualified" domain name.

Where then does the "www" come in? www stands for "World Wide Web," and by convention – but not necessity – has become a somewhat standard means of naming web sites. The address www.Microsoft.com tells your computer to connect to a server named "www" in the second level domain of "Microsoft," itself residing in the top-level .COM domain. Any name that appears before the second-level domain (such as www) is the name of a server within that second-level domain. That's why some Internet addresses start with something other than www; for example, shop.microsoft.com. The www is optional, although most web sites use it.

IP and DNS addresses

Practically all ISPs assign IP and DNS addresses dynamically (i.e. automatically), right after your computer connects to their service. In fact, even if your ISP provided you with specific IP and DNS addresses to enter (known as a "static" addresses), you could probably skip this step and still log on without error. To skip this step and use Windows 98's fully automatic log on and addressing features, click the Cancel button, then click the Next button. In the rare event your ISP requires you to use "static" IP and DNS addresses, enter them here. In the "IP address" frame, click the "Always use the following:" radio button to enable the input beside it. Then click inside the input box, and carefully type in the IP address your ISP assigned you. Similarly, in the "DNS address" frame, click the "Always use the following:" radio button to enable its input boxes. Then click inside the "Primary DNS server" input box, and carefully type in the primary and DNS addresses that your ISP uses. Follow that by clicking in the "Secondary DNS server" input box, and entering your ISP's secondary DNS addresses. When you're done, click the OK button, then click the Next button.

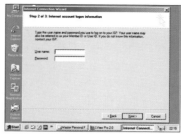

User name and password

Up comes the "Internet account logon information" dialog, otherwise known as your "User name" and "Password." Enter your user name and password exactly as provided by the ISP.

■ **Enter your** *user name and password exactly as provided by your ISP.*

Be certain to use the same upper- and lowercase letters, because some log-ons are case sensitive. If you enter your user name and password incorrectly, you won't be able to get online. Click the Next button when you're done.

Internet connection name

Finally, the ICW will ask you to give this Internet connection a name. Carefully type in the name of your ISP, then click Next. For example, my dial-up ISP's corporate name is "SNiP," so I entered "SNiP" in this dialog.

This completes your basic Internet connection setup. Make certain to note carefully your log-on name and password on a separate sheet of paper. Also note any extra settings the ISP instructed you to enter into your PC.

File the information in a safe place, and remember where you filed it! If your computer crashes and you don't have a backup, you'll need that info to get back online. You'll also need your log-on name and password if you want to sign on from someone else's PC.

E-mail setup

If you're using AOL, CompuServe, MSN, or Prodigy; if you installed your online connection using a disk provided by your Internet service provider; if you chose a national ISP using the ICW; or if your ISP handled your installation, your e-mail is already set up. Skip to the section titled web Browser Basics. If, on the other hand, you're using the Internet Connection Wizard to manually configure your Internet connection, the next screen to appear is the Set Up Your Internet Mail Account dialog. The "Yes" radio button tells the ICW that you want to set up an e-mail account. It's pre-selected, so just click Next. The ICW asks if you want to create a new Internet mail account, or use an existing account. Click the radio button beside "Create a new Internet mail account," then click Next.

E-mail display name and address

The ICW now gives you an opportunity to choose how your name will appear in e-mail messages. Click in the input box, and type in your preferred e-mail name. Enter your name, as you would like it to appear in e-mail messages. Note that this is not the same as your log-on name. For example, my Internet log-on name is RBLevin, but the name I display in e-mail messages is "RBL." You can enter virtually any name here, and can change it at any time in the future by rerunning the ICW. Click Next when you're done.

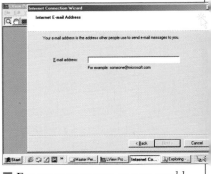

■ **Enter your name,** *as you would like it to appear in e-mail messages.*

■ **Now enter your** *log-on name, the "@" symbol, then the domain name of your ISP.*

Up comes the Internet E-Mail Address dialog. It is here that you enter your actual log-on name, followed by the domain name of your ISP. For example, if your log-on name is FUBAR, and your ISP is BARFU.com, your e-mail address would be Fubar@Barfu.com. Click in the "E-mail address" input box. Type your login name followed by the @ sign and your ISP's domain name. Then click Next.

E-mail servers

The E-Mail Server Names dialog appears. This is where you specify the names of your incoming and outgoing mail servers. Nearly all e-mail servers communicate using the default POP3 protocol standard. If your ISP uses POP3, leave the "My incoming mail server is a" drop-down pick list setting alone. If your ISP uses IMAP, click on the drop-down pick list and select IMAP as your incoming mail server type. No matter what type of server your ISP uses, you must fill out the "Incoming mail" and "Outgoing mail" server input boxes. Click on the "Incoming" input box, and enter the POP3 or IMAP server name exactly as your ISP provided it to you. Follow that by clicking on the "Outgoing" input box, and carefully typing in the name of your ISP's SMTP server. When you're done, click the Next button.

There are two kinds of mail servers for receiving mail, but only one kind of mail server for sending mail. All mail sent on the Internet is dispatched by an ISP's Simple Mail Transport Protocol (SMTP) server. Your e-mail software needs to know the name of your ISP's SMTP server, so it can connect and transfer your outgoing mail. After your outgoing mail is uploaded, the SMTP server scoots it out to one of two kinds of recipients: An ISP's POP3 or IMAP servers.

POP3 servers use the Post Office Protocol version 3 (hence the name POP3) to receive and store your mail, until you connect to pick it up. The dominant mail servers on the Internet, POP3 servers are very simple devices: They accept incoming mail from SMTP servers, and dole it out to users when they connect. Users have only two options for managing their mail on a POP3 server: Download it and delete it from the server, or download it and keep it on the server.

The latter is useful for users who are on the road, and want to keep a copy of their mail on the POP3 server for later retrieval.

Internet Mail Access Protocol (IMAP) servers are more flexible, but less common. With IMAP, you can fully manage your mail on the server, just as you can on your desktop PC. You can download some or all messages, delete some or all, move them into various folders, etc. – all on the remote server. IMAP is technically superior to POP3, but has yet to catch on in a big way. The reason: Most users are interested only in downloading their mail, and couldn't care less about IMAP's server-centric power features.

Internet Mail Log-on

Up next is the Internet Mail Log-on dialog. Click in the "Account name" input box, and enter your Internet mail log-on name. This is usually exactly the same as your primary Internet log-on name. For example, if your log-on name is FUBAR, your e-mail account name is also FUBAR. Next, click in the "Password" input box, and enter your e-mail password. This is often exactly the same as your Internet log-on password.

Note, however, that some ISPs (such as AT&T WorldNet) use separate Internet log-on and e-mail log-on passwords. Make sure you're entering the correct password here, or you will not be able to send and receive e-mail.

If your ISP requires you to use something called "Secure Password Authentication," check off the "Log on using Secure Password Authentication" checkbox by clicking on it. Note that most ISPs don't use Secure Password Authentication. Click the Next button after you complete entry of your e-mail log-on name and password.

Finishing the Internet Connection Wizard

The Internet Connection Wizard's work is now done. The ICW will display a final screen, asking if you'd like to connect to the Internet immediately.

The answer is "no," so uncheck the checkbox that reads, "To connect to the Internet immediately" by clicking on it.

Wrap things up by clicking the Finish button. And give yourself a round of applause. You just set up and configured a complex Internet connection completely on your own!

Web browser basics

BETA OR VHS? CASSETTES OR 8-TRACKS? *Macs or PCs? In every walk of life, it seems things ultimately boil down to a painful either/or decision. Browsing the World Wide Web is no different. Before you can "surf the web," you'll have to decide between two popular* web browsers: *Microsoft's Internet Explorer 5 or America Online's Netscape Navigator 4.*

Microsoft's Internet Explorer 5 is built into Windows 98. Depending upon your computer make and model, it's possible AOL's Netscape Navigator is also pre-installed on your Windows Desktop. In some ways, however, it doesn't matter which brand of browser you choose. Surfing the web works the same with virtually all web browsers, including "alternative" browsers offered by small companies and independent midnight programmers.

I'll get to the "how to" portion of web surfing in a moment. But first, some guidance to help you choose which web browser to call your own. The judgment is not as difficult as some industry enthusiasts make it seem.

Of the two major browsers, Microsoft's Internet Explorer is clearly the superior offering. Without exception, Internet Explorer 5 is faster, more reliable, and more configurable than AOL/Netscape's current release, now at version 4.

DEFINITION

A web browser *is to web surfing what a word processor is to word processing. Just as you need a word processor to create and edit documents, you need a web browser to navigate and interact with the World Wide Web. Incidentally, in cyberspeak, the terms browsing, surfing, hyperlinking, and hyper-jumping all mean the same thing: jumping around the web.*

Internet Explorer 5 is also flat-out easier to use, with a snappier user interface and tons more useful features than AOL's Netscape 4. Most important, Microsoft continues to issue regular upgrades of its IE product. Meanwhile, the next-generation of Netscape is more than a year overdue. In essence, AOL has allowed its Navigator browser to get long in the tooth, while Microsoft has continually evolved its browser's internal engine and external feature set. The result is a state-of-the-art web browsing machine.

This balance of power could change, if AOL ever delivers its promised major overhaul that Netscape's begging for, or if some other company dreams up a better browser and leapfrogs Microsoft. Until then, it makes sense to focus on Microsoft's leading browser technology. It's pre-installed on your Windows 98 PC, close to 70 percent of netizens now use it (according to most major studies), and virtually 100 percent of Internet service providers and web sites support it.

VIP

And here's the real kicker: The web is built on internationally accepted standards that dictate how computers communicate over the Internet. While features vary from vendor to vendor, all web and Internet programs must adhere to the same minimum set of standards.

That's why Macintosh users can surf the same web sites as Windows users, and Windows users can surf the same web sites as UNIX users, and so on. All web browsers must adhere to these international standards, or they simply won't work on the web. What's that mean to you? It means the IE5 skills you learn now are easily transferable to literally any other web browser. For now, though, IE5 is the way to go.

Setting up Internet auto-dial

But before you can go with IE5, or any other web browser, you first have to connect your PC to the Internet. If you're using a cable modem or DSL connection, you're already connected. Cable and DSL modems are "always on" the Internet. If you're using satellite or plain old dial-up, you first have to instruct your PC to call your Internet service provider, and activate your Internet session. Just as there are eight different ways to close a window, there are multiple ways to activate a Net connection.

INTERNET

www.W3.org
www.IETF.org
www.IAB.org
www.IANA.org
www.ICANN.org

The international bodies that develop and manage the Internet's global standards are located at these sites. The World Wide Web Consortium also offers a free web browser, called Amaya.

The easiest way is to set your computer to automatically dial your ISP whenever the PC is up and running. Here's how to do it: Click Start | Settings, and head into the Control Panel. Double-click the Internet Options icon to open the Internet Properties dialog. Click on the Connections tab, then click once on your ISP's name, which should be displayed as the "(Default)" in the "Dial-up settings" list box. If your ISP isn't flagged as the default, make it so by clicking the Set Default button. Next, select the radio button that reads, "Always dial my default connection" then click the Settings button. That puts you inside your ISP's dial-up Settings, where you can confirm that your modem's speaker and speed are cranked up. Click the Properties button, then click the Configure button. Drag the "Speaker volume" slider at least one tick-mark to the right of "Off" – and preferably all the way over to "High." This assures that you'll hear the modem working when it dials the phone.

■ **The World Wide Web**
Consortium offers its own free browser – Amaya.

Next, click the "Maximum speed" drop-down pick list, and select the highest setting, 115200 bps (that's 115kbps [kilobits per second] in a nutshell).

Technically, your Internet connection is limited by your modem at 56k, but pushing this setting to 115k will result in a slightly faster connection between your PC and the modem.

Leave the "Only connect at this speed" checkbox alone; the default is unchecked and it should stay that way. Click the OK button to accept the Modem Properties, then click OK again to accept your ISP's dial-up networking properties. Click OK once more to close your ISP's Settings dialog, and OK again to close and accept your Internet Properties. Finally, close the Control Panel window by clicking its Close button. Your PC is now properly configured to dial the Internet automatically whenever you need to get online.

Logging on to the Internet

Getting online is now a simple matter of launching your web browser. If you haven't done so already, put a copy of the Internet Explorer icon in your master personal folder. Do this by clicking Start | Programs.

Note: If you're not using the latest and greatest version of Windows 98, it's possible you'll find Internet Explorer located at Start | Programs | Internet Explorer.

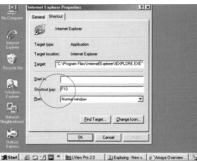

■ **Type the keystrokes** *that you want to use as your hot-key in the Shortcut key box.*

Right-click the Internet Explorer icon, and select Copy. Now open your master personal folder by double-clicking its Desktop icon, or hitting it's hot-key. With your master personal folder now open, right-click any blank area, and select Paste. The IE icon appears. If you want to assign a shortcut key to the IE icon, now's the time to do it. Right-click the IE icon, select Properties, enter the keystroke you want to use in the "Shortcut key" input box, and click OK. (I use Ctrl+Alt+F8 on my computer.)

Anytime you need to get on the Net, just open your master personal folder, and double-click the IE icon you just created – or hit its hot key combination. Go ahead and double-click it now, or hit its hot key, and prepare to enter the World Wide Web for the first time!

On some computers, Windows 98 will first ask if you want to make Internet Explorer your default web browser. Of course, the answer is yes, so click the "Yes" button.

After a moment, the Dial-Up Connection dialog will appear. If all of the options are *grayed out*, and you hear your modem dialing the phone, that means Windows 98 is automatically dialing your ISP, and logging onto the Internet.

If the Dial-Up Connection dialog isn't grayed out, check to see that your user name and password show up on the screen (if you've done everything right to this point, they should be visible). Also make certain the "Save password" and "Connect automatically" buttons are

■ **When Windows 98** *begins dialing your phone, it "grays out" dial-up options.*

checked. This tells Windows 98 to remember your password between Internet sessions, so you don't have to type it in every time. It also instructs the computer to bypass the Dial-Up Connection dialog in the future, and start dialing immediately whenever you launch IE. If the "Save password" prompt ever disappears or becomes grayed out, it means you didn't enter your Windows log-on password when you first powered-up the PC. Click Start | Shut Down | Restart | OK to reboot your computer, and make sure you enter your user name and password when Windows restarts.)

Next, click the Connect button to start the dialing process. You'll hear the modem dialing the phone, and negotiating a connection with the ISP's modem. When the connection is established, the modem will go silent. That means you're online!

> **DEFINITION**
>
> *We say that a menu item or command is grayed out when it's visible on the screen, but clicking it doesn't do anything. That's because it's temporarily not available, and Windows 98 has changed its color from normal black type to gray, to indicate the command or feature is temporarily not accessible. For example, before Windows 98 starts dialing your phone, dial-out options are available. When Windows 98 begins dialing, it disables dial-out options, and changes their color from black to gray.*

Note: The procedure for logging on to a proprietary ISP, such as America Online, CompuServe, the Microsoft network, or Prodigy is somewhat different.

There's a good chance you won't ever see the Dial-Up Connection dialog. Rather, you'll be presented with whatever proprietary log-on screen the service uses. Just look for a "Dial," "Connect," "Logon," or similar command button to initiate the connection process – and click it.

Security settings for safe surfing

Welcome to the World Wide Web! In a few moments, Internet Explorer will bring up your PC's "Home page." This is the first (or main) page that your computer displays whenever you log on to the Internet. You can change your home page at any time, as you will soon see. But first, it's important to padlock your PC to protect you from the various threats and thugs that populate the web.

Gaze closely at your Internet Explorer menu bar. One of the commands is Tools. Click it, and then click the Internet Options command. Look familiar? It's the same Internet Options dialog you can get to through Start | Settings | Control Panel. Click on the Security tab. There are four security settings available to you, through a slider control: High, Medium, Medium-Low, and Low. There are also Custom and Default buttons.

For the utmost in security – and my recommended setting – drag the slider control up until the security setting reads "High."

If you're not running the latest and greatest rev of Windows 98, the Security tab on your PC might display four radio buttons, and not a slider control. Click the radio button beside the "High" option.

While no Internet-connected computer can be said to be 100 percent secure, Internet Explorer's High security setting is as close as it gets. In fact, there's never been a report of a PC being breached while protected by IE's High Security option. That's the upside. The downside: Some web sites won't work properly when the High security option is selected. That's because they use certain technologies that are nearly always safe, but could theoretically be abused to breach your privacy or security. IE's High security setting filters out these technologies, preventing those rare web sites from operating properly with your PC.

If you'd like to decide for yourself what to run and what to avoid, choose the Medium setting. This causes IE to ask before enabling any risky technologies. If you're surfing a site you know you can trust, such as Microsoft's, your bank's, your broker's, or your best friend's, Medium lets you give IE permission to use risky technologies on a case-by-case basis. If you're surfing a web site you've never visited before, and you have no idea who is behind it – even if the site looks legit – the Medium setting lets you instruct IE on demand to disable any risky technologies and still explore the site safely.

Also available are the Medium-Low, Low, and Custom settings, all of which are not advisable for new users. Doing so exposes your PC to web-borne computer viruses, cyber-probes, security leaks, identity attacks, and other dangers. As you would expect, the Default button returns IE's security to its factory settings, which happens to be the Medium option.

Specifying your Home page

After you select your security setting, click the General tab on the Internet Options dialog. Take note of the "Home page" frame. There you'll see the address of the web site that's specified as your Home page. This is the cover page (the main page) of the web site that comes up when you first launch your browser. It also appears whenever you click the "Home" icon on your web browser's toolbar. Usually this is Microsoft's MSN site, or the main page of your ISP, such as America Online, CompuServe, or whoever.

As you wind your way around the web, you'll probably discover a site that you'd like to make your Home page. Perhaps you're an investor, and you'd prefer your broker's main page to serve as your Home page, or CBS's popular MarketWatch site. Or maybe you're a newshound, and you'd like MSNBC as your Home page. Just remember this: When you land on a site you'd like to establish as your Home page, click Tools | Internet Options on the browser's toolbar.

Then click the Use Current button on the General tab in the Internet Options dialog, and click OK. In a snap, the current web site is locked in as your Home page.

Surfing the web

THE HARD STUFF IS BEHIND YOU. *Now it's time to have some fun, and engage in your first online practice session. You're already logged on, with your Home page on the screen. All you need to know now is how to surf the web.*

Before you can learn to surf, you need to know what to surf. Look closely at the web page in your browser. You might think you're looking at words and art and graphics, but you're really only seeing two things: information that's hyperlinked, and information that's not *hyperlinked*.

Few things in life are easier than web surfing. If you think of your mouse as a TV remote control, you'll quickly see why the World Wide Web is a couch potato's dream – and why clicking on hyperlinks has come to be dubbed "surfing." From the moment you log on, simply click on anything that interests you.

If your selection is a live hyperlink, you'll be transported to a new location. If it's not a live hyperlink, nothing will happen.

To make it easier to discern hyperlinks on the screen, most browsers are preconfigured to underline them. Internet Explorer also changes the color of a hyperlinked item when the mouse pointer passes (hovers) over it.

> **DEFINITION**
>
> *A* hyperlink *is anything on the screen that "links" to something else on the web. Click on a hyperlink, and it takes you somewhere else. That page will have more hyperlinks, which in turn link to other pages with more hyperlinks. In fact, that's how the World Wide Web got its name: It's an unending web of intertwined hyperlinks that permeate the global Internet. You can jump from hyperlink to hyperlink for days on end and never run out of new links to explore.*

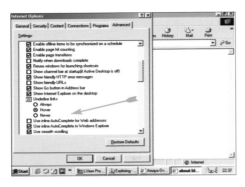

■ **After setting the** *Underline links to Hover, IE will show all links in red when your mouse pointer hovers over them.*

If you find the underlining of hyperlinks distracting (as I do), you can turn it off and still be able to see what's linked, and what's not. With Internet Explorer on the screen, click Tools | Internet Options, and hit the Advanced tab. Scroll down the list box until you see the "Underline links" option. Click the Hover radio button, and then click OK.

Internet Explorer will show unvisited links in blue, visited links in purple, and all links in red when your mouse pointer hovers over them — but they won't be underlined, which makes reading web pages easier on the eyes.

Jumping directly to a web address

Due to the large number of Home pages that new PCs are preconfigured to use, it's best to land on a specific web page to complete your basic browser training. Doing so requires that you manually enter the web address. As with everything else in Windows 98, there are a number of ways to enter a web address. You can enter it in the toolbar's "Address" box, use the File | Open menu, strike the "Open" command key combo, use the Win+Run command, and more.

DEFINITION

A web site or document's address is also called an URL (alternatively pronounced "earl," or sounded out as U-R-L), for Uniform Resource Locator — a term only techies could love. Most people just say "web address" or "document address."

The easiest way: Use the Address box on the browser's toolbar. It's that long input box that runs completely across the screen, just below the toolbar. Click once inside the Address box, and enter the name of the web site. For example, to get to my web site, enter "www.rbLevin.net" (without the quotes, of course).

Using the Address box is the easiest way to enter a web site address, but it's not the fastest. That honor goes to the "Open" command key combo, Ctrl+O. Press the Ctrl and letter O keys together to get the Open dialog, and then start typing the web address. Press Enter when done. When you use Ctrl+O, you don't even have to touch the mouse. You can also use the Windows logo key and the letter R (known as Win+R) to open the Run dialog. Once again, just type the web address into the input box, and press Enter when done; no mouse required.

You can use Win+R even if you haven't loaded Internet Explorer, which makes it the most convenient method of entering a web address.

162

After you have entered my web site, click the "Go" button, or press the Enter key on your keyboard. The little earthly globe on Internet Explorer's toolbar will spin. That means the browser is looking for or talking to another computer on the Internet.

Scrolling through web pages

In a moment, the web page will start to be drawn in your browser. As the page loads, you'll notice it's populated with text, boxes, pictures, and other stuff. You can scroll down the page by clicking the up and down arrowheads on the browser's scroll bar. You can also scroll by hitting the PageUp and PageDown keys on your keyboard, or by pressing the up and down arrow keys. If your computer's mouse features a little wheel in between the two mouse buttons, you can roll the wheel to scroll the page.

Scroll up to the very top of my web site's main page. The first line of text, which reads "[Home] [Table of Contents] [Welcome] [Software] [Search] " is actually five hyperlinks. Click on the words "Table of Contents." You're instantly transported to the web site's Table of Contents. Now click the "Welcome" link at the top of the page, and you're taken to the site's Welcome page. Click the "Software" link at the top of the page, and you're dispatched to the Software page. Each time you click a link, you're taken to the page that's described by that link.

> **Trivia...**
>
> *You'll often see web addresses preceded by the letters HTTP, a colon, and two slashes (verbalized as H-T-T-P-colon-slash-slash). Most web browsers no longer require users to enter web addresses prefixed by HTTP://. In other words, both http://www.microsoft.com and www.microsoft.com are valid web addresses. In fact, you can usually save a few extra keystrokes and drop the "www" as well. Many web sites work fine without the "http://" or "www."*

While your Windows 98 Desktop responds differently to clicks and double-clicks, the web uses only a single click. Try to get into the habit of using one click, not two, when clicking around the web.

■ **By typing** *"www.rblevin.net" in your web browser's address box, you will be sent to the author's web site.*

In fact, a double-click on the web can actually get you into trouble. For instance, if you double-click a "BUY NOW" or "SIGN UP" icon, you can end up ordering or signing up for something twice.

Conducting a web search

Give yourself a high five. You've just surfed your first web site. Now let's jump off my site, and onto another that has nothing to do with me. Click the "Table of Contents" link to arrive back at my site's Table of Contents. Look for the section titled "SEARCH ENGINES." Click the Yahoo! link. In a flash, you're transported out of my site and onto Yahoo!, one of the web's most popular search engines.

Search engines are the best way to find what you're after when surfing the web.

Click once in the Search input box, and type in anything you heart desires. Like to cook? Type in the word "cooking." Want to travel to India? Type in the word "India." Interested in Beatles memorabilia? Type in the words "Beatles memorabilia."

Whatever is on your mind, it's likely you can find it on the web using one of the popular search engines.

After you type in your search topic, click the "Search" button. Yahoo! (and all search engines) will generate a list of web pages that relate to your search request. Scroll down the page and you'll see the search engine has from one to tens of thousands of related pages. Click on one of the pages listed, and you're whisked off to that site. But what if the site isn't exactly what you were after?

■ **Just type** *"Beatles memorabilia"* in Yahoo's search input box to view a list of relevant web pages.

THE TOP TEN

www.infoseek.com	The best search engine on the web
(www.rblevin.net/infoseek.htm	My cleaner "front-end" to Infoseek)
www.excite.com	If infoseek can't find it, Excite might
(www.rblevin.net/excite.htm	My cleaner "front-end" to Excite)
www.bartleby.com	Search for famous quotes
www.dejanews.com	Search Internet newsgroups
www.go.com/white_pages	Search for people
www.link.cs.cmu.edu/dougb/ rhyme-doc.html	Rhyming dictionary
www.mapquest.com	Search for directions
www.m-w.com	Merriam-Webster's online dictionary
www.m-w.com	Merriam-Webster's online thesaurus
www.zip2.com	If MapQuest can't find it, Zip2 might

THE RUNNERS-UP

google.com	You haven't searched 'til you've Google'd
translator.go.com	Translate web sites into other languages
www.altavista.com	Alta Vista search
www.askjeeves.com	Ask Jeeves anything
www.bigyellow.com	A Yellow Pages on the web
www.citysearch.com	What to do when you go anywhere
www.dictionary.com	Great online dictionary
www.ebig.com	Encyclopedia Britannica online
www.hoovers.com	Search for information on businesses
www.house.gov/writerep	Find your US representative
www.metacrawler.com	Run multiple search engines at once
www.microsoft.com/search	Find everything about anything Microsoft
www.nandosearch.com	Search the AP and Reuters news wires
www.newsindex.com	Another news-only search engine
www.people.yahoo.com	Yahoo's White Pages search
www.randmcnally.com	Search for directions anywhere on Earth
www.restaurantrow.com	Billed as the world's largest dining guide
www.superpages.gte.net	Another online Yellow Pages
www.thesaurus.com	Great online thesaurus
www.whatis.com	Central repository of all technical definitions
www.yahoo.com	The search engine that started it all
www.yellowpages.com	Yet another online Yellow Pages
www.zagat.com	The Zagat survey online

The most up-to-date listing of my favorite search engines is always located at www.rblevin.net/toc.htm.

■ **"You haven't** *searched 'til you've Google'd."*

Retracing your steps with back and forth buttons

The nature of web surfing is such that users click here, go there, click there, and go here. After a few dozen clicks, you might find yourself dozens of web sites away from where you started. Hansel and Gretel found their way out of the forest by following a trail of crumbs. Fortunately, you won't need a bag of breadcrumbs. You have IE, which tracks your web travels automatically for you.

To retrace your steps, click the "Back" button on the IE toolbar. To move forward, click the toolbar's "Forward" button.

Try that now. Click the Back button, and the web browser will display the last page you visited. Click the Forward button, and you're returned on the most recent page you viewed. You can also hit the backspace key to go back. Each time you hit Backspace, Internet Explorer will go back one page. To move back and forth using the keyboard, hold the Alt key down, and press the left and right arrow keys. Internet Explorer's Back and Forward button are handy, indeed, but they can only remember so many web sites. After a while, the oldest sites are purged, and the browser's memory of them is gone forever. How, then, do you return to a site you've visited? The answer: your Internet Favorites.

Bookmarking your favorite sites

Whenever you come across a site you want to remember, you don't have to write it down, say it ten times aloud, or record its address into a tape recorder. Simply use the browser's Favorites feature to automatically bookmark the site's address.

To remember a site, click the "Favorites" button on the browser's menu bar. When the Favorites panel appears, click the "Add" button, and then click OK. The web site is automatically added to the Favorites panel.

When the time comes that you want to return to that site, click the Favorites button on the toolbar to reopen the Favorites panel, and scroll down the list using the up and down arrowheads, until you find the web site you're after. Then click the site, and Internet Explorer will take you there. To close the Favorites panel, click the Favorites button on the toolbar again.

You can also add and access your favorites by clicking the Favorites command on the menu bar. Or you can use the keyboard to

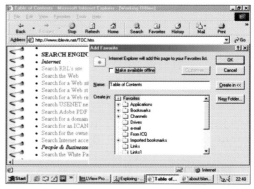

■ **Click on the** *Add button in Favorites to instantly bookmark a web page.*

bookmark sites. Press Ctrl+D to automatically add a site to your Favorites list (it will show up when you next open the Favorites panel). When you have too many Favorites to fit on the screen, you can press Ctrl+B to call up the Organize Favorites tool, which makes it easy to categorize your Favorites bookmarks by tucking them into folders you can name. (You can also get to the Organize Favorites tool by clicking Favorites | Organize Favorites on the menu bar.)

■ **All you need** *to navigate the web are the buttons on the Toolbar*

Browser buttons in a nutshell

Now that you're a wild and crazy web surfer, you'll want to know what the rest of those buttons on the Internet Explorer toolbar do.

The "Stop" button: Stops loading a page. This is useful if a page is taking too long to load, and what you want to read is already on the screen. The "Refresh" button: Reloads a web page. Use this if a web page stops loading or stops working.

The "Search" button: Brings up Internet Explorer's built-in search engine. You can use this search engine, or you can use any other. It's best to try them all, and see which one returns the most accurate results for your types of questions.

The "Full Screen" button: Makes the web browser view port as large as can be, larger, even, than clicking its Maximize button.

To really maximize your viewing area, right-click the toolbar, and select the Auto-Hide feature. This makes the toolbar slip out of the way when you're surfing the web.

To get the toolbar back, move the mouse pointer to the top of the screen. The toolbar will slide back into view. To disable Auto-Hide, right-click the toolbar again, and deselect the feature.

The "Size" button: Makes the on-screen text larger or smaller. This is a useful tool for people with crummy vision (like me). The "Print" button: Does what you'd expect; it prints the current page. The "Related" button: Supposed to bring up a list of like-minded web sites. It rarely works as expected.

■ **Web sites can** *be related, just like people.*

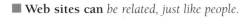

Credit card safety on the web

ONE FINAL THOUGHT ON THE TOPIC *of security: When you're surfing the web, the world is your e-oyster. You'll find many tempting offers served up by well-known and not-so-known retailers in cyberspace. For the most part, using your credit card when shopping at any e-tailers is as safe as, or safer than, using your credit card over the phone, in a store, or in a restaurant. But given the fact that, for cybercrooks, it's easier to break into PCs than it is to break open a cash register, caution is warranted.*

When shopping online, the best protection is to use one and only one credit card. Consider this credit card your "e-card." In the rare event your e-card's number is stolen online, your liability will not exceed $50 — the maximum exposure for most bank cards.

If you use multiple credit cards online, your exposure is $50 per credit card – a scenario that can quickly add up. So protect yourself and your bank account by using only one credit card for all of your online transactions.

■ **Stick to one** *credit card when shopping online.*

Prior to charging forth into the next section, it's imperative that you spend some quality time with your web browser. This falls into the "first things first" category, and is essential to achieving success with Windows 98.

Indeed, the only surefire way to guarantee computing success is to focus on one goal at a time – in this case, web browsing – and master it.

Surf to and fro on the World Wide Web, with no particular purpose in mind, other than spreading your web wings.

Ideally, you should concentrate on powering up, logging on, surfing, and searching for the next few days, before venturing into e-mail, or any other computing pursuit. When you can zip through these tasks with confidence, then and only then is it time to tackle your next computing goal.

■ **Don't perch** *on the edge of your seat, take flight on the web.*

A simple summary

✓ It's easier to protect yourself from crime online than in the real world.

✓ Most Internet service providers issue "setup" software that fully automate the process of configuring your PC for Internet access.

✓ You can use one of the ISPs featured in the Online Services folder on your Windows Desktop, or you can use the Internet Connection Wizard to choose an ISP, or set up an Internet connection.

✓ You can rerun the Internet Connection Wizard at any time.

✓ TCP/IP is the lingua franca of the Internet. All information shared between PCs is sent and received using TCP/IP.

✓ PPP and SLIP enable your PC to speak to your ISP's servers.

✓ Your IP number is your virtual address on the Internet.

✓ Your ISP's DNS servers contain the address of every known web site and e-mail system.

✓ Your ISP's POP3 or IMAP servers are where your incoming Internet e-mail is stored.

✓ Internet Autodial is your easiest connection to the Net.

✓ Crank up your Internet Explorer security settings for maximum protection.

✓ Your Home page is the first page that appears when you start your browser. You can reset your Home page at any time by going into your IE Options.

✓ To add a web site to your list of favorites, click the Favorites button on IE's toolbar, then click Add.

✓ To maximize your financial security, only use one credit card when shopping online.

✓ Focus on mastering web browsing before moving on to e-mail.

Chapter 9

All About E-mail

SINCE THE BEGINNING of computing, the success of every computing platform has been fueled by what has come to be known as "the killer app." It's the breakthrough task, or "application," that legitimizes the system, and makes it indispensable. Today, as we kick off the 21st century, the World Wide Web garners the glamour, but the Internet's real killer app is e-mail. In this chapter, you'll learn what e-mail is, how it works, the many ways you can use it, and how some people abuse it. You'll also learn how to protect yourself from e-mail abuse and how to use tricks to manage your daily e-mail more efficiently.

In this chapter...

✓ E-mail basics

✓ Using the Address Book

✓ Using e-mail folders

✓ More on SPAM

✓ E-mail attachments

✓ Creating an attachment

THINK OF THE TREES YOU'LL SAVE WITH E-MAIL

E-mail basics

THERE'S GOOD REASON *for Internet e-mail's overwhelming popularity. It's a fast, inexpensive, easy-to-use means to communicate and share information with anyone anywhere on Earth. Instead of making costly long-distance phone calls, sending expensive faxes or overnight packages, or relying on* snail mail, *people can type a message, attach any forms, contracts, pictures, or other documentation, and simply click Send.*

Moments later, the message arrives at its destination. In theory. In practice, sometimes you'll to feel as if every one of the Internet's 10 billion daily messages has ended up in your e-mail box.

Although marketed as a productivity booster, e-mail can become a bottomless time pit, if it not managed properly.

■ **According to** *eMarketer.com, Americans send over 10 billion e-mails a day.*

Within days of your signing on the Net, mountains of junk mail from direct marketers, scammers, and SPAMmers will start clogging your inbox. Add to that mindless chatter from electronic friends, endlessly circulating dumb jokes and chain letters, and utterly worthless newsletters, and it can quickly become difficult to separate the wheat from the chaff. It can, but it won't, provided you bolster your e-mail skills beyond raw composing, sending, and receiving messages, which is precisely what you're going to do, starting now. Unlike the market for web browsers, there are dozens of excellent free and for-pay e-mail clients on the market. One of the best is pre-installed on your Windows 98 PC: Outlook Express.

Any PC software that works over the Internet is referred to as a "client." Any Internet site or service is referred to as a "server." That's why you'll hear the architecture of Internet applications

DEFINITION

You can thank the immediacy of Internet mail for encouraging someone to coin the phrase "snail mail" to describe the U.S. Postal Service. In fairness, not even overnight delivery services such as UPS and FedEx can compete with e-mail's instant delivery. Thankfully for postal and parcel workers, you can't send packages through the computer – at least, not yet.

referred to as "client/server." In truth, Internet systems can be comprised of multiple servers. These are "distributed" client/server systems, because the overall software is partitioned across multiple computing "tiers." Instead of all the software residing in one big program, it's sliced up so that some runs on your PC and some on Internet servers. Your PC client becomes the "presentation" tier, while the web site or service is home to the database, business logic, and other tiers. Third-party companies might also be linking into the servers, providing "web services" such as credit card authorizations or search functions on still other tiers. All this complex inter-tier communication happens securely over the Internet and appears to you as a single cohesive program running in your web browser.

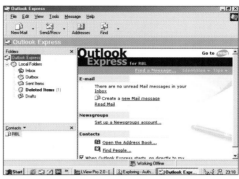

■ **Outlook Express** *is your e-mail command center.*

Outlook Express is the Chevrolet Impala of e-mail programs, outfitted with the essential features every user needs, wrapped in a stylish, well-appointed, comfortable software vehicle. It's more powerful than the stripped-down freebie e-mail Volkswagens, such as Hotmail, Juno, and Yahoo; and it lacks the bells and whistles of the e-mail Cadillacs, such as Outlook 2000, Eudora Pro, Calypso, Pegasus, and others. Regardless of which e-mail package you ultimately settle on, Outlook Express is unquestionably the best place to start. The skills you learn in Outlook Express are directly transferable to virtually any other e-mail client. Best of all, because it's the world's most popular e-mail client, every other e-mail program can *import* Outlook Express mail, folders, attachments, and address books – meaning any data you commit to Outlook Express can be migrated easily to other programs.

Any way you cut it, Outlook Express is the logical launch pad for your budding e-mail experience. So climb aboard, settle in behind the controls, and prepare to add your electronic voice to the e-mail avalanche.

DEFINITION

To import brings data into a program. Exporting sends data out of a program. This is similar to loading (importing) and saving (exporting). More information about importing and exporting data between programs is on deck in Chapter 10.

■ **Make your** *e-mail voice heard.*

If you find you don't care for Outlook Express, or don't need all its features, you can try nearly all the popular e-mail clients for free. Some work through your web browser (they're basic), while others require you to download and install their software (these are more powerful, but also more complex). Some are completely free, while others cost a few dollars after the trial period expires. Those that don't support a free or trial version (such as Microsoft's Outlook 2000) provide lots of presale information on the web.

E-mail clients

www.eudora.com	Qualcomm's Eudora ("lite" version is free)
www.mcsdallas.com	Micro Computer Systems' Calypso
www.microsoft.com/office/outlook	Microsoft's Outlook 2000*
www.netscape.com	Netscape's Messenger (free)
www.pegasus.usa.com	Pegasus Mail by David Harris (free)

*The Cadillac Eldorado (or Lincoln Continental) of e-mail clients. It's the one I use. Not for the faint-of-heart. Incredibly powerful, but aimed at heavy-duty mail users who also need to centralize and integrate their calendaring, contacts, tasks, and other personal information management requirements.

Free web-based e-mail clients

www.altavista.com	Alta Vista's client
www.eudoramail.com	Eudora's web-based client
www.hotmail.com	Microsoft's Hotmail client*
www.mail.com	Mail.com's client
www.mail.Go.com	Go Network's client
www.mail.Yahoo.com	Yahoo!'s client*
www.mailexcite.com	Excite's client
www.operamail.com	Opera's client
www.webmail.netscape.com	Netscape's web-based client
www.xoom.com/email	Xoom's client

*Hotmail is the world's largest and most popular free e-mail client. Yahoo!'s e-mail client is said to be the most powerful.

Free e-mail plus ISP services

www.altavista.com	Alta Vista free e-mail client & service
www.juno.com	Juno free e-mail client & service
www.netzero.com	NetZero free e-mail client & service

Logging on to e-mail

A neat desk is the sign of a neat mind, and a neat Windows Desktop is the sign of an organized PC. Just as you placed a copy of Internet Explorer's icon in your master personal folder, you should also clone an Outlook Express icon for instant access. First, Close or Minimize any open windows on your screen. Then click Start | Programs, right-click the Outlook Express icon, and select Copy. Next, open your master personal folder by double-clicking its Desktop icon, or hitting its hot-key.

Note: If your computer isn't running the latest version of Windows 98, you might find Outlook Express located at Start | Programs | Internet Explorer | Outlook Express.

With your master personal folder open, right-click any blank area, and select Paste. The Outlook Express icon appears. Whenever you want to compose or check e-mail, jump into your master personal folder, and double-click the Outlook Express icon. Give it a blast right now! If your Internet connection is already live, Outlook Express' main window will pop right up. If your Internet connection is not live, Outlook Express will present the Dial-up Connection dialog. On some computers, Windows 98 will first ask if you want to make Outlook Express your default e-mail client. Of course, the answer is yes, so click the "Yes" button.

If the Dial-up Connection dialog's options are grayed-out, and you hear your modem dialing the phone, that means Windows 98 is automatically calling your ISP, and logging onto the Internet. If the Dial-Up Connection dialog isn't grayed-out, make sure your user name and password appear on the screen (if you've done everything right 'til now, they will show up). Also make sure the "Save password" and "Connect automatically" buttons are checked. As with IE, these checkboxes tell Windows 98 to remember your log-on between Internet sessions, so you don't have to re-enter it every time.

It also tells the PC to skip the Dial-Up Connection dialog, and start dialing as soon as you open Outlook Express.

If the "Save password" prompt ever disappears or becomes grayed-out, it means you didn't enter your Windows log-on password when you first powered-up the PC. Click Start | Shut Down | Restart | OK to reboot your computer, and make sure you enter your user name and password when Windows restarts. Next, click the Connect button to kick off the dialing process. You'll hear the modem pick up and dial the phone, and screech its way to a satisfactory connection with your ISP. When the connection is established, the modem will go silent, and you'll be online! You'll know you're connected because the little DUN (Dial-Up Networking) icon will appear in your Taskbar. It looks like two little computers. Double-click the DUN icon to see your connection speed.

Keeping your Internet connection alive

Getting online is one thing. Staying online is another. Perhaps you've heard the horror stories of users who lose their Internet connection every few minutes, and have to log back on repeatedly – only to be forcibly logged off again. They switch to a new ISP, and the problem remains. They check their Internet connections and configuration, and everything comes up roses. Yet for some unknown reason, their computer can't maintain an Internet connection.

The problem, however, is not their computer. It's their ISP. As I explained earlier in the book, most ISPs provide what is known as "unlimited interactive access." Key word: Interactive. If you're not actively typing or clicking into your web browser, your ISP might disconnect your call.

The reason is simple: ISPs don't want to tie up one or more of their modems if you're off grabbing a corned beef sandwich or answering nature's call. It's a great strategy for the ISP and a royal pain in the neck for users.

You could dash off and buy any one of the software tools that promise to keep your Internet connection alive automatically. They work by fooling the ISP's computers into thinking you're typing and clicking in your web browser, when you're not.

But there is a better way to stay connected, and it's free. Simply configure your e-mail client to automatically check for new mail every few minutes. Every time your PC polls for new mail, your ISP's "inactivity timer" is reset to zero. Virtually all e-mail clients allow you to poll for new mail automatically, and Outlook Express is no exception. On the menu bar, click Tools | Options. On the Options General tab, make sure the "Check for new messages every [30] minute(s)" checkbox is checked.

Note the spinbox on the "Check for new messages" option. The default setting is 30 minutes, but that's too long. Most ISPs count down 15 minutes or less. When the timer strikes zero, your connection is toast.

Set the "Check for new messages" spinbox to 6 minutes. This tells Outlook Express to check for new mail ten times per hour, and will also fool virtually every major ISP's inactivity timer.

For this technique to work, you must remember to load your e-mail client (in this case, Outlook Express) whenever you go online. If you prefer, you can load your e-mail client first, followed by your web browser (Internet Explorer or Netscape). Do this, and you'll never lose your Internet connection due to an ISP's inactivity timer. OK; with this out of the way, let's stop futzing with the computer (finally!), and do something constructive.

Opening your e-mail inbox

It's empty now, but it won't be for long. "It" is your Inbox, the lifeblood of your forthcoming e-mail existence. This is the place where new messages first appear, and the control room where you'll read, reply, forward, delete, print, and save incoming mail. The standard Inbox display is organized into four main panels. Clockwise from left, they are the Folder panel, the New Messages panel, the Preview panel, and the Contacts panel. Running across the window's top are Outlook Express' menu bar and toolbar.

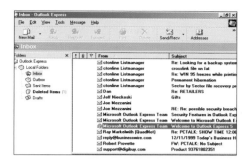

■ **New e-mail** *messages arrive in your Inbox.*

Clicking through the various menus on the menu bar will reveal some confusing commands, but even inexperienced users will likely find the big toolbar buttons self-explanatory. You'll have a chance to encounter them all as you give Outlook Express its first workout.

To be sure, the fastest way to get familiar with Outlook Express (or any software, for that matter) is to dive in and use it. Yes, I could invest page after page documenting each and every one of Outlook Express' menu items, buttons, gizmos, and so on in painful detail. Or I could put you through the paces of Outlook Express, and let you pick up the purpose of those wonderful widgets through osmosis. That's exactly how experienced users get a leg up on new software, and it exactly how you should do it, too.

Composing a message

Amazing as it might seem, even brand new users who don't know anyone else with a computer have at least one person they can send a message to: themselves. Sending a message to yourself is a great way to flex your e-mail system's muscle, and check that your entire Internet communications loop – your PC, ISP connection, POP3 server, and SMTP server – are all working as required.

■ **Send yourself** *an e-mail! Click the New Mail button and enter your own e-mail address in the "To:" input box.*

Squint at Outlook Express' toolbar, and guess which button you should click to compose a new message. If you said "New Mail," you're correct! Click the New Mail button, and the New Message window will appear. The first thing any new message gets is an e-mail address. Click in the "To:" input box, and enter your own e-mail address. This is usually your log-on name, followed by the domain name of your ISP. For example, my log-on name is RBLevin, and my ISP's domain name is RBLevin.net. That means I would enter "RBLevin@RBLevin.net" in the "To:" field of Outlook Express' New Message window.

If you want to send a copy of the message to someone else, enter their e-mail address in the "Cc:" input box. Every e-mail address listed in the "Cc:" input box gets a "carbon copy" of the message. To include other recipients, but keep their e-mail addresses hidden, enter their e-mail addresses in the "Bcc:" (Blind carbon copy) input box. You can separate multiple e-mail addresses in the "To:," "Cc:," and "Bcc:" input boxes with a comma.

After you have typed in your e-mail address, click in the "Subject:" input box (or press the Tab key to jump there) and type in any old subject. You could type in "My first e-mail message," or "God Bless America," or whatever.

Next, click in the big blank window space that takes up most of the New Message window (or press Tab to jump in there). This is called the "message body." Type in a message to yourself, such as "The quick brown fox jumped over the lazy dog." You can edit what you type using Windows 98's standard editing keys. If you don't remember them (it has been a while since the keyboard was explained), double back to the "Getting to Know the Windows 98 Keyboard" section in Chapter 5. When you're happy with your message, click the "Send" button. Outlook Express packages it up, and moves it to the Outbox folder.

The message will be automatically dispatched into cyberspace when Outlook Express next polls your ISP for new mail.

Sending an e-mail message

You could sit patiently for the next few minutes until Outlook Express polls your ISP for new mail, but why wait? Even though Outlook Express is configured to poll for new mail automatically, you can also instruct the program to dispatch and fetch e-mail on demand. Click the "Send/Receive" button on the toolbar, and Outlook Express will sling your message into cyberspace, and see if any new mail has arrived. Wait 10 to 30 seconds after clicking Send/Receive, and then click it again. The message you sent to yourself should arrive in your Inbox. Stand up and cheer! You've just joined the e-mail revolution, and added your e-mail address to the e-mail avalanche.

If your message doesn't arrive, wait a few minutes, and click Send/Receive again. If it still doesn't show up, or if you receive any error messages, rerun the Internet Connection Wizard (described in Chapter 8's "Pre-Flight Checklist" section), and double-check all of your settings. If after checking your settings, you still can't retrieve your message, contact your Internet service provider.

Reading an e-mail message

When the electronic postman arrives, there are at least seven things you can do with a new message: Read it, reply to it, forward it to one or more people, print it, sort it, file it, or delete it.

First and foremost, people read their e-mail. Before reading it, however, you'll probably want to sort it. As your mail starts to pile up, you'll appreciate being able to quickly jump to those messages that matter, and skip the junk mail. To sort messages by sender, click the "From" button in the New Messages panel. To sort by subject, click (you guessed it) the "Subject" button. Similarly, to sort by date and time received, click the "Received" button.

You can reverse the sort order by clicking the appropriate button twice in a row. Like most e-mail packages today, Outlook Express lets you read your e-mail by clicking on it once, and displaying the message in the Preview pane. You can also read your e-mail by double-clicking it, which opens the message in its own window. If you have a lot of messages, you can use the keyboard's arrow keys to work your way up and down the message list, and read each message in the Preview pane. Try that now. Click once on the message you sent to yourself, and the message body appears in the Preview pane. Double-click the message, and it pops open in its own window.

Some people find the Preview pane annoying, and prefer to read every message in its own window. If that's you, click View on the menu bar, then click Layout.

In the Window Layout Properties dialog, uncheck "Show preview pane," and click OK. You can also close the Preview pane by clicking+dragging its top border off the screen.

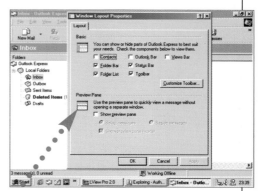

■ **Uncheck** *"Show preview pane" if you find the preview pane annoying.*

Replying to an e-mail message

Pretend the message you sent to yourself is actually a great joke that someone else sent you. You want to tell the sender how much you love the joke, and you want to share it with friends. Regardless of whether you're viewing the message in the Preview pane or in its own window, the toolbar's "Reply" and "Reply All" buttons are available. Reply responds only to the sender; Reply All responds to everyone the sender addressed the message to.

Click the Reply button, and the "Re:" window emerges. It's exactly like the New Message window, except that (1) it's already preaddressed, (2) it already has a subject, and (3) it features a reference copy of the original message. The cursor is blinking inside the message body, awaiting your reply. Type in a brief reply, and click the Send button.

Whoosh! Your reply has been transmitted to the sender (in this case, that's you, so you'll soon receive a reply from yourself).

Forwarding an e-mail message

Click the Forward button, and the "Fw:" window opens. It contains a copy of the message, and is ready to accept one or more e-mail addresses for forwarding. Type your e-mail address into the "To:" input box. That will forward the message to one person. But what if you want to forward to many people? Easy. Just enter as many e-mail addresses as you want in the "To:" input box, and separate them with a comma or a semicolon.

You can also enter multiple addresses, separated by a comma, when sending new messages and replies, as well as in the "Cc" and "Bcc" input boxes.

Give it a try. Type a comma after your e-mail address, then enter my address, RBLevin@RBLevin.net. It should look something like this: YourAddress@YourISP.com, RBLevin@RBLevin.net. That instructs Outlook Express to forward the message to both your address and mine. If you'd like to add a comment to the forwarded message, type it into the message body, above the words "Original Message." When you're done preparing your forwarded message, send it as you would any other message, by clicking the Send/Receive button. Do that now, and in a few moments, the forwarded message will arrive in your Inbox,

Using the Address Book

ENTERING ONE OR MORE *persons' e-mail addresses into the "To:" field seems straightforward enough. That is, until you have to do it 1,001 times a day. You have to first remember everybody's e-mail address – some of which can be rather, shall we say, odd. Then you have to type them in, one by one, again and again. The entire process can get rather old rather fast. That's when you begin to wonder if there isn't a better way.*

There is. It's Outlook Express' electronic Address Book. Every e-mail client provides an address book, and Outlook Express offers one of the best – if not the best. All e-mail clients let you record names and e-addresses and create bulk-mailing address lists. Outlook Express goes further, creating an Address Book automatically from messages you reply to. It's also fully integrated into the e-mail system. You can type part of an address in the "To:" field – the person's first name, last name, or portions of their e-mail address – and the Address Book will look up the entry. If it finds a match, it will automatically complete the entry. If it can't resolve the match, it will display a list of names that "sound like" what you typed in. It also provides facilities to keep bulk-mailings in sync with individual addresses that comprise your bulk e-mail lists.

To enable the Address Book's automated features, pull down the Tool menu by clicking the Tool command on the menu bar, then click Options. In the Options dialog, click the Send tab. Turn on the "Automatically put people I reply to in my Address Book," and the "Automatically complete e-mail addresses when composing" features by selecting their checkboxes. Click OK when you're done.

Now, whenever you reply to or forward a message, Outlook Express will add those persons to your Address Book, with no additional effort from you.

Advanced Address Book features

When the Address Book's automated features are enabled, you can address any message by entering all or some of a person's name in the "To:" field. When you click the Send button, Outlook Express will scan the "To:" field and validate the addresses. For example, entering "RB," "RBL," "RBLevin," or "RBLevin@RBLevin.net" all will cause Outlook Express to address the message to me. If any addresses can't be resolved, Outlook Express will display the Check Names window. Click on the correct address, then click OK. You can also click on the Show More Names button to open the complete Address Book. Scroll up or down the list by clicking the up and down arrowheads. When you pinpoint the person you're after, click the OK button.

You don't have to be working in a message to open the Address Book. It's possible to click the "Addresses" button on the toolbar at any time to flip the Address Book open. Once inside, double-click on any person's entry to bring up their contact Properties. If you want, you can click through the various tabbed dialogs, and enter detailed information about the person to your heart's content.

Creating e-mail mailing lists

On second thought, maybe it does. Imagine you're the president of the International Association of Ball-Point Penologists. Your club has 50 members, and you've decided it's time to start circulating a monthly newsletter via e-mail. You could enter 50 e-mail addresses 50 times, and have Outlook Express automatically validate them 50 times. Alternatively, you could use the Address Book's "Group" feature to create one e-mail address that sends any message to all 50 (or more) recipients. For example, you could create a group named "Penmen," and add all 50 members to the Penmen group. Then you could send your newsletter "To:" Penmen. Outlook Express would automatically scoot the message off to 50 names.

At the present time, of course, you don't have a need to practice creating Address Book Groups. But you will in the future. When you're ready, return to this section to go through the following exercise: Click the Addresses button on the toolbar, and the Address Book opens. Now click the New button on the Address Book's toolbar, and select the New Group command. In the Group Name input box, give the group a name.

SORTING GROUPS

Here's a neat idea: Preface your group names with a ` character (that's a grave accent, the first key on your keyboard, to the left of the number 1).

For example, "`Penologists." This forces your groups to appear at the top of the Address Book list, and makes it easy to find them when you open the Address Book.

If you want a group to appear at the bottom of the list, start it with a ~ (that's called a tilde). For example, "~Penologists." To type a tilde, hit the grave accent key, the one to the left of the number 1, while holding down the Shift key.

Once you've named the group, click the Select Members button. In the Select Group Members dialog, scroll up and down the list using the up and down arrowheads to find each member of the group. When you locate a member, click on his or her name, then click the Select button. Each time you click Select, that person is added to the Member list. You can even put groups inside other groups.

For example, you could create a group called "Writers," and add the "Penologists" and "Pencilologists" groups to it. This saves you the trouble of having to maintain three separate groups. Changes to the Penologist and Pencilologists groups are automatically reflected in the Writers group. When you're done populating your group, click the OK button to create the new group and close the Select Group Members dialog. Click OK again to close the group Properties dialog.

To send a message to the group, enter the group's name in the new message's "To:" field. If you don't want group members to see who else is in the group, enter the group's name in the "Bcc:" field instead. As with individual e-mail addresses, you can send messages to multiple groups by separating their names with a comma. You can also commingle individual addresses with group addresses. RBLevin@RBLevin.net, Penologists, Pencilologists is a valid entry in the "To:," "Cc:," or "Bcc:" input boxes.

■ **You can mix** *single addresses with multiple addresses using group names.*

Using e-mail folders

WHAT IF YOU ACCIDENTALLY *sent a message you didn't mean to send. If you act fast, you can save your sorry hide by preventing Outlook Express from pushing the message onto the Internet.*

Click the Outbox folder in the Folders panel, and you'll see your new message awaiting its marching orders. To stop it from being mailed, right-click it, and then click Delete. Similarly, if you'd like to make sure a message was, in fact, sent, look in "Sent Items." Click on the Sent Items folder, and there you'll find each and every message ever penned and sent by you. To clean up your Sent Items folder, right-click on any message, and select Delete. To throw out all of the Sent Items, click the Sent Items folder once. On the menu bar, click Edit | Select All, then click Edit | Delete. Note that mail you delete isn't really erased; it's moved to the Deleted Items folder. If you want your Deleted Items folder to be emptied automatically when you exit Outlook Express, click Tools | Options. On the Maintenance tab of the Options dialog, select the "Empty messages from the 'Deleted Items' folder on exit" checkbox. Then click OK. You'll find messages that you composed but didn't send stored in the "Drafts" folder. Click once to get in there, and double-click to complete and send.

Creating your own e-mail folders

You're not stuck with the standard-issue folders served up by Outlook Express. Just as you can create subfolders within your master personal folder, so too can you create subfolders (and subfolders within subfolders) on your Outlook Express *folder tree*. If you want to keep related messages together – say, messages relating to a project you're working on – it makes sense to create a folder just for them. You create a new folder on the Outlook Express folder tree in much the same way new folders are created elsewhere in Windows 98. Right-click the "Local Folders" icon in the Folders pane. Click the "New Folder" command. The Create Folder dialog opens. In the "Folder Name" input box, type in the name of the new folder. If you want the new folder to appear on the same level as other Local Folders (such as the Inbox and Outbox), click once on the Local Folders icon.

If you want the new folder to appear as a subfolder beneath another folder, click on the folder that will contain the new folder. When you're done, click the OK button. If you make a mistake and create it in the wrong location, right-click it, and select "Delete." Similarly, to rename any of your personal folders, right-click them, and select "Rename." You can also move folders by dragging+dropping them around the folder tree. To file a message in a folder, simply drag+drop it into the folder of your choice.

> **DEFINITION**
>
> *Lists of folders are called* folder trees, *because they're organized like an upside-down tree. The "root" of the folder tree is the top-level folder. Its branches cascade from the top level on down.*

More on SPAM

"IT'S PORK SHOULDER AND HAM, mostly. And spices. Secret spices."
That's how executives of Hormel Foods Corporation describe SPAM, one of the
best-known consumer brands of all time. But that's not how veteran netizens
would describe SPAM – and soon, neither will you.

SPAM makes Hormel execs smile, but SPAM in cyberspace makes them grimace, and understandably so. That's because they've watched their carefully cultivated international trademark become generic Internet slang for unwanted junk mail. How and when SPAM entered the Internet vernacular for junk mail is anyone's guess, but the fact remains that, when someone sends you unsolicited junk mail, netizens will say you've been "SPAMmed."

SPAM mail has many faces. It can be anything else that can be sent as e-mail.

Five attributes separate SPAM mail from all other e-mail you'll receive:

1 You didn't ask for it.
2 It's been sent to zillions of other users who didn't ask for it.
3 You probably don't know and can't locate the sender.
4 You delete it, and it keeps showing up in your Inbox.
5 It drives you nuts.

> **DEFINITION**
>
> *E-mail that is returned to sender is called "bounced mail," because the mail server bounced it back to you.*

SPAM mail clogs your Inbox, slows your ISP's servers, and wastes valuable Internet bandwidth. That's because each message targets millions of mailboxes, and generates millions of replies and *bounced* messages.

The more mail the Internet has to process, the slower the Internet gets. Worse, most SPAMmers are borderline crooks, or worse, trying to entice innocent users with pyramid schemes, investment scams, snake oil cures, and other dubious, even dangerous offers. You can see why the folks at Hormel aren't exactly dancing in the aisles over netizens' (and the media's) colloquial use of their SPAM brand name to describe what is perhaps the lowest form of electronic life.

Blocking junk e-mail

Fortunately, netizens and e-mail software vendors, including Microsoft, have developed ways to combat the rise of SPAM mail.

■ **Returned e-mail** *is "bounced" back to the sender.*

The most popular way to fight SPAM is also the easiest: Just delete the SPAM mail on receipt, and never, ever reply to SPAM mail.

By replying, you tell the SPAMmers that your e-mail address is valid, and they will continue to send you unsolicited messages – even if their SPAM mail says otherwise. You can also activate the anti-SPAM features in Outlook Express. This empowers Outlook Express to study your incoming mail for telltale signs of SPAM mail. Once the SPAM mail has been flagged, Outlook Express deletes it, and you never see it. Blocking mail from SPAMmers is just a right-click away. When you receive SPAM mail, open the message by double-clicking it. Then right-click on the sender's name (that's the name to the right of the "From:" field). On the context menu that pops up, select "Block Sender." This adds the address to Outlook Express' list of blocked mail. You can also block senders by clicking once on the message in your Inbox, and selecting Message | Block Sender on the menu bar. To remove senders from your blocked sender list, hit Outlook Express' message rules editor. You'll find it by clicking Tools | Message Rules on the menu bar, and selecting Blocked Senders List. Your ability to block messages isn't limited to SPAM mail. You can add any sender to the blocked mail list by right-clicking their name, and selecting Block Sender. Outlook Express will immediately delete future messages received from any address on the blocked mail list.

E-mail attachments

E-MAIL IS ALL WELL AND GOOD, *but there are times when you need to send more than a plain message. In the bad old days, when users needed to share documents, presentations, artwork, and such, there was but one option: parcel delivery. Folks had to save their data on a floppy disk, and drop it in the US mail, or pay premium for UPS, FedEx, or some other overnight delivery service to scurry their precious info across town or around the world.*

Often times, the data files didn't fit on a single 1.44M floppy disk. That necessitated all manner of hoop jumping, including the use of special software that "spanned" data files across multiple floppies or costly high-capacity proprietary storage systems. Modern Internet e-mail does away with all that nonsense. In its place: the e-mail "attachment." Just as your e-mail messages can carry your words and thoughts to another user's computer, they can also carry one or more attached data files. That is, unless you have a brain-dead ISP, like America Online, that restricts the use of attachments. AOL and proprietary services like it limit the size and number of attachments that can be sent to their members.

Nine times out of ten, when an attachment fails to go through, it's due to a restriction of the receiver's ISP.

185

Creating an attachment

BEFORE YOU CAN *send data as an e-mail attachment, you first have to create some data. Minimize Outlook Express by clicking its Minimize button. Close any open windows by clicking their Close button. Now open up your master personal folder.*

Right-click any blank area in your master personal folder, and select New | Text Document. When the new text document appears, right-click it, and select Open (or just double-click it). Now type some nonsense into it, such as "Bla bla bla." Save it by clicking the File command on the menu bar, and clicking Save. Switch back to Outlook Express by clicking its button on the Taskbar. Create a new message by clicking the New Mail button on the toolbar. When the New Message window opens, click the Attach button on the New Message toolbar. The Insert Attachment dialog opens, with a view of your Windows Desktop. Double-click on your master personal folder icon to peek inside. Once you're in, double-click on the New Text Document file.

Sending and opening attachments

Outlook Express returns you to the New Message window, which now displays the New Text Document file as an attachment. The original New Text Document file remains untouched in your master personal folder, but a copy has been attached to the message. Now type your e-mail address into the "To:" field of the new message. While you're at it, type a note into the message body (such as "Here is the attachment"). Then click the Send button on the New Message toolbar. In a few minutes, the message will arrive in your Inbox, with the attachment in tow. You can speed up the process by clicking the Send/Receive button on Outlook Express' toolbar. If the message doesn't appear, wait a minute, then click Send/Receive again.

When the message arrives, note that it's displayed in your Inbox with a small paper clip icon beside it.

That's your cue that the message has an attachment. Double-click the message to open it, and you'll see the attachment featured in the "Attach:" field. That's exactly what things will look like when someone sends you an attachment. To open the attachment, double-click it. To save it to your master personal folder for future use, right-click it, and select Save As. When the Save Attachment As dialog opens, navigate into your master personal folder, and click the Save button to save the attachment. To save the attachment on your Desktop, or to jump back to your Desktop, click the little green and white Desktop icon on the Save Attachment As dialog's toolbar first.

Sometimes the tiny green-and-white Desktop button doesn't show up on the Save As dialog. Click the Up One Level button instead (the one that looks like a little folder with a bent-elbow up-arrow on it). Keep clicking on the Up One Level button until the button turns gray, and won't let you travel up any more levels. You're now looking at a view of your Windows Desktop. Double-click the master personal folder icon to enter it.

E-mail attachments can be extremely useful, but they can also be dangerous. It's especially important that you learn how to protect yourself from a deadly form of attachment computer users have dubbed "Trojans" – double-clicking on a Trojan, can wipe out your entire system. Suffice it to say that you should NOT open ANYTHING that arrives as an attachment in your e-mail until you have read Chapter 17, "Keeping Secrets Safe." There you'll find a complete explanation of how to deal with e-mail-borne threats.

Now that you've learned how to send and open e-mail messages, it's important that you spend some quality time with your e-mail client. Send messages back and forth to yourself and anyone else whose e-mail address you know. Practice powering-up, logging on, web surfing, and sending/receiving messages for the next day or so, before moving on to other computing challenges. When you can fly through these tasks with confidence, then it's time to step up to the plate for your next computing goal.

A simple summary

✓ Setting your e-mail client to poll for new mail prevents your ISP from disconnecting your session.

✓ You send, receive, reply, forward, delete, print, and save e-mail from Outlook Express' Inbox.

✓ Address messages by entering the recipient's e-mail name in the "To:," "Cc:," or "Bcc:" input boxes.

✓ Outlook Express's toolbar manages your mail.

✓ You can send bulk mail by creating mail groups in the Address Book.

✓ Separate multiple e-mail addresses and mail group names with a comma. This works in all the address input boxes.

✓ SPAM is junk mail. Block it by adding the senders to your blocked sender list.

✓ You can share files by attaching them to e-mail messages.

Chapter 10

Sampling the Windows Software Library

YOU PROBABLY DON'T feel any different from the day you first cracked open this book and entered the world of computing. But you have changed. Your cybersense isn't fully developed yet, but it's getting there – and it gets stronger every time you boot-up your PC. Having mastered your e-mail skills, you're now ready to move on to the next phase of your e-education and explore PC software Microsoft bundles with Windows 98. In this chapter, you'll sample the vast Windows 98 software library that's lurking just a few clicks away. You'll also learn the best ways to share information between different Windows 98 programs and with other users.

In this chapter...

✓ Going for winning apps

✓ An application buffet

✓ Give your new programs a whirl

✓ Sharing data between apps

✓ Sharing data with other users

ENTER THE VAST WINDOWS 98 SOFTWARE LIBRARY

Going for winning apps

WHEN YOU'RE SITTING COMFORTABLY *behind your keyboard,
a foot or so from your PC's display, your Windows 98 Desktop looks like a
colorful collection of icons, words, buttons, and other controls. It's all a fabulous
illusion, of course. To see what I mean, look closely at your computer's screen.
Closer. Even closer still. Put your nose smack dab against the monitor's glass
tube. What do you see?*

Dots. Lots and lots of tiny dots. At least 288,000 individual dots of color, and as
many as 1,310,720 dots, depending upon the size of your Desktop area. It's similar to the
effect you get when you look at newspaper photographs under a magnifying glass. (Note:
To resize your Desktop area, right-click your Windows Desktop, select Properties |
Settings, and drag the Desktop Area slider to the left for less, or the right for more.)

In fact, examine anything closely, and it's often vividly different from what it appears
at first blush. Your Windows 98 Start Menu is no exception. The first time you clicked
on it, the sheer number of things that popped up seemed daunting, even unnerving.
Upon closer inspection, however, you'll find that the majority of programs that call
the Start Menu home are of little or no value and are, as such, utterly disposable.
What remains are system tools you'll need, and a handful of unbeatable apps worth
their weight in gold.

Apps a plenty

On my bare-bones Windows 98 system, there are about 100 items populating
various areas of the Start Menu. Your new PC might feature even more.
Amazingly, of those 100 or so stock Windows 98 offerings, most folks
end up regularly using no more than nine. Nine out of 100!

*But it can and often does take new users weeks,
even months, to explore the 91 other Start Menu apps
before they can intelligently narrow the field. That,
my friend, is a monumental waste of time. Therein
lies the key to rapidly mastering Windows 98: Take
a "big picture" approach to the Start Menu, zero in
on the indispensable tools and applications,
and temporarily pass on everything else.*

VIP

■ **Even a bare-bones**
*Windows 98 system has
over 100 tools.*

■ **Take each of** *your useful software tools for a spin.*

Those 91 other apps aren't going anywhere. They'll be ready, willing, and able to serve when and if the need arises. It would be nice if isolating the all-important Windows 98 programs from everything else on the Start Menu were as easy as separating oil and water. It's not. Quickly poking through the Start Menu and experimenting won't do it. On the contrary, doing so can get you into big trouble. You could accidentally launch a potentially destructive process, inadvertently install something you don't need that wipes out something you do, or unintentionally reconfigure a system component with negative consequences.

Or you could just totally confuse yourself. As I pointed out earlier when demonstrating the risks of exploring with Explorer, at present, your deductive computing skills are growing fast, but remain limited. For now, it's best to remain within the perfectly safe confines of your master personal folder.

With that in mind, start by adding the truly useful Windows 98 tools and applications to your master personal folder, then you can take them all for a spin.

Loading up your master personal folder

Two of Windows 98's killer apps are already in your master personal folder: Internet Explorer, and Outlook Express. To that, you should add Windows 98's standard-issue text editor, WordPad, and Windows 98's standard-issue drawing program, Paint.

Close any open programs and windows by clicking their Close button. Then open your Desktop's master personal folder by double-clicking it, or pressing its hot key. Next, click the Start button, then click Programs | Accessories.

Right-click on the Paint icon, and select Copy. Then right-click on any blank area of your master personal folder, and select Paste. Repeat these steps for WordPad. Click Start | Programs | Accessories, and right-click the WordPad icon. Select Copy, then right-click any blank area in your master personal folder and select Paste.

Drag+Drop

You can also create copies of Start Menu items using drag+drop. Open your master personal folder. Then click on the Start Menu item you want to move. Hold down the Ctrl key, and click+drag the item into your master personal folder. When you release the mouse button, a copy of the icon will appear in your folder. Make sure you press and hold down the Ctrl key when performing this drag+drop operation.

Don't drag+drop an icon off the Start Menu without pressing Ctrl; otherwise, you will erase the item from the Start Memu and move it to the Desktop – not copy it.

The Ctrl key tells Windows 98 to make a copy of the icon being dragged+dropped rather than perform a "move."

While you're at it, put a copy of the Windows 98 Calculator in your master personal folder. Click Start, then click Programs | Accessories. Right-click the Calculator, and select Copy. Then right-click on any blank area of your master personal folder, and select Paste.

Next, add Windows 98's most important system tools: Disk Defragmenter and ScanDisk. Disk Defragmenter tunes up your hard disk so programs load and run faster. ScanDisk checks your hard disk for defects, and can repair most defects automatically. You'll learn how to use both tools in a future chapter, and will come to rely on them as most users do. For now, let's move them into your master personal folder.

■ **The Windows** 98 *calculator is a must have.*

Both Disk Defragmenter and ScanDisk are located at Start | Programs | Accessories | System Tools. Right click on Disk Defragmenter, select Copy, and then click in your master personal folder. Once inside your master personal folder, right-click any blank area, and select Paste. Repeat this process for ScanDisk. Click Start | Programs | Accessories | System Tools, and right-click the ScanDisk icon. Select Copy, then right-click any blank area in your master personal folder, and select Paste.

Popular start menu items

Two of the nine most popular Windows 98 Start Menu items remain: The Windows Update icon and Control Panel. Windows Update uses your Internet connection to automatically freshen your Windows 98 system. It's a free web-based service from Microsoft, and it keeps your Windows 98 computer running on the latest version of Windows.

You should run Windows Update at least once a month, to make sure your PC is always running the most recent version of Windows 98 and contains the latest security and bug fixes.

(More on both of these topics in Chapter 17.) To clone the Windows Update icon, click Start, then right-click Windows Update. Select Copy, then right-click inside your master personal folder and select Paste.

■ **Run Windows Update** *to get the latest bug fixes.* Last up: A shortcut to the Windows 98 Control Panel, the nerve center of your Windows 98 system. Cloning Control Panel takes a little extra work, because you can't copy it from the Start Menu. Rather, minimize your master personal folder by clicking its Minimize button. Then double-click the "My Computer" icon on your Windows 98 Desktop. Inside, you'll see another icon for the Control Panel.

Right-click it, and select Create Shortcut. Windows 98 will respond by asking if you want the shortcut placed on the Windows Desktop. Click Yes. Close the My Computer window by clicking its Close button. A Control Panel icon now appears on your Windows Desktop. Right-click it, and select Cut (not Copy). Restore your master personal folder by clicking its button on the Taskbar. Once you're back inside it, right-click any blank area, and select Paste.

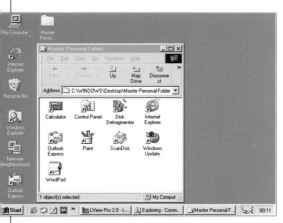

■ **Windows 98's** *nine most prominent standard-issue programs.*

Eureka! Your master personal folder is now populated with Windows 98's nine most prominent standard-issue programs. For the fun of it, organize your master personal folder by right-clicking any blank area, and selecting Arrange Icons | By Type. This groups all of the icons in your master folder by their data type. Programs will be grouped with other programs, documents with other documents, web sites with other web sites, and so on. Any time you want to organize your master personal folder, select Arrange Icons, and then choose one of the four sort options. It's taken you just a few minutes to populate your master personal folder with an arsenal of indispensable apps!

With Windows 98's most-used applications now at the ready in your master personal folder, the next logical move is to take them for a test drive.

An application buffet

ASK ANYONE TO NAME THE COMPANY that invented fast food, and they'll nearly always point the finger at one of America's premier drive-thru joints such as McDonald's or KFC.

However, the honor goes to Horn & Hardart, which opened its doors in 1902, on New York's Times Square. Every meal was served up by an H&H innovation dubbed "The Automat." The meals were prepared in a traditional kitchen, and served up fresh by rows of chrome-plated, coin-operated dispensing machines. Each fronted a column of windows, behind which a salad, sandwich, or fruit pie was displayed. Drop a coin in the slot, crank the big knob, open the window, and serve yourself. It was true fast food.

H&H closed its last Automat in 1975, but the concept lives on – in your Windows 98 PC! Instead of lunch, you have applications. Your master folder is not unlike an Automat, populated with programs that are your "application buffet." Instead of dropping in a coin, you click the mouse or stroke a key, and your master personal folder opens. Double-click the program you hunger for, and the window opens. Out slides a Taskbar button with the program's name on it.

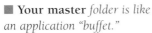

■ **Your master** *folder is like an application "buffet."*

In fact, the Taskbar becomes a sort of "cafeteria tray," where you carry around the programs you're using while they're active. To take a bite of any delectable app, click on its Taskbar button.

This "fast food computing" concept will become indispensable as you delve deeper into more advanced computing tasks. The reason: Most computing projects require the use of multiple Windows 98 programs.

Locating and loading programs quickly, switching rapidly among them, and sharing information between them is a terrific trio of skills to master. Do so, and you'll wow even the most proficient Windows 98 users as you dispatch tasks with aplomb.

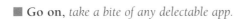

■ **Go on,** *take a bite of any delectable app.*

STAYING ORGANIZED

As you install new software programs, don't just leave their startup icons on the Start Menu. That defeats the entire purpose of getting organized, and using a centralized master personal folder. Get in the habit of copying the icon of any program you use regularly straight into your master personal folder. Just right-click the icon on the Start Menu, select Copy, right-click inside your master personal folder, and select Paste.

Give your new programs a whirl

NOW THAT YOU'RE READY *to give your new programs a whirl, start a practice round by loading up some of the programs already in your master personal folder. Open your master personal folder by double-clicking its icon, or hitting its hot key. On the master folder's menu bar, click View | Arrange Icons | By Name. This alphabetizes the icon listing. One by one, double-click some of the program icons you copied into your master personal folder. Start with the Calculator icon, followed by Disk Defragmenter, Internet Explorer, and Outlook Express.*

Double-click Paint, ScanDisk, and WordPad. (Don't load Windows Update; you're not ready to update Windows 98 just yet.)

When you're done opening the programs, your Taskbar should be stuffed to the gills with at least seven program buttons. Randomly click on the various program buttons featured on the Taskbar. As you do, each program window pops into view. This is called the "foreground" application, because it's the top-most window on your Windows 98 Desktop. Only one program can be the foreground application at any time. All other programs are said to be "background" applications, because they're running "behind" the foreground app.

If a program obscures your view of your master folder, click on any visible portion of the master personal folder to bring it back. If you can't see your master personal folder at all, click on its Taskbar button, or press its hot key on the keyboard to make it the foreground app.

Cascading and tiling windows

The Taskbar can also organize applications as well as switch between them. Right-click any blank area of the Taskbar (that's any spot above, below, or beside a button). Up pops the Taskbar's context menu. Click the Cascade Windows option, and all open windows are instantly stacked in an index card fashion. Cascading windows is useful when you want a neat and tidy way to see all the windows you have open.

You can click any exposed portion of any window to bring it to the foreground. But it's best to click a program's title bar, since that won't accidentally activate any program features.

If you click one of the program's buttons, for example, that might make the program do something you didn't intend to do. Now, right-click any blank area of the Taskbar again, and select Tile Windows Horizontally or Tile Windows Vertically. Both Tile Windows options arrange any open windows side-by-side, like linoleum tiles on a floor. This makes every open window fully visible. As you will soon learn, tiling windows horizontally or vertically is convenient when you need to drag+drop information between programs.

Multitasking programs

Once again, simply click on any area of any window to make it the foreground application. Try this now: Click on ScanDisk's window. With ScanDisk the foreground app, right-click any blank Taskbar area, and select Cascade Windows. The windows now cascade, with ScanDisk on top. Click ScanDisk's Start button, and ScanDisk starts chugging away. Immediately right-click any blank Taskbar area, and select Tile Windows Vertically. The windows tile, with ScanDisk on top. Now click on any other program's window, such as the Calculator's. Even though Calculator (or other program) is now the foreground application, notice that ScanDisk is still busy working in the background!

Windows 98 allows you to run multiple tasks at a time, a process known as "multitasking."

You can dispatch as many jobs as you like. Instead of twiddling your thumbs while you wait for each one to finish, you can switch to another program and do something else. As you get more computing hours under your belt, you'll find multitasking comes in mighty handy. For example, you can be printing one or more documents in the background, while you're writing another document or surfing the web in the foreground.

For now, click on ScanDisk's window, and click the Close button to end the program. Then right-click any blank Taskbar area, and select Cascade Windows. Now you can easily close all the open programs by clicking their Close button. (You can also close the programs by repeatedly hitting Alt+F4.)

Bottom line, just remember the dynamic trio: (1) You store and launch programs from your master personal folder, (2) you switch among programs by clicking their Taskbar buttons, and (3) you organize windows by right-clicking using the Taskbar.

Sharing data between apps

SHARE AND SHARE ALIKE. *I spent about an hour scouring the web trying to find out who first said that, and came up empty handed – which only goes to prove that the public library has nothing to fear from the web (yet).*

Regardless of whether it was Shakespeare or Superman, the concept of sharing is timeless and universal among the world's people. It's drilled into our heads from the earliest age by parents, teachers, and the media. Kids who don't share are outcasts, the subject of whispers among parents other than their own. The more willing a child is to share, the more he or she is considered warm, loving, and adorable.

Computer software is held to these same high standards. Programs capable of easily sharing their data with other applications are considered "well behaved."

Those that insist on keeping their data to themselves are chastised as being "proprietary." In the bad old days before Windows, information you entered or created in one program couldn't be used in another. If, for example, you created a database of sales orders in one program, you couldn't easily crunch its numbers using some other vendor's spreadsheet.

If you created a letterhead logo or picture in a graphic program, it was often impossible (or nearly so) to migrate that artwork from the graphic program into your word processor. Fortunately, those days are gone. Today, there are three common means of sharing information between apps. One method, dubbed "cut+paste," is nearly universal among Windows 98 programs. The others – import/export and file compatibility (covered in the next section of this chapter) – are increasingly common, but not ubiquitous.

Learn how to use these powerful techniques, and you'll rarely find yourself stuck with data that's "locked" in a proprietary program, which limits the data's overall serviceability to you.

Cutting + Pasting

You've actually used cut+paste quite a bit already. Every time you right-clicked an item, copied it to the Windows Clipboard, and pasted it somewhere else, you were using cut+paste.

Cut+paste is easy, and it's almost universally available throughout Windows 98 and the programs that run on Windows.

In a nutshell, cut+paste works like this: You first select the item you want to copy (duplicate) or cut (move). To select an item, you either click on it (if it's an object such as an icon, file, or folder), or you drag your mouse pointer over it while holding down the left mouse button (useful for selecting text, for example). Once the "source" item is selected, you can right-click it, and select Copy or Cut. Then you switch to another program (known as the "destination"), and click Edit | Paste on the program's menu bar (or right-click, and select Paste).

To illustrate the technique, open your master personal folder. Double-click the Paint icon to launch Paint. Switch back to your master personal folder (click its button on the Taskbar), and double-click WordPad. Tile both programs on the screen by right-clicking any blank area of the Taskbar, and selecting one of the Tile Windows options. This expands Paint and WordPad to fill your screen.

■ **Blue drawing** *copied and pasted into WordPad.*

Click anywhere inside of Paint's window to make Paint the foreground (active) application. Look carefully at the toolbar that extends down Paint's left side, and you'll see a paintbrush button (it's the fourth button from the top, on the right). Click it. This turns your mouse pointer into a virtual paintbrush. Press and hold your left mouse button, and drag the mouse pointer around to draw a few lines on Paint's virtual canvas. (Picasso you ain't, but who's comparing?)

Remember what I said about cut+paste? It always requires three steps: Selection, cut or copy, and paste.

■ **Mastering your mouse** *will help you cut+paste.*

Before you can cut+paste your wonderful work of art, you have to first tell Windows 98 what it is you want to cut+paste. In nearly every program, you can select a target item for cut+paste by either right-clicking it and selecting Select All, clicking Edit | Select All on the menu bar, or dragging a "lasso" around the portion of the data you want to select.

How to lasso

In this exercise, you'll learn how to lasso data. First, examine Paint's toolbar and look for a "Select" tool. It's the first icon on the top right; the one that looks like a square made up of dotted lines. Click it. This turns your mouse pointer into a selection tool. Click and hold your left mouse button down anywhere on Paint's virtual canvas, and drag it diagonally across the picture. You'll notice an expanding dotted box appears. That's you're selection "lasso."

Drag it until you have selected a portion of your drawing. If you make a mistake, simply start over by clicking and dragging somewhere else on the virtual canvas. When you have completed selecting your masterpiece, release the mouse button. Position the mouse pointer inside the lassoed area, and right-click. Up pops a context menu. Click the Copy command to put the selection on the Windows Clipboard.

■ **After creating** *a few brush strokes in Paint, use the "lasso" technique to select the painted area.*

Note: If you lasso your selection using the right mouse button, the context menu will pop up automatically. This doesn't work in all Windows 98 programs, but it's worth trying whenever you can, because it does save a step.

Now right-click anywhere inside the WordPad window. Another context menu appears. Select Paste, and a copy of your Paint artwork appears inside WordPad. So far, so good. Now that you're in WordPad, which is Windows 98's standard text editor, it makes sense to add some text to this sample project.Notice the artwork you pasted into WordPad is surrounded by a thin black border, with 8 squarish dots around it. That's Windows 98's way of showing you the size of the object you pasted into WordPad. Position your mouse pointer to the right of the picture's border, and click once. The picture's border should disappear, and a blinking line (your cursor) should appear. This represents WordPad's text insertion point; i.e. the place where your text will appear.

The quick brown fox...

Press the Enter key on your keyboard a few times, and then type "The Quick Brown Fox Jumped Over the Lazy Dog." Next, you're going to lasso both the picture and the text you just typed, and copy them back over to Paint. Position your mouse pointer at the very bottom of WordPad's window. Click and hold the left mouse button, and drag the mouse pointer up until you have selected the entire page. The text and the picture will change color as they become selected. (You can also select everything in a window by clicking Edit | Select All on the menu bar.)

When everything in WordPad's window is selected, right-click anywhere inside the selected items, and select the Copy command on the pop-up context menu. Next, right-click inside Paint's window, and select Paste. (Paint might ask if you want to resize the picture. Click the Yes button if asked.) Ta da! You've just successfully copied information from Paint into WordPad, edited it inside WordPad, and then copied it back to Paint. In a nutshell, you have shared graphical data (images) and textual data (words) between two completely different programs.

The cut+paste process you just practiced with Paint and WordPad works exactly the same way in every compliant Windows 98 program.

It's always a three step process: (1) Select the data you want to share using the mouse, (2) right-click and Copy (or Cut) it, (3) right-click inside the destination program and Paste it.

Some programs, like Paint, use a lasso to indicate selected data. Others, such as WordPad, don't use a lasso, but change the color of the target data instead.

Either way, Windows 98 programs will always provide visual cues to let you know the selection is going on.

Sharing data with other users

AS YOU LEARNED EARLIER, *one way to share data with other users is to attach files to e-mail messages and mail them to each other. That gets the data files to and fro, but there's a potential problem. All programs have at least one file format they can read and write. This is called their "native" file format. For example, Internet Explorer's native file format is .HTM (a HyperText Markup document). WordPad's native file format is .DOC (a DOCument). Notepad's native file format is .TXT (TeXT). What if you and your e-mail buddy used different software programs to create your data?*

Fret not. Import/Export, file conversion, and file compatibility are actually three ways of saying (and doing) exactly the same thing: Reading and/or writing data files created by other people, and other programs. For example, a text document that you create in WordPad can be read and *edited* in Microsoft Word 6.0, Word 97, Word 98 on the Macintosh, and Word 2000. Lotus' WordPro, Corel's WordPerfect, and a multitude of other word processors can also read it.

DEFINITION

Something edited means it has been modified in some way, and then can be resaved.

Similarly, artwork developed in Paint can be opened and accessed by virtually every graphics program on the planet. The reverse is also true, to some extent: Paint can open graphic files from many (but not all) different graphics programs. Similarly, every time your surf the World Wide Web, your web browser is actually loading and displaying data created by literally thousands of other programs. And any modern PC on Earth can display data you capture with your web browser.

■ **The standard Windows 98** *Open dialog looks like this.*

Call it what you will, the bottom line is this: With import/export you can directly share data between many different programs without having to go through the motions of cut+paste.

Unlike cut+paste, though, import and export aren't standard features of Windows 98. Some programs support import/export. Others don't. Happily, it's easy to find out if one of your programs can export data to a foreign program, or import foreign data. To export data, use the File | Save As command on the program's menu bar.

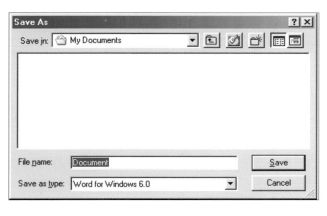

■ **Here's the Windows 98** *Save As dialog.*

Exporting data

Try this exporting exercise. Click once on WordPad's window to make it the foreground app. Click the File command on WordPad's menu bar, then click Save As. This opens the Save As dialog box. At the bottom of the Save As dialog is a "Save as type" drop-down pick list. Click on it, and WordPad will show you a list of every file type that it "knows," that is, those it can export data to. There's Word for Windows, Rich Text, Text, Unicode, and others.

Now click on Paint, then click File | Save As. Click once on Paint's "Save as type" drop-down pick list, and you'll see at least four different file types Paint can save data as. Almost every Windows 98 program features a File | Save As export function. Some programs provide dozens of different data types in their "Save as type" pick lists, while others offer a mere handful – or none at all, other than their own native file format. The only way to know for sure is to explore your program's File | Save As commands. Finding out if you have a program that can import foreign data is equally effortless. Just as most programs offer a File | Save As command for exporting, virtually all Windows 98 programs offer a File | Open command for importing.

Importing data

A program's File | Open command is normally used to load the program's native data. For example, a file you created and saved yesterday can be retrieved by clicking File | Open, and double-clicking the file. But there will be times when someone will send you a file that wasn't created by any of the software programs you own. When you click File | Open in your favorite program, either the file doesn't appear in the list or, when you double-click it, garbage appears on the screen.

Both results mean your program has no idea how to deal with the file and can't open it or display it properly. But you're not out of luck when this happens. Your program may be clueless about the foreign file type, but Windows 98 just might recognize it.

The File | Open dialog is the tool you need to get Windows 98 to import data from a foreign source.

To open an unknown file type, run or switch to any of your favorite programs (such as WordPad, Paint, or any of the Works 2000 tools). Click File | Open on the program's menu bar. In the "Files of type" drop-down pick list, select All Documents (this is sometimes referred to as All Files, or just plain All). Doing so exposes all the files available on your hard disk, including those your software can't work with.

But no matter. When you find the foreign file you want to import, simply right-click it.

On the context menu that appears, one of two options will appear: Open, or Open With. If the Open command appears, you're in luck. That means Windows 98 knows which program can be used to import and display the file. Click the Open command, and Windows 98 will launch the correct program, and open the file.

If the Open With command appears, you're out of luck. That means none of the programs installed in your computer are capable of opening the foreign file. In that case, click Cancel to close the Open dialog.

A simple summary

✓ The Windows 98 Start Menu is jam-packed with 100 or more programs, many of which are not worth learning.

✓ About nine of the Start Menu's 100 programs are worth learning right now, because they're the only ones you'll use regularly.

✓ Copy the big nine programs into your master personal folder for fast and easy access.

✓ Clicking View | Arrange Icons organizes your master personal folder when it's open.

✓ The Taskbar is your "cafeteria tray." It's the place you'll find and can switch among all of your in-use programs and data.

✓ To select data, lasso it by clicking your left mouse button, and dragging your mouse diagonally across the target data.

Chapter 11

Cranking Things Out

FROM GENERAL CORRESPONDENCE to appointment calendars, from POs and sales orders to inventory management, from flyers and advertisements to newsletters and org charts, what goes into a PC ultimately comes out again. Whether it's printed by a computer printer, faxed by a faxmodem or over the Net, or displayed on an overhead projector, knowing how to get things out of your PC is just as important as getting things in. In this chapter you'll learn the basics of outputting data in Windows 98. On deck first is output with a PC printer, which is how most of your data will find its way out of the PC. But I'll also cover the facts of faxing and the finer points of presentations.

In this chapter...

✓ Printer basics

✓ Fax me, fax you

✓ Up on the silver screen

✓ Piping out beautiful music

EXTRACTING INFORMATION FROM YOUR PC IS AS IMPORTANT AS PUTTING DATA IN

Printer basics

COMPUTER TECHNOLOGY *was supposed to usher in the paperless office, where documents and communications were exclusively digital and virtual. Instead, computers have had exactly the opposite effect.*

■ **The PaperCom Alliance**
(www.papercom.org) takes an interest in the future of paper communications.

Printers are popping up everywhere, prolifically pushing out paper at a promiscuous rate. The final tally isn't in, but according to the Information Technology Information Council, a computer industry vendor trade association, over 20 million computer printers will have shipped in 1999, nearly double the number shipped in 1992. And those 20 million new printers will join legions of other printers already in service. They'll be cranking out reams of paper, sales of which are also breaking records. According to The PaperCom Alliance, a paper industry advocacy group, paper shipments went from 87 million tons in 1990 to 96 million tons in 1995, and are climbing still.

Make no mistake about it: The paperless office is a myth of the information age. On the contrary, nearly everything that gets entered into a computer eventually ends up on some kind of printout. For you, that means printing is as important to the success of your day-to-day computing as is web surfing and e-mail. In fact, you could get away without ever surfing the web or sending e-mail.

But your PC is a worthless hulk if you don't know how to make it print. Thankfully, printing is one of Windows 98's easiest and most consistent tasks. It works the same way in literally every Windows program ever produced.

Master the printing process, and it's a skill you'll retain forever. First, close any open windows by clicking their Close button, or pressing Alt+F4 repeatedly. When you're back at the Windows Desktop, open up your master personal folder.

Printing a document

There are at least four programs in your master personal folder that create data you might want to print: Internet Explorer, your web browser; Outlook Express, your e-mail client; Paint, a graphics program; and WordPad, a text editor. Four completely different programs – all of which print in exactly the same way.

For example, to print a web page, run Internet Explorer by double-clicking it. If you're not online already, your auto-dialer will log you in. Once you're online, type this web address into the Address bar: www.nlford.com. That's the web site of Nancy Ford, an outstanding photojournalist with the *Observer-Dispatch* newspaper, in Utica, NY. Internet Explorer whisks you to Nancy's site, Photos@nlford.com, and renders the site's Home page.

There you'll find an abundance of hyperlinks that will take you to Nancy's original photographs and photo essays.

Click on any one of the links that catches your fancy. Up come the photos. Suppose for a moment, that you're awestruck by the first photo you see, and want to hang it on your computer room wall. Time to print! Here comes the tricky part. It's trickier than skydiving, trickier than tip-toeing through a mine field, and even trickier than explaining why your forgot your mom's birthday. Not!

Click the "Print" button on Internet Explorer's toolbar. That's all there is to it!

In darn near every Windows 98 program that you will ever encounter until time itself comes to an end, printing something you see on your screen is as easy as clicking the Print button. The printer will whir and the paper will feed, and in a few moments, you'll have a paper copy (also known as a "hard copy") of the web page on your screen. It's your very first printout, so hang it beside the picture frame that contains your first dollar.

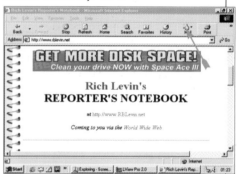

■ **No matter** *what program you're using, printing couldn't be easier. Just click the Print button.*

Generating multiple copies

Let's presume you love Nancy's photo so much, you want to print three more copies: one for your best friend, one for your worst enemy, and one for your neighbor. You could click the Print button three times, but that's kind of silly. When you need more fine-grained control over the printing process, use the active program's File | Print command instead. You'll always find this under the File command on the menu bar.

Click File, then Print, and the Print dialog appears. You'll see your printer's name in the Name box, along with a variety of printing options. Most, if not all, will be self-evident. For instance, in the "Copies" frame, you can tell Windows 98 how many copies to print. Try that now. Click in the "Number of copies" spinbox, and type the number "3" (or click the spinbox's up arrowhead). Then click the OK button. Once again, the printer springs to life, this time kicking out three identical copies of Nancy's web photo.

Setting a print range

It's conceivable that, one day, you'll need even more control over the print process. What if you print a web page, and the output you're after appears on the third of five pages? There's certainly no need to waste four pages to gain one.

■ **Click File** | *Page Setup to select Portrait orientation.*

Click File | Print, and in the "Print range" frame, you'll notice two options: "All" and "Pages from/to." You can set any logical print range by entering the first and last page numbers in the "Pages from/to" input boxes. For example, the print range can be "1" to "2," or "3" to "8." If you want to print a specific page, enter its page number in both boxes. To print page one, enter "1" to "1." To print page 3, enter "3" to "3."

Give it a shot. Enter "1" to "1" in the print range frame, and click OK. Your printer comes to life, and spits out page one. Of course, you can combine various settings on the Print dialog for additional chores. If you needed three copies of page one, enter a "3" in the "Number of copies" spinbox, enter "1" to "1" in the print range frame, and click the OK button.

Portrait or landscape?

Occasionally the information you want to print won't fit on a standard 8.5-by-11-inch letter-sized sheet of paper. You might encounter this issue if you're working with an oversized accounting table, or creating legal size (8.5-by-14-inch) or other specially sized documents. Fear not, oh printing guru! Just as every Windows 98 program features a print button and a File | Print command, just about all offer a File | Page Setup option. Click File | Page Setup, and you'll see an assortment of delectable adjustments you can apply.

■ **Use lanscape layout** *to print a landscape-orientated picture.*

The options vary with each program, but most offer at a minimum page orientation – portrait (vertical) or landscape (horizontal)– paper size, and margin settings. For all practical purposes, you'll nearly always find the adjustments you're looking for in the Page Setup dialog.

In the rare event a program doesn't offer a File | Page Setup option, there's a failsafe: You can always directly manipulate your printer's properties.

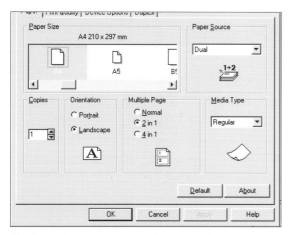

■ **The printer** *settings can be accessed in various ways. Click on File and then Print to make adjustments via the Properties panel.*

Click Cancel to close the Page Setup dialog, and click File | Print to reopen the Print dialog. Click the Properties button beside your printer's name. The printer Properties dialog appears, and it usually offers many of the same adjustments found on the Page Setup dialog. (You can also get to your printer's properties by clicking the Start button on the Taskbar, and then clicking Settings | Printers. Right-click the printer's icon, select Properties, and you're in.)

Again, the adjustments you can make vary by printer brand and model, but you'll almost always find page orientation and paper size calibrations in the Printer Properties dialog. This is also where to go for color output adjustments, or to take advantage of any special features unique to your printer. To illustrate how printing is consistent across Windows 98 programs, return to your master personal folder, and open up Outlook Express by double-clicking on it. Click on any one of the messages in your Inbox, Sent Items, or Deleted Items folders. The moment you do so, the Print button appears on Outlook Express' toolbar. You can click it to print the e-mail message. Similarly, you can click File | Print to kick out multiple copies.

Jump back to your master personal folder, and open up WordPad. Type in some text, and then click the Print button (it's a bit smaller in WordPad than it is in Outlook Express and Internet Explorer, but it's there nonetheless.) Here, too, you can also click File | Print to generate printouts in WordPad. If you're up to it, try the same steps with Paint or any other program.

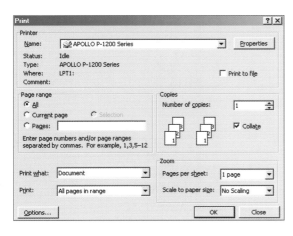

■ **The File | Print** *dialog is common to many Windows 98 applications.*

The point is, wherever you go, whatever you do, if it's a Windows 98 program, just click the Print button or File | Print to print.

Fax me, fax you

THERE ARE FOUR REASONS why people print data on their PC printer: To read it off-line, to frame it and put it on the wall, to file it for archival purposes, or to distribute it to someone else. Most of the time, reading, framing, filing, or distributing printouts doesn't require anything special in the way of PC hardware and software, beyond the PC and printer themselves. You just print the data, and do with it what you will.

All rules have exceptions, and printouts are, well, they're no exception. If the people who need your printouts aren't within arm's reach, you have to mail or fax them the paperwork. Obviously, I won't go into a tutorial on using the US Postal Service, FedEx, or UPS (although you can track your mailings over the web). But if you have a fax machine, that remains the best way to send facsimile documents to other locations.

If you need to send and receive faxes, but don't have a fax machine, consider buying one. Your PC is capable of sending and receiving faxes, but be forewarned: Desktop PC faxing is a creaky procedure that's guaranteed to drive you nuts. Virtually all PC fax software slows down your computer, often encounters trouble negotiating fax connections, regularly mangles incoming and outgoing documents, and can conflict with your online (web and e-mail) access.

■ **You can buy** *and print stamps online, for example at www.Stamps.com.*

If you must fax from your PC, consider web-based faxing. Faxing via the web is nearly 100 percent reliable, and it's largely free.

It doesn't require a phone line, doesn't incur long distance charges, doesn't slow down your PC, and doesn't conflict with your PC's modem. With web fax, outgoing faxes are transmitted by your PC to a web server somewhere in cyberspace, which handles the fax task for you. Inbound faxes show up in your Inbox as e-mail attachments, and can be viewed, printed, forwarded, or refaxed with ease.

I use CallWave for my inbound faxing, and Fax4Free for my outbound faxing. Although all three services support both inbound and outbound faxing. , I happen to prefer CallWave's inbound features, and Fax4Free's outbound features, which is why I use both services.

INTERNET

www.callwave.com

www.fax4free.com

www.efax.com

The best web-based fax services: Enter any one these web addresses into your browser, and follow the sign-up instructions on the site.

If you choose to ignore my impassioned warnings, and insist on using your PC's built-in fax software and modem to manage faxing, I am obliged by virtue of my publisher's ironclad contract to show you how. Here goes nothing. Number one, you have to install and enable the Microsoft Fax program in your PC. Microsoft Fax works in concert with Outlook Express. Once it's enabled, you'll receive faxes via the File | Print command.

■ **Sending a fax** *to or from CallWave's site (www.callwave.com) is like faxing to or from a standard fax machine.*

Setting up Microsoft Fax

Close any windows you have open on the screen by clicking their Close button. Jump into your master personal folder, and double-click the Control Panel icon (you can also get here by clicking Start | Settings | Control Panel). In the Control Panel folder, double-click the Mail icon. When the Mail dialog opens, click the Add button to start the Inbox Setup Wizard. When the Wizard opens, two checkboxes will be checked in the "Use the following information services" list box.

Uncheck (remove) the Microsoft Mail checkbox, and leave the Microsoft Fax checkbox checked (selected). When you have confirmed that only the Microsoft Fax checkbox is checked, click the Next button. The Inbox Setup Wizard will appear, asking you to select a fax modem. Your default modem should be selected. If it's not, click on it to select it, and then click Next. The Wizard will now ask if you want Microsoft fax to answer every call.

If you want auto-answering turned on, click the Yes radio button, and enter (or select) a ring count in the "Answer after [X] rings" drop-down list. Ideally, you should set this to answer on the first ring. If you're sharing the phone line with a telephone or answering machine, select the No radio button.

When the phone rings, if you pick it up and hear a fax machine, Microsoft Fax will display a button on the screen that allows you to route the call to the faxmodem.

When you're done, click Next. The Inbox Setup Wizard will give you an opportunity to enter whatever personal information you'd like to appear on the "headers" of faxes you send. (Headers are the first line of information that appears in a fax's margins.) Enter whatever info you want to appear on the fax header (such as your name or company name), and click Next. With that, the Wizard will ask you to confirm the location of your personal Address Book.

Don't change this setting; it's preselected to feature your Outlook Express Address Book.

Accept the suggested setting by clicking Next. Now the Wizard will ask you to confirm the location of your personal folders. Once again, don't touch this setting; it's preselected to feature your Outlook Express Inbox. Click Next to accept it. Finally, the Inbox Setup Wizard will confirm Microsoft Fax has been properly installed. Click Finish to exit the Wizard. After the Wizard exits, close the Mail dialog, close Control Panel, and return to your master personal folder.

■ **After you've typed** *a fax, sending it is almost as easy as printing.*

Sending a fax

With all the pieces in place, sending a fax is almost as easy as printing. Fire up WordPad, or any other print-savvy program in your master personal folder (Internet Explorer, Outlook Express, or Paint). On the program's menu bar, click File | Print. In the Printer frame in the Print dialog, click on the Name drop-down pick list, and select Microsoft Fax. This neat little switch tells Windows 98 to print using the fax software, and not the printer.

However, make sure to reset the printer Name drop-down pick-list back to specify your printer, and not Microsoft Fax, for when you next want to use File | Print. Otherwise, your computer will think you want to send another fax.

After selecting Microsoft Fax, click OK, and the Compose New Fax wizard appears. This will happen every time you send a fax using the File | Print command (so get used to it). Click the checkbox beside the "I'm not using a portable computer" (even if you are). This makes the Compose New Fax wizard skip an annoying dialing properties question when it starts again in the future. Click Next, and the address panel of the Compose New Fax wizard comes into view.

You can either enter the recipient's information manually, or you can pull up a fax name and number from your Outlook Express Address Book. To address the fax manually, enter the recipient's name in the "To:" input box. Then enter the fax number in the "Fax #:" input boxes, and click the "Add to List" button. If you want the area code dialed, make sure the "Dial area code" checkbox is checked before you click the "Add to List" button.

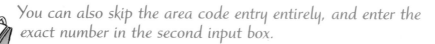

You can also skip the area code entry entirely, and enter the exact number in the second input box.

To wit: My fax number is 1-559-991-8114. Some folks find it easier to enter the entire number – in this case, 1-559-991-8114 – into the second input box, and always leave the area code box blank. When you're entering a lot of fax numbers, skipping the extra step can add up to big time savings.

You can send the fax to as many people as you like by entering their names and fax numbers individually, checking or unchecking the "Dial area code" checkbox, and clicking the "Add to List" button.

Using the Address Book with faxes

Obviously, addressing faxes this way can quickly become tedious. A better solution is to use your Outlook Express address book. Click the Address Book button to open the Address Book dialog. Click the New button to add a new fax address, and the New Entry dialog appears. In the "Select the entry type:" list box, click on "Fax," then click OK. This opens the New Fax Properties dialog.

In the "Name to show on cover page" input box, type in the recipient's name. In the "Area code and fax number:" input boxes, plug in the recipient's fax address. When you're done, don't click OK.

Click the "To:" button on the bottom left of the dialog. This adds the recipient to you fax list. After that, click OK to add the person to your Address Book. Doing so returns you to the Compose New Fax wizard. Regardless of which technique you use to address your faxes, clicking Next brings you to cover page options.

■ **You can send** *one fax to one person or a hundred, all at the same time.*

BROADCASTING FAXES

If you want to create groups of names that you can "broadcast" a fax to, simply create Address Book groups as shown in Chapter 9 in the "Creating an e-mail mailing list" section. Then address your faxes to the group, instead of to an individual.

Including a cover page

If you want to include a cover page with your fax, select the Yes radio button, and click on one of the pre-fab cover pages in the list box. Then click Next. Type a fax topic in the "Subject:" input box that appears. You can also type any comments you want to appear on the cover page by entering them in the "Notes:" input box. Click Next when you're done. Your fax is ready; click the Finish button to send it.

The Microsoft Fax Status window will pop up on the screen, and will display the fax's progress until the fax is completely sent. If you're using the telephone line, Microsoft Fax will postpone sending the fax until the line is clear. If you want to cancel the fax, click the Options command on the Microsoft Fax Status menu bar, then click Hang Up.

Receiving faxes

Receiving faxes is similar to receiving e-mail. As long as you have Outlook Express open and running, new faxes will arrive automatically as e-mail attachments in your Outlook Express Inbox.

Just open the new fax message, and double-click the attachment. In a heartbeat, you'll be reading the new fax online. To print it, click File | Print. Make sure your real printer is selected in the Printer Name drop-down pick list, and click OK. Remember, you can't receive faxes unless Outlook Express is open and running.

If you'd like Outlook Express to start automatically every time you start your computer, you can put a copy of your Outlook Express icon in Windows 98's StartUp folder.

Anything appearing in the StartUp folder is loaded automatically as soon as your PC turns on. Open your master personal folder, right-click Outlook Express, and select Copy. Next, click the Start button, then click Programs, and you'll see the StartUp folder on the list. Right-click the StartUp menu entry, and select Paste.

The Outlook Express icon will suddenly appear to the right of the StartUp folder's entry. That's your confirmation that it is now featured in the StartUp folder, and will load automagically every time you log on to Windows 98.

■ **Paste the** *Outlook Express shortcut into the StartUp folder in the Start menu and Outlook Express will automatically open when you start up your computer.*

Up on the silver screen

CRANKING DATA THROUGH your printer and sending out faxes through a modem are the most common means of getting info out of your PC, but they're not always the most effective paths. Sometimes you'll have to present data on transparencies, projectors, TVs, and other nonstandard displays. For this, a printer or faxmodem alone won't do. Your information will either have to be piped directly from your PC's video-out port into the presentation device or printed on transparencies (clear plastic sheets) for use with an old-fashioned overhead projector. (Yes, your plain old printer can render output directly on plastic transparencies, provided they're certified for use with ink-jet or laser printers.)

■ **Sometimes you** *might want to output data to a TV, it's easy to do.*

A better approach: Always consider your final output destination when developing a presentation, whether it's a straightforward letter or an intricate presentation production. For paper-based output, the sky is the limit. Small type. Big type. One column. Ten columns. Tiny pictures. Bold pictures. High contrast colors. Low contrast colors. With paper and its siblings (fax and e-mail), you're limited only by your skill and creativity. When targeting public or group presentations, however, keep both feet squarely on the ground. Use large, bold type faces. Apply as few colors as possible, and make sure they're complementary. Never use light text against a dark background. Always use dark text against a light background.

And make sure your finished product fits perfectly within the display area of your target output device.

Specialized tools

Often such presentation are prepared with specialized tools, such as Microsoft PowerPoint, Adobe PageMaker, or Corel Draw. But there's no reason for not using your ordinary word processor, spreadsheets, and databases to do the same thing. When preparing data to be presented on a device other than a printer or a fax, the software you use doesn't matter as much as how you use it. For printing, faxing, or e-mailing, you can use darn near any combination of texts and colors. Even if you decided to draft a letter using Day-Glo colors and teeny-weeny type faces, folks with poor vision would still be able to read it. They'd just have to clean their glasses and squint a little.

Tiny type and garish color

Try those same tiny type sizes and garish color combinations with an overhead transparency, projection, or TV image, and your presentation will be wholly unreadable. That's because your computer screen, printer, fax, and e-mail are high-resolution devices. They can show even the smallest details clearly and sharply, even when using horrendous color schemes. Transparencies, projectors, PC-to-TV feeds, and other nonstandard presentation schemes, on the other hand, are low-resolution devices. Small or thin types will be rendered as fuzzy, quivering blobs. Bad color combinations will make text and pictures impossible to read. And data formatted for 8.5-by-11-inch pages will *bleed* straight off the bottom of the display.

■ **This version** *may look good on screen, but the small fonts and light text on the dark background will make it hard to read from a distance.*

> **DEFINITION**
>
> *Professional printers have dubbed text or graphics that spill over into margins* bleeds.

A good rule of thumb is to assume the output device can clearly display 12-point text at no greater than 40 letters (columns) across, and 24 lines of text (rows) down. (In Chapter 13, you'll learn how to adjust point sizes.) Adhere to these basic rules of presentation output, and your presentations are sure to be crowd pleasers.

Piping out beautiful music

WHAT'S BLACK AND WHITE *and heard all over? If you said "music," you're right. It's the only form of computer data that can be sent to virtually any output device – including your speakers – and one of the few you can actually listen to. You can take a musical score and print it, fax it, e-mail attach it, or display it on your PC screen, overhead projector, or TV. But there's one thing you can do with a musical score that you can't do with other data: Listen to it. Which means you can use musical data to dress up personal and business presentations, to provide a soothing background while you work at the PC, or to kick back and relax after a long session in front of the computer screen.*

■ **Drop your favorite** *CD in the tray and crank up the volume.*

Playing music CDs

To play an audio CD on your computer all you have to do is press the Eject button on your CD-ROM or DVD drive, drop the audio CD onto the tray, and press the Eject button again. The drive loads the CD and, in seconds, Windows 98 starts playing it. You can adjust the output volume by double-clicking the little speaker icon on the Windows Taskbar. That opens the Master Out dialog. Drag the Master Volume and CD Volume slider controls up or down, to adjust the volume to your liking. Generally, it's best to crank the CD Volume slider all the way up, and control the output volume using the Master Volume control.

By the way, once you've pegged the CD Volume control at its highest setting, you won't have to change it again. Windows 98 will remember it. Close the Master Out dialog and, in the future, access the Master Volume by clicking the little speaker icon just once.

■ **Download the free** *version of Real Jukebox from proforma.real.com/real/jukebox/.*

Downloading real jukebox

It's also possible to record your audio CDs, and convert them into digital audio files that you can organize into music libraries for playback at any time.

The software for this is available free at www.real.com. (I'm sure this has been vetted, but in the copyeditors humble opinion, we're instructing the reader to violate copyright laws.) If you'd like to get it, hop on the Internet by switching into your master personal folder, and double-clicking Internet Explorer. In the Address bar, type in www.real.com, and click the Go button (or press Enter).

This takes you to the home page of Real Networks, the software company behind Real Jukebox, one of the best free CD recording tools available. Look carefully for a *Download* link on the home page. When you find it, click on it, and work your way to the "Download Real Jukebox" section of the web site. Real Networks will probably ask you to fill out a form that provides company marketers with your name, e-mail address, and other basic information. After that, the site will want you to select a server from which to download the Real Jukebox software.

DEFINITION

To Download *means to get data, to upload is to send data. When data is coming into your PC, it's being "downloaded." When you're sending data, you're "uploading."*

Real Jukebox Installer

Choose any domestic USA server by clicking on it. Internet Explorer's File Download dialog will appear. Click the radio button that reads "Run this program from its current location." When the download is complete, the Real Jukebox installer will launch. Accept the program's default settings by repeatedly clicking the Next button.

SAFE DOWN-LOADING

It's always safe to download and run software from "trusted" web sites, such as Microsoft, Apple, IBM, Real, and other major software companies. Never, ever, ever download or run programs from "untrusted" web sites run by companies you've never heard of.

When all of the default selections have been entered, complete the installation by clicking the Finish button. When the installer is done, it might ask if you would like to restart your PC. Click the Yes button if asked.

Using Real Jukebox

After Windows 98 restarts, you'll notice two small blue icons on your Taskbar. One is Real Player, which plays back audio and video you encounter on the Internet. The other is Real Jukebox, which plays back and records audio CDs. To start Real Jukebox, insert an audio CD into your CD-ROM or DVD drive. Real Jukebox will automatically open and start recording the CD.

When the recording is complete, Real Jukebox will prompt you to save it. You can replay the recording at any time, without having to insert your CD into the computer.

Simply double-click the Real Jukebox icon on your Taskbar, and then click File | Open on the menu bar. You'll find all of your recorded CDs listed there. Click on the CD recording you want to play, and click the Open button.

If you want to use Real Jukebox for automatic playback of CDs only, and not recording, that's doable, too. Just double-click the Real Jukebox icon on your Taskbar, and select Options | Preferences on Real Jukebox's menu bar. On the General tab, uncheck the "Start recording the CD" checkbox. Now, when you insert an audio CD into the computer, Real Jukebox will play it back, but won't record it automatically. Should you choose to record an audio CD, click Real Jukebox's red Record button on the toolbar to kick-start the process.

A simple summary

✓ Data that goes in must come out. And come out it does, via the Windows 98 Print command.

✓ You can print whatever appears on your screen using any Windows 98 program by clicking the Print button on the toolbar.

✓ The toolbar's Print button generates one printout per click.

✓ The File | Print command provides more control over printouts, enabling you to print multiple copies, specific pages, a range of pages, set margins, change paper size, switch page orientation, and more.

✓ PC faxing is far from perfect. It slows down your PC, causes crashes, and often flat-out doesn't work right. The best way to fax a document you created in your PC: Buy a cheap fax machine.

✓ If you don't want to buy a fax machine, free web-based faxing services remain your next best option for fax send and receive.

✓ If you insist on using your PC to send and receive faxes, you have to first set up Microsoft Fax.

✓ To receive faxes on your PC using Microsoft Fax, Outlook Express must be running at all times.

✓ The Outlook Express Address Book is the place where your Microsoft Fax names and phone numbers are stored.

✓ What looks good on your PC screen, printouts, and faxes can look terrible when displayed on overhead transparencies, projectors, and TVs. Always consider how your data will be displayed when formatting it for a presentation. Large type and conservative color combinations work best when using transparencies, projectors, and TVs.

✓ Your PC is also a CD player, and it can record, too.

✓ Install Real Networks' Real Jukebox to record audio CDs.

PART THREE

WELCOME TO PRODUCTIVITY CITY

NOW THAT you're online and successfully keeping up with the www.Joneses.com, it's time to tap your PC's full potential. In Part III, I'll show you how to lever the *richness* of the Internet with the power of your PC. That goal is made *easier* by Windows 98, which is the first computing platform that aims to seamlessly integrate the Internet and PC worlds.

First, I'll help prepare you and your Windows 98 environment for a fast and busy business workday. Then I'll delve deep into the world's most *popular* desktop software categories: word processing, spreadsheets, database, and calendar.

Chapter 12

Getting Down to Business

THE AVERAGE American's PC focused on word processing, accounting, database management, desktop publishing, and games. Then came the World Wide Web. Attracted like moths to a porch light, the public flocked to this newfangled communications medium. Online use skyrocketed from five million users in 1995 to 120 million by January 2000, according to market researcher NetRatings. And there's no end in sight. Five years ago, few people knew what e-mail was, the Web was a novelty, and only business users and enthusiasts could justify a hefty PC investment. Today, people are lining up like lemmings to buy PCs and cannot wait to get online.

In this chapter...

✓ Fast access to favorite apps

✓ Secrets of the "Win" key

✓ Common commands

✓ Meet the Lincoln Log

THE WEB IS WONDERFUL, BUT YOUR PC CAN DO MUCH MORE

Fast access to favorite apps

IT ALL COMES *to a grinding halt when you have to use your PC. Consider this scenario: You have to quickly create a presentation built with a spreadsheet, an accounting program, a word processor, various collected e-mails, web research, a graphics tool, and the presentation software itself. You also need to pull data from a* mainframe *terminal window. One way to do this is to activate each program by clicking the Start button, then traversing the entire Start Menu until you locate the various software titles you need. Let's see – you'd need to do that at least eight times, once for each program.*

> ### DEFINITION
>
> *Personal computers kicked the old-fashioned* mainframe *computer terminal off the office desktop, but they didn't muscle the mainframe out of the corporate computer room (a-k-a the data center). Instead of terminals, most companies now use software that makes their mainframe think the powerful desktop PCs are really just dumb terminals. PC software allows information displayed on the terminal software to be cut+pasted into PC software.*

Or you could create icons for all eight programs in your master personal folder – but you'd still have to double-click the first one, wait for it to load, minimize it, double-click the next one, minimize it, and so on, and so on . . . until all eight are loaded. After they're loaded, you could switch among them by grabbing the mouse, and clicking their buttons on the Windows Taskbar.

Or, try cycling through the programs until you find the one you want, using Windows 98's "task switching," or shortcut, keys.

Windows' magic shortcut keys

What if you could load or switch among programs and open documents simply by pressing a key? Better yet, what if you could automate your program switching without spending a penny, without having to install special software, and without programming? Imagine this: You press F3, and your word processor pops up. Hit F11, and there's your e-mail program. Ding F8, and your web browser appears, ready for surfing. Tap F5, and you're tapped into the mainframe.

No Start Menu . . . no Desktop shortcuts . . . no Taskbar buttons. And no finger-crossing magic keyboard combinations required. It's all made possible by one of Windows 98's least known, most powerful features: Shortcut keys. With shortcut keys, loading and moving between programs becomes "keystroke easy." But there is a catch: Windows 98 shortcut keys only work with icons that appear on the Desktop or the Start Menu. That means you can add a shortcut key to your master personal folder, because it

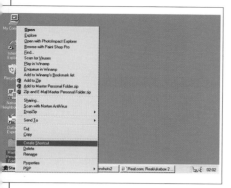

presently resides on the Windows 98 Desktop. But to activate any of the icons that reside inside your master personal folder, you'll first have to relocate the folder to the Start Menu. Here's how to do it.

Moving your master personal folder

Right-click on *your master personal folder and select Create Shortcut.*

Remember that this procedure is optional. If you don't desire one-key access to your most-used programs and data files, you can skip this exercise and move on to the next section.

You can also choose to enable shortcut key support at a later date. But if you, like me, want to gain a productivity boost from shortcut keys, start by clicking the Close button on any open window. Then right-click your master personal folder, and select Create Shortcut. This creates an *alias* (or a shortcut, in Microsoft-speak) of your master personal folder on the Desktop.

You'll see why the shortcut is required in a moment, Next, right-click your master personal folder again, and this time select Cut, not Copy. Now click the Start button, then click Programs. With the Programs submenu open, right-click (that's a right-click, not a click) the item named "StartUp." Select Paste. Your master personal folder disappears from the Desktop, and reappears as a submenu of the StartUp submenu. If you click Start | Programs | StartUp, you'll see your master personal folder, and its contents, now integrated into the Start Menu Notice that the shortcut you created to the master personal folder remains on the Desktop.

> **DEFINITION**
>
> *An alias or a shortcut is literally a mirror image of the original. Changes made to the original are reflected in the shortcut, and vice versa.*

Essentially, you now have two images of your master personal folder: The original, which now resides in the Start Menu's StartUp submenu (to enable the power of shortcut keys); and its alias, which conveniently appears on the Desktop (an easy way to click into your master personal folder).

Moving your master folder from the Windows Desktop to the StartUp submenu on the Start Menu enables shortcut key support, and means that your master folder will automatically open whenever you turn your PC on.

As well as being able to open your master personal folder by clicking its new Desktop alias or pressing its hot key, you can now get to it by clicking Start | Programs | StartUp.

Assigning shortcut keys to program icons

On to setting up some shortcut keys. First, close any open windows by clicking their Close buttons. Then open your master personal folder by double-clicking its Desktop icon, or pressing the hot key you defined for it earlier (if you did so). Remember, your master folder will eventually house icons for literally all your important stuff. Right

now, there are icons in it for at least five programs you'll use regularly: Calculator, Internet Explorer, Outlook Express, Paint, and WordPad. To assign a shortcut key to Internet Explorer, right-click the Internet Explorer icon. This brings up the icon's context menu. Click the Properties command, and then click inside the "Shortcut key" input box. Now press the key or key combination you want to use to load or switch to Internet Explorer. If you press the F8 key, "F8" will appear in the "Shortcut key" input box. Almost any key or key combination can be used, including the letter keys, number keys, arrow keys, function keys, Shift, Ctrl, Alt, and Backspace keys, and so on.

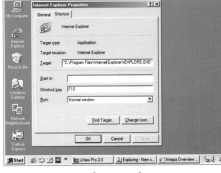

■ **Assigning a shortcut** *key to Internet Explorer.*

For example, you can use F8, Ctrl+F8, Ctrl+Alt+I, Shift+Ctrl+I, Shift+Ctrl+Alt+I … the possibilities are too numerous to mention. But as long as the keyboard combination you enter isn't in use by another icon, it will be accepted by the "Shortcut key" input box.

When you're satisfied with your key or key combination, click the "Run" drop-down pick list, and select one of the options. "Normal" runs the program in a window. "Maximized" expands the program window to fill the entire screen. "Minimized" loads the program as a button on the Taskbar. Experienced users prefer the "Maximized" setting. When you're done, click the OK button. Now press the key or key combination you setup for the icon. Voila! The program immediately pops-up on your screen. Whenever you press that shortcut key or key combination, the program will load and run.

Better still, if the program is already loaded, Windows 98 will switch to it, and make it the foreground application.

Adding shortcut keys to document icons

If you want to open a document instead of launching a program, you need to create a shortcut icon for the document, put the icon in your master personal folder, and assign a shortcut key. For example, suppose you composed a form letter in WordPad that you plan to use repeatedly. You would first save it in your master personal folder using WordPad's Save As command. When the Save As dialog opens, click the little green and white Desktop icon on the Save As dialog's toolbar. Then double-click the shortcut to your master personal folder. Finally, give the document a file name by typing it in the "File name" input box.

Sometimes the green-and-white Desktop button doesn't show up on the Save or Open dialogs. Not to worry. There are two buttons with beige folder icons on them. One has an up-arrow icon on it; the other has a *sparkling folder* icon. Slowly and repeatedly click the up-arrow folder button until your Desktop appears in the dialog window. You'll know you arrived at the Desktop because the word "Desktop" will appear in the dialog's drop-down pick list. Alternatively, click its up-arrow button until you arrive at the "Desktop" entry.

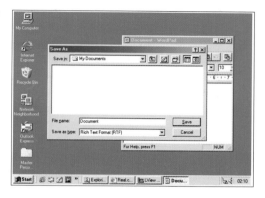

■ **Saving a WordPad** *document using File | Save As.*

Click OK, and the file is saved to your master personal folder. It's now ready to have a shortcut icon created, and a shortcut key assigned. Jump into your master personal folder by double-clicking its Desktop icon, or hitting its hot key. Right-click the WordPad document you just created, and select Create Shortcut. That brings up the icon's context menu. Click on the Properties command, click inside the "Shortcut key" input box. Press the key or key combo to open and switch to the document.

Set the document's Run state from the "Run" drop-down pick list. Click OK, and the shortcut key is ready for action.

Secrets of the "Win" key

BACK IN THE BAD *old days, getting started with a computer literally meant learning another language: Computerese. To get the computer to do anything, you had to spend months learning how to talk to it. For example, to open a directory named "MyStuff" on the C: drive, you would have to type this command: CHDIR C:\MyStuff, with CHDIR standing for CHange DIRectory.*

Naming drives

Every disk drive in your computer is labeled with a letter. Your floppy drive is referred to as "Drive A." If you had a second floppy drive, it would be called "Drive B." The main hard drive in your system is always called "Drive C." Additional drives, be they hard drives, CD-ROMs, DVDs, or any other type, are lettered D to Z.

The drive letters are helpful for users who wish to open files and programs the old-fashioned way: By entering computerese. For example, you can open the Windows Calculator by clicking Start | Run, typing C:\Windows\Calc.EXE, and then pressing Enter. This tells the computer to look on the C drive, in the Windows folder, for a document or program named Calc.EXE. When entering computerese, a colon (:) always follows the drive letter, and backslashes (\) always separate items.

The problem with this archaic approach is that it requires users to know and memorize the drive letter and folder path to files and programs. It's also crazy to be typing C:\My Documents \Taxes\ Year1999\ Document.TXT, when a few mouse clicks will do.

Graphical user interfaces

So there once was a lot of typing for what today requires a double-click. There were hundreds of these arcane commands tucked away in PCs. Computer magazines, publishers, and consultants based an entire cottage industry on creating and documenting computerese. Today, thanks to the Macintosh and Windows, almost anyone can sit down at a computer and become productive within minutes. Instead of having to learn computerese, users point and click their way around computers' *Graphical User Interfaces*. But that doesn't mean modern PCs aren't replete with hidden commands. Some are carry-overs from the computerese era. Others are as simple as an undocumented keyboard combination that ignites a Windows 98 feature. One of the best examples of an undocumented Windows 98 feature is sitting right in front of you. Every modern PC today includes a Windows 98 logo key (a-k-a the "Win" key) on the keyboard. It's the one wedged between the Ctrl and Alt keys on either side of the keyboard. Pressing the Win key brings up the Windows 98 Start Menu, but the key also harbors some secret computing powers.

DEFINITION

The term Graphical User Interfaces, *or "GUIs" (pronounced "gooeys"), refers to a computer's ability to communicate with users by way of pictures, such as icons, instead of text-based commands*

■ **You can still** *open a program the old-fashioned way by selecting Run from the Start Menu.*

Managing Windows with the Win key

To see what else the Win key can do, first close any open window by clicking its Close button. Open your master personal folder by double-clicking it, or hitting its hot key. Once the folder is open, double-click a few program icons, such as Calculator, Paint, and WordPad (or hit their hot keys). Your Windows Desktop will now be quite cluttered. But no matter how many windows are on the screen, pressing Win+D flips you back instantly to the Windows Desktop. In fact, from here on in, I won't ask you to close all open windows by clicking their Close buttons. Instead, I'll ask you to hit Win+D to return to the Desktop – because it's the better way! Pressing Win+D again returns you to the last program you were working on.

Finding files and running programs with the Win key

Need to find a file? Press Win+F, and Windows 98's Find Files dialog steps up for service. Punch in some or all of the file name or text you're looking for, click the Find Now button, and Windows 98 will scour your hard disk for what you're after.

Business users take note: If you need to find a computer on the company LAN, try Win+Ctrl+F. Type in the computer's name, click Find Now, and Windows 98 will present any matching systems connected to the company LAN.

You can even navigate buttons on the Windows Taskbar using nothing more than your keyboard. Use Win+Tab to cycle through any visible Taskbar buttons. When the button you want to use is depressed, press Enter to activate it.

WIN KEY COMBINATIONS

Win	Pops up the Windows 98 Start Menu
Win+D	Returns you to the Windows Desktop
Win+D again	Returns you to the last program you were working with
Win+E	Opens the Windows 98 Explorer
Win+F	Opens Windows 98's Find File dialog
Win+Ctrl+F	Opens Windows 98's Find Computer dialog
Win+M	Minimizes all open windows
Win+Shift+M	Restores all minimized windows
Win+Tab	Cycles through Taskbar buttons (press Enter to select a button)
Win+Shift+Tab	Cycles through Taskbar buttons . . . backwards!
Win+Break	Displays the System Properties dialog (for advanced users)

Common commands

"WIN" KEY COMBINATIONS aren't the only speed keys you can use with your PC. Quite the contrary. Windows 98 is jam-packed with keystrokes, dubbed "alternate" keys, designed to keep your hands on the keyboard, and off the mouse.

Which raises the question of why you'd want to stay off the mouse in the first place. When it comes to pointing and clicking, dragging and dropping, manipulating on-screen objects, drawing, and lassoing the mouse is the ideal device. It's also far easier to get new users up to speed with the mouse's point+click approach. But for certain jobs, frankly, the mouse stinks.

When it comes to the most common computing tasks — navigating menus, zooming windows, switching programs, printing documents, and so on — the keyboard can dramatically accelerate your productiviy.

That is, if you're willing to invest the time to discover and memorize the various keyboard commands. Fortunately, Microsoft makes it easy for savvy Windows users to figure out a program's alternate keys.

Exposing the Alt keys

First, hide all open windows by pressing the Win+D hot key. Back at the Windows Desktop, open your master personal folder by double-clicking it or hitting its hot key. Next, double-click either Paint or WordPad. Take a good look at the menu bar. Notice anything unusual? Each command has one letter underlined. File has the letter "F" underlined. Edit has "E," View has "V," and Help has "H" underlined.

■ **Any menu** *command with a letter underlined can be activated using the Alt key.*

The highlighted letters are your alternate keys (or "Alt" keys for short). Now that you know how to identify your Alt keys, how in tarnation do they work? A simple question with a simple answer. Turn your gaze to your keyboard. There, beside your Win key, and bracketing your Space Bar, are not one, but two keys labeled "Alt." They're your "alternate" power keys. Used in conjunction with any underlined command letter, the Alt keys can activate menus, buttons, pick-lists, list boxes, spin boxes, and just about any other on-screen control Windows 98 serves up. Use your left thumb to depress the left Alt key. With the Alt key held down, press the letter "F." The File menu drops down. To close the File menu, hit the Esc key (that's the topmost key on your keyboard, located at the upper left-hand corner). Now try Alt+E, and the Edit menu drops down. Hit Esc to close. Take a moment to try all of the Alt key commands you can see on the foreground window's menu bar. Hit Esc to close them.

Using Alt keys for more than menus

The Alt key is good for more than just accessing top-level menus. You can also use it to navigate throughout a program or process. Here's an example of how to do it: First, use your mouse to make WordPad the foreground app by clicking WordPad's button on the Taskbar. If WordPad isn't featured on the Taskbar, hide all open windows by pressing the Win+D hot key. Open your master personal folder by double-clicking it, or hitting its hot key. Then double-click WordPad. Click anywhere inside WordPad's document window (that's the main blank white area), and type in some dummy text, such as "The quick brown fox jumped over the lazy dog." Now press and hold the Alt key, and tap the letter "F." The File menu opens. Keeping the Alt key depressed (or just press it again), strike the letter "P." The Print dialog opens. Notice that all of the options on the Print dialog have letters underlined. Try this test: Press and hold the Alt key, and then press N, A, G, and S. Notice the dialog's focus switches to a different option every time. Now press Alt+P, and the Properties button gets pressed, exposing the Properties dialog.Hit Esc repeatedly to close both dialogs. As you can see, simply pressing and holding Alt, followed by an underlined command letter, allows you to navigate through any Windows 98 screen, without ever touching the mouse.

Switching between open windows with Alt

Most alternate keystrokes available in Windows 98 are obvious, thanks to the fact their command letters are underlined on screen. But a considerable number of alternate commands don't appear on any menus. Windows 98's "Task Switch" alternate keystroke is a perfect example. When you're composing a document with clippings from e-mail, the web, and other programs, it would be nice to switch among them using the keyboard. You can, thanks to the "task switch" Alt key. Press the Alt key with your left thumb and keep holding it down while you tap the Tab key with your left middle finger. Still holding the Alt key down, tap Tab again. And again. And again. As long as the Alt key is held down, Windows 98 displays the Task Switch menu every time you press Tab, cycling through a list of icons that reflect every open file or program window. You'll see the name of the selected window at the bottom of the Task Switch menu. When the focus (the square blue box) surrounds the program or file icon you want to switch to, release the Alt key. Windows 98 will switch to that window. Practice switching between windows using Alt+Tab now.

Remember to hold down the Alt key the entire time, as you hit the Tab key to cycle through the Task Switch menu list. Release the Alt key to switch to a selected window.

Alternatives to the Alt Key

Now that you have the hang of the Alt key, it's a good opportunity to show you other alternate key combinations. Documenting them all is a book in itself; there are literally thousands embedded into Windows 98. Thankfully, the most useful alternate keys fit quite nicely within the confines of these pages. Others are actually documented on the menus, alongside their underlined alternate key counterparts. For all practical purposes, what follows is as complete a guide as you'll need to Windows 98's alternate keys. Combining the keystrokes in the order noted will result in the stated action. The best way to approach this lengthy list is to circle those keystrokes that strike your fancy, and practice using them regularly. When a keystroke combo, such as Alt+Tab, becomes second nature, it's time to tackle a few more. Remember, there's no law that says you have to memorize these alternate keystrokes, or even use them. If you're happy using the mouse for your man/machine interaction, by all means, do so.

KEY ACTIONS

- **F1** Launches the Help system. Press F1 whenever you're confused about something.
- **Shift+F1** Displays help text about the item which has the focus.
- **F2** Renames the selected item.
- **F3** Displays the Find Files dialog.
- **F4** Displays the drop-down pick list box on any Explorer or Internet Explorer toolbar. Press F4 again to close the pick list.
- **Alt+F** Closes the active program window.
- **F6** Switches between open panes within a document window.
- **Ctrl+F6** Switches to next open document in the foreground program window.
- **F8** Selects the current item. Press F8 to select adjacent items. Each press of F8 expands the selection's scope.
- **F10** Switches the focus to the foreground window's menu bar.
- **Shift+F10** Like right-clicking an object.

- **Shortcut key** (located between Win and Ctrl keys) Same as Shift+F10.
- **Esc** Cancels the current action.
- **Ctrl+Esc** Displays the Start Menu.
- **Ctrl+Alt+Del** Displays the Close Program dialog. Press this keyboard combination twice if your computer "freezes." Doing so will restart Windows 98.
- **Ctrl+N** Creates a new document.
- **Ctrl+O** Displays the File+Open dialog.
- **Ctrl+P** Displays the File+Print dialog.
- **Ctrl+S** Saves the current file to disk.
- **Ctrl+A** Selects all of the text in a document.
- **Ctrl+C** Copies the selected item.
- **Ctrl+X** Cuts the selected item.
- **Ctrl+V** Pastes the selected item.
- **Ctrl+F** Displays the Find text dialog within programs.
- **Ctrl+H** Displays the Search & Replace text dialog within programs.
- **Ctrl+Z** The "Undo" key. In programs that support it, will reverse (undo) the last action.

- **Ctrl+Y** The "Redo" key. The inverse of Undo. In programs that support it, will reverse (undo) the last undo (confusing, isn't it?).
- **Alt+Shift+Backspace** Same as Ctrl+Y.
- **Ctrl+F4** Closes the active document window.
- **Alt+Space Bar** Displays the program menu for the active window.
- **Alt+Hyphen** Same as Alt+Space Bar
- **Alt+Tab** Switches to the last-used program. If the Alt key is held down, displays the Task Switch menu.
- **Alt+Esc** Switches to the next open program among all open programs.
- **F10 or Alt** Switches the focus to the foreground window's menu bar. Press F10 or Alt again to take the focus off the menu bar.
- **Arrow keys** Allow you to navigate a menu bar. First press F10 or Alt, then use the arrow keys to move the focus. Press Enter to activate the command. When using the arrow keys to navigate menus, you can also press the command's alternate key, without having to use the Alt key.
- **Enter** Activates the selected command.
- **Tab** Moves the focus to the next object or on-screen item.
- **PageUp & PageDown** Scrolls the display up or down one full page at a time.
- **Home & End** Moves the focus or cursor to the beginning (Home) or end (End) of a line.
- **Delete** Moves the selected item to the Recycle Bin.
- **Shift+Delete** Deletes the selected item permanently.

- **Alt+Enter** Displays the selected item's properties dialog.
- **Print Screen (or PrtScr)** Captures the screen to the Windows Clipboard. To save or print the screen capture, load Paint, and select Edit + Paste. Then save the image using File+Save, or print it using File+Print.
- **Alt+Print Screen (or Alt+PrtScr)** Captures the foreground window to the Windows Clipboard. To save or print the window capture, load Paint, and select Edit + Paste. Then save the image using File+Save, or print it using File+Print.
- **Backspace** When surfing the web, the same as clicking the Back button in Internet Explorer.
- **Alt+Left Arrow** When surfing the web, the same as clicking the Back button in Internet Explorer.
- **Alt+Right Arrow** When surfing the web, the same as clicking the Forward button in Internet Explorer.
- **Ctrl+D** When surfing the web, bookmarks the current web page.
- **Alt+Home** When surfing the web, jumps back to your Home page.
- **F5** When surfing the web, reloads the current web page.
- **F11** When surfing the web, toggles the screen between full-screen and normal modes.

■ **Shift+Delete** *sends the selected item to the Recycle Bin.*

Meet the Lincoln Log

NEW YACHT or old tug, aircraft carrier or outboard, when a captain first takes a vessel's command, the chief order of business is to embark on a shakedown cruise. It's during this inaugural journey that captain and crew assess a ship's components and document any problems. Home and car buyers do the same thing. Those first few months in a new home or car are the shakedown cruise. You're noting any problems, compiling your punch list and, ultimately, working with the builder, realtor, or dealer to resolve any warranted items.

In the world of computing, your shakedown cruise never ends. To get the most from your Windows 98 PC, it's wise to keep a pen and notepad at the ready.

Jot down any error messages, odd behaviors, bugs, or other problems you encounter. This process is known as "maintaining a User Log." Over time, your User Log will prove to be an indispensable aid in troubleshooting and resolving technical problems, and in fleshing out your next round of application requirements.

No matter how diligent you were in compiling your initial application requirements list, there were certain requirements you missed. You don't know what these requirements are, because you're just now starting to use your computer. Over time, you'll discover certain shortcomings in programs. Unless you keep track of these shortcomings, you won't be able to recall them all when the time comes to upgrade your computer's capabilities (and it will come sooner than you think).

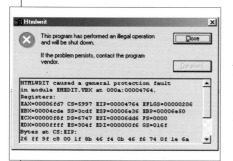

■ An "illegal operation" *message probably means that a program has crashed.*

For example, perhaps you discover a need to print banners, and it turns out your word processor doesn't support such a feature. Jot it down: "Requirement: Need to print banners!" Or let's say you're working happily, when the screen suddenly turns blue, and a message appears saying, "Windows has given up the ghost. Error #4,098,185 in file FUBAR.VXD in System32. Bang your head on the wall, then press any key to close Windows and reboot."

Jot down the date the problem occurred and the error message: "Windows has given up the ghost. Error #4,098,185 in file FUBAR.VXD in System32. Bang your head on the wall, then press any key to close

Windows and reboot." If the error doesn't recur, great. If it does, you're armed with the critical information a tech support guru will need to quickly troubleshoot your problem. Also, error messages that occurred weeks ago can sometimes help solve a later problem.

You'll be in good shape either way, because your User Log will have a record of every negative event that occurred during your computing hours. So before you click another click or enter another keystroke, grab a pen and notebook and inaugurate your User Log. It will turn out to be one of the simplest, yet most powerful weapons in your computing arsenal.

A simple summary

✔ Computers are good for a lot more than mere web surfing.

✔ Compared to clicking icons and menus, Windows Shortcut keys (also known as hot keys) are a faster and more convenient means to load and switch between programs.

✔ You can add a Windows Shortcut key to any icon that appears on the Windows Desktop or Start Menu.

✔ The secret "Win" key combinations can be used to quickly zoom back to the Windows Desktop, Minimize and Maximize windows, and streamline many other useful functions.

✔ Every program can be controlled using Alt key commands. Simply press and hold the Alt key in combination with any on-screen command that features an underlined letter.

✔ Alt+Tab is used to rapidly switch between open programs.

✔ There are hundreds of other keyboard commands that can be used in place of pointing and clicking.

✔ Boning up on your keyboard commands is important preparation for serious work, but keeping a log of your keyboard activity is even more important. Anytime you encounter a stumbling block, jot it down.

Chapter 13

Wonderful Word Processing

T HERE'S NO BETTER way to start your Windows 98 workout than by running through the major types of productivity apps you're sure to use. No matter how specialized your application requirements are, practically everyone uses a core set of common tools – word processing, spreadsheets, databases, and calendars. Every major application suite features them, and they all work the same way. The exercises in this chapter assume you're using Microsoft Works 2000 suite, the most popular package among new users.

In this chapter...

✓ Wrangling with words

✓ Composing a Word document

✓ Polishing your document

✓ Saving and printing

Wrangling with words

WORD PROCESSING WAS *one of the original killer apps. It remains so today, surpassed in popularity and importance only by web surfing and e-mail. If you're planning to use your PC to create resumes, proposals, reports, or any other printed matter, your word processor is the place to start. If you don't own a word processor, consider purchasing one, such as Microsoft Works 2000 or Microsoft Word 2000. Contrary to popular belief, the WordPad program built into Windows 98 doesn't qualify as a bona fide word processor.*

WordPad is actually a text editor, which is different from a word processor.

A text editor is used for basic text entry, modification, and printing. It offers little more than an old-fashioned typewriter, in terms of features and capabilities.

A word processor not only does all of the above, it also provides important tools that improve document quality, such as spelling and grammar checkers, a thesaurus, automatic table of contents and footnote generation, automated bullets and numbering, outline assistants, and

■ **WordPad offers** *little more than an old-fashioned typewriter.*

more. You'll find that WordPad and other simple text editors quickly run out of gas when you try to use them as a word processor.

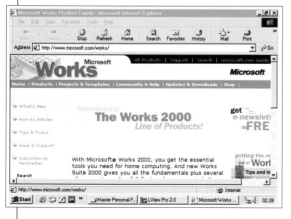

If, on the other hand, you invest a mere $45 to $55 for a copy of Microsoft Works 2000, you'll get all of Works 2000's integrated tools.

That is a word processor, spreadsheet, database, and calendar program – plus a free copy of Microsoft Word 2000, the world's #1 word processor. That's

■ **You can purchase** *Microsoft Works online at www.microsoft.com/works.*

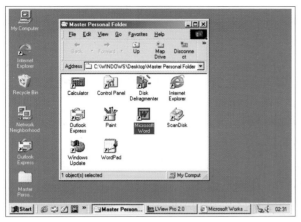

■ **Copy the icon** *for Microsoft Word into your master personal folder.*

right: Works 2000 gives you two word processors for the price of one. The reason: Microsoft's flagship word processor, Word 2000, is so popular, company product managers have decided to emphasize it over the functional, but less capable word processor that's long been a part of Works. Eventually, I expect the "classic" Works 2000 word processor will be discontinued, with Microsoft Word completely taking its place. For that reason, this chapter will focus exclusively on word processing using Microsoft Word.

Before you run off to buy Works 2000, check to see if it's been pre-installed on your PC. Click Start | Programs, and see if there's a program group named "Microsoft Works." If there is, point to it, and the Microsoft Works submenu will slide out. If one of the items on the submenu is labeled "Microsoft Works Calendar," you're the proud owner of Microsoft Works 2000. If not, I urge you to rush to your local computer retailer right now, and pick up a copy of Microsoft Works 2000. Follow the instructions in Chapter 19's "Installing (adding) new software" section.

Copy your Word icon

Once you have confirmed that Works 2000 is installed in your PC, the first order of business is to copy the icon for Microsoft Word into your master personal folder. Press Win+D to return to the Windows Desktop. Then click Start | Programs, right-click the Microsoft Word icon, and select Copy. Switch to your master personal folder by double-clicking it, or hitting its hot key. Right-click any blank area in your master personal folder, and select Paste.

If you want to assign a hot key to the Microsoft Word icon, now is a great time to do it. Right-click the Word icon, select Properties, enter the keystroke you want to use in the "Shortcut key" input box, and click OK. (I use Ctrl+Alt+F3 on my computer.)

You're now ready to process thoughts and words. Fire up Word by double-clicking its icon or hitting its hot key. When Word finishes loading, zoom the window to full screen size by double-clicking its title bar, or clicking its Maximize button.

Composing a Word document

WORD IS A DEEP *and powerful program. Before you get going, though, carefully review the accompanying chart to bone up on Word's main keystrokes.*

WORD'S MAIN KEYSTROKES

✓ To start a new line, press the Enter key.
✓ To create a blank line, press Enter twice.
✓ To type a blank space, hit the Space Bar.
✓ To capitalize a letter, press and hold the Shift key while typing the letter.
✓ To type characters such as !, @, $, press and hold the Shift key while typing a number.
✓ To type other "shifted" characters, press and hold the Shift key while hitting their key.
✓ To indent a word or line, press the Tab key.
✓ To "out-dent" a word or line, delete the Tab by double-clicking it, and pressing Delete.
✓ To make Tabs and paragraph markers visible, press Shift+Ctrl+8.
✓ To make Tabs and paragraph markers invisible, press Shift+Ctrl+8 again.
✓ Use the mouse or the arrow keys to move around within the document window.
✓ Use the scroll bars or the PageUp/PageDown keys to flip through multiple pages.
✓ To jump to the next word, press Ctrl+LeftArrow or Ctrl+RightArrow.
✓ To jump to the beginning of a line, press Home.
✓ To jump to the end of a line, press End.
✓ To jump up one page, press PageUp.
✓ To jump down one page, press PageDown.
✓ To jump to the beginning of a document, press Ctrl+Home.
✓ To jump to the end of a document, press Ctrl+End.
✓ To select a letter, click+drag your mouse pointer over it.
✓ To select a word, double-click it (or click on it and press F8).
✓ To select a paragraph, triple-click it (or click on it and press F8 twice).
✓ To select an entire document, press Ctrl+A (or press F8 three times, or click Edit | Select All).
✓ To cancel a selection, press Esc, then click anywhere.
✓ To select a letter, press Shift+LeftArrow or Shift+RightArrow.
✓ To select a word, press Shift+Ctrl+LeftArrow or Shift+Ctrl+RightArrow.
✓ To select a line, press Shift+End or Shift+Home.
✓ To select a page, press Shift+PageUp or Shift+PageDown.
✓ To select a document from the current letter on up, press Shift+Ctrl+Home.

✓ To select a document from the current letter down, press Shift+Ctrl+End.

✓ To extend a selection, keep pressing the arrow, PageUp/PageDown, Home, or End key.

✓ To cancel a selection, press Esc.

✓ To delete a letter, select it, then press the Delete key.

✓ To delete a word, select it, then press the Delete key.

✓ To delete a paragraph, select it, then press Delete.

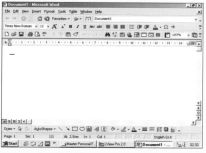

■ **Word's toolbars** *are packed with useful functions.*

✓ To delete a letter you just typed, press the Backspace key.

✓ To make text bold, select it, then press Ctrl+B (or click the Bold toolbar button).

✓ To make text italic, select it, then press Ctrl+I (or click the Italic toolbar button).

✓ To underline text, select it, then press Ctrl+U (or click the Underline toolbar button).

✓ To center text, select it, then press Ctrl+C (or click the Center toolbar button).

✓ To align text left, select it, then press Ctrl+L (click the Left toolbar button).

✓ To align text right, select it, then press Ctrl+R (or click the Left toolbar button).

✓ To justify text, select it, then press Ctrl+J (or click the Justify toolbar button).

✓ To change fonts, select the text, then choose a font from the Font drop-down pick list.

✓ To change size, select the text, then choose a size from the Size drop-down pick list.

✓ To copy text, select it, then press Ctrl+C (or click the toolbar's Copy button, or click Edit | Copy).

✓ To cut text, select it, then press Ctrl+X (or click the toolbar's Cut button, or click Edit | Cut).

✓ To paste cut or copied text, press Ctrl+V (or click the toolbar's Paste button, or click Edit | Paste).

✓ To find text, press Ctrl+F (or click the Find toolbar button, or click Edit | Find).

✓ To search and replace text, press Ctrl+H (or click Edit | Replace).

✓ To check your spelling, press F7 (or click Tools | Spelling).

✓ To set your preferences, click Tools | Options, and explore the Options dialog.

✓ To see other tools, click the Tools menu, and select a tool to use.

✓ To undo a mistake, press Ctrl+Z (or click Edit | Undo).

✓ You can undo multiple mistakes, too. Just keep pressing Ctrl+Z (or Edit | Undo).

✓ To save the file, press Ctrl+S (or click the toolbar's Save button, or click File | Save).

✓ To print the file, press Ctrl+P (or click the toolbar's Printer button, or click File | Print).

✓ To open a saved file, press Ctrl+O (or click the Open button, or click File | Open).

✓ To close a file, click File | Close.

✓ To get Help, press F1 (or click Help | Works Help).

That's it. To use Word effectively requires "only" about 50 of the over 1,500 or so keystrokes and commands the program supports. Using the "basic editing" keystrokes described in the chart, type in the following practice document. (All you'll really need to use are the letter keys, Shift, Tab, space, and Enter.) Take your time, and expect to get confused. The document on the screen should look exactly like the one you see here.

January 01, 2000

Mr. John Doe
National Federation of Shoehorn Manufacturers
1234 Main Street
Anywhere, NJ 12345

Dear Mr. Doe:

Enclosed please find a copy of my resume, which I have sent to you in response to your advertisement for a shoehorn engineer, as seen on page H9 of the Sunday, January 1, 2000 edition of the *Philadelphia Inquirer*. I am a seasoned engineering professional with 20 years of diversified shoehorn design and manufacturing experience. I would be happy to meet with you personally, at your convenience, should you decide to follow up on this initial application.

Sincerely,

Richard B. Levin
P.O. Box 1234
Anywhere, PA 54321

RBL: rbl
Enclosure

Polishing your document

BASIC TEXT ENTRY *is one thing. Making your document presentable is another. After you bang in your basic text, the next step is to polish it up. Perhaps you want to underline some of the copy, or have it stand out by making it bold, or increase the type size to make it more readable. Or maybe you need* *to center some text on the page, while leaving the rest of the text left-justified. These and other changes to the appearance, or format, of a document are called formatting changes, and they're easy to implement using Microsoft Word. Once you've formatted your document, and before you print it out, you'll want to make sure every word is spelled correctly.*

Word can also handle this job for you, through its automatic spell-checking feature.

Selecting and formatting text

Changing the format of a text is always a two-step process: First, select the text you want to change, then select the formatting you want to apply. The easiest way to select text is with the mouse. On your practice document, position the mouse pointer just before the word "Enclosed." Click and hold the mouse button, and drag the pointer diagonally across the entire paragraph, ending with the word "Inquirer." You can also press F8 to select text. Each time you press F8, it expands the selection (i.e. it selects more of the document). The first time you press it, F8 selects the current word, then the line, then the paragraph, and finally, the entire document. To cancel the selection, press the Esc key.

If you mess up your text selection, press Ctrl+Z to fix the text, or click Edit | Undo. When you get it right, the entire paragraph will be reverse-colored (usually white letters with a black background). That means the text is selected. You can select a single letter, word, paragraph, or the entire document. For now, leave the one paragraph selected. Click on the Font drop-down pick-list, and choose a different typeface.

> *Trivia...*
>
> *With each new release of Word, Microsoft increased the number of available commands. Microsoft officials tell me the current version of Word has about 1,000 commands, but I suspect the number is closer to 1,500. Here's how the numbers grew from 1992 to 1997, according to Scientific American (July '97, p. 88):*
> *1992: 311 commands (Word 2.0C)*
> *1997: 1,033 command (Word 97)*
> *2000: 1216 commands (Word 2000)*

If you're not sure which drop-down pick-list controls the Font setting, hover your mouse over the various controls on Word's toolbar. The control's name will appear in a little box, or "tool tip." Look for the control that displays a tool tip called "Font."

When you click the Font drop-down list and choose a different typeface, the text you selected changes to that typeface. Now click on the Size drop-down pick-list, and choose a different size. Same thing happens again. If you're unsure where the Size control is, hover your mouse over all the toolbar controls. When you see a tool tip that reads "Size," you've found the Size control.

Formatting entire documents

Since we're just experimenting, click Edit | Undo twice to undo the changes (or press Ctrl+Z twice). Next, select the entire document by pressing Ctrl+A (or clicking Edit | Select All, or dragging the mouse over all the document's text, from upper left to lower right). When the entire document is selected, click the Font drop-down pick-list again, and choose a different typeface. Now click the Size drop-down pick-list again, and choose a different size. Here again, you've changed the selected text's formatting, this time impacting the entire document!

While you have the entire document selected, play around with the other formatting controls on the toolbar. Click the bold, italic, and underline buttons, and witness their effects. Check out the align left, right, and center buttons. Sample the numbering and bullets buttons, and watch what happens. Remember, just hover your mouse over the toolbar controls to receive a description of what the control does. To undo any formatting, click the control a second time (they all act as toggles). Don't be afraid to explore! It's your key to opening new vistas with Word, or any software, for that matter. If you get tripped up, just press Ctrl+Z (or click Edit | Undo) to repair the mistake.

And remember, no matter what formatting change you're after — font style, size, centering, bolding, italicizing, etc. — the steps remain the same. First select the text you want to change, then choose the formatting you want to apply.

Moving text around

Word processing essentially boils down to typing blocks of text at the keyboard, formatting the text, and moving those text blocks around on the screen until you're happy with the layout. Then you spell-check your document, save it, and print it. Moving text around on the screen requires the use of cut+paste. You select the text you want to move, cut or copy it, point to the text's new destination, and paste it. You can move text exclusively with the mouse, or exclusively with the keyboard. Give it a whirl: Position the mouse pointer just before the word "Enclosed." Click and hold the left-mouse button, and drag the pointer across the paragraph, ending with the word "Inquirer." You can also click anywhere in the paragraph, and press F8 three times to select it.

Now press Ctrl+X (or click the Edit | Cut command on the menu bar). The paragraph disappears. Reposition the mouse pointer after the word "application" and before the word "Sincerely.") Then press Ctrl+V (or click the Edit | Paste command on the menu bar).

■ **Example of** *highlighted text with typeface and size changed.*

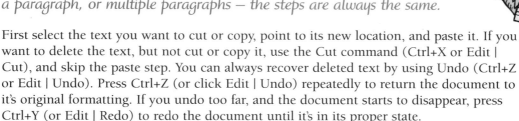

The paragraph reappears in its new location. To undo the cut+paste operation, press Ctrl+Z (or click Edit | Undo). To copy text instead of moving it, use Ctrl+C instead of Ctrl+X (or Edit | Copy instead of Edit | Cut).

No matter what text you want to cut or copy — a letter, a word, a line, a paragraph, or multiple paragraphs — the steps are always the same.

First select the text you want to cut or copy, point to its new location, and paste it. If you want to delete the text, but not cut or copy it, use the Cut command (Ctrl+X or Edit | Cut), and skip the paste step. You can always recover deleted text by using Undo (Ctrl+Z or Edit | Undo). Press Ctrl+Z (or click Edit | Undo) repeatedly to return the document to it's original formatting. If you undo too far, and the document starts to disappear, press Ctrl+Y (or Edit | Redo) to redo the document until it's in its proper state.

Spell-checking a document

Spelling errors are embarrassing, but thanks to Microsoft Word, they can largely be avoided. Word offers a feature, called a "spell-check," that automatically scans your document and flags errors in spelling. It's a good practice to run a spell-check before printing or e-mailing a document. To launch a spell-check, press F7, or click Tools | Spelling and Grammar. The Spelling and Grammar dialog appears. Word will flag every misspelled or improperly used word, and allow you to change it.

To change a word to its suggested correction, click on the correct word featured in the "Suggestions" list box, then click Correct (or hit Alt+C).

To ignore the suggested change, click the Ignore button (or hit Alt+I). If the word is spelled correctly but Word flags it as misspelled (for example, Word will flag my last name, "Levin," as misspelled), add the word to your personal dictionary so it's not flagged as misspelled in the future. Click the Add button (or hit Alt+A). To edit the text manually, click in the top input box, and edit it as you see fit. Click the Correct button (or

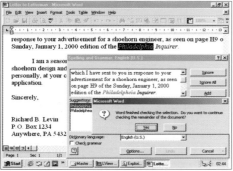

hit Alt+C) when you're done. When the spelling check is complete, Word will display a dialog that reads, appropriately enough, "The spelling check is complete." Click the OK button to close the dialog. To cancel a spell-check that's in progress, press the Esc key, or click the Cancel button.

■ **After Word** *has corrected a selected word, it will prompt you to check the rest of the document.*

Saving and printing

THE FINAL PHASE *of word processing involves saving and, ultimately, printing your work. The first time you save a document, you'll have to give it a name. In Windows 98, document names are also known as "file names." To save a document, just press Ctrl+S (or click the Save icon on the toolbar, or click File | Save). The first time you do this, the Save As dialog will appear. Click in the "File name" input box, and enter a name for the file.*

You can name the file anything you like, such as "Document1," "Resume," "My Resume," "Test Resume," "FUBAR," "Bill Gates Hairdo," or whatever. Note that some punctuation characters can't be used in file names. But don't worry. If you use a so-called "illegal" character, Windows 98 will warn you, and ask you to choose a different file name, or remove the illegal character that's giving it fits.

Here's the most important part of saving a file for the first time: Make absolutely certain you save it into your master personal folder.

If you don't, you might misplace the file and have a hard time locating it in the future. Click the little green-and-white Desktop icon on the Save As dialog's toolbar. You're now looking at a mini-view of your Windows Desktop, scrunched into the Save As dialog's window. Double-click your master personal folder to open it. Now that you're inside, you can safely click OK. The file is saved to your master personal folder.

Sometimes the green-and-white Desktop button doesn't show up on the Save or Open dialogs. Not to worry. There are two buttons with beige folder icons on them. One button has an up-arrow icon; the other has a sparkle icon. Slowly and repeatedly click the up-arrow folder button until your Desktop appears in the dialog window. You'll know you arrived at Desktop because the word "Desktop" will appear in the dialog's drop-down pick-list. Alternatively, you can traverse the drop-down pick-list by clicking its up-arrow button until you arrive at the "Desktop" entry. It's a good idea to save your document every few minutes. The easiest way to do this is to get in the habit of hitting Ctrl+S after every few lines you type. In the event of a power failure or some other problem, the latest version of your document will be stored on the PC's hard disk, and can be easily retrieved. Once the file is saved, there are two ways to retrieve it. You can

■ **To retrieve a document** *press Ctrl+O or select File | Open.*

double-click the file from inside your master personal folder, or you can open the file from inside your word processor. Press Ctrl+O (or click the Open toolbar button, or click File | Open), and the file you just saved will be listed in the Open dialog. Double-click it, and it's loaded. It's that simple. If your document doesn't appear in the Open dialog, it simply means you're not looking at your master personal folder. Click the little green-and-white Desktop icon on the Open dialog's toolbar. There's your mini-view of the Windows Desktop, scrunched into the Open dialog's window. Double-click your master personal folder to open it, and your previously saved documents will appear.

Note, too, that a list of your most recently accessed documents always appears on the File menu. Click the File menu, and you'll see them at the bottom of the File menu's commands.

To print any open document, just press Ctrl+P, or click the Print button on the toolbar. You can also click File | Print. Advanced printing options are covered in painful detail in Chapter 10's "Printer basics" section.

A simple summary

✓ Works 2000 features a killer word processor: Word 2000.

✓ Go out and buy Works 2000.

✓ Text editors lack all the tools essential to preparing documents.

✓ Entering and Edit text with the various word processor keys.

✓ You can always undo a text entry error by pressing Ctrl+Z.

✓ Move text around with the various cut+paste commands.

✓ Always spell-check your documents.

✓ Save files as you work.

✓ Always save your documents to your master personal folder.

✓ To open a previously saved document, press Ctrl+O, or click the Open toolbar button, or click File | Open.

✓ To print an open document, press Ctrl+P, or click the Print button on the toolbar.

Chapter 14

Summing Things Up

NUMBER CRUNCHING isn't a new breakfast cereal. It's the serious business of accounting. Juggling the numbers, balancing the books, exploring "what if" financial scenarios – all are numbers crunching activities made possible by the PC. Or more correctly, made possible by the original killer app that put the PC on the map: the spreadsheet. Best of all, spreadsheets are among the easiest programs to master. The skills you acquire when learning Microsoft Works 2000's Spreadsheet carry over perfectly to other products, such as Microsoft Excel 2000, Apple Works' spreadsheet, or Lotus 1-2-3.

In this chapter...

✓ What's a spreadsheet?

✓ Creating a spreadsheet

✓ Formatting a spreadsheet

✓ Formulating formulas

✓ Saving and printing

YOUR SPREADSHEET MAKES NUMBER CRUNCHING SO MUCH EASIER

What's a spreadsheet?

A spreadsheet is a collection of rows, numbered one through infinity (theoretically), and columns, labeled A through Z.

A spreadsheet cell is any intersection of a row and a column. In other words, location A1 – that's column A, row 1 – is one spreadsheet cell. Likewise, B7 refers to the contents of column B, row 7. C9 equals column C, row 9. Each spreadsheet cell can contain text, a number, or a formula. When a spreadsheet is properly wired with numbers and formulas, a change to any of the numbers will automatically activate the formulas and recalculate the spreadsheet's results.

Imagine if simply writing information in your checkbook would cause it to recalculate your balance.

Before you get to explore the marvels of spreadsheets, and of the Microsoft Works 2000 Spreadsheet in particular, you need to copy the program into your Master Personal Folder.

■ **Works 2000** *spreadsheet cannot handle all accounting tasks. You might need software such as Quicken (www.quicken.com).*

Setting up the Works icon

First, press Win+D to return to the Windows Desktop. Then click Start | Programs | Microsoft Works. Right-click the Microsoft Works Spreadsheet icon, and select Copy. Switch to your master personal folder by double-clicking it, or hitting its hot key. Right-click any blank area in your master personal folder, and select Paste. If you want to assign a hot key to the Microsoft Works Spreadsheet icon, do it now. Right-click the icon, select Properties, enter the keystroke you want to use in the "Shortcut key" input box, and click OK. (I use Shift+Alt+F3 on my computer.) You're now ready to crunch numbers. Fire up the Works 2000 Spreadsheet by double-clicking its icon or hitting its hot key. When it finishes loading, zoom the window to full screen size by double-clicking its title bar, or clicking its Maximize button.

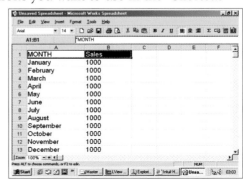

MICROSOFT WORKS 2000
SPREADSHEET TOOLBAR

Creating a spreadsheet

THE WORKS 2000 SPREADSHEET *is a deep and powerful program that would take an entire book to fully document, but is easy to get started with. It's a good idea to review the accompanying chart to consider the brief rundown of the Works 2000 Spreadsheet's standard keystrokes.*

They're similar to those used in Word, but geared to working with numbers in cells, as opposed to free-flowing text.

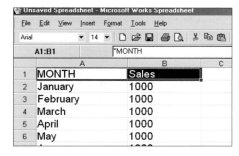

■ **Selected cells** *are displayed in reverse color.*

STANDARD KEYSTROKES

✓ Use the mouse or arrow keys to move up, down, left, and right within the spreadsheet.

✓ Use the scroll bars or the PageUp/PageDown keys to flip through multiple pages.

✓ You can also use Tab and Shift+Tab to move around cells.

✓ To jump to the beginning of a row, press Home.

✓ To jump to the end of a row, press End.

✓ To jump up one page, press PageUp.

✓ To jump down one page, press PageDown.

✓ To jump to the beginning of a spreadsheet, press Ctrl+Home.

✓ To jump to the end of a spreadsheet, press Ctrl+End.

✓ To edit the active cell, press F2, and start typing (or click inside the cell or formula bar).

✓ All standard word processing editing/selecting keys work when editing inside a cell.

✓ The active cell (the one with the thick black border around it) is automatically selected.

✓ To select adjacent cells, click+drag the mouse pointer over the cells you want to select.

✓ To select a row, click on the row's number button.

✓ To select a column, click on the column's letter button.

✓ To select an entire spreadsheet, press Ctrl+A (or click Edit | Select All.)

✓ To cancel a selection, press Esc, then click anywhere.

USEFUL COMMANDS

Deleting cells

✔ To delete a cell, select it, then press the Delete key.
✔ To delete a range of cells, select the range, then press Delete.

Formatting cells

✔ To make cells bold, select them, and press Ctrl+B (or click the Bold toolbar button).
✔ To make cells italic, select them, and press Ctrl+I (or click the Italic toolbar button).
✔ To underline cells, select them, and press Ctrl+U (or click the Underline toolbar button).
✔ To center cells, select them, and press Ctrl+C (or click the Center toolbar button).
✔ To align cells left, select them, and press Ctrl+L (click the Left toolbar button).
✔ To align cells right, select them, and press Ctrl+R (or click the Left toolbar button).
✔ To justify cells, select them, and press Ctrl+J (or click the Justify toolbar button).
✔ To change fonts, select the cells, and choose a font from the Font drop-down pick-list.
✔ To change size, select the cells, and choose a size from the Size drop-down pick-list.

Copying, cutting, and pasting cells

✔ To copy cells, select them, and press Ctrl+C (or click the toolbar's Copy button, or Click Edit | Copy).
✔ To cut cells, select them, and press Ctrl+X (or click the toolbar's Cut button, or click Edit | Cut).
✔ To paste cut or copied cells, select them and press Ctrl+V (or click the toolbar's Paste button, or click Edit | Paste).

Managing cells

✔ To find a cell, press Ctrl+F (or click the Find toolbar button, or click Edit | Find).
✔ To search and replace cells, press Ctrl+H (or click Edit | Replace).
✔ To check your formulas, press F9 (or click Tools | Recalculate).
✔ To sort cells, click Tools | Sort.
✔ To create a chart, select the cells you want to chart, and click Tools | Create New Chart.
✔ To check your spelling, press F7 (or click Tools | Spelling).

✓ To set your preferences, click Tools | Options, and explore the Options dialog.
✓ To see other tools, click the Tools menu, and select a tool to use.
✓ To undo a mistake, press Ctrl+Z (or click Edit | Undo).
✓ You can undo multiple mistakes, too. Just keep pressing Ctrl+Z (or Edit | Undo).

Saving, opening, printing, and closing spreadsheets

✓ To save the file, press Ctrl+S (or click the toolbar's Save button, or click File | Save).
✓ To print the file, press Ctrl+P (or click the toolbar's Printer button, or click File | Print).
✓ To open a saved file, press Ctrl+O (or click the Open button, or click File | Open).
✓ To close a file, click File | Close.
✓ To get Help, press F1 (or click Help | Works Help).

Entering data and formulas

Once you're familiar with the keystrokes, it's time to create your first spreadsheet. With the Works 2000 Spreadsheet maximized on the screen, click in column A, row 1 (that's cell A1). Type in the text, "MONTH." Hit the right arrow key once, and type in the word "Sales." Press the down arrow key once, which takes you to column A, row 2 (that's A2). Type the text, "January." Press the down arrow key again, and move to cell A3. Type "February." Press the right arrow key again, and in cell A4, type "March." Continue doing this down column A until you have entered all 12 months of the year, January through December.

After you have entered the names of all 12 months in column A (that's A2 through A13), press Ctrl+Home to return to cell A1 (or hit PageUp a few times).

Click on cell B2, and enter the number 1000. Press the down arrow key, and enter 1000 again. Keep doing this until all 12 months in column A have the number 1000 beside them, in column B. When you have entered the last 1000 entry in cell B13, click on cell B15 (that's column B, row 15).

■ **Enter your** *"Month" and "Sales" columns.*

So far, you've only entered raw data. Now type the following formula, inside cell B15:

=Sum(B2:B13)

and press Enter.

Your spreadsheet now looks like this:

	A	B	C	D	E
1	MONTH	Sales			
2	January	1000			
3	February	1000			
4	March	1000			
5	April	1000			
6	May	1000			
7	June	1000			
8	July	1000			
9	August	1000			
10	September	1000			
11	October	1000			
12	November	1000			
13	December	1000			
14					
15		12000			

Notice the number 12000 appears in cell B15. You have just instructed the spreadsheet to display the sum total of all the numbers listed in cell B2 through cell B13. Use the arrow keys to go back to cell B5, and enter the number 5000. Press Enter to complete the change. Amazingly, the total in cell B15 now reads 16000.

That's because any changes you make to the numeric data are automatically factored in by the formula and reflected in the total.

Duplicating cells and formulas

You've just witnessed the power of a spreadsheet: It's the ability to factor in changes and recalculate results on the fly. But there's more. You can also duplicate cells and formulas, and link formulas to create entirely new ones. To illustrate this, use your arrow keys to move back to cell A1. Change the wording from "MONTH" to "1999." Hit the right arrow key to get over to cell D1. Once there, type in "2000." Then hit the right arrow key again, and type in "Sales."

Arrow back over to cell A2. Press and hold the Shift key, then arrow over to cell B2. Keeping the Shift key depressed, arrow down to cell B15 (the formula cell).

You've just selected an entire block of cells. After the cells are selected, release the Shift key, and press Ctrl+C to copy the block (or click Edit | Copy). You can also use your mouse to select cells, if selecting cells with the keyboard is hard for you to do.

Position the mouse pointer over cell B2, and drag it to cell B15. Arrow over to cell D2. Press Ctrl+V to paste the cell block (or click Edit | Paste).

Your spreadsheet now looks like this:

	A	B	C	D
1	1999	Sales	2000	Sales
2	January	1000	January	1000
3	February	1000	February	1000
4	March	1000	March	1000
5	April	5000	April	5000
6	May	1000	May	1000
7	June	1000	June	1000
8	July	1000	July	1000
9	August	1000	August	1000
10	September	1000	September	1000
11	October	1000	October	1000
12	November	1000	November	1000
13	December	1000	December	1000
14				
15		16000		16000

Arrow over to cell E5, and change the 5000 to 9000. Press enter to accept the change. When you do, the total for year 2000 sales changes to 20000. Copying the cells not only duplicated their value; it also intelligently duplicated the formula.

Linking formulas

The sales figures for 1999 are calculated independently of the sales figures for 2000. The next logical step is to create a formula that calculates sales for the entire two-year period you're dealing with.

To do this, you need to link the two existing formulas with a third new one. Arrow over to cell A15, and type in "Year End."

Next, arrow over to cell G15, and type in an = (equal) sign. The equal sign tells the spreadsheet you're about to enter a formula.

After you enter the equal sign, don't press Enter. Instead, arrow over to cell B15.

Notice that the Works 2000 Spreadsheet is building the formula for you, as you arrow around the cells! Look in the cell, or in the formula bar, and you'll see that it reads "=B15." Don't press Enter yet. Instead, type + on the numeric keypad (that's the big + key on the far right of your keyboard). Don't press Enter yet! Arrow over to cell E15. When you're on E15, press Enter. The formula bar reads "=B15+E15." And cell G15 reads 36000 – that's cell B15 plus cell E15. Congratulations. You just created a complete, working spreadsheet, which looks like this:

A	B	C	D	E	F
1	1999	Sales	2000	Sales	
2	January	1000	January	1000	
3	February	1000	February	1000	
4	March	1000	March	1000	
5	April	5000	April	9000	
6	May	1000	May	1000	
7	June	1000	June	1000	
8	July	1000	July	1000	
9	August	1000	August	1000	
10	September	1000	September	1000	
11	October	1000	October	1000	
12	November	1000	November	1000	
13	December	1000	December	1000	
14					
15	Year End	16000		20000	36000

Formatting a spreadsheet

DEVELOPING A SPREADSHEET *is about more than numbers, calculations, and results. It's also about making the numbers easy to read and results easy to find. That's done by formatting the spreadsheet for maximum readability. For example, it's a good practice to format cells so that negative numbers are printed in red and positive numbers in black. It's also common practice to format subtotals and totals in bold and to underline totals. Formatting a spreadsheet is similar to formatting text in a word processor document. It always takes two steps: First, you select the cell or cells you want to change, then you choose the formatting to apply.*

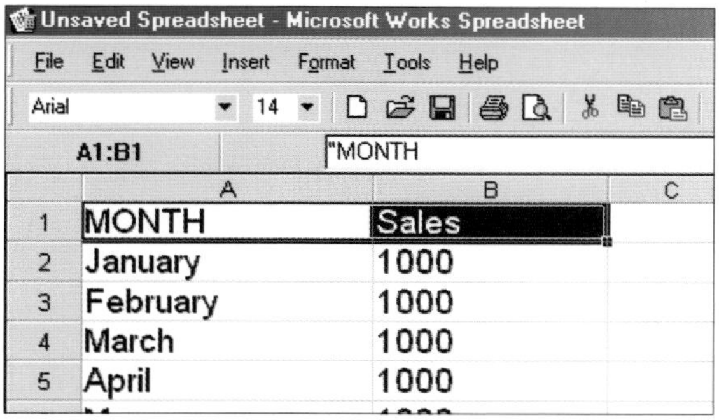

FORMATTED CELLS

Selecting and formatting cells

The easiest way to select cells is with the mouse. Click on cell A15. Keeping the left mouse button depressed, drag the pointer to the right, until cells A15 through G15 are selected. You can also select cells using the keyboard. Click on a cell, then press and hold the Shift key down while using any of the arrow keys, PageUp/PageDown, or Home/End. See the chart, "Moving around a Spreadsheet," for a complete list of keyboard commands.

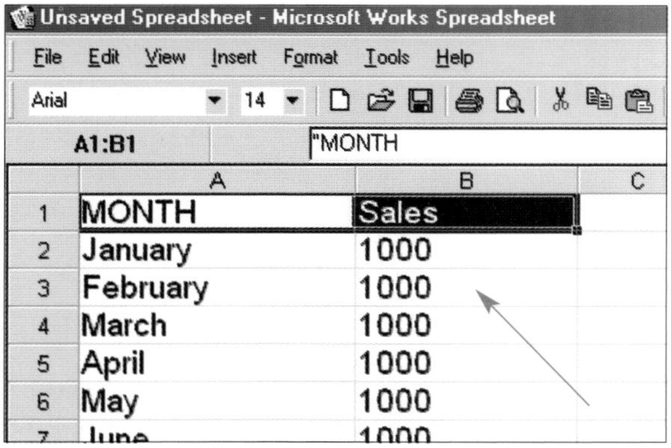

If you mess up, click on any unselected cell (or press any arrow key) to remove the selection. When you get it right, the cells will be reverse-colored (usually white letters with a black background). That means the cells are selected.

■ **If you mess up,** *click on any unselected cell.*

257

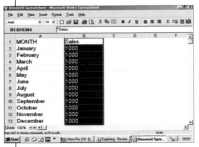

In the example shown here, seven cells have been selected, A15:G15, but there's no limit to the number or type of cells that can be selected. You can select one cell, multiple cells, combinations of data cells and formula cells, a row, multiple rows, a column, or multiple columns.

The fastest way to select an entire column is to click the column's letter panel.

■ **Click on the** *column's letter panel to highlight the column.*

Similarly, the fastest way to select an entire row is to click the row's number panel. You can select multiple columns or rows by clicking+dragging the mouse pointer over the column letter panels or row number panels.

Now that the cells are selected, you can format them. Click the "$" icon on the Works 2000 Spreadsheet toolbar. The cells are transformed from plain numbers to cash values (i.e. 36000 becomes $36,000). Click "$" to change them back to plain numbers. Press Ctrl+U to underline the selected numbers (or click the toolbar's "U" icon). This underlines the cells. Press Ctrl+B to make the cells bold (or click the toolbar's "B" icon). Press Ctrl+U or Ctrl+B again to reverse (remove) the formatting.

If you're not sure what purpose a toolbar control serves, remember what you learned when exploring the word processor: Just hover your mouse over the toolbar controls to view a tool tip that describes the control's function.

Advanced cell formatting

You must drill down into the Format menu to change cell formatting beyond the Works 2000 Spreadsheet's basic toolbar or keystroke options. With your target cells still selected, click the Format command on the menu bar, then click Number. The Format Cells dialog appears. Here you will find a cornucopia of delicious formatting options for cells of all varieties. Feel free to explore these tempting options in the future. For now, click the "Negative numbers in red" checkbox, then click the OK button.

Now click on the sales figures for January 2000, and type in -30000. Press Enter, and the Year End total for 2000 becomes a bunch of red "#" signs. That means the Works 2000 Spreadsheet wants to display

■ **Tooltips also** *work in Works 2000 Spreadsheet.*

a negative number, but the cell isn't wide enough. Click Format | Column Width, and then click the Best Fit button in the Column Width dialog. The cell expands to fit resulting data, and now displays "($11,000)" in red. (You can also format rows using the Format | Row Height dialog's Best Fit button.)

Formatting an entire spreadsheet

Sometimes you'll need to format all of a spreadsheet's cells. Easier done than said! First, select the entire spreadsheet by pressing Ctrl+A, or clicking Edit | Select All. (You can also select all active cells using the mouse.)

With the entire spreadsheet selected, click the Font Name drop-down pick-list on the toolbar, and select "Ariel Black." Next, click the Font Size drop-down pick-list on the toolbar, and select "16" as the point size. The entire spreadsheet changes to Ariel Black, 16 point font. But wait! The spreadsheet is once again showing "#" signs, indicating some cells need to be resized. Click Format | Column Width, click the Best Fit button, then click OK to automatically size all columns.

Repeat the process for the rows by hitting Format | Row Height, clicking the Best Fit button, and then OK. This time, instead of automatically sizing one cell, all the spreadsheet's cells have been perfectly sized to fit. Now click on any cell, or hit an arrow key, to unselect the entire spreadsheet. If the Year End totals aren't underlined, click the number "15" panel to select row 15. Then press Ctrl+U, or click the "U" icon on the toolbar, to underline the totals.

No matter what formatting change you're after – font style, point size, bolding, underlining, numeric type, etc. – you always have to do the two step. First select the cell or cells you want to change (or even the entire spreadsheet), then choose the formatting you want to apply.

And remember, the easiest way to set a lot of formatting options at once is to drill into the Format | Number menu.

Of course, you can also use the toolbar buttons, or their keyboard alternates, to lay out one or more cells using a single formatting feature at a time.

■ **Drill down** *into the Format menu for formatting options.*

Creating a chart or graph

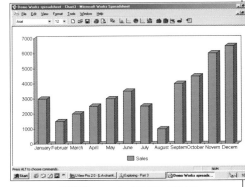

A WORKS 2000 SPREADSHEET CHART

Accountants, clerks, and other number crunchers are happy to immerse themselves in mountains of raw spreadsheet data, but for non-accounting folks, numbers make more sense when compiled into a chart or a graph. Charting and graphing in the Works 2000 Spreadsheet is a straightforward technique, requiring only a selection and a click. First, select the range of cells you want to represent as a chart or graph.

In this case, select cells A2 through B13. To do so, click on cell A2, and drag the pointer diagonally to cell B13. (You can also move to cell A2, and use the Shift+Arrow keys to select the cell block.) With the cell block selected, click the New Chart button on the toolbar (or click Tools | Create New Chart). The New Chart dialog appears, and gives you a choice of 12 ready-made chart types.

Click once on the various chart types featured in the "Chart type" frame to see previews in the Your Chart panel. After you have sampled all of the charts, click once on the very last chart type, the 3D Pie Chart. Next, click in the Title input box featured in the "Finishing touches" frame, and give the chart a name, such as "SALES FOR 1999." Click the Border and Gridlines checkboxes if you'd like to preview or use those visual elements. Click the OK button when you're done. Presto! A beautiful chart of your design appears on the screen.

Again, you can convert any collection of spreadsheet cells into a chart or graph, as long as the data contained within them relates sensibly.

In this case, the data makes perfect sense: It's a listing of sales activity from January through December 1999. The Works 2000 Spreadsheet has no trouble deducing that the pie slices relate to months of the year.

However, if you select data that doesn't make sense (such as the entire spreadsheet), you'll end up with a nice looking chart that doesn't make sense – a perfect example of computing's oldest maxim: Garbage in = garbage out.

If you ever encounter trouble generating a sensible chart or graph, carefully review the cells you're selecting. Virtually all charting and graphing problems can be traced back to the selection of nonsensical data.

To switch away from the chart and back to the spreadsheet, press Ctrl+F6 (the switch document window command), or click the Window menu and choose the spreadsheet (item 1) from the list. When you return to the spreadsheet, click on any cell (or press any arrow key) to unselect the entire spreadsheet.

The Ctrl+F6 keystroke works in most Windows programs. Whenever you're working with more than one file, you can press Ctrl+F6 to cycle through them easily.

Formulating formulas

SPREADSHEETS ARE A SIMPLE *yet powerful way to organize and calculate numbers. Any formula you can punch into a calculator can be punched into a spreadsheet. Addition, subtraction, multiplication, and division are all supported. All you have to do is enter the numbers you want to work with, and calculate your results using one or more formula cells. To create a formula cell, simply type in an equal sign, followed by the formula. You can even use the arrow keys to move around the spreadsheet, and let Works 2000 assist you in building the formula. After landing on each cell you want to include in the formula, enter the "operator" (or calculation) you want to use.*

To add cells, use a plus sign:
=A1+B1+C1

To subtract cells, use a minus sign:
=A1-B1-C1

To multiply cells, use an asterisk:
=A1*B1*C1

To divide cells, use a slash:
=A1/B1/C1

You can even mix and match operators:
=A1+B1-C1*E1/D1

To give one calculation priority over another, enclose it in parenthesis: =(A1+B1)*(E1/D1). In this case, the program first calculates the total of A1 and B1, then divides E1 by D1, and finally, multiplies the result of A1+B1 by the remainderof E1/D1. You can even enclose formulas that are in parenthesis within additional sets of parenthesis, in order to control the order of calculation operations: =((A1+B1)*(E1/D1))+300+(A1*D1). Here, the program first multiplies the sum of A1 plus B1 by the remainder of E1 divided by D1, adds 300, then adds the result of A1 times D1. Formulas can also contain combinations of cell names, numbers, and calculations. For example, all of the following are valid formulas:

```
=A1+100
(That's A1 plus 100)
=A1/2
(That's A1 divided by 2)
=A1*.06
(That's A1 times .06)
=A1+B1+1000
(That's A1 plus B1 plus 1000)
=(A1+B1)*(E1/D1)-5
(That's the result of A1 plus B1, times the remainder of E1 divided by D1, minus 5)
=((A1+50)*(F2+G3))+(1.79*R58)
(That's too complicated to explain!)
```

Remember, you can create formulas that calculate against one cell, groups of cells, and other formulas. There's practically no limit to the number of mathematical interdependencies you can create with a spreadsheet.

Using functions

You can live 1,001 years and never have to use any of the Works 2000 Spreadsheet's advanced functions – or any spreadsheet's functions, for that matter. Once you discover spreadsheet functions, though, you'll wonder how you got along without them.

Remember the =Sum(B2:B13) function used in the spreadsheet example earlier? That saved you the trouble of having to enter =B2+B3+B4+B5+B6+B7+B8+B9+B10+B11+B12+B13

Both formulas return the same result, but =Sum is a lot easier. Every spreadsheet program, Works 2000 Spreadsheet included, contains a slew of prebuilt functions you can use in formulas.

There are functions for financial information, dates and times, trigonometry, statistics, logical operators, lookups, and much more. In particular, Microsoft Works

2000 Spreadsheet makes it laughably easy to apply functions to the calculations at hand. You don't have to memorize manuals, comb through the Help menus, or run your finger down any charts. Instead, just click the Easy Calc button on the Works 2000 Spreadsheet toolbar (or click Tools | Easy Calc). It's the button that looks like a tiny calculator. (If you can't find it, just hover your mouse over each one of the toolbar controls until you see a tool tip that reads "Easy Calc.") Clicking the Easy Calc button calls up the Easy Calc wizard. Unlike most other features, Easy Calc doesn't require you to select any cells first. It will instruct you on selecting cells and building formulas.

Using the Easy Calc wizard

With the Easy Calc wizard on the screen, click the Average button. Easy Calc will prompt you to click the individual cells you want to average, or to select a range of cells using your mouse. Click on cell E2, and it appears in the Range input box. Notice Easy Calc has also started to craft a formula, "=AVG(E2)," in the grayed-out "What your formula will look like" input box. Now click cell E3. Easy Calc kicks in once again, adding cell E3 to the Range input box, and expanding the formula to read "=AVG(E2,E3)." You could continue to click the rest of the cells in column E one at a time, but it's faster to select them all.

Begin by erasing Easy Calc's partially built formula. Do this by double-clicking in the Range input box, and pressing either the Delete or Backspace key on your keyboard. (You can also click the Back button to return to Easy Calc's main menu.) Click on cell E2 and, while holding the mouse button down, drag the mouse pointer down to cell E13. The Range input box reads "E2:E13," and the formula reads "=AVG(E2:E13)." Click the Next button. The Easy Calc wizard will ask you to define where you want to display the result of the Average calculation, and will suggest cell D16. Click on cell D20, just for fun; then click Finish. The average of all monthly sales, -916.6666667, appears in cell D20. The result is correct, but it sure is ugly. Click Format | Number to pretty it up. In the Format frame, select the Currency radio button. In the options that appear in the Options frame, make sure the number "2" appears in the "Decimal places" input box (if it doesn't, type it in). Click on the "Negative numbers in red" checkbox, then click OK. The average sale is properly reformatted, showing up as "($916.67)" in red. Click on cell C20, type in the words "Average Sale in 2000," and press enter. Click Format | Column Width, click the Best Fit button, and your spreadsheet is complete.

In short, you can construct any formula using the Easy Calc wizard, without knowing a thing about spreadsheet programming.

> ## Trivia...
>
> *Works 2000 Spreadsheet's Easy Calc wizard is the friendliest formula builder available in any spreadsheet on the market, bar none. It's even friendlier than the one featured in Microsoft's top-of-the-line spreadsheet, Excel 2000.*

Saving and printing

THE FINAL PHASE *in developing spreadsheets is to save and print your work. As with word processing, the first time you save a spreadsheet, you'll have to give it a name. In Windows 98, spreadsheet names (as with everything else that gets saved) are also referred to as "file names." To save a spreadsheet, press Ctrl+S (or click the Save icon on the toolbar, or click File | Save). The first time you do so, the Save As dialog will appear. Click in the "File name" input box, and enter a name for the file.*

■ **The first time** *you save your spreadsheet, the Save As dialog will appear.*

You can name the file anything you like, such as "Spreadsheet1," "My Spreadsheet," "Test Spreadsheet," "FUBAR," "Steve Ballmer's Hairdo," or whatever. Again, as is the case with saving documents, some punctuation characters can't be used in file names. If you try to use a so-called "illegal" character, Windows 98 will warn you, and ask you to choose a different file name, or remove the illegal character that's causing the problem.

Keep your file safe

The most important aspect of saving a file for the first time: Be absolutely certain you save it in your master personal folder. If you don't, you could misplace the file, and have a terrible time locating it in the future. Click the green-and-white Desktop icon on the Save As dialog's toolbar. You're now looking at a mini-view of your Windows Desktop, squeezed into the Save As dialog's window. Double-click your master personal folder to open it. Once you're inside, you can safely click OK. The file is saved to your master personal folder.

Sometimes the green-and-white Desktop button doesn't show up on the Save or Open dialogs. Not to worry. There are two buttons with beige folder icons on them. One has an up-arrow icon on it (that's the Up One Level button); the other has a sparkle icon (the Create New Folder button). Slowly and repeatedly click the up-arrow folder button until your Desktop appears in the dialog window. You'll know you arrived at Desktop because the word "Desktop" will appear in the dialog's drop-down pick list. Alternatively, you can traverse the drop-down pick list by clicking its up-arrow button until you arrive at the "Desktop" entry.

It's wise to save your spreadsheet every few minutes. Get religious about hitting Ctrl+S after every few cells you edit.

In the event of a power failure or other problem, the latest version of your spreadsheet will be safely tucked away in the PC's hard disk. After a file is saved, there are two ways to retrieve it. You can double-click the file from inside your master personal folder, or you can open the file from inside the Works 2000 Spreadsheet. Press Ctrl+O (or click the Open toolbar button, or click File | Open), and the file you just saved will be listed in the Open dialog. Double-click it, and it's loaded.

If your spreadsheet doesn't appear in the Open dialog, it means you're not viewing your master personal folder. Click the green-and-white Desktop icon on the Open dialog's toolbar. That returns you to a mini-view of the Windows Desktop, crunched into the Open dialog's window. Double-click your master personal folder to open it, and your previously saved spreadsheets will appear. In addition, a list of your most-recently accessed spreadsheets will always appear on the File menu. Click the File menu, and you'll see them at the bottom of the File menu's commands. To print a spreadsheet, press Ctrl+P, or click the Print button on the toolbar. You can also click File | Print. For more on advanced printing options, turn to Chapter 10's "Printer Basics" section.

A simple summary

✓ Spreadsheets are simply a collection of cells, organized into rows and columns.

✓ Each cell can contain text, a number, or a formula.

✓ You can navigate and edit data using many of the same keyboard commands you learned with word processing.

✓ You start a formula by entering an = into a blank cell.

✓ The easiest way to format cells is through the Format menu.

✓ Use the New Chart dialog to turn your spreadsheets into informative charts and graphs.

✓ Use the Easy Calc wizard to create formulas and use mathematical functions automatically.

✓ Get in the habit of saving files as you work, by pressing Ctrl+S.

✓ Always save your documents to your master personal folder.

✓ To print, press Ctrl+P, or click the Print button on the toolbar.

Chapter 15

Doing the Database Deed

USUALLY PROJECTS somehow end up as a word processor document or a spreadsheet table. Need to track sales orders or inventory? Spin up the spreadsheet! Need to do a mass-mailing or print address labels? Whip out the word processor! Then again, a buzz saw can clip supermarket coupons. The fact is, the perfect tool for managing forms, data entry, merging, and large information sets isn't the word processor or the spreadsheet. It's the database.

In this chapter...

✔ What is a database?

✔ Creating a database

✔ Activating the database

✔ Navigating and populating

✔ Using and updating

✔ Saving and printing

THE DATABASE IS THE MOST POWERFUL AND FLEXIBLE KIND OF SOFTWARE

What is a database?

THINK OF A DATABASE as a virtual file folder. Each folder contains a limitless stack of database forms. They can be credit applications, customer contacts, sales orders, inventory control, shipping labels, or anything else that typically gets entered on a form. But unlike paper-based forms, database forms are capable of "reacting" to data as it's typed in. For example, entering a quantity and a unit price on a sales order database form will cause the subtotal, tax, freight, and total amount due to be filled in completely automatically. Multiple databases can be stitched together, using what's known as "relational database" technology.

Entering an item description and quantity shipped into a sales order database can automatically update a separate inventory database.

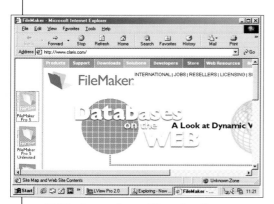

■ **Find out about** *Filemaker Pro at www.claris.com/.*

Three kinds of databases

There are essentially three kinds of database programming technology available to the average PC user: Relational, flat-file, and free text. The Microsoft Works 2000 Database is a flat-file database, meaning all the database information you enter is stored in a single file. Flat-file databases are good for addressing basic database requirements. Many users never outgrow them.

Relational databases store information in multiple databases, creating one "virtual" database from many smaller database files. They're used when the database requirements are too complex to be expressed and implemented in a simple flat-file database, such as Works 2000's (for example, an inventory system for an auto dealer with 25 franchises). Also, most flat-file databases are single-user programs, meaning only one user at a time can access data. Relational databases can support thousands of simultaneous users over LANs, WANs, and the web – a must for larger business settings. Programs such as FileMaker's FileMaker Pro offer larger businesses the same ease of use as the Works 2000 Database, but also support relational databases, multi-user access, and web access. Interestingly, all relational database programs can create multi-user flat-file databases, for addressing less demanding requirements.

Free text databases operate almost exactly like your word processor: You simply type information in, without any programming whatsoever, and can retrieve it using the database's search tool. This type of database is easy to use, but it's usually extremely slow and does not support multi-user access. Users say a database's most useful function is its "lookup" feature. This allows the database to automatically fill out a form whenever it encounters a certain unique code, such as a customer's account number, last name, or telephone number. (Unfortunately, this feature isn't supported by entry-level databases such as Works 2000 Database, but can be found when you step-up to products such as FileMaker's FileMaker Pro.) Best of all, databases make it easy to collect and find all kinds of useful information. Instead of having to rummage through 1,000 unrelated spreadsheets or documents, you can open your database, and ask it to find what you're after. The database will scan its forms and display those that match your query. In this way, databases are similar to web search engines, except that they work with your personal data and not data on the web.

If diamonds are a girl's best friend, and dogs are man's best friend, then the database is your information's best friend. The best way to illustrate the database's fundamental power is to create a classic database application: a sales order entry database. Even if you have nothing to sell, once you've worked your way through the development of this classic database solution, you'll understand how to apply database technology to solve dozens of other uses. Eventually, you can even use your database skills to build databases that work over the web. And even though entry-level databases, such as Works 2000 Database, don't support web access, your Works 2000 Database skills will serve you well as you upgrade to the more powerful database software, such as FileMaker's FileMaker Pro, which you'll need when and if you decide you want to create a web database.

Setting up the Works 2000 Database

As with all of your other mission-critical applications, the first step is to clone the Microsoft Works 2000 Database icon into your master personal folder. Press Win+D to return to the Windows Desktop. Then click Start | Programs | Microsoft Works. Right-click the Microsoft Works Database icon, and select Copy. Switch to your master personal folder by double-clicking it, or hitting its hot key. Right-click any blank area in your master personal folder, and select Paste.

If you want to assign a hot key to the Microsoft Works Database icon, do so now. Right-click the icon, select Properties, enter the keystroke you want to use in the "Shortcut key" input box, and click OK.

■ **Clone your Works 2000** *Database icon into your master personal folder.*

Planning a database

A database is simply a "smart" computerized form. The first step in planning a database form is to define a table of data fields – placeholders, if you will – that will be used to store information that's typed into the finished form. Surprisingly, the best way to plan a database table is with a pencil and paper, and not the PC. Layout your database manually and ahead of time, and you'll avoid tricky design snafus later. That said, grab a pencil and paper, and start writing down all of the information you believe a sales order entry form should capture. Obviously the buyer's name, address, and telephone number come to mind.

■ **First plan** *your database on paper.*

Jot this down:

First name
Last name
Title
Company
Address 1
Address 2
City
State
Zip
Telephone

You can already see the database taking shape, and you haven't even touched the computer keyboard. Also, note how each data element is broken down into its discrete components. In other words, instead of having a "Name" *field*, you're breaking it down into "First name," "Last name," and "Title" fields. It's not an absolute necessity to break your data fields down this way, but it's certainly a good design approach. If the database had only a "Name" field, you wouldn't be able to alphabetize database reports by last name, for example. The more fine-grained your database table, the easier organizing and searching information will be.

> **DEFINITION**
>
> *A placeholder in a database is called a* field. *How long the name of a field can be depends on the program you're working with. Microsoft Works 2000 Database limits field names to 15 characters.*

Next on the list of sales order entry fields are shipping, product, and billing information for two line items. Jot these field names down on your database sketch sheet:

Ship address
Product 1   Quantity 1   Unit price 1   Total price 1
Product 2   Quantity 2   Unit price 2   Total price 2
                                           Subtotal   Tax
                                           Freight
                                           Amount paid
                                           Balance due

Invoice number   Order date

That pretty much wraps up all the information a basic sales order entry form should have. If there are other fields you believe should be included, jot them down now. When you're done, grab your pad, and turn your attention to your PC.

Creating a database

FIRE UP THE WORKS 2000 *Database by double-clicking its icon or hitting its hot key. When it finishes loading, the Microsoft Works Database startup dialog will appear. This obtuse dialog offers three choices: Blank Database, Template, and Open an Existing Database.*

After you've created your database, you can select "Open an Existing Database" to retrieve it.

You can also open a Template to load pre-fab databases for many common home, school, and business requirements. Once you learn how to create a database, you can use the Templates as a starting point, and customize them using your database programming skills. But for now, since you're creating a new database, click the radio button beside the default setting, Blank Database, if it's not already selected. Click OK, and the Create Database wizard appears. Creating the database is now a simple matter of entering the various field names you jotted down on paper, and telling the database what kind of data should be attached to the field name. Click on the "Field name" input box, and type in the first field of your database table, "First name." Click the Add button, and the "First name" field appears in the background. Your database table is now taking shape. Click on the "Field name" input box again, and type in the next field of your database table, "Last name." Click the Add button, and the "Last name" field appears in the background. Repeat this process for the Title, Company, Address, City, and State fields.

When you're ready to enter the Zip and Telephone fields, don't press the Add button.

Since these are numeric fields, select the Number format in the Format frame by clicking its radio button. In the Appearance frame, enter a "0" in the "Decimal places" input box. When you're done, click the Add button. This tells the database that only numbers should be entered into the Zip and Telephone fields. Users will now be prevented from accidentally entering non-numeric data in either of these fields.

Why was Numeric format specified for the Zip and Telephone fields, but Text format wasn't for the First name through State fields? Because the default format, "General," is appropriate for nearly all data. You could conceivably create a database without ever specifying formats other than General. Specifying fixed data formats is absolutely optional, and is best used only when you want to force users to enter a specific data type (or protect yourself from accidentally entering text where numbers should be, and vice versa).

271

Assigning database fields

That's ten fields created, with 11 fields to go. Using the Create Database wizard, enter all of the remaining fields into the database table, taking care to specify the correct data formats featured in the Format frame. Again, for each field entered, first type the field name in the "Field name" input box, then click the radio button beside the appropriate format in the Format frame. Then click the Add button. Repeat this for each field, until all 11 remaining fields have been created:

Field	Format	Appearance
Ship address	General	None
Product 1	General	None
Quantity 1	Numeric	0 decimal places
Unit price 1	Numeric	2 decimal places
Product 2	General	None
Quantity 2	Numeric	0 decimal places
Unit price 2	Numeric	2 decimal places
Total price 1	Numeric	2 decimal places
Total price 2	Numeric	2 decimal places
Subtotal	Numeric	2 decimal places
Tax	Numeric	2 decimal places
Freight	Numeric	2 decimal places
Amount paid	Numeric	2 decimal places
Balance due	Numeric	2 decimal places
Invoice number	Serialized	1000, increment by 1
Order date	Date	Your choice

Setting the "Invoice number" field to "Serialized" means the database will automatically enter a number with every new database record created.

That guarantees that each invoice will have a unique invoice number, which is useful for tracking purposes. Select the Serialized format, and the Appearance frame offers up two options: "Next value" and "Increment." "Next value" is the initial number that will form the basis of all other automatically generated numbers for the "Invoice number" field. Click on the "Next value" input box, and enter the number 1000. Leave the increment set to 1 (the default).

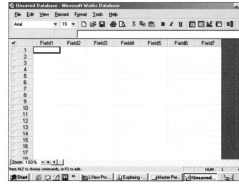

THE WORKS 2000 DATABASE TOOLBAR

Specifying a Date format for the "Order date" instructs the database to display any data entered in that field as a date. Choose whatever date style you prefer for your "Order date" field in the Appearance frame, then click Add. When you're finished creating database fields, click the Done button. Shazam! Your database table stands before you. Zoom the window to full-screen by double-clicking its title bar, or clicking the Maximize button.

Designing your database form

Right now your database looks suspiciously similar to a spreadsheet. The only difference appears to be the columns running atop the screen. Instead of being labeled A to Z, they're labeled with your field names. Running down the left are row numbers, from 1 to who knows how many? But don't be deceived by the outward appearance. Those aren't row numbers. They're "database records."

Each database record contains placeholders for all of the fields you created.

Think of these database records as akin to a stack of index cards. The database is the card file. The database table defines the kind of info you'll note on the cards. The database records are the individual index cards, from card #1 to however many fit in the box. Contrast that to a spreadsheet or a word processor document which, in the context of this analogy, are nothing more than a single oversized index card.

When you think of managing information, a project, or a business, you need much more than one index card.

It takes but one keystroke to drive this "index card" concept home. Press the F9 key to switch the database from the "table" view it's in now (known as "List" view in Works 2000 Database vernacular) to "Form" view. Bada-boom, bada-bing: Now the database form looks a lot more like, well, a form! There, listed top to bottom, are your database fields. But even though the form layout is readily apparent, it's not exactly the world's most professional looking sales order entry form.

■ **Think of a database** *as a set of smart index cards.*

THE PLAIN DATABASE FORM

To jazz up the form requires little more than few clicks and drags. First, put the database into "Form Design" mode by hitting Ctrl+F9 (or clicking View | Form Design). This mode allows you to make changes to the underlying database schema (that's database-ese for "design"). Click+drag the "Invoice number" field from the bottom of the form to the upper right. Next, grab the "Order date" field, and line it up directly below the "Invoice number" field. Drag+drop the remaining database fields to put them in any layout that makes sense to you. To move multiple fields at once, click+drag a lasso around them to select. Then click on any of the selected fields, and drag+drop to their new location.

If any field doesn't line up properly, click Format | Snap To Grid to disable the invisible positioning grid. This allows you to position fields fluidly and precisely.

When all fields are positioned to your liking, click Format | Snap To Grid to "lock" the fields in place. While you're at it, you might want to resize the "Ship address" field. As it stands now, the "Ship address " is too small to contain an entire shipping address. To widen it, click the little gray block on the far right edge of the "Ship address" field. That little gray block is called a field's "handle." Drag it to expand the field's border to the right. Then click and drag the handle on the "Ship address" field's bottom border to make the field taller. There are a total of three handles for every field: A width handle on the right border, a height handle on the bottom border, and a diagonal sizing handle on the bottom right corner. Grab the diagonal sizing handle to simultaneously change width and height. Come to think of it, the First name, Last name, Title, Company, Address 1, Address 2, and Product 1 fields could be a little wider as well. Click+drag their right-most handle to widen their respective fields.

Remember, you can move fields around by clicking+dragging them. You can also make them longer, shorter, taller, or shorter by clicking+dragging their handles. When you're done arranging the form's layout, press F9 (or click View | Form) to return to Form view.

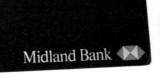

■ **It's not worth** *using a database just to balance your checkbook...*

Activating the database

SOME THINGS ARE *better off left uncomputerized. Your personal checkbook, for example. There are plenty of programs available to computerize your checkbook – and every one of them overcomplicates the plain and simple process of writing and logging checks. If databases were merely the electronic equivalent of index cards, there'd be little reason to commit data to them. But index cards can't react to or dynamically change data. A database can.*

Case in point: The sales order entry database you're building right now. Were you taking orders manually, using index cards, you'd have to whip out your calculator every time you clinched a sale. That's because you'd have to multiply the quantity ordered by the unit price, and tack on sales tax and freight charges. Then you'd have to deduct any cash deposit made at the time of order, and scribble in the balance due on delivery. And oh yes, you'd have to run the calculations twice, just to be sure they're entered correctly. Chances are good that when your order gets submitted to the home office, some clerk will rekey it from your index card into – yep! – a database!

You can save yourself time and trouble by programming your database to automatically perform and validate calculations as data is being entered. And this good news gets even better: Programming database formulas is exactly like building spreadsheet formulas. Well, almost. The only difference: Spreadsheets use cell letters and numbers to identify data. To add two cells in spreadsheet, you would program "=A1+B1." Unless you know what A1 and B1 represent, the formula is clear as mud. Databases, on the other hand, use field names. To add two fields in a database, you reference the field names. For example, "=Quantity 1+Unit price 1" is a valid database formula.

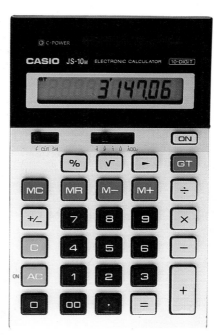

As an added benefit, if you use self-explanatory field names when designing your database, you'll have less trouble maintaining and debugging your database formulas in the future.

■ ...**But for taking** *sales orders, a database beats a calculator any day.*

Programming database formulas

The only drawback to database formulas over spreadsheet formulas: Unlike Works 2000 Spreadsheet, the Works 2000 Database doesn't offer an Easy Calc wizard. You'll have to look up formulas in the Help system to learn them, and again if you forget them. That's not a huge hurdle, though. Just hit F1 (or click Help | Works Help). Click the Contents button (that's the one sandwiched in between the magnifying glass and binoculars). Click on the entry titled "Calculate with Formulas and Functions."

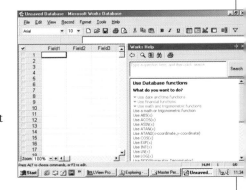

When the entry expands, click on "Works with Database Functions." You'll next see an entry titled "Use Database functions." Click it, and the function help guide will appear. In it you'll find a complete list of all 53 database functions, and tips on how to use them. Thankfully, for most database functions, you'll need only the four basic mathematical operators: addition, subtraction, multiplication, and division. They're coded the same way in the database as they are in the spreadsheet:

■ **Learn about Works 2000**
Database formulas in Help.

+ = addition   - = subtraction
* = multiplication   / = division

As with the spreadsheet, you precede a function with an equal sign. This tells the database that the field will return a value based on some sort of calculation.

But if you try to enter a formula while the database is in Form View, it won't work. That's because Form View is used exclusively to enter, update, search for, and retrieve data.

You can't do any database programming in Form View. If you try, the database will simply treat the formula as raw data. Microsoft, in its infinite wisdom, confuses matters by preventing formulas from being entered in Form Design mode. Even though this is the place where database forms are programmed, laid out, and reformatted, Form Design mode won't accept formulas. No, to create or modify formulas requires switching to the database table. Press Shift+F9 (or click View | List) to re-enter the database table. Now click on the "Total price 1" panel at the top of the database column. The entire "Total price 1" column gets selected. Type an equal sign, and then click on (or arrow over to) the "Quantity 1" column. When you do, Works 2000 Database starts to build the "Total price 1" formula. Now type a multiplication operator (that's the * sign). Then click on the "Unit price 1" column. When you're done, press the Enter key.

The entire formula has now been built, simply by your pointing and clicking, and typing in the various operators.

A "0.00" appears in the "Total price 1" column. The formula is now active. Now you have to repeat the above steps for the "Total price 2" formula. Click the "Total price 2" panel at the top of the database column. The "Total price 2" column is selected. Type an equal sign, and click on (or arrow over to) the "Quantity 2" column. Now type a multiplication operator (that's the * sign), and then click the "Unit price 2" column. Press the Enter key when you're done, and a "0.00" appears in the "Total price 2" column. At this point, the "Total price" functions – which tally the quantity purchased by a single unit price – are operational. But there remains much work to be done. You still have to build formulas for the "Subtotal," "Tax," and "Balance due" fields. You could build the formulas using the point+click approach detailed above. That's helpful when building spreadsheets, because you have to make certain the column letters and row numbers are precisely entered.

Dealing with named database functions, however, means you can also safely enter formulas right off the top of your head.

For example, click on the "Subtotal" panel to select the entire column. Then type the following formula: **= Total price 1 + Total price 2**

Press Enter, and the formula comes alive. The "Subtotal" field now reads "0.00." Click on the "Tax" field, and type: **= Subtotal * .06**

Press Enter, and the "Tax" field will assess a six percent sales tax whenever the "Subtotal" field contains a value greater than zero. Lastly, click on the "Balance due" field, and type in this formula:
= (Subtotal + Tax) - Amount paid

■ **If you go into** *Form View, you can't enter formulas.*

Enclosing the first part of the formula in parenthesis instructs the database to perform that calculation first, then subtract the amount paid from the result. Enclose formulas in parenthesis when you want greater control over the formula's processing. Press Enter, and all of the database's formulas are ready to rumble.

■ **Enter formulas** *carefully, remembering to begin each one with an equal sign.*

Functions

The 53 documented functions supported by Works 2000 Database, listed in the appendices (see page 367), can handle most database needs. If your requirements demand more power than you can squeeze out of Works 2000 Database, you can upgrade to Microsoft Access 2000, FileMaker Pro, or Corel Paradox – all of which support hundreds of advanced functions. To learn how to apply any of these functions, press F1 (or click Help | Works Help). Click the Contents button (between the magnifying glass and binoculars icons). Click the "Calculate with Formulas an Functions" entry, click "Works with Database Functions," and then click "Use Database functions." The function help guide will appear.

Navigating and populating

TAKE A PEEK *at the status bar on the bottom of the screen. You'll see it reads "Record 1." That means your database contains one record, and an empty one at that. Let's populate it together. Before you can populate your database forms, however, you need to learn how to navigate them.*

Fortunately, navigating a database form is similar to walking down the street. It takes two feet to walk, and two keystrokes to navigate: Tab and Shift+Tab.

Setting the tab order

Press Tab a few times, and you'll see the database form focus move forward, from one field to the next. Press Shift+Tab, and the database form focus moves backwards, from one field to the previous field. Filling out a database form consists of nothing more than filling out a field, pressing Tab, filling out the next field, pressing Tab, and so on. When all the fields are filled out, pressing Tab will automatically open a new blank database record page. Similarly, if you have more than one record in your database, pressing Shift+Tab enough times will bring you back to the previous record.

Notice, though, that pressing Tab doesn't always move the focus to the next logical field. That's because Works 2000 Database has no way of knowing in what order you want the fields traversed.

Press Ctrl+F9 to jump back into Form Design mode (or click View | Form Design). Then click Format | Tab Order to open the Format Tab Order dialog. There you'll see the current tab order displayed in list box. Click on any field that's out of order, and then click the Up or Down buttons to relocate it to its proper position. Click the up and down arrow buttons on the scroll bar to review the overall tab order. If you make a mistake and want to start over, click the Reset button. To quit without saving your changes, click the Cancel button. To accept and save your changes, click the OK button. Hit the F9 key to return to Form view.

Entering data into a database

Your database is now ready to be pressed into service. Click on the "First name" field if it's not already selected, and type in your first name. Press Tab, and the focus jumps to the next field in your tab order. Fill in the field by typing in it, and press Tab. (Note that if you press Enter instead of Tab, the data you entered into the field will still be accepted, but the focus will remain on the current field.)

To change a field's contents, you can Tab or Shift+Tab into the field and retype over its contents — but it's easier to press the edit key: F2.

Keep filling in fields and pressing Tab until all of the record's fields have been completed. At that point, pressing Tab will leave the current database record, and open a new blank record. Creating new records with the Tab key is the logical choice when you have to enter lots of data. But to create just one new record, click Record | Insert.

Keep going: Fill in the first field in the new record, hit Tab, fill in the second field, hit Tab, and so on. As you arrive at each field, punch in some information that makes sense for that field. In other words, enter a product description for "Product 1," a number for "Quantity," etc. Hit Tab after entering your info, and keep going until you have filled out at least five database records. You'll know you've completed five or more records when the status bar reads "Record 5" or greater. After you have completed five or more database records, you're ready to practice searching for, retrieving, editing, and deleting database records.

■ **It takes two** *feet to walk, and two keystrokes to navigate.*

Using and updating

WHEN MANAGING *information with file folders and file cabinets, it can be like searching for a needle in a haystack. Not so when your haystack is digital, and stored in a PC database. It takes but one keystroke – and less than one second – to retrieve any information stored in your database.*

Also, as your database requirements evolve, so can your database. Perhaps you may discover the need to include three products on each sales order entry form. Or maybe your business goes international, and you now need to include a country and international postal code on the database. To make these and other changes, all you have to do is go back to the database's Form Design mode.

Finding information in a database

The whole point of building and maintaining a database is the ability to retrieve, organize, and generate reports based on your data set. Right now, your test database is small: a mere five or so records. But assuming you were running a booming business, your sales database could quickly balloon to hundreds, even thousands of records.

Yet you can pinpoint any one of those records in a flash, using your database's Find feature.

Press Ctrl+F (or click Edit | Find) to call up the Find dialog. Type in the last name of one of your dummy database records, and then press Enter (or click OK). In no time, the Works 2000 Database zeros in on the information you asked for. Even if your database was populated with thousands of records, all it takes is a hit of Ctrl+F to find the record you're looking for. Try it again: Press Ctrl+F (or click Edit | Find), and this time type in a company name or product description. Press Enter (or click OK), and if any database record supports a perfect match, the database displays it. To repeat your last Find without having to re-enter it, press F3. You can also use Ctrl+H (or click Edit | Replace) to search and replace data with different information. For argument's sake, you could search for "Widgets," and replace all occurrences with "Fidgets." It should be obvious what a powerful and useful tool this is: instant access to names, addresses, telephone numbers, transactions, product descriptions, call logs, purchase orders. If it can be translated to a database form, it can be at your fingertips via Ctrl+F.

Revising and formatting a database form

As you gain experience building and using databases, your reliance on them will increase. Before you know it, you won't be able to get though a computing day without tapping into one or more of your databases. As your database dependency grows, so will the number of cool ideas you'll have for improving your various forms. In the paper-based world, when the need to change a form arises, you first redesign the form, then spend a pretty penny getting it printed. Oh, and you also have to toss the old forms in the trash (a capital offence if ever there was one) or use them for scrap paper. Thankfully, you're now in the digital domain. Changing a database form won't cost you anything but time. Press Ctrl+F9 to enter Form Design mode (or click View | Form Design). To add a new database field, click in any blank area of the form, and type the name of the new field followed by a colon. Here's an example: Click at the bottom of the form, and type: **Notes:**

Make sure to end the field name with a colon (entered by typing Shift+;). The colon tells the Works 2000 Database that you want to enter a new field.

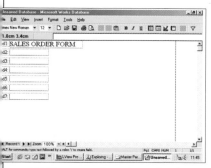

■ **You can alter** the style of text in a database object.

Press Enter, and the Insert Field wizard appears. Look familiar? It's the same dialog used by the Create Database wizard. Select your field's Format and Appearance (in this case, you can leave it set to General), and click OK. The all-new "Notes" field materializes on your form. At this point you can position it, resize it, and set its tab order just like any other field. It's also possible to enter text into the database that's not tied to a field. Click in any blank area, and type **SALES ORDER FORM** and press Enter. Notice there's no colon used. This plain text, without a colon, is called a "label," and can be relocated anywhere on your database form. Labels are useful for adding instructions on how to use the database, or to dress up a database so it can be used as a paper-based form when it's printed. For instance, you might want to use this sales order entry database as an invoice. That would require your adding a "Remit To" address, and other basic information. All that can be added as plain text labels, simply by clicking, typing, and moving the label. Remember, to create a new field, end your field name with a colon. To create a label, don't use a colon.

While you're in Form Design mode, you might also want to dress up your database fields and plain text labels. Right-click on any database field, and the object's context menu pops up. You can modify the object's alignment, font, and style, just as you can in word processors and spreadsheets. You can also add borders to fields and labels, or apply 3-D shading effects.

All of these formatting options are available through the straightforward use of a right-click – but only while you're in Form Design mode.

Deleting database fields or records

The day will come that you discover one or more fields in your database table are no longer needed. Perhaps you've decided to give all of your customers free shipping. That kills the need for a "Freight" field. To snip a field out of the database, head into Form Design by pressing Ctrl+F9 (or click View | Form Design). Click on the field you want to delete, and press the Delete key (or click Edit | Delete Selection). If you'd like to delete multiple fields, click+drag a lasso around all of the fields you'd like to delete, then press the Delete key (or click Edit | Delete Selection). It's even more likely that you'll want to delete records. Simple enough. First find the order by pressing Ctrl+F (or clicking Edit | Find). When the order comes up, click Record | Delete Record.

■ **That could be** *a customer calling to cancel his orders!*

If you delete the wrong record, immediately hit Ctrl+Z to Undo the deletion (or click Edit | Undo). If you don't the data is gone forever.

Now assume a customer goes bankrupt and cancels all his orders with you. First you'll want to print out all of the company's bills, so you can file a claim with the bankruptcy court. And eventually, you'll want to delete all of their records from your database. Click Ctrl+F to open the Find dialog (or click Edit | Find). Enter your search argument. Before clicking OK, select the "All records" option by clicking its radio box. This tells the Works 2000 Database to find all of their records, and to temporarily hide all records that don't match. Click OK, and the Works 2000 Database processes your request.

Now the only records showing are those that match the company's. You can print them all by pressing Ctrl+P (or click the Print button on the toolbar, or click File | Print). Only the found record set will print; all other records remain hidden. You can visually review the records by using the "VCR buttons" at the bottom of the database's window. You can also jump among records by pressing Ctrl+UpArrow (or Ctrl+PageDown). To go backwards, press Ctrl+DownArrow (or Ctrl+PageUp). As you view each record, you can delete it by clicking Record | Delete. You can resume displaying all records by clicking Record | Show | All Records.

Saving and printing

THE FIRST TIME *you save a database, you'll have to name it. To save a database, press Ctrl+S. If this is the first time you're saving it, the Save As dialog will appear. Click the "File name" input box, and enter a name for the file.*

AUTO-SAVE

Most flat-file databases, such as Works 2000 Database, require you to manually save the database by pressing Ctrl+S or clicking File | Save. Relational databases save your work automatically. (FileMaker's FileMaker Pro auto-saves in both flat-file and relational modes.)

You can give the file any name you like. As is the case with saving documents and spreadsheets, certain punctuation characters are off-limits in file names. If you try to use a so-called "illegal" character, Windows 98 will hiccup, and ask you to decide on a different file name, or remove the illegal character.

The single most important aspect of saving a file for the first time: Be absolutely certain you save it in your master personal folder.

If you don't, you could misplace it, and have a tough time locating the file in the future. Click the small green-and-white Desktop icon on the Save As dialog's toolbar. You're now looking at a miniature view of your Windows Desktop, scrunched into the Save As dialog's window. Double-click your master personal folder to open it. After it opens, click OK. The file is saved directly to your master personal folder.

It's wise to save your database every few minutes. Hit Ctrl+S periodically. In the event of a power failure, the latest version of your database will be safely tucked away in the PC's hard disk. After the file is safely saved, there are two ways to retrieve it. You can double-click the file from inside your master personal folder, or you can open it from inside the Works 2000 Database. Press Ctrl+O (or click the Open toolbar button, or click File | Open.) The file you just saved will be listed in the Open dialog. Just double-click it.

Make sure you *use "Save As" to save your file into your master personal folder.*

If your database doesn't appear in the Open dialog, it means you're not looking at your master personal folder. Click the little green-and-white Desktop icon on the Open dialog's toolbar. This returns you to a tiny view of the Windows Desktop, squeezed into the Open dialog's window. Double-click your master personal folder to open it, and your previously saved databases will appear. (A list of your most recently accessed databases always appears on the File menu.) To print a database, press Ctrl+P, or click the Print button on the toolbar. You can also click File | Print.

USEFUL KEYSTROKES AND COMMANDS

✓ To move to the next database field or record, press Tab.

✓ To move to the previous database field or record, press Shift+Tab.

✓ To accept a field change without moving to another field, press Enter.

✓ To move to the next record, press Ctrl+UpArrow or Ctrl+PageDown.

✓ To move to the previous record, press Ctrl+DownArrow or Ctrl+PageUp.

✓ To jump to the first record, press Ctrl+Home.

✓ To jump to the last record, press Ctrl+End.

✓ To jump to the beginning of a record, press Home.

✓ To jump to the end of a record, press End.

✓ To edit the active field in Form view, press F2, and start typing (or click inside it or the formula bar).

✓ To select fields in Form Design mode, click on them, or click+drag a lasso around them.

✓ To cancel a selection in any View model, press Esc, then click anywhere.

Explanation of the database modes

✓ Form View is for entering and printing data.

✓ Form Design view is for programming the database.

✓ List View is used to build and enter database formulas and to view the database table.

Changing database modes

✓ To view the database form, press F9.

✓ To view the database table, press Shift+F9 (or click View | List).

✓ To program the database, press Ctrl+F9.

Adding and deleting

✓ To add a new record, click Record | Insert.

✓ To delete the current record, click Record | Delete Record.

✓ To undo a deletion, press Ctrl+Z (or click Edit | Undo).

✓ To add fields or labels, press Ctrl+F9 to enter Form Design, and click Insert | Field or Insert | Label.

✓ To delete a field, press Ctrl+F9 to enter Form Design, select the target field(s), then press the Delete key. Field deletions are NOT undoable.

Formatting fields

✓ To format fields, first press Ctrl+F9 to enter Form Design mode.

✓ To make a field bold, select it and press Ctrl+B .

✓ To make a field italic, select it and press Ctrl+I .

✓ To underline a field, select it and press Ctrl+U.

✓ To change fonts, select the field and choose a font from the Font drop-down pick-list.

✓ To change size, select the field and choose a size from the Size drop-down pick-list.

Copying, cutting, and pasting fields

✓ Copying, cutting, and pasting works in all View modes.

✓ To copy a field, select it and press Ctrl+C .

✓ To cut a field, select it and press Ctrl+X.

✓ To paste a cut or copied field, select it and press Ctrl+V.

Managing data

✓ To set tab order, press Ctrl+F9 to enter Form Design, and click Format | Tab Order.

✓ To find data, press Ctrl+F (or click the Find toolbar button, or click Edit | Find).

✓ To repeat the last Find, press F3.

✓ To search and replace data, press Ctrl+H (or click Edit | Replace).

✓ To find and select multiple records, press Ctrl+F, and choose "All records."

✓ To sort the database, click Record | Sort.

✓ To check your spelling, press F7 (or click Tools | Spelling).

✓ To set your preferences, click Tools | Options, and explore the Options dialog.

✓ To undo a mistake, press Ctrl+Z (or click Edit | Undo).

Saving, opening, printing, and closing databases

✓ To save the file, press Ctrl+S (or click the toolbar's Save button, or click File | Save).

✓ To print the file, press Ctrl+P.

✓ To open a saved file, press Ctrl+O .

✓ To close a file, click File | Close.

A simple summary

✓ Database formulas use field names as variables instead of cell rows and columns.

✓ You navigate database forms using Tab and Shift+Tab.

✓ To enter data into a database field, Tab or Shift+Tab into the field, type the data, and then press Enter.

✓ Retrieve information using the Find and Find Again commands.

✓ Right-click any database field to format it while in Form Design mode.

✓ You can restore deleted database fields by hitting Ctrl+Z.

✓ Get in the habit of saving files as you work, by pressing Ctrl+S.

✓ Always save your documents to your master personal folder.

✓ To print, press Ctrl+P.

Chapter 16

Penciling Things In on the Calendar

HAD LEWIS CARROLL been born in the 1990s instead of the 1830s, childhood would be all the poorer for not having his classic fantasy, *Alice's Adventures in Wonderland*, to read. Fast forward to 2000: that busy rabbit wouldn't be at the mercy of a low-tech pocket watch, no sir! He'd have a hot new desktop PC in his high-tech rabbit warren, chugging away with Windows 98, running the latest version of the hot hot hot new Works 2000 Calendar. Mr. White Rabbit would have punched his very important date into the Calendar weeks ago. When the big day arrived, the Works 2000 Calendar would have automagically reminded him of his impending appointments – and made sure the high-tech hare had plenty of time to spare. Unlike that pesky wabbit, you have the Works 2000 Calendar at your disposal.

In this chapter...

✓ A computerized calendar?

✓ Using the calendar

A computerized calendar?

AFTER SCALING THE *word processing, spreadsheet, and database learning curves, tackling the Works 2000 Calendar is going to seem like a walk in the park. That's because you already know how to use it. The Microsoft Works 2000 Calendar is essentially the computerized equivalent of a paper-based calendar. It takes the same familiar calendar design that's been used for ages, and enhances it with the natural benefits of computerization.*

For example, you can pencil in an appointment on a paper-based calendar, and you can pencil in an appointment on the Works 2000 Calendar. But what if the appointment is five years from today? You'd be lucky if you could find a paper calendar or date book that goes out beyond 18 months.

The Works 2000 Calendar, on the other hand, can book appointments up to the year 2099!

Booking appointments is one thing. Remembering them (and getting to them on time) are quite another. With the Works 2000 Calendar, you'll never forget an anniversary or birthday again – not to mention legal holidays, business luncheons, deadlines, meetings, and anything else that gets pegged to a date, time, and place. Reminders for any type of appointment can be set to pop up on your screen minutes, days, weeks, even months in advance.

■ **A paper calendar** *is fine for a year – but then you have to get another one.*

Setting up the Works 2000 Calendar

The first step is to copy the Microsoft Works 2000 Calendar icon straight into your master personal folder. Press Win+D to return to the Windows Desktop. Then click Start | Programs | Microsoft Works. Right-click the Microsoft Works Calendar icon, and select Copy. Switch to your master personal folder by double-clicking it, or hitting its hot key. Right-click any blank area in your master personal folder, and select Paste. If you want to assign a hot key to the Microsoft Works Calendar icon, do that now. Right-click the icon, select Properties, and enter the keystroke you want to use in the "Shortcut key" input box. Then click OK. (I use Ctrl+Alt+F11 on my computer.)

■ **Clone your Works 2000** *Calendar icon into your master personal folder.*

Using the calendar

CALL UP THE WORKS 2000 *Calendar by double-clicking its icon or hitting its hot key. When it finishes loading, zoom its window to full screen size by double-clicking the title bar, or clicking the Maximize button.*

Looks just like the calendar magnetically stuck on your refrigerator, doesn't it? Therein lies the strength of the Works 2000 Calendar, and most PC-based calendars. In Works 2000 Calendar, you grab the mouse (not a pencil), and click through electronic pages until the appointed date appears. Then you click on the date and type in the appointment. When the time comes, the Works 2000 Calendar will automatically remind you of the appointment.

Entering appointments

The Works 2000 Calendar gives you three different ways (or "views") to book and review appointments, and other time-and-date sensitive reminders: Month view, Week view, and Day view. Switching among views is as easy as clicking the appropriate view button on the toolbar. For Day view, click the toolbar button with the number "1" on it. For Week view, click the "7" button. For Month view, click the "31" button. Yes, you have to click "31" for Month view even when the month has 28, 29, or 30 days!

You can also use keyboard alternates or menu commands to switch views.

To hit Day view, press Alt+1, or click View | Day. For Week view, press Alt+- (that's Alt plus the minus key). For Month view, hit Alt+= (that's Alt plus equal), or click View | Month. Most people find Day view the most flexible and convenient of the three views. Day view shows a day at a glance, broken down by the hour. Through Day view, you can set and adjust hourly or daylong appointments, and skip through the calendar one day or month at a time. Week view

displays your week at a glance. Week view also lets you set and adjust hourly or daylong appointments, and skip through the calendar a week or month at a time. Month view is the traditional calendar view. It's best for taking in your schedule's big picture. Month view displays all appointments, but only supports setting or changing of daylong appointments. Month view is also limited to traversing the calendar a month at a time.

■ **Guess what?** *Works 2000 Calendar looks exactly like ... a calendar.*

Setting appointments in Day view

Let's say you want to set a reminder for 4:00 p.m. Friday. This reminder could be for an appointment, a deadline, or just something to jog your memory (e.g. perhaps you want to remember to pick up milk on the way home from work). Put the calendar into Day view by clicking the "1" button (or pressing Alt+1, or clicking View | Day). Click the big date display at the top of the Works 2000 Calendar screen. Down drops a miniature calendar, which can be used to select days in the future and past.

■ **You can insert** *a new appointment for any time of the day.*

At the top of the mini-calendar are right- and left-arrow buttons. Click the left arrow to go back in time. Click the right arrow to move forward in time. Do that now: Click the right arrow, and next month appears. Click the left arrow, and you're returned to the current month.

A slower but easier way to traverse the calendar is to click the "Previous Day" and "Next Day" buttons. You'll find them to the left and right of the large date display.

Now click on the next available Friday, and the Works 2000 Calendar displays that date in Day view. Click anywhere on or across the 4:00 p.m. block, and the New Appointment dialog appears. If you clicked on the top half of the 4:00 block, the new appointment will be set to start at 4:00 sharp. If you clicked in the bottom half of the 4:00 block, the new appointment will be set to start at 4:30. It doesn't really matter; you can change the start and end times easily enough using the New Appointment dialog tools. But first, click in the Title input box and then type in a name for the appointment.

The name of the appointment will become the text of the reminder that will pop up on your screen when the appointment reminder is set to go off, so make sure it's something that will make sense to you. For example, "Pick up milk," or "Teleconference with Joe G"

You can also enter a location and category for the appointment. These bits of extra info are entirely optional. Most folks (including me) ignore them in the interest of rapid data entry, but some people find them extremely handy. To enter a location, type one into the Location input box. To assign the appointment to a category, click the Change button, and select one of the categories from the list box. Click its check box to select it, then click OK. You can also create your own categories by clicking the Edit Categories button, and entering the category name into the input box. Click the Add button to add your custom category to the list.

There will be times when you need to clip some additional information onto an appointment, such as driving directions or a teleconference dial-in number. Click in the Reminder input box, and type in any information you want to attach to the appointment.

If the appointment's start and end times aren't exactly correct (and they often won't be), fine tune them by clicking on the "Appointment starts" and "Appointment ends" drop-down pick-lists. You can edit the start and end times right down to the minute. For instance, a start time of "4:00 p.m." can be edited to read "4:02 p.m.". You can even change the month, day, and hour using the "Appointment starts" and "Appointment ends" pick-lists.

Setting all-day events in Day view

■ **Use Works 2000** *Calendar to remind yourself to pick up essential groceries.*

Click OK when you're satisfied with all of the new appointment parameters. That returns you to the Day view screen, where your appointment now appears. Now suppose you wanted to set an all-day appointment or reminder. This is a reminder that isn't tied to a specific time, but rather to a specific date. Examples of all-day appointments are things such as project deadlines, vacation or sick days, company holidays, and so on. Click the gray bar at t he top of the Day view screen that reads "Click here to add an all day event." A long input box opens. Type in a title for the all-day event (such as "Off today! Yippee!"), and press Enter.

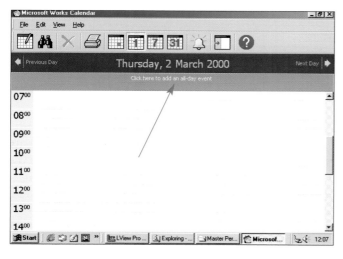

The title you enter will form the text of the reminder that pops-up as your all-day event approaches.

■ **In Day view**, *you can click to add an all-day event.*

Setting appointments in Week view

Now lets assume you're booked to the walls, but your boss insists on a lunch meeting with you, to congratulate you on your outstanding progress in learning Windows 98. You could travel one Day view at a time looking for an opening. A better choice: Use Week view. First, go back to the current date by clicking Edit | Go To | Today. Switch the calendar into Week view by clicking the toolbar's "7" button (or press Alt+-, or click View | Week). Click the big date display at the top of the Works 2000 Calendar screen. Once again the miniature calendar drops down, but this time, it's used to select weeks in the future and past – not days.

■ **Adding a new** *appointment in Week View.*

As before, the mini-calendar features right- and left- arrow buttons. Click the left arrow to go back, the right arrow to move forward in time. Try that now: Click the right arrow, and next month appears. Click the left arrow, and you're back in the current month. Now click on any week, and the Works 2000 Calendar displays it in Week view. Alternatively, you can click the "Previous Week" and "Next Week" buttons to traverse the calendar week by week.

You might think that to add an appointment you should click where it reads "Click here to add an appointment." Don't.

That will open an appointment for the first available time slot that day. Instead, double-click any blank area on the date you want to set, or right-click and select New Appointment. The New Appointment dialog appears. Fill out the New Appointment dialog with your appointment's information, and click OK to set it.

Week view also supports all-day appointments and reminders. Double-click the actual date text (i.e. where it reads "Monday, July 4" or whatever), and the New Appointment dialog opens. This time, however, it's preset to accept only an all-day event. Complete the dialog, and click OK to set it in stone.

Setting all-day events in Month view

It happens to the best of us: Get the hang of the Works 2000 Calendar, and suddenly you're booking all of your important birthdays, anniversaries, and other personal and religious events on the computer. Try to get that big job done using day or Week view, and your wrist will fall off from all the pointing and clicking. It takes 52 clicks to scan a year in Week view, and 365 clicks to do the same in Day view. Sure, you could use the mini-calendar to expedite the process. But a better approach is to use Works 2000 Calendar's

Month view feature. Zip back to the current date by clicking Edit | Go To | Today. Switch the calendar into Month view by clicking the toolbar's "31" button (or press Alt+=, or click View | Month). Before running off to enter holidays, take advantage of a little gift from mother Microsoft.

Microsoft's engineers and **beta testers** *figured out early on that users immediately wanted to enter holidays and other special events soon after they mastered the Works 2000 Calendar.*

■ **You can select** *the religious holidays you want added to your calendar.*

Rather than force users to enter all this data manually, Microsoft added not one, but two cool features that automatically populates the calendar with important dates. Click Edit | Add Holidays, and the Works 2000 Calendar will display the "Add Holidays" dialog. Review the list of countries featured in the list box, and click on those whose national and religious holidays you want added to your calendar. You can select as many countries as you like, and can return to the Add Holidays feature at any time to add more. When you're done, click the OK button to add the holidays to your calendar. They'll show up as all-day events in Day, Week, and Month view for every year through 2099.

If you have entered any birthdays in your Outlook Express address book, you're in luck. Click Edit | Birthdays to have the Works 2000 Calendar clone them into your calendar as well. Do this once, and Works 2000 Calendar will automatically clone any new birthdays it finds in your address book every time you start it up.

■ **Keep track of** *birthdays with Works 2000 Calendar!*

It's also a snap to add events to the calendar using Month view. Click the big date display at the top of the Works 2000 Calendar screen. The mini-calendar drops down. Click the left arrow to go back in time, and the right arrow to move forward. You can also click the big "Previous Month" and "Next Month" buttons. When the month you're after is in view, click any date to set an all-day event. Note that you can only set daylong events while in Month view.

Setting recurring appointments

You can cause any appointment to recur by clicking the "Make this appointment repeat" checkbox that appears in the New Appointment dialog.

The Recurrence button will suddenly come into view. Click it, and you can set your recurrence options in the Recurrence Options dialog. Point and click your instructions to make the appointment recur daily, weekly, monthly, or yearly. As you click the various selections, the Works 2000 Calendar will provide further logical options to fine-tune the recurrence. For example, if you choose a monthly recurrence, the software will allow you to set a specific date or a certain week of the month. You'll also be able to set a start and end date for the series of recurring events, or set a maximum number of recurrences before the Works 2000 Calendar automatically cancels the event. When you're finished, click OK to accept them, and then OK again.

Changing and deleting appointments

There's more than one way to change appointments and events. You can double-click them to open the Edit Appointment dialog, which is essentially the same as the New Appointment dialog. You can also drag+drop appointments from one date to another in Month or Week view, or from one time slot to another in Day view. Also, while in Day view, you can visually make an appointment longer or shorter by clicking+dragging its borders. Appointments and events can also be deleted. Deleting any entry in Works 2000 Calendar is a simple matter of right-clicking it, and selecting Delete. You can also click on an item and press Delete.

■ **When your reminder** *pops up you have to choose one of the following: Dismiss, Cancel or Open.*

Dealing with reminders

At the time an appointment comes due, it will pop up on your screen. You can set reminders to pop up anywhere from a few minutes in advance, to months ahead of time. When you first set up an appointment, you'll see the option to set its advance reminder in the New Appointment dialog's Reminder drop-down pick-list. For established appointments and events, you can get this pick-list through the Edit Appointment dialog. Select the advance notice you prefer, and click OK. If the advance notice you're looking for doesn't show up on the drop-down pick-list, type it in yourself. The Works 2000 Calendar will figure out what you're after, and adjust its settings accordingly.

After the sands of time run out on your reminder and Works 2000 Calendar pops it up, you can choose to Dismiss Item (cancel it), Close the dialog (ignore it), or Open the item to edit.

Saving, opening, and printing the calendar

In contrast to all other Works 2000 productivity tools, you never have to save or open the calendar. Loading the Works 2000 Calendar automatically opens the data set, and changes you input are automatically saved. To print your calendar, press Ctrl+P, or click the Print button on the toolbar. You can also click File | Print. For advanced printing options, see chapter ten's "Printer Basics" section.

A roundup of the calendar keystrokes and commands

Here's a helpful roundup of the main keystrokes and commands available in the Works 2000 Calendar.

✓ Use the mouse or arrow keys to move up, down, left, and right within the calendar.
✓ Use the scroll bars or the PageUp/PageDown keys to flip through multiple pages.
✓ To jump up one page, press PageUp.
✓ To jump down one page, press PageDown.
✓ To enter Day view, press Alt+1 (or click the toolbar's "1" button, or click View | Day).
✓ To enter Week view, press Alt+- (or click the toolbar's "7" button, or click View | Week).
✓ To enter Month view, press Alt+= (or click the toolbar's "31" button, or click View Month).
✓ To delete an appointment, select it, then press the Delete key (or right-click it, and select Delete).
✓ To find an appointment or event press Ctrl+F (or click the toolbar's Search button, or click Edit | Find).
✓ To quickly hit a specific date, press Ctrl+G (or click Edit | Go To).
✓ To jump to the current date, click Edit | Go To | Today.
✓ To get Help, press F1 (or click Help | Works Help).

A simple summary

✓ The Works 2000 Calendar manages your time and commitments.

✓ The Calendar offers three views: daily, weekly, and monthly.

✓ You can set appointments by the hour, day, week, or month.

✓ Use the Add Holidays feature to °automatically populate your Calendar with national holidays.

✓ Appointments can be set to recur automatically at specific times.

✓ You will be automatically reminded of appointments.

PART FOUR

IT MAKES SENSE TO KEEP YOUR PC DATA SAFE

TO PROTECT AND PRESERVE

YOUR PC IS YOUR *virtual* HOME. It will ultimately contain some or all of your personal electronic artifacts, such as credit card information, resumes, love  letters, business correspondence, photos, legal matters, personal thoughts, and other digital gems. If you fail to lock down your PC data, your computer remains an open book for thieves, computer crackers, Internet probes, family members, curious friends, and even your favorite computer repair person.

1	2	3	4	5	6	7
8	9	10	11	12	13	14
15	16	17	18	19	20	21
22	23	24	25	26	27	28
29	30					

In part 4, you'll *learn* how to protect your PC from all manner of cyber-threats, from natural disasters such as system crashes, to man-made nasties and the computer repair guy or gal.

Chapter 17

Keeping Secrets Safe

TODAY, THERE ARE over 45,000 nasty bugs that target, attack, destroy, or otherwise foul your PC – and more arrive daily. Over 1,025 new live viruses were identified as circulating in the wild by technicians at the Symantec Antivirus Center (SARC) in 1999 alone. Sadly, viruses are not the only threat PC users face. Merely logging on to the Internet exposes your computer to cyber-crooks, whose only goal in life is to break into your PC and make off with your personal data. In this chapter, you'll learn what data security and integrity are and why they matter. Then you'll learn how to protect your personal data and how to ward off computer viruses and other germs.

In this chapter...

✓ Data security and integrity

✓ Protect your data

✓ Shielding yourself online

✓ Computers catch colds too

GIVE YOURSELF THE COMFORT OF KNOWING THAT YOUR DATA IS SECURE

Data security and integrity

THEY SAID *it couldn't be cracked. Cartes Bancaires, a consortium of 176 French financial institutions, invested years of effort and piles of cash to create an unbreakable "smart" card system. The cards, distributed to bank patrons, are secured by a tiny computer chip. Unlike "dumb" magnetic strips, which are easily duplicated and mass-produced by counterfeiters, the smart card's embedded chip can't be inexpensively cloned, Cartes Bancaires officials said. Moreover, the cards use "digital signatures" to electronically validate the cardholder every time they're used.*

■ **The idea that**
*Cartes Bancaires'
"smart" card was
secure sank
without trace.*

The combination of a high-tech chip and electronic validation turned out to be as unbreakable as the *Titanic* was unsinkable. In January 2000, Serge Humpich, a 36-year-old programmer, used a homemade counterfeit smart card to buy ten train tickets. He was arrested soon after proving his point. That same month, hackers purloined data from credit card giant Visa International's systems. This occurred only days after a cyber-thief illicitly downloaded credit card data from e-retailer CD Universe and posted the info on the web for all to steal.

If organizations like Visa International, Cartes Bancaires, and CD Universe can't protect their corporate jewels from hackers, crackers, crooks and schnooks, how in the world can you? Rest assured you can. It turns out that securing your personal PC is a trivial task, when compared to locking down huge web servers such as Visa's, or designing "uncrackable" smart cards. It's even easier than securing your home, car, or office.

Before you can fully protect your PC and its data, you need to understand the difference between data security and data integrity. Data security is the ability to isolate and protect your PC's electronic contents from the outside world.

That means restricting access to your computer through the use of passwords and shielding your data from unauthorized contact via firewalls, encryption and obfuscation.

Even the most secure systems, however, can be compromised. If your data is corrupted, infected, or otherwise tampered with, it is said to lack integrity. Maintaining data integrity refers to your ability to detect tampering and corruption and rapidly repair damaged data.

If you adhere religiously to computing practices that ensure total data integrity — such as creating emergency "backup" copies of your data — you'll be able to laugh in the face of data disasters that literally cripple, even bankrupt, less prepared users.

Data security and data integrity go hand in hand. As a matter of fact, the first rule of preserving your data's integrity is to maximize your PC's security. For that, you'll have to . . .

■ **An unprotected PC** *is an invitation to cyber-thieves.*

Protect your data

IN ITS NATURAL out-of-the-box state, your PC is a gilded invitation to cyber-thieves — technologically-sophisticated criminals who can penetrate your PC while you're online. While no security system is foolproof, there are standard procedures you should implement.

Topping the list is setting a main system password. This is set through the PC hardware itself. Nearly every computer sold today provides a means to set a main system password. The problem is that they all use a different keyboard command to run the software program that lets you set the system's password. Most computers display this command when you first power-on the system.

Setting a power-on password

Unfortunately, most users never notice this command, also known as the "hardware Setup" command. Here's how to gain access to your PC's hardware Setup program and set a system password. First, shut down your computer by clicking Start | Shut Down. When the Shut Down Windows dialog appears, click the "Shut Down" radio button, then click OK. Allow Windows 98 to shut down completely, then restart the computer. Watch the screen carefully. As the system goes through its power-on self-test, you should see a message on the screen that reads something like this: "Press <keystroke> to enter Setup". The <keystroke> could be any key or keyboard combination.

If you see a prompt to press any key or keyboard combo, that's your Setup key. If you don't see a prompt for a Setup key, check your owner's manual, or call your PC manufacturer.

The most common Setup keys are F1, F10, Del, Ctrl+Esc, Ctrl+Alt+Esc, and Alt+S. Regardless of what the keystroke is, press it immediately after the on-screen prompt appears. Your PC's Setup program will appear on the screen. If you see the keystroke prompt but hit the keys too late, turn your computer off, wait a second, and turn it on again. When the prompt reappears, quickly hit the keystroke to load the Setup program.

Sometimes computers are pre-set at the factory or by your dealer not to display their Setup keystroke at startup. If your computer doesn't display its Setup key or key combo at startup, try all of these keystrokes. Hit one of them immediately after you turn your computer on and hear its beep (PCs always beep after they successfully complete their power-on self-test). If the keystroke doesn't work, turn the computer off and on again, and try another keystroke or key combo from the following:

Alt+?	Ctrl+Esc
Alt+Enter	Ctrl+Insert (or Ins)
Alt+S	Ctrl+S
Ctrl+Alt+=	Ctrl+Shift+Esc
Ctrl+Alt+Esc	Delete (or Del)
Ctrl+Alt+Insert (or Ins)	Esc
Ctrl+Alt+S	F1
Ctrl+Alt+Shift+=	F10
F2	Insert (or Ins)

■ **Find the right key** *combination to enter Setup.*

. . . and last but not least, hit the "Reset" button twice (if your PC features a reset switch). If none of the above keystrokes work, press and hold any key down on your keyboard while powering up the PC. Keep the key depressed while the computer starts up. This will cause most PCs to generate an error, followed by the message "Press F1 (or F2) to enter Setup." Hit the key as instructed, and you're in!

Be extremely careful while poking around in the Setup program. It's possible to change settings here that can cause your PC to stop operating properly. If you even think you've screwed up, stop in your tracks! Then turn off the PC's power, wait a second, and turn it on again. That will revert the PC to whatever settings it had before you entered the Setup program.

Let's assume you haven't screwed up! Now look for a menu named "Security," "Password," "Access Control," or something similar. Your mouse probably won't work in the Setup program, but your arrow and Tab keys will. In most Setup systems, the arrow keys are used to move between options, and Tab, Shift+Tab, and Enter are used to select (activate) options.

■ **Take care** *when poking around in Setup.*

Some Setup programs use the + and - keys to select options, and use Enter to activate them. As always, RTFS (read the fine screen) for clues as to what keys cause what actions when working within the Setup program.

When you find the password settings, follow the instructions on the screen for establishing and enabling the password. Most Setup programs offer two settings: User password and supervisor password. The user password controls access to the computer. The supervisor password controls access to the Setup program. It's best to set both of these passwords to the same code word. When choosing a password, take care to use something singularly unique that you and you alone will know.

Never use your last name, your initials, your kid's or spouse's names, sporting teams, rock bands, birthdays, nicknames, and so on. Don't use "password" as your password.

(Don't laugh. It's the most common password.) All of these are easily exploited by what are called "brute force attacks." They're the first passwords spies type in when they're trying to break into your PC.

Also, for some computers, passwords are case sensitive. That means a password entered in uppercase letters, such as "FUBAR2000," is treated differently from "fubar2000," which is treated differently from "FuBaR2000."

To avoid locking yourself out of your system by accidentally entering an all uppercase or reverse-case password, make sure the "Caps Lock" light on your keyboard is off.

Caps Lock reverses your keyboard's output, so that lowercase letters are capitalized and caps are not. If Caps Lock is lit up, press the Caps Lock key on the left-hand side of the keyboard, below Tab, and above Shift, to return the keyboard to its normal state. Passwords that are hardest to crack are eight to ten characters long, with a random mix of numbers, letters, and punctuation. For example, XAV-5722 is a meaningless, yet excellent password.

Entering a password usually requires nothing more than arrowing into the password option and pressing Tab or Enter. Then type in a password. The computer will ask you to enter it again, to make sure you typed it correctly. Repeat the process for any additional password settings the Setup program offers. When you're done, review the screen for a SAVE option. This is usually labeled "Save Setup and Exit," "Save and Exit," or "Save Changes and Exit." If you don't see a SAVE option, try hitting the Esc key. That will usually bring up the SAVE options, or feature an "Exit Saving Changes" option. Select a SAVE option. The PC will store the new password setting, reboot, and start its power-on self-test.

A moment later, you'll be greeted by an "Enter password" or "Input password" prompt of some kind. Type in the password exactly as you entered it in Setup, and press Enter.

Your PC will continue its startup process. Note that some computers provide an extra level of security by not displaying an "Enter password" prompt. Instead, they'll display a picture of a key, a question mark, a blinking underscore, or nothing at all. If your PC reboots and just sits there, without going into Windows 98, it's waiting for your password. Type it in, and press Enter. Your PC will merrily resume its startup process, and drop you into Windows 98.

If you enter your password incorrectly, your computer will reject it, and will repeatedly ask you to enter your password again. Some PCs lock up by design after three incorrect password entries. If this happens to you, first make sure your keyboard's Caps Lock light is off. If it's lit up, press the Caps Lock key to turn it off. Turn off the PC, wait a second, and then turn it on again.

Once you've established a power-on password, anyone who doesn't know the password won't be able to get into your PC. To protect yourself from a memory lapse, write your password down, and store it in your wallet or purse.

■ **Never stick** *your password on your monitor.*

BYPASSING THE PASSWORD

No security system is foolproof, and power-on passwords are no exception. Most PCs have secret "backdoor" passwords that some crooks know. These backdoor passwords are used by the PC manufacturer to gain access to protected PCs when they need service, or when users forget their password and accidentally lock themselves out of their computer. Type in the backdoor password and the PC opens up.

Also, if a spy has enough time, he can disassemble your PC, remove the battery on the motherboard, and restart the computer. Other models have something called a "jumper" (a small plastic cap that covers two electrical pins on the motherboard) that allows the power-on password to be bypassed. Remove the jumper and the password is removed. The best PCs, such as certain models offered by Acer and IBM, are tamper resistant. They'll require a power-on password even if the battery is removed, or if the motherboard is tampered with. If you're very concerned about security, check out IBM's line of secure PCs at www.ibm.com/security. They're tops.

Whatever you do, don't jot your password down on a Post-It or notepad that's kept by your computer. That defeats the entire purpose of password-protecting your PC.

Setting a screen saver password

■ **For top-of-the-range** *secure computers, check out IBM at www.ibm.com/security.*

Preventing access at power-on is one thing. Stopping people from peeking at your work while the PC is running is quite another matter. Even if your PC is protected by a power-on password, when your PC is running and you step away, your data is vulnerable. The solution is to enable your screen saver password. A screen saver is a built-in utility that blanks the screen and displays some entertaining animation whenever your PC is idle for an extended period of time.

As an added bonus, the screen saver can be configured to activate a password when it starts up. Here's how: Click Start | Settings | Control Panel. When the Control Panel opens, double-click the Display applet. In the Display Properties dialog, click the Screen Saver tab. (You can also open the Display properties dialog by right-clicking your Windows Desktop, and selecting Properties.)

Select one of the available screen savers featured in the Screen Saver drop-down pick-list. After you select the screen saver, check the "Password protected" checkbox. The Change Password dialog will appear. Click in the "New password" input box, and type in a password. Hit Tab, and type the same password in the "Confirm password" input box. Click OK, and Windows 98 will report that the screen saver has been set. Click OK again to return to Display Properties.

Ideally, your screen saver password should be different from your power-on password. As before, when choosing a password, take care to use something singularly unique that you and you alone will know.

Remember, never use your last name, your initials, your company name, your kid's or spouse's names, sporting teams, rock bands, birthdays, nicknames, and so on. And don't use the word "password." All are easily cracked by experienced spies.

■ **Don't use your** *kid's name for a password.*

The passwords hardest to crack are eight to ten characters long, with a random mix of numbers and letters. For example, FOO*2280 is a meaningless, yet superb password.

Also, don't forget to check the state of Caps Lock before entering your password. This prevents you from accidentally locking yourself out of your own PC. If the Caps Lock light is lit, press the Caps Lock key to turn it off.

If the "Password protected" checkbox is grayed-out, the screen saver you selected does not support a password. Choose a different screen saver, one that supports the password feature. If you want to change your screen saver password, return to the Display Properties dialog, and click the Change button.

■ **You can change** *your screen saver password.*

Next, set the "time-out" for the screen saver. This is the amount of time your PC has to be idle before the screen saver will kick in and activate its password protection. Click in the Wait spin box, and type in a value for the screen saver time-out. Ideally, this should be somewhere between 5 and 15 minutes. You can set it as low as 1 minute, and as high as 60 minutes. Some screen savers have various options that can also be tweaked, such as which colors to use, whether sound effects should be on or off, how fast or slow they should playback any animation, and so on. Click the Settings button to examine and configure any available screen saver options.

When you're done, click OK to accept the settings and enable the screen saver password. After the time-out period, the screen saver will gear up. Unauthorized persons will be prevented from accessing your PC after the screen saver kicks in. Even if they reboot your computer in an effort to get around the screen saver password, they'll be stopped cold by your system's power-on password.

In fact, if you ever step away from your PC, and return to find it powered off or waiting for a power-on password, you'll know someone tried to get a peek at your data.

To get past the screen saver and back to your Windows Desktop, press any key on the keyboard. The Windows Screen Saver dialog will appear. Type in the password, and press Enter (or click OK).

Bulletproof security

■ **Even the cleverest** *criminals can't crack your data if it's scrambled.*

Power-on and screen saver passwords afford an effective level of security for home and office environments. If your PC is lost or stolen, however, sophisticated thieves know how to bypass these safeguards. There are two paths to follow if you're interested in the utmost in data security: data file encryption software and system security software.

Data file encryption software creates one or more areas on your hard disk that are electronically scrambled. Only people who know the access password can get to the scrambled data. If you save all of your sensitive data files to these automatically scrambled areas, the chances of the data being compromised by even advanced cyber-criminals are slim to none. That's because the scrambling technology is the same or similar to that used by the Central Intelligence Agency (CIA), the Department of Defense (DoD), the National Security Agency (NSA), and other super-secret US government agencies. It would take a supercomputer, or hundreds of interconnected PCs, to crack the scrambled data without a password.

INTERNET

www-08.nist.gov/cryptval/des.htm

The National Institute of Standards and Technology's Computer Security Division maintains this resource on U.S. data encryption standards.

There are also software packages that offer total system protection. Such packages provide password-protected access to various resources in your PC, such as folders, files, drives, programs, and so on. This means you can set additional passwords beyond just the standard power-on and screen saver passwords. For example, you can allow people to access your word processor and create or edit their own documents, but prevent them from accessing documents created by you or other users of your PC. Similarly, you can permit access to computer games, but prevent access to the Internet. The software goes into action after the power-on password and before Windows 98. Once again, these sophisticated tools offer extraordinary levels of protection that few, if any, spies and crooks can defeat.

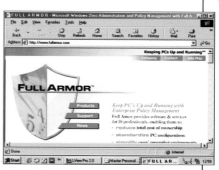

■ **The best range** *of security system products can be found at Full Armor (www.fullarmor.com).*

You can evaluate, sample, or purchase some of the better data and system security products at these web sites.

Data security (file encryption)
www.att.com/secure_software AT&T Security Software (yes, *that* AT&T)
mikkoaj.hypermart.net Mikko's File Protector
www.pgp.com PGP Desktop data security product
www.winability.com Folder Guard

System security (password protection)
www.encoreSoftware.com Encore's Security 98
www.fullarmor.com Full Armor (the best there is)
www.securewin.com SecureWin

Shielding yourself online

THERE'S GOOD REASON *why technology analysts and software vendors carp incessantly about the security risks of web surfing. The more dangerous the web appears to be, the more security software, books, seminars, and consulting services they can sell. It turns out that web surfing is actually the safest activity you can pursue with your PC. Reading e-mail, on the other hand, is the riskiest. The reasons are simple: web browsers can be adjusted to block dangerous content from ever hitting your PC. Because e-mail clients currently offer no such protection: they require add-on security software, such as anti-viruses and firewalls. As you will learn in the next section, if your e-mail system isn't protected by an anti-virus, simply reading an e-mail can destroy your PC.*

Safe web traveling, on the other hand, requires little more than a few tweaks of your web browsers settings. If you have carefully followed every exercise in this book, your web browser is already configured for maximum security. This happened back in chapter 8, in the "Security Settings for Safe Surfing" section, when you were first preparing to go online. If you haven't activated the security settings suggested in that section, go back and punch them in now.

Once your web browser's security settings are cranked up to "High," you can surf the web to your heart's content, without worrying about malicious computer programs getting into your PC by way of a web site. Any "unsafe" content will be prevented from entering or coming to life inside your PC. Clean, safe, and *pure web content* will get through. Everything else won't.

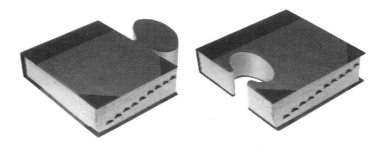

■ **Plug-ins enhance** *the capability of your browser.*

Some computer users will tell you that cranking up your web browser's security to its highest setting reduces the richness of the web experience. They're right. The sources of that extra eye candy are small programs called "scripts," "applets," and "plug-ins" that some web sites transmit to your web browser in an effort to dress up their web pages. Some of these programs animate buttons and text, or play movies. Others generate sound and music, while still others control menus and navigational systems.

It all sounds pretty innocuous. Why, then, would anyone want to block such web-enhancing programs? The answer is simple. If the world were populated by saints, then scripts, applets, and plug-ins would be loved by users everywhere. But the world is a mix of saints and sinners. The sinners use *scripts*, *applets*, and *plug-ins* to wreak havoc on innocent users' PCs. These programs can monitor your web travels, steal your personal data, plant bugs in your computer, or even wipe out entire hard drives. None of these "enhancing" technologies required to browse the web; they're all optional add-ons marketed by various technology vendors. Frankly, the risk from scripts, applets, and plug-ins far outweighs their benefit to users.

It's no wonder that the Computer Emergency Response Team (CERT) at Carnegie-Mellon University recently issued an advisory warning users to disable scripts, applets, and plug-ins in their browsers. CERT's warning was echoed by officials of the U.S. Department of Defense Joint Task Force for Computer Network Defense, the Federal Computer Incident Response Capability, and the National Infrastructure Protection Center. The bottom line: To protect yourself online, make sure your web browser security settings are cranked up, as shown in Chapter 8's "Security settings for safe surfing" section.

DEFINITION

There are many different kinds of scripts, applets, *and* plug-ins. *The most common scripting languages are AOL/Netscape's JavaScript and Microsoft's JScript and VBScript. They're essentially programming languages used to control browser behavior and activity. Applets are self-contained programs, usually written as Microsoft ActiveX components, or in Sun Microsystems' Java language. Popular plug-ins include Macromedia's Shockwave and Flash players, and Real Networks' RealPlayer.*

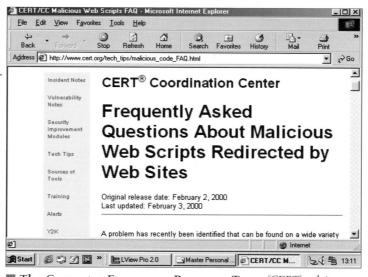

■ **The Computer Emergency Response Team** (*CERT*) *advises users to to disable scripts, applets, and plug-ins.*

Computers catch colds too

■ **An e-mail virus** is *the software equivalent of a Trojan horse.*

YOU'RE PROBABLY FAMILIAR *with the story of the Trojan War. In this mythical Greek tale, the Greeks besieged Troy for ten years, yet failed to conquer the walled city. Finally, they gave up and retreated – or so the Trojan people thought. Outside the city's walls, the Greek army left behind a giant wooden horse. The curious Trojans wheeled it inside the city in the wake of the Greek retreat. But come nightfall, Greek warriors hidden inside the giant horse came out and unlocked the city gates. The waiting Greek army marched on Troy and burned the city to the ground.*

Over 3,200 years later, the Trojan horse trick remains as potent as ever. Rogue programmers get their kicks by sending unsuspecting users the software equivalent of a Trojan horse. It can appear as an innocuous attachment to an e-mail message. Sometimes the message is actually sent – or appears to be sent – by someone you know. Open the attachment, and a software time bomb is released and starts ticking in your computer.

It's also possible for you to bring the bomb in yourself. Poking through the various "free" software offerings on the web, you download what appears to be an interesting program, game, or screen saver. You run it, and unknowingly release the time bomb into your computer.

Sometimes the bomb explodes immediately, and wipes out some or all of your files. Other times the bomb slips into your system unnoticed and starts rifling through your personal data, sending it back to the rogue programmer over the Internet. Or perhaps the bomb sends your personal data as e-mail attachments to random people plucked from your Outlook Express Address Book.

No matter how it operates, the bomb takes great pains to ensure it gets secretly attached to every e-mail you send. That way, your friends, family members, and associates will also be struck when they innocently open an attachment that appears to have been sent – by you!

Technically, these software time bombs go by many popular names. They're called worms, germs, viruses, macro viruses, time bombs, chameleons, Trojans, and a dozen other techie buzzwords. But they all boil down to one thing: a huge security risk that you, and every other Internet user on Earth, have to deal with.

Fortunately, it's easy as pie to protect yourself from software bombs. All you have to do is target the Achilles' heel all rogue programs share: In order for a bomb to impact your computer, you (yes, YOU) have to personally release it into your system. Learn to recognize the telltale signs of encroaching software bombs and you'll (hopefully) never make the mistake of double clicking on one. You'll need two powerful tools to realize this goal: an antivirus program and common sense.

Antivirus software

Antivirus software continuously monitors your PC, both on and off the Net. It scans new programs and data and defuses 99.999 percent of all software bombs circulating in the wild. Windows 98 does not include an antivirus program, but third-party software vendors offer many fine solutions to choose from. In my experience, Symantec's Norton Antivirus provides the highest level of protection against software bombs. It's the easiest of all the antivirus products to use, and it's acknowledged by leading virus research organizations as the product most likely to identify and neutralize virtually all viruses circulating over the Net.

Regardless of which vendor's antivirus product you acquire, be absolutely certain to keep the antivirus engine up to date.

Rogue programmers put hundreds of new software bombs into circulation every few months. If you don't keep your antivirus engine up to date, it won't be able to detect the latest software bombs – and that means you could get hit, even if you have an antivirus program active.

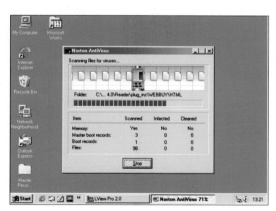

■ **Symantec's Norton Antivirus** *is the easiest of the antivirus products to use.*

All of the leading antivirus packages, include Symantec's Norton Antivirus, provide "live" update features that keep your antivirus engine current with little more than a click of the mouse. The best packages, such as Symantec's, also automatically remind you to run the live update feature every so many days, weeks, or months.

Flip a coin: From the wide range of respected vendors, any one of these leading antivirus programs will provide rock-solid protection:

www.ca.com	Computer Associate's Inoculate IT
www.mcafee.com	McAfee's VirusScan
www.sarc.com	Symantec's Norton Antivirus (it's the one I use)

Installing an antivirus

Adding an antivirus and activating it is extremely complicated (NOT!). All it takes is (1) buying the software, and (2) inserting the software CD-ROM into your CD-ROM drive. The antivirus' Setup program will start automatically. Answer any questions the Setup program asks in the course of installing the antivirus (such as your name). Accept all of the default settings by clicking the Next button in the various Setup dialogs.

Unless you know exactly what you're doing, don't change any of the recommended settings. They're preset to provide maximum protection from all manner of software bombs. Changing these settings can fatally reduce your level of protection.

When the Setup program is finished, your computer will reboot (restart), and your antivirus will automatically kick in. You don't have to run the antivirus to activate its protection; the antivirus will start on its own whenever you power-up your PC. Once the antivirus is installed, you can adjust any of its options by clicking Start | Programs, and then clicking the program's entry on the Start Menu. Or, you can put a copy of your antivirus program's icon in your master personal folder.

To copy the antivirus, press Win+D to return to the Windows Desktop. Then click Start | Programs, and your antivirus program's Start Menu entry. Right-click the program's main icon, and select Copy. Switch to your master personal folder by double-clicking it or hitting its hot key. Right-click any blank area in your master personal folder, and select Paste. If you want to assign a hot key to the antivirus icon, do so now. Right-click the icon, select Properties, enter the keystroke you want to use in the "Shortcut key" input box, and click OK. (I use Ctrl+Alt+V on my computer.) When you're done, it's a good idea to run the antivirus' update feature.

■ **After installing Norton Antivirus,** *you can clone its icon into your master personal folder.*

Check your antivirus software owner's manual for instructions on how to activate your particular vendor's update feature. If you're using the Symantec Norton Antivirus, run the program by clicking Start | Programs | Norton Antivirus. In the submenu that opens, click the Norton Antivirus icon. (Of course, if you put a copy of this icon in your master personal folder, you can double-click that or hit its hot key.) Click the LiveUpdate button on the toolbar, and the update process will proceed.

Safe computing practices

Automated antivirus software will snag 99.999 percent of all software bombs circulating in the wild, but it's that .001 percent they miss that can really bite you in the neck. Just such a virus slipped through the antivirus net in 1999. The "Melissa" virus attached itself to e-mail messages and spread over the Intenet faster than any other bomb seen before. Hundreds of thousands of PC users saw their data corrupted in its wake. Worse, entire corporate networks had to be shut down to contain the Melissa virus.

Even Microsoft had to disconnect its corporate computer network from the Internet to corner and clean out the Melissa virus.

■ **It's a jungle out there** – *some viruses will really bite you in the neck.*

How did Melissa slip by the powerful antivirus systems installed by many of the effected users and companies? Simple, really. Melissa was a brand-new, never-seen-before virus designed to spread at lightning speed. Melissa entered systems by way of users' e-mail, as an attachment. Antivirus software programs, even the latest antivirus engine updates, didn't recognize Melissa as a virus, because as a brand-new strain, Melissa did not have an identifiable "fingerprint."

■ **Just as infected** *cells mutate, so do software programs.*

HUNTING VIRUSES

Antivirus software programs catch viruses three ways. Every virus has a unique fingerprint that antivirus programs continuously scan for. When they find a match, they know a system is infected.

Antiviruses also monitor programs, web sites, e-mail, and the Internet for suspicious virus-like behavior. When they see it, they stop it.

Lastly, antiviruses scrutinize programs under a virtual microscope, looking for evidence of morphing. Just as healthy human cells morph when they become cancerous, so do infected programs. Programs that morph are flagged as infected, and isolated from the rest of the PC by the antivirus.

Protecting yourself from that .001 percent of software bombs requires a little knowledge, a little common sense, and a little practice. Again, the key to protection is to target the Achilles heel all software bombs share: You have to double-click them to set them off. Raise your awareness of the various types of files that can harbor viruses, and you'll think twice before clicking twice.

That means never, ever, ever, ever open attachments that include these codes as part of their filename:

BAT   - BATch command file
CHM   - Compiled Hypertext Markup language file
CMD   - CoMmanD file (Windows NT and 2000 only)
COM   - COMputer memory image file
DOC   - DOCument file
EXE   - EXEcutable program
HTM   - HyperText Markup language file
HTML   - HyperText Markup Language file
JS   - JavaScript file
PPT   - PowerPoint file
SCR   - SCReen saver program file
SHS   - SHell Scrap file
XLS   - eXceL Spreadsheet file
VBS   - Visual Basic Script file
XML   - eXtensible Markup Language file

■ **Listen to the alarm bell** *in your head before you open a dubious e-mail attachment.*

These codes, called "filename extensions," identify the file type to the PC. For example, a file named GAME.EXE is a program. A file named FUN.SCR is a screen saver. All of the file types listed above can harbor computer viruses. Your computer is actually bursting at the seams with files that end with these extensions – yet they're all safe. The problem arises when files with these extensions appear as attachments in your e-mail

That's when the alarm bells should go off in your head. Whatever you do, don't open attachments in e-mail that end with any of the above file extension seven if you know the person who sent them to you (because it could be a Trojan masquerading as that person). Instead, ask the sender to resend the attachment as a different file format. For example, a DOCument file can be saved as an RTF file (or some other format) using the "Save as" menu command. Doing so kills any lurking software bombs, yet maintains the DOC file's readability. You'll find instructions on exporting data in Chapter 10's "Sharing data with other users" section.

If you have Microsoft Office 2000, Word 2000, or Excel 2000 installed on your computer, make sure the macro security is set to High. To activate Microsoft Office's virus protection shield, click Start | Programs | Microsoft Word. Click on Word's Tools menu, then click Macro | Security, and set the security level to High.

Lastly, be extremely careful when downloading programs and documents over the Internet. It's generally safe to download files from trusted sites, such as Microsoft.com, IBM.com, Symantec.com, Intel.com, your bank, your broker, and so on. The last thing any established corporation is going to do is try to infect your system with a virus.

But when you're surfing untrusted sites — that is, web sites managed by people or companies you never heard of — your risk of contracting a software bomb goes up. Way up.

Earlier in the book you set your Internet Explorer security settings to "High." That will protect you from most web-borne bombs. Installing and using an antivirus will protect your from 99.999 percent of the rest. Using your head will protect you from the remaining .001 percent.

A simple summary

✓ It's up to you to adopt and apply the proper security measures to protect your PC and its data.

✓ Data security measures protect your data from theft. Data integrity measures protect your data from loss due to tampering, viruses, or corruption.

✓ Set a power-on password to keep casual snoopers out of your PC.

✓ It is a good idea to set a screen saver password to shield your PC when you walk away from the keyboard.

✓ If you're storing personal or business data, seriously consider buying and using add-on system and data security software.

✓ Keep your web browser security settings cranked up to "High" to prevent rogue codes from entering your PC by way of the web.

✓ Computer viruses are the greatest risk to your computing. Buy, install, and use a leading antivirus software program.

✓ Keep your antivirus software up to date.

✓ Never, ever, ever open e-mail attachments unless they're first scanned by an up-to-date antivirus program.

Chapter 18

Tool Time

JUST AS ENGINES need regular maintenance, tune-ups, repairs, and pampering, so do PCs. If you neglect your PC's maintenance, and performance and reliability will suffer. Eventually, it too will fail to start – and you'll be facing a hefty repair bill. Fortunately, the tools you need to keep your PC running smoothly are pre-installed in Windows 98. In this chapter, you'll learn how to keep your PC purring by applying basic housecleaning and maintenance techniques. You'll also bone up on the tools Microsoft offers for system maintenance, and the dos and don'ts of cleaning your PC.

In this chapter...

✓ Machine or mind?

✓ Keeping your system running smoothly

✓ Housework homework

✓ Tools to use, tools to avoid

✓ A clean computer is a happy computer

NEGLECTING YOUR CAR'S MAINTENANCE IS ASKING FOR TROUBLE. DITTO ... YOUR PC

Machine or mind?

BRITISH MATHEMATICIAN *Charles Babbage conceived the computer in 1812, while still an undergraduate laboring over complex formulas at Cambridge University. He was soon perfecting a device that generated logarithmic tables. On June 14, 1822, he presented his "Note on the application of machinery to the computation of astronomical and mathematical tables" before the Royal Astronomical Society. He also conducted what has to be the first computer demo, when he put his computing "engine" through its paces. (It didn't crash.)*

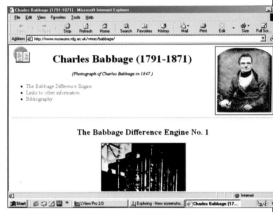

■ **You can find** *out about Charles Babbage at www.museums.reading.ac.uk/vmoc/babbage/.*

Babbage's creativity didn't stop there. He went on to design the world's first general purpose computer, which he dubbed the Analytical Engine. Unfortunately, Babbage never raised enough money to build the giant steam-powered machine. Twentieth-century computer scientists have since built Babbage's designs to scale. They found that they worked, proving Babbage's designs correct.

INTERNET

Visit these sites for more on Babbage and his legacy.

www.museums.reading. ac.uk/vmoc/babbage

The Virtual Museum of Computing.

www.fourmilab.to/ babbage

John Walker's Analytical Engine site.

Development of computers continued at a glacial pace until the 1940s, when the first electronic systems appeared. With thousands of glowing tubes, miles of wires, and wall-to-wall panels, the early electronic computers looked more like giant electronic brains than the simple mechanical calculators of the day. Indeed, by 1950 the public ceased thinking of computers as mere calculating machines. That year, the celebrated mathematician Alan Turing published a paper titled "Computing Machinery and Intelligence" in the journal *Mind*. The notion of artificial intelligence was born, and the computer would forevermore be compared to the human mind.

Anyone who works with computers will tell you: Babbage was right, Turing was wrong. Maybe someday a computer will be able to carry on what feels like a conversation with its user, but that day remains far in the distant future. For now, computers are like engines, not minds.

Keeping your system running smoothly

COMPUTERS AND CARS *have more in common than their maintenance requirements. Both are hybrid devices. They're part mechanical, part electrical, part electronic, and part virtual. Think about it: Your PC's disk drives, mouse, and keyboard are mechanical. Its power supply is electrical. The motherboard, add-in cards, and screen are electronic. And everything you do with your PC is virtual, because software, e-mail, and the web have no physical form in the real world. They exist . . . without actually existing.*

■ **Keep your PC** *running smoothly with a software toolkit.*

Keeping those parts running smoothly and in sync requires a variety of tools – and I don't mean the hammer and screwdriver variety. Such tools are fine for shade tree mechanics, but they won't get you far when it comes to keeping your PC running in tip-top shape.

In the cyber world, PC maintenance tools have no physical form, either. They're programs used in the care and feeding of the PC. Among them are tools to clean and repair disk drives, tools to solve hardware problems, and tools to optimize PC performance.

There are so many different products available, that visiting the software tools and utilities section of your local computer dealer or e-commerce site can be downright overwhelming. Fortunately, nearly all of the basic tools required to maintain your PC are already included in Windows 98. Those that aren't are just a download away. Best of all, you can configure those crucial maintenance tasks once, and they'll run automatically thereafter. Keeping your PC running smoothly starts with the basics of Housework Homework.

Housework homework

IMAGINE HOW LIBERATING *life would be if you owned a robot that did housework. Press a few buttons on the robot's remote control, and it dashes off to fetch the vacuum cleaner. One hour later, your carpets are fresh and clean. Punch more buttons, and the robot grabs cleanser and paper towels, and scrubs the bathroom tiles until they shine. While it's at it, the robot notices some tiles need caulking. It fetches a caulk gun and lays down a perfect bead. On its way back to the garage, the robot collects the trash and drops it on the curb.*

■ **The Maintenance Wizard** *is your housekeeping robot.*

Fantasy? Not quite. When it comes to your PC, nearly all critical housekeeping chores can be put into action by the software equivalent of a housekeeping robot. Its name: the Windows 98 Maintenance Wizard. Of the 17 system tools included in Windows 98, the only one you need to know and love is the Maintenance Wizard. Sure, you could dabble with any and all of the 17 system tools individually. But that would be a colossal waste of time.

The Maintenance Wizard automates literally all of the core system maintenance requirements served up by Windows' system tools, and does so though a single easy to use, easy to understand user interface.

And that's not all: Over time, as Microsoft upgrades and updates Windows 98, you can rest assured that the Maintenance Wizard will embrace any new system maintenance tools essential to the daily health of your PC.

Setting up the Maintenance Wizard

Before running off and trying the Maintenance Wizard, put a copy of its icon in your master personal folder. That keeps it readily accessible, never more than a click or hot key away. Press

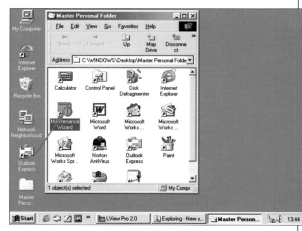

■ **Click on the** *Maintenance Wizard's icon to mop up Windows 98's chores.*

Win+D to return to the Windows Desktop. Then click Start | Programs | Accessories | System Tools. Right-click the Maintenance Wizard icon, and select Copy. Switch to your master personal folder by double-clicking it or hitting its hot key. Right-click any blank area in your master personal folder, and select Paste. To assign a hot key, right-click the Maintenance Wizard icon, select Properties, and enter a keystroke in the "Shortcut key" input box. (I use Ctrl+Alt+M on my PC.) Then click OK.

The Maintenance Wizard can safely be used when other programs are loaded, but it won't be able to tune up areas of the computer that are being used by other programs.

For this reason, it's wise to unload other programs before firing up the Maintenance Wizard.

Doing so gives the Maintenance Wizard free rein over the PC, and allows it to go about its business without being slowed down by, bumping into, or otherwise interfering with other programs.

Click any one of the buttons on the Taskbar (or press Alt+Tab) to switch into and expose the window of an open program. Click the window's Close button. Repeat this process for every program that appears on the Taskbar.

Configuring the Maintenance Wizard

You're ready to launch the Maintenance Wizard when there are no program buttons on the Taskbar, other than the Start button. At that point, open your master personal folder by double-clicking its Desktop icon, or hitting its hot key. Then double-click the Maintenance Wizard. (Of course, if you assigned a hot key to the Maintenance Wizard, you can skip all of that pointing and clicking and just hit its hot key.)

The Maintenance Wizard appears, and gives you a choice of two maintenance modes: Express or Custom. Express settings are preprogrammed by Microsoft to conduct the preferred standard maintenance tasks on your PC. Custom settings allow you to adjust the overall behavior of the Maintenance Wizard, and are provided for people who just can't leave well enough alone. For 99.999 percent of users (that's you), the Express settings are ideal.

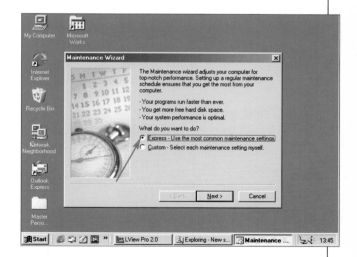

■ **For most users,** *Maintenance Wizard's Express settings are ideal.*

Select the Express radio button, and then click Next. The Maintenance Wizard asks you to select a maintenance schedule. That's because the Maintenance Wizard is a "set it and forget it" kind of program. Once you activate and configure it, it will load automatically, and run silently in the background, until its work is done. Of the three available settings – Nights, Days, Evenings – the preferred choice is Nights, for the simple reason that it will launch the Maintenance Wizard after midnight, when your computer usually isn't busy doing anything else. This assumes, of course, that you leave your computer on and running all the time (as advocated in Chapter 5's "Burn in & backup" section). If you turn your PC off every day, selecting Days or Evenings is obviously a better approach. Select the radio button beside the maintenance schedule you prefer, and click Next.

The final Maintenance Wizard screen appears. This is actually just an informational display that lets you know the Maintenance Wizard is properly configured and ready for use.

■ **You can set your** *Maintenance Wizard to launch after midnight.*

Before wrapping up the Maintenance Wizard setup, you can instruct the Wizard to get busy right away. Since your PC has never been optimized (computerese for "tuned up"), it's a fine time to give the system its first automated tune-up. To do this, click the checkbox that reads "When I click Finish, perform each scheduled task for the first time." Then click Finish. The Maintenance Wizard will pop up a dialog that shows you the status of its activities.

■ **For a thorough cleanout** *of unwanted files on your hard disk, try the author's own Space Ace III, a free trialware download at www.spaceace.net.*

The Maintenance Wizard's First Job

The first job the Maintenance Wizard handles is cleaning your hard disk of unnecessary files, which are nothing more than debris left behind by programs. These files will never be accessed again, yet they consume gobs of space on your hard disk. Maintenance Wizard targets such files and erases them. Other windows will also appear. You'll see ScanDisk load and run, for example.

This utility checks your disks for data errors (stuff that can't be reliably retrieved) and automatically repairs them.

After ScanDisk is done, Disk Defragmenter will launch and give your hard disk a major league work out.

Disk Defragmenter analyzes literally all the data on your hard drive and reorders it for maximum efficiency.

Programs and data files that are stored piecemeal by the computer are collected and laid out in one long contiguous chain. This lets the hard disk access the programs and data faster, because it doesn't have to jump all over the disk collecting their pieces first. Disk Defragmenter also puts your most-used programs at the front of the disk, where the computer can retrieve them faster. Note, however, that Disk Defragmenter can take a long time to finish its work the first time out. Subsequent runs will take less time.

When the various maintenance tasks are complete, your PC will have more disk space available for storage, and will be running at top speed. You'll also be able to rest easy, knowing that the Maintenance Wizard has checked your hard disk for errors and permanently repaired any problems it encountered.

Running Maintenance Wizard

■ **Disk Defragmenter** *will give your hard disk a major workout.*

In a perfect world, you'll never have to run Maintenance Wizard manually again. It remembers your settings and automatically cleans and tunes your PC according to the schedule you set. The reality is, it's possible you'll want to change your Maintenance Wizard schedule in the future. Or perhaps, as you become more proficient with your PC, you'll want to scratch the custom configuration itch.

Simply run Maintenance Wizard again by double-clicking its icon in your master personal folder, or hitting its hot key. This time, however, instead of the Wizard itself opening up, you'll be presented with two options. You can choose to perform your automatic maintenance tasks immediately or reopen the Wizard to adjust its settings. To force the Maintenance Wizard to clean and tune your system immediately, select the "Perform maintenance now" radio button, and click OK.

To tweak your Maintenance Wizard options, select the "Change my maintenance settings or schedule" radio box, and click OK. The Maintenance Wizard will reopen, and provide full access to the options you preset earlier.

Tools to use, tools to avoid

COMPUTERS ARE LIKE CARS *in more ways than one. You have to maintain your car and your computer to keep both running in tip-top shape. And just as there are "car nuts," there are "computer nuts." The neighborhood car nut is easy to spot. He's the guy with his backside beaming from under the open hood, or his legs jutting out from beneath the chassis.*

The neighborhood computer nut is much the same. He's spent most of his computing time optimizing performance, tweaking settings, and adjusting configurations, all to ensure that his computer looks its coolest and runs its best. His software library will probably include an e-mail program, a web browser, a word processor – and 742 different system utilities. Some of these tools will be commercial favorites, such as Symantec's Norton Utilities. Others will be shareware or freeware products downloaded over the Internet. There are tools that analyze and optimize hard disks, tools that monitor memory use, tools that intercept crashes, and tools that uninstall programs.

■ **Just like the** *"car nut," the "computer nut" is easy to spot.*

Software tool distribution

In common with all software products, tools and utilities are now packaged and distributed in several different ways. You'll find most software today falls into the commercial, e-ware and trialware categories.

✓ **Commercial or "shrink wrap"**
Software products sold through stores and online retailers. They come nicely packaged, with a CD, documentation, and a registration card. You cannot legally share this form of software with anyone.

✓ **E-ware**
Commercial software distributed electronically over the Internet with documentation provided electronically. You don't get a box or a CD. Registration happens automatically by virtue of the electronic purchasing process. You cannot legally share this kind of software with others.

✓ **Shareware**

If you continue to use shareware beyond the free trial period, you are expected to pay for it. It can be legally shared with friends. But if they use it, they're also expected to pay for it.

✓ **Trialware**

Like shareware, you can download and use trialware products for free. After the trial period expires, so does the software. It stops working unless you pay for it.

✓ **Demoware**

Programs that advertise software or services, but can't be used to get any real work done.

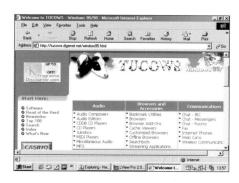

■ **Shareware can be** *downloaded from web sites such as tucows.digenet.net.*

✓ **Freeware or "open source"**

Freeware programs are free, with no strings attached other than occasional copyright limitations. They may even include the program's source code (hence the term "open source").

✓ **Public Domain**

Software in the public domain is completely free of all restrictions. You can use it, share it, modify it, and resell it to your heart's content.

With few exceptions, PC tools and utilities are the software equivalent of a timing light. The neighborhood car nut has three (his favorite, a backup, and his Dad's). Most car owners don't need one, don't own one, and don't want one.

Likewise, unless you're a die-hard PC enthusiast compelled to fiddle aimlessly, you'll never need to spend a penny on third-party software tools.

The basic apparatus required for total PC maintenance – the Maintenance Wizard – is included with Windows 98. Unlike automotive tools, practically all PC tools are solutions in search of a problem. They'll run the entire time your computer is on, checking the hard disk, memory, and all manner of stuff.

If your computer ain't broke, don't spend money on tools that claim to fix it. The only time you'll need a third-party tool is in the rare event your system crashes and can't be resurrected through standard failsafe practices (described in Chapter 20).

325

A toolbox of utilities

Although most tools and utilities do little more than separate you from your money, a handful of utilities (as you'll see below) are worth having. Be forewarned, however:

System tools mess around with areas of your computer that are, in general, best left undisturbed.

It's not uncommon for inexperienced users to nuke their systems when playing around with system tools. Again, if it ain't broke, don't fix it. That said, here's a list of those utilities worth having:

✓ Antivirus – a must have

This is a must-have because it protects your system from all manner of rogue software. The industry's best offering is Symantec's Norton Antivirus (www.symantec.com/nav). It's fast, easy to use, and cures the most viruses and other germs. Plus, its "Live Update" feature makes it easy to keep your antivirus current with the latest virus-fighting info. Windows 98 does not include an antivirus system tool.

✓ Compression tools – included with Windows 98

■ **You can use** *Disk Defragmenter manually, or let the Maintenance Wizard run it automatically.*

When you're running low on disk space, a compression tool can be used to "squeeze" folders and files into smaller sizes. Doing so can double or triple the amount of free disk space, at the expense of slowing down your computer. Windows 98 includes an excellent disk compression tool, called DriveSpace. But don't use it unless you're dangerously low on free disk space, because it will make your computer run slower. A better solution: Have your dealer add another hard drive to your PC.

✓ Disk Cleanup tools – worth having

Windows 98's Disk Cleanup wizard sweeps your hard disk clean automatically. Unlike most tools included in Windows 98, the Disk Cleanup Wizard doesn't do as thorough a job as it should. For maximum space gains, try a free trialware download at www.SpaceAce.net.

✓ Disk Defragmenter – included with Windows 98

Windows 98 already has Disk Defragmenter, and it works just as well as any other. It's located at Start | Programs | Accessories | System Tools | Disk Defragmenter. But you don't have to run it manually. The Maintenance Wizard automatically runs Disk Defragmenter.

✓ Disk repair utilities – included with Windows 98

You can repair damaged disks by running Windows 98's ScanDisk utility. It's located at Start | Programs | Accessories | System Tools | ScanDisk. The maintenance Wizard runs ScanDisk automatically, so you'll rarely if ever have to access it manually.

✓ **Rescue and recovery tools – included with Windows 98**

Windows 98's ScanDisk program can diagnose and repair most forms of disk corruption. If you're one of the unlucky few who encounter disk corruption that ScanDisk can't fix, and you don't have backup copies of the damaged data, then it's time to consider investing in a third-party disk recovery tool. Norton's Disk Doctor, a component of the Symantec Norton Utilities, is the gold standard for hard and floppy disk recovery software. It's available at www.symantec.com/nu. For failed Zip disks, use Norton's Zip Rescue, available at www.symantec.com/specprog/nzr. All is not lost if Norton can't recover your data. For a hefty fee, emergency recovery services, such as Ontrack Data International (www.ontrack.com), can scrape important data off disks that have been tossed overboard, burned to a crisp, or run over by an 18 wheeler.

CRASH PREVENTION TOOLS (A-K-A "CRASH GUARDS")

Interestingly, programs that claim to prevent your computer from crashing often increase the number of crashes. It is wise to avoid crash prevention software at all costs. If Windows 98 crashes, it means the computer is in a severely unstable condition, and should be rebooted (restarted).

✓ **Scheduling utilities – included with Windows 98**

Some system tools can be run automatically and unattended when the PC is idle. This is made possible by a scheduling agent, a small system utility that watches the clock and launches programs at their appointed hour. That's precisely how Windows 98's Maintenance Wizard works: It uses Windows 98's built-in Task Scheduler. You can use Windows 98's Task Scheduler to launch any process according to any appointed schedule. To do so, click Start | Programs | Accessories | System Tools | Scheduled Tasks. Then double-click the Add Scheduled Task command, and follow the instructions in the Scheduled Task Wizard.

✓ **System Information tools – included with Windows 98**

These programs inspect, and generate reports on, your system's hardware and software. They're useful when you're trying to troubleshoot a problem and a support technician asks, "Whose modem is installed in your computer?" or "Who makes your PC's hard drive?" All the same, it's foolish to pay extra for this kind of tool when Windows 98 includes one for free. To load Microsoft's System Information utility, click Start | Programs | Accessories | System Tools | System Information.

✓ Undelete (a-k-a unerase) tools – worth having

If you accidentally delete a folder, file, or icon, you can bring it it back by double-clicking the Recycle Bin icon on the Windows Desktop. Inside, you'll find a list of every item you've recently deleted. To restore a file, right-click it, and select Restore. Occasionally, though, deleted files won't be sent to the Recycle Bin, because the program you're using to delete the files ignores the Recycle Bin feature. If a deleted file doesn't show up in the Recycle Bin, and you don't have a duplicate backup copy, an undelete (unerase) tool can often recover them.

Unfortunately, undelete tools are almost always bundled with a larger tool set, such as the Norton Utilities (www.symantec.com), or Mijenix Fix-It Utilities (www.mijenix.com). Such toolsets can slow your computer to a crawl whenever it has to access a disk. One excellent undelete tool that stands on its own and doesn't slow down a PC is PowerQuest's Lost & Found (www.powerquest.com). If you do make the mistake of buying and installing a bloated utilities suite just to gain an undelete tool, take care to disable all the excess features of the suite except the undeleter. This ensures your PC runs at peak performance.

■ **Check out** *Lost and Found – PowerQuest's undelete tool – at www.powerquest.com.*

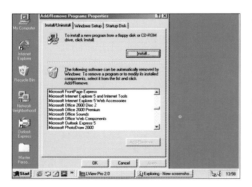

■ **Windows 98** *has a built-in uninstaller: Add/Remove Programs.*

✓ Uninstallers – included with windows 98

There's a built-in uninstaller in Windows 98. To remove any program, click Start | Settings | Control Panel | Add/Remove Programs.

✓ Zip tools – worth having

Many files on the Internet are "zipped" to save space. One Zip file can contain dozens, even hundreds, of other files. The data in the regular files is compressed (made smaller) before being stored inside the Zip file. That means Zip files are typically half the size of the files they contain, and so they travel over the Internet twice as fast as uncompressed files. When you "extract" files from a Zip file, they're uncompressed (expanded) back to their original, larger sizes. But you can't extract files from a Zip file unless you own an "unzipping" utility. Similarly, you can't create your own Zip files unless you own a "zipping" tool. For instance, perhaps you need to send ten large documents to a friend via e-mail. Zipping those ten documents first reduces their size, making the e-mail faster to send. It also puts them into one easy-to-mail Zip file, instead of ten separate files. Clearly a Zip utility is well worth having. The world's most popular Zip utility is WinZip, available at www.winzip.com. (Note: Don't confuse Zip files with Iomega Zip disks. They're two entirely different things. Zip files are compressed data. Zip disks are storage media.)

■ **"Zipped" files:** *Here, many files have been compressed into one file called Windows.zip.*

A clean computer is a happy computer

THERE'S STILL MORE MILEAGE *to be gleaned from the "cars and computers" analogy (no pun intended). Maintain your car and computer, and both will deliver years of reliable service. Car nuts and computer nuts both love to tinker with their respective tools. And every car owner, and every computer owner, can take pride in giving their beloved transportation or information vehicle a good detailing.*

On second thought, perhaps this is one area where the comparison between autos and PCs doesn't completely hold water. After all, you can drive a dirty car and the only thing you'll damage is your pride. Drive a dirty computer, and one day that grime will cause a critical system component to fail. Keep your PC parts clean as a whistle, and they'll turn in years of reliable service.

PC cleaning basics

Plan to clean your PC's components at least once a month, and no less than four times a year.

The reason: From the moment you power up to the second you power down, your PC is getting filthy. To keep the system from overheating, the PC's cooling fan spins up and maintains a constant airflow over the internal electronics. The fan draws air in through vents and disk drive openings, and forces it out the same way. It's also sucking in and circulating dust, pollen, mold, mildew, and other contaminants.

Over time, these contaminants can gum up disk drives and electrical connections. As they build up and blanket internal electronics, they can even cause components to overheat.

■ **While you're typing,** *skin and clothing fibers are dropping between the keys.*

Every time you open your CD or DVD drive, or slide a disk into a floppy or Zip drive, you introduce finger oils, dust, and other debris into the drive mechanism. These can gum up a drive's read/write heads or lenses, and prevent it from accessing disks. While you're busy banging out a letter on your keyboard, microscopic skin particles, eye lashes and other hair, and clothing fibers are working their way between and underneath the keys. This crud can block key contacts and stop one or more keys from operating. And one look at any user's screen will reveal a mess of fingerprints and little dots and stray lines from pen points – not to mention the occasional gooey spots from exploding soda cans or accidents with coffee cups.

Always shut down Windows 98 and turn off your PC before cleaning your computer.

Failure to do so can damage sensitive PC components and result in electric shock or even death. To shut down Windows 98, click Start | Shut Down. When the Shut Down Windows dialog appears, click the "Shut Down" radio button, then click OK.

There's one thing no PC owner should be without: a can of compressed air. Truly the product with 1,001 uses, compressed air is used to clean the screen, keyboard, disk drives, media, and even internal PC components. Compressed air is sold under a variety of brand names, including Dust-Off, Endust, and Fellowes Duster. In my experiences, Fellowes Duster (www.fellowes.com) beats the others cold. Its product lasts longer and maintains a strong "blast" until the very end. Regardless of which brand you choose, make sure it's environmentally friendly, contains no harmful ozone-depleting CFCs or HFCs, and is nonflammable.

Cleaning the screen

■ **Clean your screen** *with cleaner designed for eyeglasses.*

It doesn't matter whether your PC's screen is a conventional glass tube or a new-fangled flat panel; the cleaning process is the same. First, blast the screen with compressed air to remove any particles that could scratch the surface if rubbed. Then get a soft, clean, lint-free cloth (an old T-shirt is ideal), and spray it lightly with a cleaning agent specifically designed for eyeglasses. Don't soak it; just apply a fine mist to moisten the cloth.

Never use household glass cleaners, such as Windex or Glass Plus, on computer components.

Chemicals in these household cleaners can damage your PC. Also avoid cleaners "designed" for PC monitors. Many damage the antiglare finish that coats glass tubes, or harm sensitive flat panel displays. You'll find eyeglass cleaners in the contact lens or eye care sections of your neighborhood drug store. One outstanding national brand to look for: Visaclean, from Pfizer Consumer Healthcare (www.pfizer.com/chc/visacl).

Kiwi brands distributes pre-moistened wipes that contain the same cleaning agent as Visaclean (isopropyl alcohol). They're sold under the "Endust for Electronics Anti-Static Wipes" brand. Their only drawback: The continuous feed package often dries out before all the wipes are used. You'll find them at most computer stores, or call 1-800-392-7733 for the name of a store near you.

No matter what cleaner you use, always spray the cloth and not the screen. The reason: Spraying the screen causes small droplets to roll down the display. You can short-circuit the monitor if any of the droplets work their way inside.

Start at the center of the display and gently clean the screen with a circular motion. Repeat the process until all scum is removed from the display. When you're done, blast the screen with compressed air to blow away any remaining lint or dust.

Cleaning the keyboard

Shut down Windows 98, then disconnect the keyboard by carefully removing its plug from the computer. Take the keyboard and a can of compressed air outside or into another room, to avoid getting dirt into other computer components. Hold the keyboard upside down and over your head, and insert the compressed air can's needle nose into the groove between the bottom two keys (Ctrl and Shift) at the far left end of the keyboard.

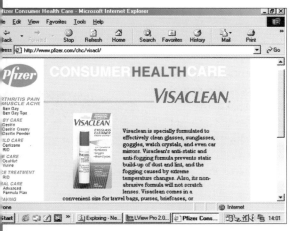

While dragging the needle nose from left to right along the groove between the bottom two rows of keys, repeatedly pull the compressed air's trigger to issue a series of short, powerful air bursts. You'll be amazed at how much gunk is ejected from the keyboard. Repeat this process until you have dragged the needle nose across all the grooves between keys on the keyboard. Reconnect the keyboard when you're done, and power up the PC.

■ **A fine cleaner** *for your monitor is Visaclean from Pfizer Consumer Healthcare (www.pfizer.com/chc/visacl).*

Cleaning the mouse

There are dozens of different kinds of mouse devices, from conventional two-button mice to trackballs, infrared pointers, gyroscopic devices, and so on. Refer to your device's owner's manual for specific cleaning instructions. For standard-issue mice, turn the mouse over and twist off the cap covering the mouse ball. Clean the rollers inside with foam-tipped swabs that have been moistened with a few drops of isopropyl alcohol. You'll find the swabs and the cleaning solution at any local Radio Shack store, packaged as a "mouse cleaning kit."

Note: Never use cotton swabs or rubbing alcohol to clean electronic components. Cotton swabs contaminate components with tiny cotton fibers. Rubbing alcohol can cause lasting damage to electronics, as it contains a gum that permanently coats components.

Cleaning removable media drives and disks

There are cleaning kits for all manner of removable media drives – simply follow the instructions included with them. Floppy disk and CD/DVD drive cleaning kits are available at your local computer store, office supply retailer, or electronics shop. Keep your disk drives clean, and you'll never lose data due to dirty read/write heads or lenses.

There is no way to clean magnetic media, such as floppy and Zip disks, but optical media, such as CDs and DVDs, should be kept clean. You clean CDs and DVDs the same way you clean your monitor. First, blast the disk with compressed air to remove any stray particles. Then, spray some eyeglasses cleaner on a soft, lint-free cloth (not on the disk), and clean the media from the center hole outward, using a smooth, circular motion. Use another compressed air blast to blow away any lint left behind.

Cleaning the PC's innards and other devices

Once a year, completely disconnect all the external components (keyboard, screen, mouse, etc.) from your PC. Unplug your PC from the AC outlet, and move it outside or to your garage. Carefully remove the PC's case, and blast the insides with short, powerful bursts from your trusty can of compressed air.

■ **You'll find mouse** *cleaning kits at any local Radio Shack store (www.radioshack.com).*

After the insides are relatively dust-free, carefully insert the compressed air's needle nose into the AC power supply, where the fan is visible. Give the fan a long, smooth stream of compressed air. You'll see big puffs of dust rocketing out of the AC power supply as the fan whirrs. Keep blasting the fan until most of the dust is removed. When you're done, put the PC's cover back on, reconnect all the components, and power it back up.

Use common sense when cleaning other PC devices. For example, blast the printer's innards occasionally with some compressed air. Use eyeglasses cleaner to clean a scanner's glass plate.

And never use household cleaners or solvents of any kind for any PC cleaning.

A simple summary

✓ Computers are machines not minds.

✓ If you don't perform regular maintenance, computers will slowly deteriorate over time.

✓ There's only one system tool that matters: The Maintenance Wizard included in Windows 98.

✓ Use the Maintenance Wizard to keep your system running at peak performance.

✓ Always shut down all programs before using any system tools.

✓ Don't get suckered into buying unnecessary third-party tools and utility suites.

✓ Dirt, dust, and grime conspire to reduce the lifespan of your data, disk drives, and PC components.

✓ Physically clean your computer's components no less than four times a year. Clean your PC's case out at least once a year.

✓ Compressed air, isopropyl alcohol, a lint-free cleaning cloth, and foam swabs are the recipe for a sparkling clean computer.

Chapter 19

The Never-Ending Upgrade Chase

THE MOMENT YOU BUY your computer, it's already obsolete. Computer technology has always evolved rapidly, and it will be decades before the state of the PC art stabilizes – if ever. But the industry won't pass you by, and you won't outgrow your new PC. The reason: PCs are designed to be expandable. In this chapter, you'll learn how to face down the unavoidable PC upgrades in your future. You'll also learn when it makes sense to do an upgrade yourself, and what types of upgrades are best handled by your neighborhood dealer. Lastly, you'll discover how easy it is to install new and remove old software, and upgrade existing programs over the Internet.

In this chapter...

✓ Facing the unavoidable

✓ A trip to the hardware store

✓ In with the new

✓ Installing software over the Internet

AS YOUR PERSONAL APPLICATION REQUIREMENTS EVOLVE, YOU'LL NEED TO UPGRADE...

Facing the unavoidable

DEATH. TAXES. PC UPGRADES. Some things in life are unavoidable. Today, your PC is fast and peppy, chugging on the latest software offerings with nary a hiccup. At some point down the road, however, you'll notice your PC is slowing down. It might happen later this year. It might take two years or more. But suddenly, the trusty PC that zipped through tasks with abandon will be feeling more like a ball and chain. No, the CPU, hard drive, RAM haven't worn out.

Rather, the world of software will have passed your PC by. Programs being released today are designed to run on today's PCs.

Software that's released in two years will be designed to run on future era PCs.

Older PCs will be unable to deliver the punch that future software will need to deliver perky performance. The solution: upgrade. Unlike death, upgrades aren't painful. Unlike taxes, many upgrades are affordable, even free.

When the time comes that your PC needs a power boost, it's as easy as having your dealer snap in a new, faster CPU. If disk activity feels sluggish, your dealer can install a faster hard drive in minutes. Need more powerful 3-D video to play the latest games? No problem. Snap out the old video card, snap in a new one. There's virtually no hardware component in your computer that can't be upgraded as the need arises.

Software is even easier to upgrade, and that's good – because most users need to upgrade software far more often than hardware. Software vendors are continuously fixing bugs and adding features to their offerings. To take advantage of bug fixes and feature enhancements, usually all you need to do is hit the vendor's web site and download the updated wares. Snatch the update, run the installer, and your software is purring with their latest and greatest.

Upgrades fall into two categories: hardware and software. Upgrading software is easy. You just run the installation program. Hardware upgrades range from a simple plug-in connection you can do yourself to jobs that are best left to skilled technicians.

■ **Benjamin Franklin:** *"Nothing is certain but death and taxes."*

A trip to the hardware store

■ **Help is at hand** *in your hardware store.*

THERE ARE HARDWARE PEOPLE, *and there are software people. Hardware people don't break a sweat when they tear open their PC's case and rip and replace chips, cards, cables, and drives with nary a hint of hesitation. Yet they cringe at the thought of installing new software, lest one errant app screw up their carefully balanced electronic world. Software people, on the other hand, shudder at the mere thought of cracking open their PC, but don't think twice about downloading, installing, experimenting, and removing 22 cool programs found on the web in the course of an hour. These counterbalancing skills are a fact of computing life and offer reciprocal benefits for hardware and software folks.*

■ **Install a downloaded** *update and your software will be purring.*

When hardware people have intractable software problems, or need a recommendation, they turn to a software person for help. When software people have hardware problems, or need a hardware upgrade, they turn to a hardware person for help.

Most PC users are software people. When the time comes that your PC is in need of a hardware upgrade, you'll need to ask yourself whether the upgrade is something you're capable of handling.

Internal and external hardware upgrades

The general rule of thumb for most software people: If the upgrade requires opening the PC case, turn to a hardware person. If the upgrade can simply be attached to the computer by way of the computer's connection ports, it's a DIY (do-it-yourself) project. Opening the PC and installing add-in cards, disk drives, CPU upgrades, and other enhancements are tasks that require skill, experience, and special tools. They are also projects that can go terribly wrong if you lack any of the requirements.

■ **Many a PC** has *been fried by a seemingly simple hardware upgrade gone wrong.*

Many a computer has been fried by a software person trying to apply what appeared to be a trivial hardware upgrade. Perhaps they intended to slide a new modem card into a slot, pop a new CPU on the motherboard, or add some RAM. What they ended up with was an utterly dead, dead, dead computer.

A better approach: Spend the few extra dollars — about $25 to $100 — that it costs to have a hardware person handle the internal upgrade for you.

Internal hardware upgrades for experts

You'll find experienced hardware people at literally every national computer and consumer electronics store in town. You can also contact your PC's manufacturer and ask them for a list of authorized service centers in your area.

Whoever does the job, make sure to get a written estimate of the cost of the upgrade and a copy of the store or service center's upgrade warranty in writing.

An upgrade warranty protects you in the event the upgrade later fails or if the upgrade fries your PC (yes, even hardware people screw up). Make sure your PC is covered for any problems that occur as a result of the upgrade. Any time your PC is opened and its innards tinkered with, there's a risk of collateral damage. For example, installing memory, a CPU, or hard drive can cook the PC's main circuit board (motherboard). If the warranty only covers the component being installed, you're on the hook for a new motherboard — and in the hole for $500 or more.

Don't be afraid to shop around and ask questions. You'll eventually find a reputable hardware person who puts quality and integrity first, and guarantees his work. When you do, hand over the PC and indicate what you need done. Within hours, your PC will be back in your hands, empowered by its new hardware.

External hardware upgrades for software people

If the hardware upgrade you need can be addressed by products that simply plug into your PC, by all means, go that route. For example, you can add or upgrade hard and Zip disks, CD-RWs and DVDs, networking interfaces, modems, and more, simply by plugging them into your PC's serial (COM), parallel (LPT), or USB (Universal Serial Bus) ports. Windows 98 will automatically detect the new hardware, and walk you through the process of installing its supporting software. On the off chance the new hardware isn't detected, you can install its software using the technique described in the next section in this chapter.

■ **You'll find state** *of the art USB hubs at Belkin Components (www.belkin.com).*

Whenever you're considering a hardware upgrade, always try to find a solution that simply plugs into a port on your PC. It's only when an external hardware upgrade is not an option that you should consider opening the PC and upgrading its internals.

And if at all possible, look for an upgrade that uses the PC's USB ports.

Most PCs have two USB ports, and you can add more USB ports as needed, simply by connecting a box called a "USB hub." This device can add two, four, eight, or more USB ports to a computer without opening the case. If you run out of extra USB ports on the hub, you can add another hub for even more ports – up to 127 in all!

For hardware devices that require super-high-speed connections (such as hard drives), consider using a SCSI interface. You'll have to have a hardware person install a SCSI card in your PC, but once done, you can chain up to 30 SCSI devices to one SCSI card. In the unlikely event you need to connect more than 30 devices to your PC, just slap in another SCSI card.

■ **Adaptec leads** *the world in SCSI technology.*

Certain hardware enhancements are only available as internal upgrades, while others are available in both internal and external flavors.

✓ **Internal only (best to have trained personnel install)**

CPU (your Pentium, AMD, or other central processing chip)
Ethernet networking cards
Firewire cards
USB ports (not to be confused with USB hubs)
Master (bootable) hard disk (the one your PCs "boots" from)*
Motherboard (your PC's main circuit board)
Parallel (LPT) ports
Power supply and fan
RAM (memory)
SCSI cards
Serial (COM) ports
Sound card and audio memory
Video card and video memory

* If you use a SCSI hard disk, you can boot from external SCSI hard drives.

✓ **External or internal (go for external if you can, and DIY)**

CD-Rs
CD-ROMs
CD-RWs
DVDs
Floppy drives
Hard drives
Modems
Removable disks
Scanners
Tablets (pen-based drawing devices)
Tape (backup) drives
Video cameras
Web cams
Zip disk

✓ **External only (always DIY)**

Digital snapshot cameras
Keyboards
Mice (pointing devices)
Printers
Routers
Speakers
Switch boxes (allows two devices to share the same port)
USB hubs

■ **Connecting a video** *camera to your PC is a safe DIY procedure.*

In with the new

YOUR HEART BEATS 60 TO 70 TIMES *every minute of every day of your life, pumping five liters of life-sustaining blood through your cardiovascular and respiratory systems. Just as a heartbeat is the pulse of human life, installing and removing software is the pulse of computing life.*

The ebb and flow of software through your computer sustains your ability to solve problems, tackle projects, and get your work done. Right now, your PC seems unlimited in its power. You can surf the web, send and receive e-mail, create documents, crunch numbers, and caress data with ease. But you'll soon find your PC lacks the ability to perform many required tasks.

Windows 98 doesn't include software for a host of potential requirements. For example, if you buy a digital camera, you'll need to add software for editing and cataloging digital photographs.

But what Windows 98 doesn't have, you can add – that's the beauty of computing. When you have a new requirement, simply shop around for a software program that fits the bill. Once found, it's a simple matter to install it into your Windows 98 PC.

In addition to addressing new application requirements, the time will come when you'll want to update existing software programs. Case in point: Windows 98 itself.

Microsoft's issue of its 2000 update to Windows 98 is dubbed Windows ME (Millennium Edition).

The new release will improve performance, fix bugs, and add cool new features you'll surely want to take advantage of. There will also be times when you no longer need a particular program and want to extricate it from your system. Getting software out of your PC is just about as easy as putting it in.

Installing (adding) new software

Installing software into a Windows 98 PC can often be this simple: Press the Eject button on the front of the CD drive, drop the program's CD or DVD into the platter, then press the Eject button again to "mount" (load) the disk. Windows 98 will scan the disk for an installation program, launch the installer, and display it on your screen. At that point, all you need to do is follow the instructions on the screen.

Alas, installing new software is not always this easy. Some CDs and DVDs don't include the automatic installation routines that Windows 98 requires to automatically fire up the installer. And though it's rare these days, some programs are still delivered on floppy disks. Due to technological limitations of the floppy disk drive, Windows 98 can't tell when a new floppy disk has been inserted and can't automatically scan it for an installation program. But fear not. Once again, Microsoft planned ahead, and provided a way to install software manually.

■ **You can clone** *the icon for Add/Remove Programs into your master personal folder.*

The Add/Remove Programs applet

Use the Add/Remove Programs applet to add software to your PC when the program's installer doesn't appear automatically. You'll find the Add/Remove Programs applet in your Windows 98 Control Panel. Since you'll be using the Add/Remove Programs applet often, it's smart to put a copy of it into your master personal folder. Press Win+D to get back to your Windows Desktop, and jump into your master personal folder by double-clicking it, or hitting its hot key. Double-click the Control Panel icon (you can also get to Control Panel by clicking Start | Settings | Control Panel). There you'll see the Add/Remove Program applet. Right-click it, and select Copy. Then right-click any blank area of your master personal folder, and select Paste.

If you like, you can assign a hot key to the Add/Remove Programs applet. Right-click the icon, select Properties, and enter the keystroke you want to use in the "Shortcut key" input box. Then click OK.

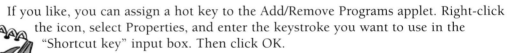

Note, however, that most people don't use hot keys with Add/Remove Programs.

Even though you'll use Add/Remove Programs often, it's not something you'll use every day. Most folks reserve hot keys for programs they use daily.

Installing software with the Add/Remove Programs applet

To install software using the Add/Remove Programs applet, double-click the icon, or hit its hot key. The Add/Remove Programs dialog appears. You'll see a big button labeled "Install" at the upper-right of the dialog. Click it. This activates the Add/Remove Programs Wizard, which will prompt you to insert the new software's floppy disk, CD, or DVD into the appropriate disk drive. After you have mounted (inserted) the disk, click the Next button. The Add/Remove Programs Wizard will scan your system's disk drives, and will display the Run Installation Program dialog when it finds it. You should see the name of the installation program highlighted in blue in the input box just above the Browse button.

Click the Finish button to launch the installation program. Most will use a wizard to walk you through the installation process. You'll soon grow accustomed to clicking Next, Next, Next a few times, until you reach a Finish button. Remember though that every installation program is ever so slightly different from those that preceded it.

Always read the on-screen instructions carefully before clicking the Next button (in other words, remember to RTFS!).

If an installer gives you a choice between automatic (also called "recommended" or "default"), manual, or custom settings, always choose the automatic installation settings.

Troubleshooting installation problems

Sometimes a new program gives Windows 98 fits. It won't be able to automatically display its installation program when you mount the disk, and the Add/Remove Programs applet will be unable to locate a valid installation program. Nine times out of ten, this means you inserted the wrong disk or put the disk in upside down.

If the disk is part of a multi-disk set, eject it and make sure you're inserting disk #1 of the set. Installation programs never reside on a disk other than #1 of a set.

Similarly, make sure the CD or DVD is inserted with the label side up, that is, facing you. If everything checks out, and you still can't get a new program installed, contact the program's vendor.

Locating and cloning icons for new software

When you're done installing the new software, you'll usually find its icons somewhere on the Start Menu or on the Windows Desktop. Check both. If you plan to use the software every day, clone a copy of its icon or icons into your master personal folder. As always, right-click the icon and select Copy. Then open your master personal folder by double-clicking it or hitting its hot key. Right click any blank area inside the master personal folder and click Paste.

And of course, you can assign a hot key to new programs by right-clicking their icon, selecting Properties, and entering the keystroke you want to use in the "Shortcut key" input box. Click OK when you're done.

■ **New software** *can be installed using the Add/Remove Programs Install applet.*

■ **You can also use**
*Add/Remove Programs to
uninstall a program.*

Removing software

Getting software out of Windows 98 is as easy as getting it in.
Once again, fire up the Add/Remove Programs applet by double-
clicking its icon in your master personal folder or hitting its hot
key. This time, instead of clicking the big Install button, examine
the huge list box that takes up most of the dialog. It's a laundry list
of every program that's installed in your computer.

Click the up and down arrowheads to work your way
through the list. When you locate the program
you want to remove, click it to select it. Then
click the Add/Remove button that appears. The
program's uninstaller will appear.

*As with installers, each uninstaller is slightly different from the
next. Carefully read and follow the instructions on the screen to get
the software out of your PC.*

Like installers, uninstallers use wizards. That means uninstalling programs is usually just
a matter of clicking the Next button a few times. If an uninstaller offers you a choice of
automatic, manual, or custom uninstallation options, always choose automatic.

Sometimes, an uninstaller will display a dialog that asks if you want to remove a
"shared" file. It will say the file is no longer in use by any other programs and
will encourage you to allow its deletion.

*Never, ever, ever delete shared files. Such files are used by more than
one program. Even though you're removing a program that uses the
shared file, other programs might still require access to the file.*

If you allow the uninstaller to remove it, other programs you're still using might fail.
That's why uninstallers ask this question in the first place: Software vendors know it's
risky to delete shared files.

Upgrading to new software

Upgrading means installing a new version of a program you already own. Contrary to
popular belief, you do not have to uninstall the previous version before installing the
new one. Simply install upgrades as you would any other software. The installation
programs are intelligent enough to detect a previous version on your PC, and will
automatically remove it before bringing in the update. All of your previous settings will
be preserved, and all of your data will remain untouched. But the program itself will be
seamlessly upgraded to the latest components provided by your software vendor.

Installing software over the Internet

VIDEO KILLED THE RADIO STAR,
*and e-commerce threatens to kill the retail star.
Just a few years ago, there was only one way to
acquire a commercial software program: at your
local dealer. Software was packaged in attractive
shrink-wrapped boxes that included a manual,*

■ **You have to** *download software before you can try it out.*

registration card, and installation disks. Users unfortunately had to run to the dealer's store, buy the program they needed, take it home, break open the box, and install the product.

Today, all it takes is a web browser to electronically purchase and download software directly into your PC. Minutes after buying a new program, it's up and running in your computer – and you never have to leave the comfort of your PC chair. Sounds great, but downloading and installing new software is one of the tasks that consistently baffles new users. That's because, after years of trying, the computer industry still hasn't figured out a way to make downloading brain-dead easy.

No matter. While others struggle, you'll survive. Why? Because the PC computing environment you established in the past 18 chapters makes electronic software installation a fast, easy, and reliable solution.

Installing software over the Internet is a three-step process: Locating the software you're after, downloading the program's installer, and running the installer.

Three steps to download success

Most people don't have any trouble finding or downloading the software they want. It's the last step that trips them up: running the installer. That's because they have no idea where the installer goes after it's downloaded, and they're baffled when they can't find it. You'll encounter no such mysteries, because your downloads will go to the same place you put everything else: your master personal folder. Press Win+D to return to your Windows Desktop. Then open your master personal folder by double-clicking it or pressing its hot key.

Once inside, create a sub-folder named "Downloads" by right-clicking any blank area of your master personal folder and selecting New | Folder. Name the folder Downloads by typing the word "Downloads" into the folder's input box. Press Enter to accept the folder's name.

If you mess up, you can try again by right-clicking the folder and selecting Rename. Doing so allows you to re-enter a name for the folder. Once you've created a central storage location for your downloads, you're ready to give web installations a try.

■ **Create a new** *"Downloads" folder inside your master personal folder.*

Hop on the World Wide Web by firing up Internet Explorer. Double-click the IE icon, or hit its hot key to load it up. If you're not already online, IE will display the Dial-up Connection dialog and begin the Internet logon process. Suppose you wanted to download and install my Space Ace program, which automatically cleans your hard

■ **The author's** *Space Ace III Automatic Win95/98/NT4/2K HD Cleaner program does a better job of cleaning your hard disk than the Windows 98 Maintenance Wizard.*

drive more efficiently than Windows 98's Maintenance Wizard. Jump to Space Ace's web site by clicking in Internet Explorer's Address bar, and typing www.spaceace.net. Then click the Go button, or press Enter to instruct IE to go to and load the Space Ace web page.

To download a program requires little more than finding the program's download link and clicking it.

Some software vendors might present a link that reads "Download now." Others might present a link that reads "Click here to download." The wording will vary wildly, but will almost always include the word "download.". If you're carefully reading the screen (remember, RTFS!), you'll find the download link. Practice now. Scan the Space Ace page for a download link. When you find it, click it.

If you clicked on the link that reads "Download NOW," you clicked the right place. Internet Explorer will display the File Download dialog. You'll have two options: "Run this program from its current location," or "Save this program to disk." The default is to save the program to disk. Make sure that radio button is selected, then click OK. The Save As dialog will appear.

This is the point in the process at which most users screw things up, but fear not — you will now sail through with flying colors.

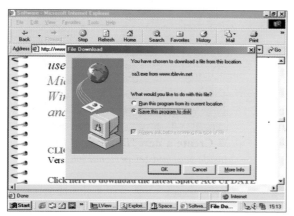

Click the little green-and-white Desktop icon on the Save As dialog's toolbar. Then double-click the shortcut to your master personal folder, and double-click the Downloads sub-folder.

Note: sometimes the green-and-white Desktop button doesn't show up on the Save As dialog. In that case, click the Up One Level button instead (that's the button that looks like a little folder with a bent-elbow up-arrow on it). Keep clicking on the Up One Level button until the button turns gray and won't let you travel up any more levels. You're

■ **The File Download** *dialog tells you that a download is about to begin.*

now looking at a mini-view of your Windows Desktop, compressed into the Save As dialog's window. Double-click the shortcut to your master personal folder, and double-click the Downloads sub-folder.

Whichever way you got to it, take a look now at the "Save in" drop-down pick list. Your Downloads sub-folder should appear as the destination for the saved file.

If you hadn't specified a destination folder for your downloaded program, the transferred file could well have ended up anywhere on your hard disk.

That's why you'll hear inexperienced or disorganized users complain about downloads. They'll tell you every time they download a file, it just "disappears" into their computer. You'll never "lose" downloads because they'll all be in your Downloads sub-folder.

Click the Save button to initiate the download. Internet Explorer will start to bring down the remote file. Be patient. Downloads can take a while – a l-o-o-o-ng while. You'll know the download was successfully completed when Internet Explorer reports "Download Complete."

Once the download is finished, click the Open button to automatically launch the downloaded software's installation program. It's that easy! When the installation is complete, you can choose to keep the downloaded program on your hard drive for future use, or you can delete it to free space.

Deleting downloaded software

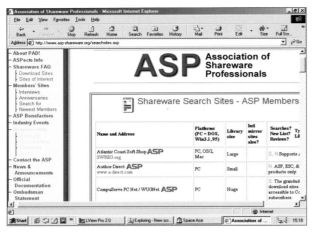

To delete a downloaded program, press Win+D to return to your Windows Desktop. Then open your master personal folder by double-clicking it or hitting its hot key. Double-click the Downloads sub-folder, then right-click the installer you just downloaded, and simply select Delete.

■ **Visit the** *Assocation of Shareware Professionals (ASP) web site at www.asp-shareware.org/.*

Think twice before deleting downloaded software programs, however.

Keeping them doesn't take that much space, and in the event your system crashes (i.e., breaks down), you can re-install your downloaded programs by double-clicking their installers in your master personal folder's Download sub-folder.

This is certainly faster and more convenient than having to remember all of the programs you downloaded and installed, returning to their web sites, and transferring them one at a time back into your PC.

INTERNET

www.asp-shareware.
org/searchsites.asp

www.filemine.com

www.jumbo.com

www.microsoft.com/
windows98/downloads

www.shareware.com

Build your download skills! You'll find the latest and greatest in free and low-cost programs at these excellent software libraries.

■ **At Shareware.com,** *you can search for over 250,000 downloadable programs.*

A simple summary

✔ Upgrades are the only way to preserve and extend your PC investment. They fall into two categories: hardware and software.

✔ Some hardware upgrades you can do yourself. Others are best handled by an experienced computer technician.

✔ Make sure an upgrade has a guarantee that covers all PC components that could be adversely effected.

✔ The easiest and most reliable upgrades are those that use your PC's USB ports.

✔ For high-performance upgrades, have a SCSI card installed in your PC.

✔ To adapt your PC to meet new, previously unforeseen application requirements, you'll have to install new software.

✔ To install a new program, slide its installation disk into the appropriate disk drive. Windows 98 will automatically run the installer.

✔ To install software manually, use the Add/Remove Programs applet.

✔ After installing a new program, you can clone its icon into your master personal folder.

✔ To free up hard disk space, remove software using the Add/Remove Programs applet.

✔ Always RTFS when installing or removing software.

✔ To install software over the Internet, simply click the software's "download" link, and follow the browser's on-screen instructions (RTFS!).

✔ To avoid "losing" Internet downloads somewhere on your hard disk, create a "Downloads" sub-folder in your master personal folder, and save all Internet downloads there.

Chapter 20

Computing's Golden Rule: Back-up!

NOTHING'S PERFECT. In the event your PC is lost, stolen, damaged by flood or fire, or simply gives up the ghost, you can easily replace the various hardware components. But your personal data will be lost with no hope of recovery in the event of a computing catastrophe. That is, if you don't have a backup plan. It consists of up-front preparation, a dash of specialized software and hardware, and a disaster recovery strategy. In this chapter, you'll learn how to protect yourself from the ever-present threat of data loss. You'll learn about the threats to your PC's data, what kind of hardware and software you'll need to protect it, and how to devise and implement a disaster recovery strategy.

In this chapter...

✓ Murphy's first law of computing

✓ Types of backup systems and software

✓ Devising your backup plan

✓ When all else fails

DISASTER CAN STRIKE AT ANY TIME SO START YOUR DATA BACKUP STRATEGY NOW

Murphy's first law of computing

IT'S IRONIC. One of the world's favorite axioms on the inevitability of failure is itself an example of such inevitability. It's Murphy's Law, most often stated as "anything that can go wrong, will." The irony: That's not Murphy's Law at all. It's "Finagle's Law of Dynamic Negatives," devised by the famous science fiction author Larry Niven. The real Murphy's Law was coined sometime around 1949 by USAF engineer Edward A. Murphy Jr.

Murphy was part of a team of USAF engineers working on a project that tested the effects of extreme G-forces on the human body. One such test involved mounting 16 sensors to 16 different parts of the test subject's body. Each sensor could be connected in one of two ways: Correctly or incorrectly. On the first run, a technician installed all 16 sensors backwards, after which Murphy issued his now-famous maxim: "If there are two or more ways to do something, and one of those ways can result in a catastrophe, then someone will do it." Someone did, and now Finagle's Law is almost always misrepresented as Murphy's.

The moral of this story for PC users: He who fails to plan for system failure, plans to fail. Or to put it bluntly, if you don't have a data backup plan in place, you'll be sorry.

Your computer contains a few million components, and hundreds of billions of software bits. The mechanical, electronic, and architectural complexity of your PC is mind boggling. Considering Finagle's and Murphy's laws, it's amazing your PC boots up at all. But it does, at least for the time being. Inevitably, your computer will fail. It might be a "hard" failure, such as an expired hard disk, chip, or circuit board. It could be a "soft" failure, such as a program that runs amok and scrambles the data on your hard disk.

Or it could be a user error, in which you or someone you know (like a two-year-old) accidentally deletes an

■ **Disaster scenario #1:** *"junior" deletes a file while you are out of the room.*

important file or folder, spills coffee on the keyboard, or jams a peanut butter sandwich into the floppy disk drive (it's happened!). Any way you cut it, your PC is destined for a crash.

Users who have a backup plan are never more than minutes away from recovering whatever data was temporarily lost or damaged.

Those who don't take planning seriously will have no options other than to tip their hat to Finagle and Murphy – that is, after they're done kicking themselves.

Types of backup systems and software

YOUR BACKUP PLAN STARTS *with hardware and software, and ends with a course of action. The hardware: a backup device to copy your data from your PC onto some form of removable media, such as tape, disk, or CD. The software: A backup program, designed to do nothing more than clone your data to removable media, and restore it in the event of a catastrophe or lesser disaster. Before you can choose the software, you must first decide on the hardware.*

■ **Disaster scenario #2:**
"junior" is fast asleep, but you pour coffee over the keyboard.

That's because some backup programs only work with certain kinds of hardware. For example, Adaptec's brand-new Take Two program can back up your system to any disk drive that appears in your My Computer folder, including CD-Rs and CD-RWs. But it can't back up to tape. Iomega's 1-Step Backup program does a fine job backing up data from and to removable floppy and hard drives – provided those drives are manufactured by Iomega. No Iomega drive? No backup.

Adaptec and Iomega aren't alone. This scenario gets repeated again and again in the backup products world. With rare exceptions, backup software products are tied to the backup hardware being used.

Translation: Choose your backup hardware carefully, because you'll be stuck with it for a long time, and you'll be dependent on it to provide a critical digital lifeline in the event of an emergency.

Backup hardware

■ **Wherever** *you work, don't neglet your backup options.*

There are literally dozens of different backup hardware products, technologies, and services at your disposal. Boil them down, and they fit neatly into the following four categories.

✓ Streaming tape drives

The classic approach to backup hardware, streaming tape drives use cassette-like tapes to store your backup data. Most include a basic but serviceable backup utility to create and restore backup sets. The software allows you to stream (send a continuous flow of) data off your hard drive onto the tape cassette. Streaming tape drives have one advantage over all other backup mediums: They store the most data. One streaming tape can hold up to 70G of data – many times the size of the average hard disk. Tape is also the least expensive backup medium, costing between $1 and $2 per G. That's convenient and cost-effective, because one streaming tape can contain months, even years of backup data. But that's where tape's advantages end. On the downside, they're slow and proprietary. Generally speaking, streaming tape cassettes only work with one manufacturer's tape drives, even when they're advertised as being compatible across multiple vendor offerings. Worse, if your tape drive hardware ever fails, you'll be the owner of worthless backup tapes.

INTERNET

www.hp.com/ tape/colorado

www.onstream.com

www.tecmar.com

www.valitek.com

For the highest-capacity backups, streaming tape is the answer. The industry's best streaming tape drives can be found at these sites.

✓ Removable disks

There are two varieties of removable disks: Floppies and hard disks. Neither provides a cost-effective backup solution. The 3.5-inch 1.44M floppy disk drive included with most computers is woefully inadequate for backup needs. With a storage capacity of 1.44M per disk, it would require close to 7,000 floppy disks to backup a 10G hard disk

■ *Hewlett-Packard Colorado drives can be found at www.hp.com/tape/colorado/.*

(and some computers today are shipping with 20G, 25G, or larger hard drives). That's $4,200 in floppy disks! High-capacity 120M and 250M floppies from vendors such as Iomega, Sony, and 3M don't do much better. Backing up a 10G drive will cost you $500 for 83 120M floppies, and $800 for 40 250M floppies. The high-capacity floppy disk drives themselves run $100 to $200.

The cost/benefit ratio for removable hard drives is similarly unattractive. The largest industry-standard removable hard drive, Iomega's Jaz, holds 2G of data.

Using one requires a $350 removable Jaz drive system and five 2G cartridges costing $125 each. Total bill: $475, about half the cost of a new PC.

Worse, with the exception of the 1.44M floppy disk, all removable floppy and hard disk formats are, to greater or lesser degrees, proprietary. If the backup hardware device fails, you're stuck with boxes of unusable disks. Any way you cut it, removable floppy and hard disks are an expensive, unwieldy backup option.

✓ Compact discs

Every computer sold today already has 50 percent of the best backup solution: A CD-ROM or DVD reader. You have to supply the other 50 percent, a CD-R (Compact Disc Recordable) or CD-RW (Compact Disc Re-Writable) drive. They cost between $200 and $400, and enable you to "burn" (record) your own CDs. CD-Rs can be written to (recorded on) once and played back an infinite number of times. CD-RWs can be written to and erased, which means the media can be reused over and over again, just like a cassette tape. This saves money, because you can buy a supply of CD-RW disks and reuse them practically forever. Each CD stores up to 650M of data, and costs between $.80 and $2 in bulk, depending on brand – and the prices continue to decline. It takes only 16 CDs to backup a 10G hard drive which, worst case, adds up to $32.

■ **Iomega Zip and Jaz** *drives are viable backup media. Find out more at www.iomega.com/.*

In stark contrast to tapes and removable disks, CDs are pure media; they contain no moving parts that can fail over time. Best of all, CDs can be accessed on any type of PC with a CD-ROM or DVD drive.

Even if your computer is crushed by an asteroid, you'll be able to recover your data without having to shell out for a proprietary device to read the CD media.

Also, CDs store information optically, not magnetically. That means they're far less susceptible to fluctuations in temperature during long-term storage (only extreme heat or scratches from mishandling can harm them). They're also immune to data corruption resulting from static, magnetic fields, or radio emissions. According to scientists at Kodak's digital and applied imaging group, when CDs are stored in their plastic case, and in a cool, dry location, they can retain backup data for over 200 years! (The Kodak white paper on CD data longevity is located at www.cd-info.com/cdic/technology/cd-r/media/kodak.html.)

✓Internet backup

The new kid on the block, Internet backup (also referred to as "network-attached" backup) uses your Internet connection to replicate (backup) your data to a server somewhere in cyberspace. Because your backup data is stored on the Internet backup service's computers, Internet backup involves no up-front hardware expense, no media costs, and no storage limitations (in theory). But that doesn't mean it's the cheapest way to go. Internet backup services charge monthly or annual access fees that add up to $100 to $500 a year. In the long run, Internet backup is the most expensive approach of all, because you're coughing up cash as long as you use it. It's also slow, inconvenient, and potentially risky. Most users will be sending their data over slow modem connections, which can take forever to send a few megs of data. Also, most services limit the amount of data you can backup to between 100M and 500M, far short of the gigabytes of data housed in a typical new PC today. Perhaps most important, to use Internet backup means you have to trust some faceless corporation with your crown jewels, and transmit your personal data over the Internet, where it can be peeked at and poached by hackers.

■ **Internet backup** *is the new kid on the block and growing by the minute!*

INTERNET

www.adaptec.com

www.panasonic.com

www.plextor.com

www.sony.com

www.yamaha.com

The best CD-RW drives are made by the vendors listed here.

Backup software

You might be wondering why I haven't mentioned specific backup software programs. There's a reason: All of the backup solutions discussed above include a decent backup software package. The packages are not flashy, but they work, which is just what good backup software should be – simple and uncomplicated. All it has to do, after all, is copy your data to the backup media and reliably restore (recover) it in the event of a disaster.

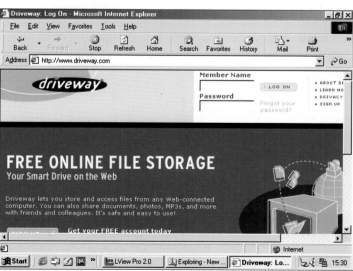

Still, if you're not satisfied with the free backup software bundled with your backup hardware device, consider investing in the Veritas Backup Exec Desktop for Windows (www.veritas.com).

This state-of-the-art backup package supports literally every backup hardware device mentioned here. It's not perfect (no software ever is), but it's the closest thing to a perfect backup solution the industry offers. Plan to spend between $70 and $100.

My recommendation for plan B: Buy a CD-RW drive as the foundation of your backup strategy.

Stick with one of the vendors noted above. Specify a unit with a USB port if you'd like to do the installation yourself. For the utmost in backup speed, have your dealer add a SCSI card to your PC if it doesn't feature one already, and plug a SCSI-based CD-RW drive into the SCSI card. Once that's out of the way, you're ready to start ...

INTERNET

www.atbackup.com

www.backupmystuff.com

www.docspace.com

www.driveway.com

www.connected.com

Some of the leading Internet backup service providers are located at these sites.

■ **Internet backup** *means that you can also share your files with family, friends, and colleagues. Check out Driveway at www.driveway.com/.*

Devising your backup plan

BACKING UP is like exercise: It's hard to get into the habit, but once you do, it's hard to quit. As with your exercise regimen, you'll need to decide exactly when you will perform your system backups. Some people exercise in the morning, while others prefer an evening workout. And even folks who exercise daily will occasionally visit the gym for an extended session or run an extra mile or two.

Backing up is similar. There are two kinds of backup approaches, both of which must be applied regularly to keep your system data protected.

"Total" system backups copy everything on your hard disk to the backup hardware device. "Incremental" backups copy only the data that's been modified (changed) since your last total backup.

Depending upon how much data is stored on your hard disk, total backups can take from a few minutes to a few hours to complete. Incremental backups generally take only 5-to-15 minutes, because even the busiest computer users don't "touch" more than a few megabytes of data per day.

■ **Like daily exercise**, *a backup routine is good for you.*

Think of incremental backups as "daily" backups and total backups as "monthly." A solid backup plan includes both daily and monthly backups, beginning with a complete system backup when you first install your backup hardware device.

The backup cycle

■ **Few computer** *users "touch" more than a few megabytes of data in a day.*

Using a 3M Post-It® or other removable label, mark each backup tape or disk with the backup date and a number, starting with #1. The first tape or disk is #1, the second is #2, etc. Every day thereafter, instruct your backup software to perform an incremental backup of modified files only. Add these backed up files to the last backup tape or disk in your total backup set.

For example, if your initial total backup consumed ten tapes or disks, use #10 as the first of the daily

backups. When #10 is filled up, your backup software will ask for the next tape or disk. Insert #11, and label it as such. Some people prefer to do their daily backup in the morning, while others like to cap the day with a backup (I'm a nightcap person).

As long as you're backing up every day, it doesn't really matter when you do it.

The monthly backup

Continue to add tapes or disks to your backup set until one full month has passed. At that point, it's safe to stop buying new tapes or disks, and begin reusing the ones you have acquired over the past 30 days. Instruct your backup software to perform a full backup, and overwrite tape or disk #1 in the process. This restarts the entire backup cycle anew. When the total backup is complete, you're ready to resume daily backups for another 30 days.

Observing this monthly backup cycle guarantees you'll always have at least the last 30 days of data at your disposal, which is usually an adequate safety net for

1	2	3	4	5	6	7
8	9	10	11	12	13	14
15	16	17	18	19	20	21
22	23	24	25	26	27	28
29	30					

■ **Develop a monthly** *backup routine.*

most users. If need be, you can adapt the backup cycle to cover a 60 or 90 day range, or even greater.

Maintaining an intelligent backup cycle also reduces your media costs, because you're continually reusing the tapes or disks.

If you're not using CD-Rs or CD-RWs, however, replace the tapes or disks after a year, as magnetic media do wear out with use.

■ **CDs have a** *longer life than magnetic media.*

When all else fails

SOMETIMES A BACKUP PLAN ISN'T ENOUGH. Consider electrical generators powered by nuclear reactors. If one system fails, a backup system kicks in. But what happens if the backup system fails? Yet another backup system kicks in. Backups for backups are called "redundant backups," and they are essential for systems that can't fail under any circumstances, such as heart/lung machines, air traffic control systems, the White House telephone network, and so on.

Computer users should take a cue from nuclear power plant engineers: Even your backup plan should have a backup plan. It's the only sure-fire way to guarantee you won't suffer a catastrophic loss of data. Backing up daily, weekly, and monthly are critical steps on the path to total data protection, but they're not enough. Backups provide a safety net for your PC data, but you must also implement measures to protect the backups themselves. Here are the essential elements of a complete disaster plan:

A fire-proof safe

As soon as your daily, weekly, or monthly backup is done, store the backup media (tapes or disks) in a UL-rated fire-proof safe. Make sure the safe is impact tested, and can withstand the collapse of a roof or floor during a fire. Underwriters Laboratories has a rating system that designates a safe's ability to protect its contents from heat and fire damage. The UL class 350 rating, for example, applies to safes that can withstand fire and heat from a half-hour to two hours. The UL ratings also cover impact protection.

■ **Sentry provides** *information on UL-rated safes at www.sentrysafe.com/.*

INTERNET

www.ul.com/info/
uldirs.htm

www.nfpa.org

www.meilinksafe.com

www.mutualsafes.com

www.sentrysafe.com

Always look for a safe that's UL rated; don't trust vendor promises. For more information on UL-rated safes, hit these web sites.

A disaster drill

Fire drills are a regular occurrence at elementary and high schools nationwide. There's good reason for this: If schools didn't test and practice their fire escape plans, the risk of a fire disaster increases dramatically. Practice does make perfect, and it's especially important in matters of life and death – and data. For that reason, it makes sense to periodically test the integrity of your backups by performing a practice restore.

With repeated use, magnetic backup tapes and disks wear out, and optical CDs become scratched from handling. Both scenarios can result in tape or disk media that accept backup data, but are incapable of restoring it.

On the off chance that your backup data is corrupt and can't be recovered from your tapes or disks, it's essential to find out about it now, rather than in the heat of an emergency restoration.

Once a month, after you complete your total system backup, instruct your backup software to restore the last file in your backup set. That's the last file your backup software copied to tape or disk. Restoring the last file in the backup set forces the backup software to read the entire tape or disk "catalog" (the backup software's equivalent of a file and folder director). Doing so will flush out any corruption that could prevent a successful restoration of data. For users working with tape drives, this process also forces the backup software to scan the entire tape, and verify the integrity of all the tape headers and markers. Any damage here can also prevent a successful restore. Lastly, performing a disaster drill ensures that your data is actually being backed up and making the transition from the PC to removable tape or disk. If the backup software successfully restores the test file, you can be 99 percent sure your backup is sound.

After the successful completion of your monthly disaster drill, move the complete backup set to an off-site location, such as a safe deposit box at your bank. This is the redundant backup component of a well-devised disaster plan.

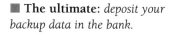

In the event you lose everything — your PC, your backups, and even the contents of your fireproof safe — you'll still have a copy of the only thing that really matters: your data. At that point it's a simple matter to buy a new PC and resume your electronic life.

■ **The ultimate:** *deposit your backup data in the bank.*

Insuring your PC

Alas, even the backup plan's backup plan should have a backup plan.

Contact your insurance company and inquire about their computer system coverage. Most major homeowner's insurance policies today offer some token PC coverage. Take your homeowner's or renter's policy to the next level, and work with your agent to define an appropriate amount of PC coverage. Ideally, your PC system should be insured for its replacement value in the event of fire, theft, flood, or acts of God.

■ **To insure your PC,** *call your insurance company about computer system coverage.*

INTERNET

www.safeware.com

Some companies even specialize in PC insurance policies. One of the most experienced is Safeware. You can reach them at this address, or call them at 800-800-1492.

And here's the ultimate backup: In the event you get yourself into a pickle, keep my e-mail and BBS addresses handy. Some folks call me a glutton for punishment, but I have always enjoyed helping users work their way through computer problems – and so do the volunteers on my BBS. So feel free to write to me at RBLevin@RBLevin.net whenever you have a computer question, or hit my BBS at http://www.rblevin.net/bbs. I'll be there to help.

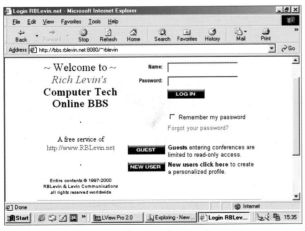

■ **If you're really stuck,** *try the author's free Computer Tech Online BBS (www.rblevin.net/bbs).*

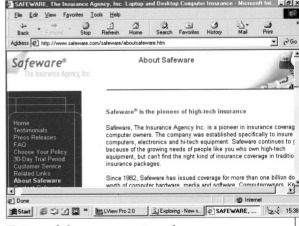

■ **One of the most** *experienced companies specializing in PC insurance is Safeware (www.safeware.com).*

A simple summary

✓ Your computer is the storehouse for all your digital information. That means your PC is a disaster waiting to happen. If the hardware or software fails, you lose your data.

✓ Plan for the inevitable disaster by devising and implementing a disaster recovery strategy, a-k-a your backup plan. Users who adopt a backup plan will never be crying over lost data.

✓ There are many different types of backup hardware and software. The best existing technology is probably the CD-RW drive, because the backups it creates can be accessed on almost any PC, and the backup medium itself is inexpensive and reusable.

✓ Do a total backup of all your data once a month.

✓ Every day, backup all the files and folders you worked on.

✓ At the end of a month, perform another full backup. Repeat this daily/monthly backup cycle every 30 days.

✓ Have a backup plan for your backup plan, in case your backup plan fails.

✓ Keep your monthly and daily backups in a fireproof safe.

✓ Perform a disaster drill once a month, by restoring at least one file from your backup set. This makes sure your backup set is valid.

✓ Get your backups off-site at least four times a year, and preferably monthly. A bank's safe deposit box is the best place for this kind of archival storage.

✓ Check with your insurance agent to see if you have adequate coverage for your PC.

✓ Write to me at RBLevin@RBLevin.net whenever you have a computer question. Yes, I'll really write back.

More resources

Rich's Picks

As time goes on, you'll discover you need a variety of different hardware and software tools to get various jobs done. To make it easier for you to choose the right products, I've compiled this list of my favorite products in a variety of categories. Feel free to use this as a starting point when you begin your search for a new hardware or software solution.

Antivirus
Symantec Norton Antivirus   www.sarc.com

Backup power
APC	www.apc.com
Tripp-Lite	www.tripplite.com

Backup software:
Veritas Desktop Backup   www.veritas.com

Computer manufacturers:
Acer America	www.acer.com
Compaq Computer	www.compaq.com
Dell	www.dell.com
Gateway	www.gateway.com
Hewlett-Packard	www.hp.com
IBM	www.ibm.com
NEC	www.nec.com
Sony	www.sony.com
Toshiba	www.toshiba.com

CD-RW:
Hewlett-Packard	www.hp.com
LaCie	www.lacie.com
Panasonic	www.panasonic.com
Plextor	www.plextor.com
Ricoh	www.ricoh.com
Sony	www.sony.com
Yamaha	www.yamaha.com

CPUs (processors):
Evergreen Technology	www.evertech.com
JDR Microdevices	www.jdr.com
Kingston Technology	www.kingston.com

CRT or flat-panel displays:
Acer	www.acer.com
CTX	www.ctxintl.com
IBM	www.ibm.com
Mag InnoVision	www.maginnovision.com
Mitsubishi	www.mitsubishi.com
NEC	www.neccomp.com
Princeton Graphics Systems	www.princetongraphics.com
Samsung	www.samsung.com
Sony	www.sony.com
Viewsonic	www.viewsonic.com

Database
Microsoft Works 2000	www.microsoft.com/works
FileMaker	www.filemaker.com
FileMaker Pro	

Data security
Pretty Good Privacy	www.pgp.com
Folder Guard	www.winability.com

Desktop publishing:
Microsoft Home Publisher	www.home-publishing.com
Microsoft Publisher 2 000	www.microsoft.com/office/publisher

Digital cameras:
FujiFilm	www.fujifilm.com
Kodak	www.kodak.com

DNS/Lifetime E-mail Address:
NameSecure   www.namesecure.com

DVD:
Pioneer	www.pioneer-america.com
Toshiba	www.toshiba.com

Fax software/services:
CallWave	www.callwave.com
Fax4Free	www.fax4free.com
Symantec WinFax Pro	www.symantec.com

Firewall:
Symantec Norton Internet Security	www.symantec.com
Zone Labs	www.zonealarm.com

Game controllers:
Logitech	www.logitech.com
Microsoft	www.microsoft.com/products/hardware

Hand-held PC companions:
Microsoft Windows CE	www.microsoft.com/windowsce
Palm Computing	www.palm.com

Hard disk cleaning:
Space Ace — www.spaceace.net

Hard disk drives:
Maxtor — www. maxtor.com
Seagate — www.seagate.com
Quantum — www.quantum.com
Western Digital — www.westerndigital.com

Internet service providers (ISPs):
Argos Networks — www.argosweb.net (regional service area)
AT&T WorldNet — www.att.net (national)
DirecPC — www.direcpc.com (national)
EarthLink — www.mindspring.com (national)
Excite@Home — www.home.net (regional service area)
SNiP — www.snip.net (regional service area)

Keyboards:
BTC — www.jdr.com
Microsoft — www.microsoft.com/products/hardware
Unicomp (formerly Lexmark) — www.pckeyboard.com

Memory (RAM):
Kingston Technology — www.kingston.com
Viking Components — www.vikingcomponents.com

MLPPP modems:
Diamond Multimedia — www.diamondmm.com

MLPPP routers/hubs:
Linksys (modems extra) — www.linksys.com
Netopia (includes modems) — www.netopia.com
Ramp Networks (includes modems) — www.ramp.com

Modems:
Diamond Multimedia — www.diamondmm.com
USRobotics — www.usrobotics.com

Multitrack recording:
Sonic Foundry Vegas — www.sonicfoundry.com

Music loops:
Sonic Foundry Acid — www.sonicfoundry.com

Network hubs:
3Com — www.3com.com
SMC — www.smc.com

Network interface cards:
3Com — www.3com.com

Office suite:
Apple Works — www.apple.com
Microsoft Office 2000 — www.microsoft.com/office
Microsoft Works 2000 — www.microsoft.com/works

Photo editing software:
Adobe Photo Deluxe — www.adobe.com
Microsoft Picture It! 2000 — www.home-publishing.com

Pointing devices:
Interlink Electronics — www.interlinkelec.com
Logitech — www.logitech.com
Microsoft — www.microsoft.com/products/hardware

Portable music players:
Diamond Multimedia — www.diamondmm.com
Sony — www.sony.com

Printers:
Canon — www.ccsi.canon.com
Hewlett-Packard — www.hp.com
Lexmark — www.lexmark.com
Xerox — www.xerox.com

Programming:
Microsoft Visual Basic — msdn.microsoft.com/vbasic
PowerBASIC — www.powerbasic.com

Removable disk drives:
Iomega — www.iomega.com
MicroSolutions — www.micro-solutions.com

Scanners:
Hewlett-Packard — www.hp.com
Visioneer — www.visioneer.com

Scanner software:
Paper Port Deluxe — www.scansoft.com

SCSI adapters:
Adaptec — www.adaptec.com

Sound/audio cards:
Creative Technology — www.creative.com
Yamaha — www.yamaha.com

Sound/audio editing:
Sonic Foundry Sound Forge — www.sonicfoundry.com

Speakers:

Altec Lansing	www.alteclansing.com
Benwin	www.benwin.com
Bose	www.bose.com
Creative Technology	www.creative.com
Yamaha	www.yamaha.com

Switchboxes:

Belkin Components	www.belkin.com

System security:

Encore Software	www.encoresoftware.com
Full Armor	www.fullarmor.com
Secure Win	www.securewin.com

Tape backup drives:

MicroSolutions	www.micro-solutions.com

USB hubs:

Belkin Components	www.belkin.com
I/O Networks	www.ionetworks.com

Video capture/editing/TV cards:
(See also: video cards)

Hauppage	www.hauppage.com
Pinnacle Systems	www.pinnaclesys.com

Video cards:

3dfx	www.3dfx.com
ATI	www.ati.com
Creative Technology	www.creative.com
Diamond Multimedia	www.diamondmm.com
Matrox	www.matrox.com
Nvidia	www.nvidia.com
Number Nine	www.nine.com

Web cams:

Logitech	www.logitech.com

Web page editors:

Adobe PageMill	www.adobe.com
Microsoft Front Page	www.microsoft.com/frontpage
Symantec Visual Page	www.symantec.com

Tech Support Links

When the going gets tough, the tough go surfing. There are hundreds of superb technical support facilities available on the web. The hard part is sorting through them all when you're in need of a quick answer to a technical problem. Most users avoid the confusion by calling their hardware and software vendors directly. That's usually a mistake. The reason: Tech support by phone usually entails long waits on hold, and a service charge on a per-incident or per-minute basis. Worse, computer industry tech support is notoriously bad. More often than not, users are given the wrong advice, or guided into "sledge hammer" solutions, such as erasing the entire hard drive and starting anew.

Before you make the mistake of turning to a software or hardware vendor for support, hit some of these free tech support services on the web. You'll probably be able to resolve your problem without ever having to deal with a live human being. And when it comes to tech support, that's a plus.

Rich Levin's Computer Tech BBS*
www.rblevin.net/bbs

*This is free service provided by yours truly

InfiniSource
www.windows-help.net

J. Helmig's World of Windows
www.helmig.com

Microsoft Troubleshooters
support.microsoft.com/support/tshoot

Microsoft Personal Support Center
support.microsoft.com/support

Microsoft Knowledge Base
search.support.microsoft.com/kb

Microsoft FAQ (Frequently Asked Questions)
support.microsoft.com/directory/faqs.asp

No Wonder
www.nowonder.com

PC Support Center
www.pcsupport.com

Tom's Hardware Guide
www.tomshardware.com

Works 2000 Database Functions

Date & Time Functions

DATE(Year,Month,Day)
DAY(DateSerialNumber)
HOUR(TimeSerialNumber)
MINUTE(TimeSerialNumber)
MONTH(DateSerialNumber)
NOW( )
SECOND(TimeSerialNumber)
TIME(Hour,Minute,Second)
YEAR(DateSerialNumber)

Financial Functions

CTERM(Rate,FutureValue,PresentValue)
DDB(Cost,Salvage,Life,Period)
FV(Payment,Rate,Term)
PMT(Principal,Rate,Term)
PV(Payment,Rate,Term)
RATE(FutureValue,PresentValue,Term)
SLN(Cost,Salvage,Life)
SYD(Cost,Salvage,Life,Period)
TERM(Payment,Rate,FutureValue)

Informational Functions

ERR( )
ISERR(x)
ISNA(x)
NA( )

Math and Trigonometric Functions

ABS(x)
ACOS(x)
ASIN(x)
ATAN(x)
ATAN2(x-coordinate,y-coordinate)
COS(x)
EXP(x)
INT(x)
LN(x)
LOG(x)
MOD(Numerator,Denominator)
PI( )
RAND( )
ROUND(x,NumberOfPlaces)
SIN(x)
SQRT(x)
TAN(x)

Text Functions

EXACT(TextValue0,TextValue1)
FIND(FindText,SearchText,Offset)
LEFT(TextValue,Length)
LENGTH(TextValue)
LOWER(TextValue)
MID(TextValue,Offset,Length)
PROPER(TextValue)
REPEAT(TextValue,Count)
REPLACE(OldText,Offset,Length,NewText)
RIGHT(TextValue,Length)
STRING(x,DecimalPlaces)
TRIM(TextValue)
UPPER(TextValue)
VALUE(TextValue)

A simple glossary

Address book A central repository of all e-mail names and addresses, and other contact information.

Alias *See Shortcut.*

ALT keys Any key pressed in combination with the ALT key.

Analog Recording and playing back data as continuous electrical fluctuations that can be seen as wiggly lines on an oscilloscope.

Antigen *See Antivirus.*

Antivirus A program that detects computer viruses and other rogue software, and prevents them from damaging a computer or data.

Applet A small program.

Application(s) *See Software.*

Arrow keys The keyboard's four-key cluster with up, down, left, and right arrows on the key caps.

Asymmetric Data is sent and received at different speeds.

Attachment One or more data files sent along with an e-mail message.

AUX Auxiliary port.

Backup Creating copies of computer programs and data for safe keeping.

Backup plan Also called *backup cycle*. A formal policy that defines a timetable and process for backing up a computer on a regular basis.

BASIC Beginners All-purpose Symbolic Instruction Code, a computer programming language.

Batch files Lists of commands compiled into a single text file that's read and executed by the computer.

BCC Blind Carbon Copy, a list of e-mail addresses hidden from view on all copies of a message.

Beta Also called *beta test, beta code*. Pre-release software or hardware products being developed by a vendor and tested by the public simultaneously.

Bleed Text or graphics that spill over into a document's margins.

Bookmarks *See Favorites.*

Bit One element of data.

Blocked sender list A list of e-mail addresses whose mail is prevented from entering a user's Inbox.

Boot Also called *boot up* or *bootstrap*. Jargon for *startup*. The act of starting up a computer. The first program a computer executes is called a *bootstrap loader*, because the computer is turning itself on by its boot straps.

Bounced mail E-mail that's returned to sender.

Byte Eight bits of data (one alphanumeric character requires a byte of storage).

Cable modem A high-speed means of accessing the Internet that uses TV cable lines.

Cancel Stopping the computer from completing a task.

CC Carbon Copy, a list of e-mail addresses that receive a copy of an e-mail message.

Cell A placeholder for data in a spreadsheet. *See* also *Formula* and *Spreadsheet*.

Context menu The pop-up menu that appears when the right-mouse button is clicked.

Cursor The blinking vertical or horizontal line that indicates where text is being typed.

CD-ROM Also called *CD*. Compact Disc Read-Only Memory, music CDs that contain up to 650M software programs or other computer data.

CD-R/CD-RW CD-Recordable/CD-Read/Writeable, disk drives that create (or *burn*) new CDs, using the appropriate CD-R or CD-RW media.

Centronics port *See LPT port*.

Chipset A generic term used to describe the constellation of support chips and circuitry that make a PC tick.

Client A desktop computer or terminal that's connected to and works over the Internet.

Click The act of pointing at an on-screen item, and pressing the left mouse button.

Click+drag The act of pointing at an on-screen item, pressing and holding the left mouse button down while simultaneously moving the mouse.

Clipboard An invisible area where data is temporarily stored during a copy+paste or cut+paste operation.

Clock speed The pace of a computer's processing performance, measured in ticks. Higher clock speeds equate to faster computer performance.

Close Un-loading a program or data file.

Commercial software Software products sold through stores and online retailers.

COM ports Also called *modem ports* or *serial ports*. Communications ports; receptacles where devices such as modems are connected.

Configure Adjusting the settings of hardware or software.

Control keys Any key pressed in combination with the CTRL key.

Copy To duplicate an item in the computer.

Copy+paste Cloning a file or information from one location to another.

CPU The Central Processing Unit, also known as the processor. Marketed under a variety of brands, such as Intel Pentium and AMD Athlon, it's essentially the computer's electronic brain.

Crash A hardware or software failure.

Cut To remove an item from the computer.

Cut+paste Moving a file or information from one location to another.

Cyberspace *See Internet*.

Database A collection of data records. *See also Field and Record*.

Defragment *See Disk Defragment*.

Demoware Software that advertises other software or services, but can't be used for real work.

Desktop *See Windows Desktop*.

Dialog box A window that asks a question or requests the user to make a choice.

Digital Recording and playing back data as a stream of binary numbers (1's and 0's).

Disk defragment Also called *disk defragmenter*. The process of running a utility program that reorganizes data scattered about the hard disk so that the computer can fetch the data faster.

DNS Domain Name System, translates numerical IP addresses into meaningful names (such as www.RBLevin.net).

Double-click The act of pointing at an on-screen item and pressing the left mouse button twice in rapid succession.

Download Also called *downstream* or *downlink*. The act of retrieving data from another computer.

Drag+drop The act of using the mouse to move an on-screen item using click+drag. *See also Click+drag.*

DSL Digital Subscriber Line, a high-speed means of accessing the Internet.

DVD Also called *DVD-ROM*. Digital Versatile Disk Read-Only Memory, an enhanced CD-ROM that can store up to 4.7G of software and data.

Edit To modify a document or data file it in some way, and then re-save it.

E-mail Text messages sent between two or more computers, and retrieved at the recipient's leisure using e-mail software.

E-mail filter *See Blocked sender list.*

E-mail list *See Group.*

Endless loop *See Loop.*

Enter *See OK.*

Esc Or, *Escape. See Cancel.*

E-ware Commercial software distributed electronically over the Internet.

Export Sending data out of a program.

Favorites Saved locations (addresses) of web sites.

Field A place to enter and display data in a database record. *See also Record and Database.*

File Any form of digital data that's saved to a disk, such as a word processor document, spreadsheet, database, web page, program, and so on.

Filename extension The last three characters of a file or folder name, appearing after a period (dot). For example, DOC is the filename extension of MyLetter.DOC.

Firewall Software programs that sit between a computer and the Internet, shielding the system and other computers connected to it from outside attack and infiltration.

Flat-file database A database that stores all information in one file.

Floppy disk Also called *floppy drive, FD, FDD*. The standard removable magnetic media storage device used with computers.

Focus Whatever element on the screen that has the computer's attention.

Folder The computer equivalent of a file folder. A means of organizing named collections of digital data files.

Folder tree A list of folders organized like an upside-down tree, where the folder root is the top-level folder.

Font A typeface.

Foreign data A data file that's not recognized by the computer's installed software.

Formula A calculation in a spreadsheet or database. *See also Spreadsheet and Database.*

Freeware Free software, with no price tags, time limits, or strings attached, other than occasional copyright limitations.

Free-text database A database that operates much like a word processor, with automatic indexing and fast retrieval of stored information.

Function A built-in spreadsheet or database formula that returns a value. *See Formula.*

Function keys The keyboard keys labeled F1 through F12.

Game pad A hand-held thumb-controlled pointing device used to interact with computer games.

Gigabit Also expressed as *g, gb, Gb*. One billion bits.

Gigabyte Also expressed as *G, GB*. One billion bytes

Group A named list of e-mail addresses (such as Friends, Beatles Fans, and so on).

GUI Graphical User Interface, the visual design of a software program. It's pronounced goo-ey

Hot keys Pressing a specific function key or combination of keys on the keyboard to generate a computer action or command.

Hover The act of holding a mouse pointer over an item, without clicking.

HTML HyperText Markup Language, the standard file format of web documents.

Human interface *See GUI*.

Icon A small drawing that represents a program, command, data file, service, function, or web site.

IMAP Internet Mail Access Protocol, an e-mail standard that allows users to remotely manage their e-mail.

Install Adding new hardware or software to a computer.

Instant messaging Also called *IM*. Text messages that pop-up on a computer screen the moment they're sent.

Internet service provider Also called *ISP*. Companies that sell access to the Internet, such as America Online, CompuServe, the Microsoft Network, and AT&T WorldNet are all examples of Internet service providers.

Hard disk Also called *hard drive, HD, HDD*. Magnetic mass storage device where all software and user data is stored.

Hardware The electronic, electrical, and mechanical components (keyboard, mouse, chassis, disk drives, monitor, printer) that make up a computer.

http HyperText Transport Protocol, the common language spoken between web browsers and web servers.

Hyperlink A word or picture on a web page that, when clicked, transports the user to another web page.

Import To bring foreign data into a program.

Inbox The electronic place where Internet mail arrives.

Information superhighway *See Internet*.

Input box An on-screen box where characters are typed.

Internet The world standard communications network for computers.

I/O Input/output. *See also Port*.

IP Internet Protocol, the standard means by which data is transmitted between computers over the Internet.

IP address Internet Protocol address, a set of up to 12 numbers (nnn.nnn.nnn.nnn) that define a computer's unique numerical identity on the Internet.

IrDA The Infrared Data Association, a standards body that ensures devices can reliably communicate using infrared beaming (wireless) technology.

Joystick A control stick used to interact with computer games.

Junk e-mail *See Spam*.

Keyboard The standard data entry device used with computers.

Kilobit Also expressed as *k, kb, Kb*. One thousand bits.

Kilobyte Also expressed as *K, KB*. One thousand bytes.

LAN Local area network, two or more computers connected using NICs or home networking systems.

LCD Liquid crystal display, a technology used to manufacture ultra-thin flat-panel screen used in notebook computers, and high-end desktop monitors.

Legacy free Computers that replace classic PC technologies, such as expansion slots, serial ports, and parallel ports, with modern alternatives including USB and FireWire ports.

List box An on-screen box that offers a menu of items for selection.

Load *See Open*.

Loop *See Endless loop*.

LPT port Also called *parallel port*. Line printer port, the computer's receptacle where the printer gets plugged in.

Macintosh A computer that runs Apple's Mac OS.

Mainframe The largest and most powerful computers made.

Master personal folder The central (main) folder for user programs and data.

Maximize Expanding an open window to fill the screen by clicking the window's Maximize button.

Media Consumable computer products such as floppy disks, CD-Rs, CD-RWs, printer ink cartridges, paper, and so on.

Megabit Also expressed as *m, mb, Mb*. One 1 million bits.

Megabyte Also expressed as *M, MB*. One million bytes.

Menu bar The list of commands that run across every program window from left to right.

MIDI Musical Instrument Digital Interface, the musical equipment industry's standard for connecting instruments keyboards, sequencers, and other instruments with computers.

Minimize Shrinking an open window by clicking the window's Minimize button.

MLPPP Multi-link Point-to-Point Protocol, a high-speed means of accessing the Internet that uses multiple modems and telephone lines.

Modem A device that connects your computer to other computers over the Internet using a telephone line.

Modem ports *See COM ports*.

Mouse The standard pointing device used with computers.

Mouse pointer *See Pointer*.

Motherboard The main circuit board in a computer.

MP3 Digital music files.

MPEG Digital movie files.

MS-DOS Microsoft Disk Operating System, an OS that predates Windows 98.

Multitask Also called *multitasking*. To run more than one program at a time.

Network *See LAN, WAN*, and *Internet*.

NIC Network interface card, an add-on expansion card used to connect a computer to a network.

OK Approving a computer's request to perform a task.

Open Activating a program or a data file.

Open source Freeware that include the program source code. *See also Freeware*.

Open technology Technology that can be used by any person or company to create derivative products without paying royalties or other licensing fees.

Operating System Also called *OS*. The main program that controls your PC. Popular operating systems include Windows 98, Windows 2000, the Macintosh OS, Solaris, UNIX, Linux, BeIA, OS/2, MS-DOS, OS/400, and MVS.

Parallel port *See LPT port*.

Password A unique word known only to the user, which acts as a key, providing secure access to the computer, the OS, a program, data, or a web site.

PC cards Credit-card sized add-in expansion cards, such as modems and network adapters, that confirm to the Personal Computer Memory Consortium International Association standards.

PCMCIA cards Personal Computer Memory Consortium International Association. *See* also *PC cards.*

Platform Any software or hardware pivotal to a person or companies ability to accomplish tasks. Platforms include Intel's Pentium, Microsoft's Windows, Microsoft's Office 2000, and others.

Plug-in A small program that runs inside a web browser. Popular plug-ins include Adobe's Acrobat Reader, Macromedia's Shockwave and Flash players, Real Networks' RealPlayer, and Microsoft's Windows Media player.

Pointer The arrow that moves when the mouse is jostled.

Point size The measurement (or scale) of a font. *See* also *Font.*

POP3 Post Office Protocol 3, the standard that defines how e-mail is retrieved by remote computers.

Port Input/output receptacles which enable your PC to connect to other hardware resources, such as a keyboard, mouse, disk drive, network, and so on.

Power cycle The act of turning a device off and on.

PPP Point-to-Point Protocol, a standard that enables bi-directional, error-free communication between desktop computers and Internet service providers. In other words, PPP gets a computer connected to an ISP, which then connects the computer to the Internet.

Programming The art of writing (designing, authoring, creating, testing) software.

Proprietary technology Technologies owned and controlled by a single company, or group of companies.

Protocol A defined set of standards that dictate how two or more computers communicate or otherwise interoperate.

Public domain software Software in the public domain that is completely free of all copyright restrictions.

RAM Random Access Memory, the chip memory in a computer.

Reboot Restart the computer.

Record One entry in a database, comprised of a collection of database fields. *See* also *Field* and *Database.*

Relational database A database that stores information in multiple databases, creating one virtual database from many smaller database files.

Restore Expanding a minimized window by clicking the window's Restore button. Also, recovering lost or damaged data from backup disks or tapes.

Right-click The act of pointing at an on-screen item and pressing the right mouse button.

ROM Read-only memory, computer programs stored on a chip

RTFM Read The Fine Manual, a favorite saying of experienced computer trainers who urge novices to thoroughly read manuals before attempting to use new software or hardware.

RTFS Read The Fine Screen, a popular maxim among trainers who remind new users that most computer software can conquered by simply reading the on-screen commands and controls.

Run *See Open.*

Save Also called *Save as.* Storing a data file on disk.

Scanner A device, similar to a copy-machine, that allows documents and photographs to be converted into a digital computer data file.

Script A list of computer written in a programming language such as JavaScript, JScript, or Visual Basic Script, often used to control a web browser's behavior and activity.

Scroll bars Vertical and horizontal borders that frame most program windows. The buttons on these borders can be used to move up, down, left, and right through a document.

Scroll wheel The small wheel in the middle of a mouse, used to move up and down through a document.

SCSI Small Computer System Interface, or scuzzy. A high-speed I/O port for connecting disk drives, scanners, and other high-performance devices to computers.

Selection Also called *selected.* Data that is highlighted on the screen.

Serial ports *See COM ports.*

Server Any computer that runs an Internet web site or provides a Net-based service, or access to shared files, printers, or other network resources.

Setup *See Install.*

Shareware Software provided on the honor system.

Shift keys Any key pressed in combination with the Shift key.

Shortcut An icon that serves as a placeholder for a program or data file stored elsewhere. Acts as a remote control for the program or data file. Double-clicking the shortcut causes the associated program or data file to open.

Shortcut keys *See Hot keys.*

Shrink wrap *See Commercial software.*

Shut down The process of preparing a computer to be turned off.

SLIP Serial Line Internet Protocol. Similar to PPP, except that SLIP communicates in one direction at a time (transmit or receive) and lacks error detection. It is therefore slower than PPP.

SMTP Simple Mail Transport Protocol, the standard that defines how e-mail is sent from one system to another.

Snail mail A letter sent via any traditional overland letter or parcel delivery service, such as the US Postal Service, UPS, or FedEx.

Software Programs that run in a computer, such as a word processor, spreadsheet, database, web browser, or e-mail system.

Spam Junk e-mail.

Spreadsheet A data file comprised of a collection of cells and formulas. *See* also *Formula* and *Cell.*

Start menu The menu that appears when the Start button on the Taskbar is pressed.

SVGA Super VGA, a marketing term dreamed up by video card makers who improved on the IBM VGA standard. *See VGA.*

Symmetric Information sent and received at the same speed.

System tray The indented area of the Windows Taskbar that features the clock.

Tabbed dialogs Multiple dialog boxes organized into a single master window, with descriptive folder-style tabs used for navigation and selection.

Tape drive A hardware device that stores and

plays back data using cassette-style tapes.

Taskbar The area of the Windows Desktop that features the Start button.

Task switch To jump from one program to another.

TCP/IP Transmission Control Protocol/Internet Protocol, the computer's common language on the Internet.

Time-out The period it takes a screen saver or other scheduled program to kick in. A screen saver that kicks in after 60 minutes is said to have a 60-minute time-out.

Trialware Software that expires after a limited time if not purchased.

Trojan horse A program that appears to be a normal piece of software, but actually contains a deadly payload, such as commands that erase all data on a computer's hard disk.

UI Aso called *user interface. See GUI.*

Upload Also called *upstream* or *uplink*. The act of sending data to another computer.

Upgrade Replacing or updating old hardware and software with newer versions.

URL Uniform Resource Locator, a web site or document's address (such as www.RBLevin.net).

USB Universal Serial Bus, the standard I/O port for connecting devices to computers.

USB hub A junction box used to connect multiple USB devices to a single USB port.

VCR buttons Icons that that appear similar to the fast-forward, rewind, play, and stop buttons found on a video cassette recorder.

VGA Video Graphics Array, a marketing term coined by IBM for the PC video standard it invented. *See Super VGA.*

WAN Wide Area Network, which is two or more LANs connected together. *See LAN.*

Web address *See URL.*

Web browser The software program that used to navigate the World Wide Web.

Web browsing *See Web surfing.*

Web cam A video camera connected to a PC that broadcasts its pictures over the Internet.

Web server A program that runs a web site.

Web surfing Traveling around various web sites.

Windows Desktop Windows 98's main workspace screen.

Windows Update Windows 98's automatic updating facility, located at Start | Windows Update.

WIN keys Any key pressed in combination with the Windows logo key.

Wizard Interactive guides that break complex technical tasks into easy step-by-step processes.

World Wide Web A global marketplace of interconnected multimedia publications, software, and services that are accessible through a computer's web browser.

Index

A

access control 302
accessibility options 105
active matrix LCD 48
add new hardware 98, 105
add printer 96
add programs applet 342
add/remove programs 105
add-in cards 338
adding new software 341
ADSL (Asymmetrical Digital Subscriber Line) 70
advanced address book features 181
airborne pointer 54
ALT key 230, 231
analytical Engine 318
antivirus software 311
antivirus tools 326
appearance tab 109
applications requirements 31, 32
arrow keys 92
assigning database fields 272
assigning program icons 226
assigning shortcut keys 226
association of Shareware Professionals 348
Athlon 41
audio 44
audio circuitry 44
auxiliary port 68

B

Babbage, Charles 318
background tab 108
backspace keys 91
backup 100
backup cycle 358
backup device 50
backup hardware 354
backup power 49
backup software 353, 357
backup systems 353
bad advice 76
bandwidth 61, 71
bare bones Internet plans 61
barrel distortion 46
basic text entry 242
Berners-Lee, Tim 308
Better Business Bureau 80
bits 38
blocking junk mail 184
boot 93
bootstrap loader 93
broadcasting 213
browser buttons 167
bulletproof security 306
burn in 100
burn-in test 101
burning-in process 101
bus speed 45
bypassing the password 304
bytes 38

C

C> prompt 118
cable 61, 71, 148
carpal tunnel syndrome 88
Cascade Windows 196
CD Read/Writeable 50, 339
CD-Rom drives 43, 88, 99
Celeron 41
central Intelligence agency 307
central Processing Unit 41
centronics 47
CERT (Computer Emergency Response Team) 309
chameleons 310
chip memory 42
cleaning removable media drives 332
cleaning the keyboard 331
cleaning the mouse 332
cleaning the screen 330
clock speed 42
cloning icons for new software 343
color LCD 48
color photographs 31
colors 110, 216
COM ports 97, 339
command line 118
compact disks 355
composing a message in E-mail 177
composing a Word document 240
compression tools 326
computer frustrations 34
computer name 90
computer shopping 75-85
Computer Support Plans 82
computing requirements 30
configuration 103
Connection Properties 150
context menus 120
control panel:
　accessibility options 105
　add new hardware 105
　add/remove programs 105
　date/time 105
　desktop themes 105
　display 105
　fonts 105

Acknowledgements

This book would not have been possible without the support and encouragement of five people, and two companies.

Currently an editor for CMP Media's Planet IT web site, Jerry Lazar has written for scores of high-tech trade rags over the past 20 years. Jerry is also the editor of my "Desktop Computing" column, which appears monthly on Planet IT (www.PlanetIT.com).

A woman of few words – and always the right ones – Beth Adelman is the acquisitions and managing editor of the KISS series at DK (Dorling Kindersley) Publishing. Beth is the person who saw the need for a new kind of computer book, one that respects users, instead of denigrating them. It's a vision Beth and I share.

When friends Jerry Lazar and Beth Adelman were chatting one day about DK's upcoming line of KISS books, Jerry dropped my name. Thank you, Jerry, not only for thinking of me, but for thinking of me as the right guy for a book that aspires to embrace, educate, and elevate the average computer user. And thank you, Beth, for your unwavering KISS vision, and for convincing me to sign on.

Once the writing was underway, two superb editors entered the fray: Joseph Gonzales, who took on the formidable task of line editing my manuscript (and did a stellar job), and James Lubin, who handled the copyediting with aplomb under intense deadline pressure (I never met a deadline I couldn't miss).

To my amazing and beautiful wife, Ellen: Thank you, sweetie, for your love, support, and unshakable encouragement. You are my only constant in a constantly changing world.

And then there's the folks who had the greatest impact on this book: the listeners and callers on my weekly talk radio show, PC Talk, which airs every Saturday on CBS Talk Radio 1210 AM WPHT Philadelphia; the members of my PC Talk Posse; and the regulars that hang at my Computer Tech Online BBS, at www.RBLevin.net/BBS. These outstanding guys and gals keep me tightly focused on the real-world issues that matter most to computer users – which, it turns out, are remarkably different from the issues that matter most to editors, writers, and industry pundits. Thanks, gang. You're the best. ;-)

A heartfelt "thank you" to the engineers and product managers at Microsoft, and the rapid response team at Microsoft's PR agency, Waggener Edstrom. This book simply would not have been possible without the outstanding level of support and access you provided. No request was too small or large, and they all were turned around in a flash.

Lastly, a big bear hug for everyone at Dorling Kindersley Publishing, for having the courage to field a new computer book for everyday users in an already crowded field. The folks at DK still care about the creative process and the art of publishing.

God bless you all.

RICH LEVIN
Philadelphia
January 2000

Picture Credits

All pictures courtesy of
  Dorling Kindersley except:

Allsport: pp. 114
Comstock: pp. 2, 16-19, 24,
  86, 188, 204, 222, 266,
  298, 334, 352, 354
Foundry Arts: pp216, 288,
  359(b), 38, Alf Cutts 167,
  Josephine Cutts 279,
  Karen Fitzpatrick 208,
  Helen Courtney 305, Ian
  Powling 47, 48, 51, 73(b),
  78, 91, 139, 140, 190, 270,
  273, 274, 282, 304, 330,
  353, 358
Greg Evans: pp.26, 28(all),
  29(b), 32, 36, 40, 46, 52,
  59(all), 64, 70, 103, 104,
  130, 134, 144, 191, 194(t),
  248, 259, 275, 293(all),
  302(b), 310, 316, 323,
  337(all), 340, 350
Mary Evans: pp. 74, 286,
  300, 361
NASA: pp. 236
Nokia: pp. 132
Patrick Eagar Photography:
  pp 220
Pictorial Press: pp. 33
Still Pictures: pp. 170, 296,
  313
Topham: pp. 29(t), 34, 116,
  127, 320, 336